SUMMARY OF DOS COMMANDS*

COMMAND	DESCRIPTION	FORMAT	PAGE
DEBUG	Invokes the assembly-language debugging program	[*D*:*Path*]DEBUG [*FileSpec*] [*Param1*] [*Param2*]	571
DEL	Removes a file from the disk	DEL *FileSpec*	572
DIR	Lists files on a disk or in a directory	DIR [*FileSpec*][/P][/W]	574
DISKCOMP	Compares two diskettes	[*D*:*Path*]DISKCOMP [*D1*:[*D2*:]][/1][/8]	575
DISKCOPY	Duplicates complete diskette	[*D*:*Path*]DISKCOPY [*SourceD*:*DestD*:][/1]	576
EDLIN	Line editor supplied with DOS	[*D*:*Path*]EDLIN *FileSpec* [/B]	578
ERASE	Removes a file from a disk	ERASE *FileSpec*	579
EXE2BIN	Converts an .EXE file to a .COM file	[*D*:*Path*]EXE2BIN *SourceFile* [*DestFile*]	580
FASTOPEN	Speeds up file opening	[*D*:*Path*]FASTOPEN *D1*:[= *Size*] ...	581
FDISK	Partitions a hard disk	[*D*:*Path*]FDISK	583
FIND	Finds strings in files	[*D*:*Path*]FIND [/V][/C][/N]"*String*" [*FileSpec*...]	584
FORMAT	Prepares a disk to accept data	[*D*:*Path*]FORMAT *D1*:[/S][/1][/8][/V][/B][/4][/N:*xx*][/T:*yy*]	586
GRAFTABL	Displays ASCII characters on CGA	[*D*:*Path*]GRAFTABL [437 ¦ 860 ¦ 863 ¦ 865 ¦ /STATUS]	588
GRAPHICS	Enables PrtSc to print graphics screens	[*D*:*Path*]GRAPHICS [PrinterType] [/R][/B][/LCD]	589
JOIN	Merges two disks into one	[*D*:*Path*]JOIN [*Drive2*[*Drive1*]][/D]	591

*See Part 6, "DOS Command Reference," for a complete description of subcommands and their parameters.

This summary of DOS commands, plus summaries of EDLIN commands, configuration file commands, and batch-file subcommands, continues at the back of this book.

Bill Anderson

752-1619

UNDERSTANDING DOS 3.3

UNDERSTANDING DOS® 3.3

Academic Edition

JUDD ROBBINS

San Francisco • Paris • Düsseldorf • Soest

Acquisitions Editor: Dianne King
Editors: Fran Grimble, Deborah Craig, Kay Luthin
Technical Editors: Robert Campbell, Michael Gross
Word Processor: Christine Mockel
Graphic Artists: Julie Bilski, Lucie Živny
Illustrator: Rick Van Genderen
Screen Graphics: Delia Brown, Michelle Hoffman
Typesetter: Elizabeth Newman, Bob Myren
Proofreader: Lisa Jaffe, Aidan Wylde
Indexer: Anne Leach
Cover Designer: Thomas Ingalls + Associates
Cover Photographer: Mark Johann
Screen reproductions produced by XenoFont.

Library of Congress Card Number: 90-70511
ISBN: 0-89588-718-5

Manufactured in the United States of America
10 9 8 7 6 5 4 3 2 1

to

BALANCE

CONTENTS AT A GLANCE

Introduction xxiii

PART 1: GETTING STARTED

Chapter 1: The Fundamentals of DOS 1
Chapter 2: Your First Steps with DOS 17

PART 2: MAKING DOS DO MORE

Chapter 3: Manipulating Files 49
Chapter 4: Understanding the DOS Directory Structure 81
Chapter 5: Working with Hard-Disk Directory Structures 109
Chapter 6: Using the DOS Editor 131
Chapter 7: Printing 153

PART 3: REVVING IT UP

Chapter 8: Communications 173
Chapter 9: Backups and Restorations 195
Chapter 10: Custom Configurations of DOS 223
Chapter 11: International Setup of DOS 245
Chapter 12: Redirecting the Action 277

PART 4: LIFE IN THE FAST LANE

Chapter 13: The Power of DOS Batch Files 313
Chapter 14: Subcommands in Batch Files 327
Chapter 15: Sophisticated Batch-File Examples 349
Chapter 16: Advanced DOS Commands 387

APPENDICES

Appendix A: DOS Prompt, Batch-File, and Configuration Commands 415
Appendix B: Glossary 463
Appendix C: ASCII Codes 479
Appendix D: Partitioning Your Hard Disk 485

Exercises 499

Index 532

TABLE OF CONTENTS

INTRODUCTION *xxiii*
Necessary Hardware and Software for This Book xxiii
How to Use This Book xxiii
How This Book Is Organized xxiv
Icons Used in This Book xxvii

PART 1 GETTING STARTED

CHAPTER 1 *THE FUNDAMENTALS OF DOS* *3*
What DOS Does 4
What You Need to Know about DOS 6
The Fundamental Hardware 6
Input and Output Devices 9
How Disks Are Set Up 9
The Disk Commands 10
Disk Organization 10
Taking Care of Your Diskettes 13
Summary 15

CHAPTER 2 *YOUR FIRST STEPS WITH DOS* *17*
Getting Started 18
Setting the Date and Time at Startup 18
How the DOS System Gets Going 19
Giving Commands to DOS 20
Editing Controls 21
Correcting Mistakes 22

Canceling a Command 24
Repeating a Command 24
Correcting Part of a Command 25
Clearing the Display 25
Changing the System Date and Time 26
Preparing Your Disks for Use 27
Formatting a Diskette 28
Making a System Diskette 29
Backing Up an Existing Diskette 32
Backing Up Your DOS Diskettes 33
Checking the Disk for Available Space 38
Summary 42

PART 2 *MAKING DOS DO MORE*

CHAPTER 3 *MANIPULATING FILES* *49*
The Disk Directory 50
Long Directory Lists 54
Referring to Files on Other Drives 56
Changing the Default Drive 57
Limiting the Directory Display 57
Making Copies of Files 60
Making Secondary Copies 61
Making Backup Copies 61
Making Multiple Copies 62
Making Complete Disk Copies 63
Copying Data to Other Devices 63
Combining File Copies 64
Verifying Accurate Data Transfers 65
Using the XCOPY Command to Transfer Files 67
Other Fundamental Activities 73
Typing Out a Text File 74
Changing the Name of a File 74
Erasing a File 77
Summary 78

CHAPTER 4 UNDERSTANDING THE DOS DIRECTORY STRUCTURE 81

A First Look at a Disk's Directory Structure 82
Creating a Subdirectory 85
Accessing Files in a Subdirectory 86
Changing the Default Directory 87
Copying Files into a Subdirectory 88
Returning to the Root Directory 88
How Subdirectories Work 90
Multilevel Directories 91
  Applying DOS Commands to Subdirectories 91
  Understanding the Concept of Paths 92
  Moving Files Between Directories 94
Maneuvering Around the DOS Directory Structure 98
  Viewing the Structure 98
  Searching Paths 99
  Setting Up a Complex Path 102
  When the PATH Command Isn't Enough 102
  Checking the Path 103
Pruning the Tree 103
Summary 105

CHAPTER 5 WORKING WITH HARD-DISK DIRECTORY STRUCTURES 109

Formatting the Disk 110
A Place for the DOS Files 110
  Creating New Directories 111
  Copying Files Between Disks and Directories 111
  Listing a Subdirectory 112
  Changing the Active Directory 112
  Returning to the Root Directory 113
Changing the Prompt 113
Loading Your Word Processor onto the Hard Disk 114
  Creating Your Word-Processing Directory 115
  Copying Word-Processing Programs to the New Directory 115
  Running Your Word Processor from the New Directory 116
Loading Your Spreadsheet Program onto the Hard Disk 117
  Subdirectories for Data 118
  Configuring Programs 119

	Creating Multiple Subdirectories for Your Data Files	119
	Running Programs from Within Subdirectories	121
	Running Your Database Management System	122
	Running Any Program on Your Hard Disk	123
	Limitations of the PATH Command	125
	Mapping Your Hard Disk	126
	Summary	128
CHAPTER 6	***USING THE DOS EDITOR***	***131***
	Getting EDLIN Started	132
	Starting a New File	132
	Changing an Existing File	133
	Bringing New Text into Memory	134
	Combining Separate Text Files	134
	Making Space for Large Files	135
	Displaying EDLIN Files	136
	Listing Your Text File	136
	Listing Your Text File Rapidly	137
	Editing EDLIN Files	137
	Inserting New Lines	139
	Changing Existing Lines	139
	Moving Lines (Cutting and Pasting)	141
	Copying Lines	143
	Searching for Text Strings	144
	Search and Replace Capabilities	146
	Deleting Lines	147
	Ending the Editing Session	147
	Quitting the Editing Session Without Saving	148
	Saving Your Work and Exiting to DOS	149
	Summary	150
CHAPTER 7	***PRINTING***	***153***
	Printing Screen Images	154
	Printing Files	158
	Printing Files with the COPY Command	159

Indirect Printing and Spooling 160
  Printing Files with the PRINT Command 160
  Dual Tasking with PRINT 161
  Using Switches with PRINT 163
Summary 168

PART 3 *REVVING IT UP*

CHAPTER 8 *COMMUNICATIONS* *173*
System Communications in General 174
Parallel Versus Serial Communications 176
DOS Devices Versus Files 179
Initializing Devices and Ports 182
  Controlling the Printer 183
  Initializing the Serial Communications Port 185
  Connecting a Serial Printer to a COM Port 188
  Controlling the Mode of the Video Display 188
Summary 192

CHAPTER 9 *BACKUPS AND RESTORATIONS* *195*
Special Commands for Your Disks 196
How Backup Files Are Stored 197
Making Backup Copies of Your Files 199
  Backing Up a Complete Directory 200
  Backing Up a Partial Directory 200
Other Types of Backup Processing 202
  Adding Files to an Existing Backup 202
  Backing Up Subdirectories 207
  Performing Multiple Operations with One Command 208
  Backing Up Modified or New Files 209
  Backing Up by Date and Time 211
  Creating a Log File of the Files Backed Up 211

Restoring Files from a Backup Disk 213
  Restoring Only Some of Your Backed-Up Files 216
Summary 218

CHAPTER 10 *CUSTOM CONFIGURATIONS OF DOS* *223*
Using the CONFIG.SYS File 224
  Specifying the Number of Active Files 225
  Specifying the Number of Internal DOS Buffers 226
Using Device Drivers to Customize DOS 227
  Creating a RAM Disk 228
  Using a RAM Disk 231
  Adding Power with the ANSI System Driver 233
ANSI.SYS and the PROMPT Command 233
  Controlling the Screen Display 234
  Using Meta Symbols 235
  Combining Multiple Attributes 237
  Redefining Keys 240
Summary 242

CHAPTER 11 *INTERNATIONAL SETUP OF DOS* *245*
Character Sets for Different Countries 246
  ASCII Codes 246
What Country Do You Call Home? 247
Understanding Code Pages 249
  The Keyboard Translation Table 250
  Code Pages 253
  Devices and Their Drivers 255
  Translation Tables and Device Drivers 256
Working with Code Pages 259
  Loading Code-Page Support Routines 260
  Loading Specific Code Pages 260
  Loading a Keyboard Translation Table 263
  Switching Between Available Code Pages 266
  Displaying Extended ASCII Codes on a Color Graphics Adapter 267

Preparing an International DOS System Disk 268
Installing Country and Keyboard Information 268
Modifying the Required System Files Yourself 270
Updating the CONFIG.SYS File for International Support 270
Updating Your AUTOEXEC.BAT File 271
Summary 272

CHAPTER 12 ***REDIRECTING THE ACTION*** ***277***
Controlling the Flow of Information by Redirection 277
Sending Screen Output to the Printer 278
Storing Screen Output in a Disk File 278
Adding Output to an Existing File 279
Receiving Input from Text Files 281
Processing Your File Information with DOS Filters 282
Arranging Your Data with the SORT Filter 282
Performing Text Searches with the FIND Filter 285
Connecting DOS Operations with Pipes 289
Combining Piping and Sorting 290
Customizing Your DOS Sorts 293
Combining Redirection with Filters and Pipes 296
Sophisticated Text Searches Using Redirection 298
Saving Time by Combining Filters 303
Controlling Screen Output 305
Pipes, Filters, and Redirection: An Example 306
Summary 308

PART 4 ***LIFE IN THE FAST LANE***

CHAPTER 13 ***THE POWER OF DOS BATCH FILES*** ***313***
Building a Batch File 314
Rules for Batch Files 314
Creating Your First Batch File 317

Editing a Batch File 318
Variables in Batch Files 320
Summary 325

CHAPTER 14 *SUBCOMMANDS IN BATCH FILES* *327*
Incorporating Messages into Batch Files 328
Interrupting Batch Files During Execution 329
Decision Making in Batch Files 333
An Example Branching Program 333
Using Looping and Repetition in Batch Files 337
Using Batch Chains and Batch Subroutines 342
Summary 346

CHAPTER 15 *SOPHISTICATED BATCH-FILE EXAMPLES* *349*
Automating System Jobs 350
Automating the System Startup 350
Changing the Default System Prompt 352
Other Possibilities with AUTOEXEC.BAT 352
Creating Your Own Menu System 353
Improving Performance with Batch Files 356
Simplifying Consistent Sequences 357
Repeated Automatic Invocation 359
Program Setup and Restoration 360
Chaining for Diskette-Switching Applications 363
Initializing Your RAM Disk 364
Initializing Your Color Monitor 365
Sophisticated Batch Files 367
Customized System Help Screens 368
Appointment Reminder System 370
Broadcasting System Messages 374
Using Batch-File Subroutines for Status Tracking 375
Tips, Tricks, and Techniques 378
Using RAM Disks Effectively 378
Controlling User Access 380
Summary 382

CHAPTER 16 **ADVANCED DOS COMMANDS** **387**
Advanced File Manipulation 387
Changing a File's Attributes 388
Updating Sets of Files 390
Rescuing Lost Files 393
Improving Disk and Directory Referencing 394
Treating Disks As Directories 394
Treating Directories As Disks 397
Rerouting Disk Input and Output 404
Speeding Up Disk Access 404
Influencing the Command Processor and Its Environment 405
Renaming Commands 406
Creating a Second Command Processor 409
Summary 412

APPENDIX A **DOS PROMPT, BATCH-FILE, AND CONFIGURATION COMMANDS** **415**

APPENDIX B **GLOSSARY** **463**

APPENDIX C **ASCII CODES** **479**
Character Sets 479
ASCII Codes 479
Mapping One Character Set onto Another 480
Numbering Systems 482

APPENDIX D **PARTITIONING YOUR HARD DISK** **485**
Configuring a DOS Partition 486
Creating a Partition 487

Changing the Active Partition 493
Displaying Partition Information 493
Deleting DOS Partitions 495

EXERCISES ***499***

INDEX ***532***

INTRODUCTION

You and I probably select our software based on what each package offers, and whether we need it for our business. DOS is usually a required part of your system. Just as surely as you need a printer to produce hard-copy reports and a screen to display intermediate results, you need a disk operating system (DOS) to provide the key management capabilities for your hardware. This allows each software package to deal only with its own application needs.

You may have bought DOS because you were told you had to, or simply to run your application software (Lotus 1-2-3, dBASE III PLUS, WordPerfect, and so on). The great wealth of software being advertised, sold, and used in the business world today requires that MS-DOS, PC-DOS, or another DOS manage the overall hardware and operating environment. You will find that using DOS can be remarkably easy.

NECESSARY HARDWARE AND SOFTWARE FOR THIS BOOK

This book assumes that you have an MS-DOS or PC-DOS microcomputer. Although most of the fundamental capabilities are available in earlier versions of DOS, many of the more advanced features seen later in this book are only available to you in the most recent versions. This book uses DOS 3.3, although you will be told when a particular feature is unavailable in earlier versions. In fact, this book will be useful if you are using any version of DOS from 2.X upward; version 2.X introduced the key feature of hierarchical directories.

HOW TO USE THIS BOOK

You may have a computer with diskette drives only, or you may have a hard-disk machine. This book is appropriate for you in either case. Many examples are provided for either situation, and commands are explained in terms of what they can do on *any* disk drive. While you read through the book, you should stop as often as possible to try the commands and features on your computer. Seeing them work immediately will give you the reinforcement necessary for quickly sharpening your skills.

A WORD ABOUT THE ACADEMIC EDITION

Practice, practice, practice is the advice given to students of any subject, physical or mental. This principle also applies to learning about DOS. This Academic Edition of *Understanding DOS 3.3* provides a series of supplemental exercises, beginning on page 530, that offer you the opportunity for additional practice.

The exercises included in this book are grouped by chapter, and are designed to reinforce your understanding of DOS's principal concepts and techniques. If you are studying DOS as part of a class, your instructor may assign readings to go along with specific chapter exercises. Or, if you are studying DOS on your own, you can work the related exercises into your study of each chapter.

In some of the chapter exercises, you can save the time needed to type in the text files if you use the diskette that accompanies the instructor's manual. If your teacher doesn't have the companion diskette, he or she can contact SYBEX for a complimentary copy. However, if you are studying the book on your own, you can type in the text yourself since all referenced files appear in the respective chapters. The instructor's disk will save you time, but you don't need it to perform the exercises.

HOW THIS BOOK IS ORGANIZED

You don't need any background at all to get the most out of this book. As in all things, however, experience will help you to learn some things more easily, and to skip other things that you already know. *Understanding DOS 3.3* is structured so that you can jump to the section or chapter that's right for you.

Understanding DOS 3.3 emphasizes the power available to you within DOS itself. Although additional utility programs are available, this book can save you money by showing you how to implement utility capabilities with DOS commands alone. A well-written

DOS command can often take the place of a piece of additional software. You'll learn how to use DOS to set up your own menu system, file-sorting capability, diskette-cataloging mechanism, backup procedure, text-searching facility, and much more.

This book has four parts. Part 1, "Getting Started," presents the strong foundation necessary for any user. Chapter 1 presents the fundamental pieces of hardware and software used when working with a disk operating system. Chapter 2 focuses on your first steps with the DOS diskettes, in preparation for running programs. Beginners must read and become comfortable with the information presented in Part 1. Those with some experience are urged to read this part to review fundamentals and to learn basic skills that might have been overlooked before.

Part 2, "Making DOS Do More," is a self-contained tutorial on how DOS stores and uses information in files on disks. Chapter 3 concentrates on the commands and features used to manipulate files in a host of ways. You then learn in Chapter 4 how a directory structure is created and maintained, as well as the commands necessary to create, name, modify, and manipulate your files. Chapter 5 takes a special look at the elements of a directory system as they pertain to application programs. If you intend to set up your hard disk for running a word processor, a database management system, a spreadsheet program, or almost any other application package, you should read this chapter carefully.

Chapter 6 prepares you to create and modify text files using the DOS line editor, EDLIN. You will need this skill throughout the rest of the book to generate and update certain system files properly, as well as to write your own simple programs with the DOS batch-file mechanism. Finally, in Chapter 7 you will examine the ways you can produce printed output with your system.

Part 3, "Revving It Up," picks up the pace quite a bit. Some advanced capabilities are discussed for those of you who want to learn more than the basics. The general arena of DOS communications is explored in Chapter 8. The flow of data between the central processor and peripheral devices is critical to any successful computer system; you will learn in this chapter the terminology and technology for data transmission, and you will see how certain DOS commands give you complete control over the flow of information.

An important, but often neglected, capability of DOS is its ability to back up and restore all or portions of your hard disk. Chapter 9 introduces the appropriate backup commands and discusses effective techniques for using them. In Chapter 10, you will also learn how to customize your system by means of DOS configuration and startup options. They can significantly improve the performance of your DOS system, as well as its ease of use.

Unique features for the international use of your computer are presented in Chapter 11. These tools enable you to initialize your keyboard layout, printer, and screen for a foreign flair. Chapter 12 examines advanced features—pipes and filters—that give you precise control over the flow of information throughout your entire system.

Part 4, "Life in the Fast Lane," deals primarily with advanced commands and features. It focuses on the sophisticated arena of batch files. You will learn of the possibilities and limitations of these files in Chapter 13, and in Chapter 14, you will extend this knowledge with subcommands and parameters. You'll learn how to combine all of the elements of batch files in creative and powerful ways.

Many actual batch files and techniques are presented in Chapter 15. You can type in any of these batch files and run them immediately on your system, or you can send for a companion diskette that contains all of the batch files in this book. An order form for this purpose is included at the end of this book.

Chapter 16 deals with the commands available to an advanced DOS user. These powerful commands can connect multiple disk drives into directory superstructures, simulate nonexistent drives with subdirectories, and reroute disk requests from one drive to another. You'll also see uncommon commands that influence the command processor itself and modify the DOS environment. In addition, you'll study a group of specialized commands that provide you with advanced file-manipulation capabilities.

Four appendices are also included to make your use of DOS a little easier. Appendix A, the "DOS Command Reference" has been included for easy access to all of DOS's commands. The text of *Understanding DOS 3.3* presents the most important DOS commands. You won't find your learning impeded by a blind presentation of all commands and all of their parameters and switches, some of which are not essential. Appendix A fills in the gaps by providing you with a quick, alphabetized reference to all commands, all parameters, and all possible switches. You are encouraged to return to this reference chapter over and over as you use DOS. A quick overview of both the usage and format of each command may be all you'll need to speed you on your way with DOS applications. Appendix B is a complete glossary of relevant computer terms. Appendix C is an extended table of ASCII codes, with an explanation of character sets and numbering systems. Appendix D will come in handy when you need to configure or reconfigure fixed disks.

DOS is now a stable product; it is expected to be a principal operating system for years to come. This book will be a useful companion as you work toward your goal of making effective use of the software available.

ICONS USED IN THIS BOOK

Three visual icons are used in this book. The Note icon

indicates a note that augments the material in the text. The Tip icon

represents a practical hint or special technique. When you see the Warning icon

pay particular attention—it represents an alert or warning about a possible problem or offers a way to avoid the problem.

PART 1

GETTING STARTED

In Part 1, you will get a sense of what DOS is and what it can do. If you're just beginning to use DOS, you should read and become comfortable with the information presented here. Even if you have some experience, you should read Part 1 to refresh your memory and perhaps learn some basics you missed elsewhere.

Chapter 1 explains the fundamental pieces of hardware you will use with DOS: the central processing unit, the disk drives, hard disks and floppy diskettes, and other devices such as printers. It introduces the two types of DOS commands, resident and transient. It also explains how DOS stores data on disks.

In Chapter 2, you will get down to work with DOS. You'll load and start up DOS, and you'll learn how to give commands, set the system date and time, and prepare your disks for use. You'll also learn how to back up diskettes, starting with your DOS master diskettes.

THE FUNDAMENTALS OF DOS

CHAPTER 1

EVERY COMPUTER THAT USES DISKS (HARD OR floppy) must have a master program that coordinates the flow of information from computer to disk and from disk to computer. This is called the *disk operating system,* or *DOS*. In this book, you'll learn about the operating system used on the IBM PC and compatible microcomputers. This operating system is manufactured by Microsoft Corporation and licensed to IBM and other microcomputer manufacturers. The name of this system, when purchased from Microsoft, is *MS-DOS*—that is, *M*icro*s*oft *D*isk *O*perating *S*ystem. When it is purchased from IBM, it is called *PC-DOS*.

What does all this mean? Simply that the terms *DOS, MS-DOS,* and *PC-DOS* really refer to the same thing, and in fact are often used interchangeably. In this book, the term *DOS* refers to the disk operating system used on IBM microcomputers and the wide range of IBM-compatible microcomputers.

This chapter will teach you how DOS is used and what useful functions it can perform. You will also learn about the fundamental parts of the computer sitting on your desk and about a number of computer devices (peripherals) that you might not own yet but might be interested in acquiring. You'll learn the differences between input and output devices, as well as their purpose.

Most importantly, you'll acquire an understanding of what disks and diskettes are, how they're set up, and how DOS provides you with commands to manage them. You'll see how data is organized on them, so you can make better decisions later about which disks are appropriate for your use. You'll learn a host of good techniques for caring for your disks, so you can significantly reduce the odds of losing critical data through disk failure.

Since the manufacturer of each new computer may make minor adjustments to DOS before releasing it for that machine, you may occasionally notice slight differences between your DOS's messages and those in this book. However, since DOS is virtually the same from machine to machine, you will probably never see any variation other than in the startup message.

WHAT DOS DOES

The disk operating system is assigned the task of integrating the various devices that make up a computer system. There are three major tasks the operating system must carry out. It must

- Coordinate the input and output devices, such as monitors, printers, disk drives, and modems;
- Enable the user to load and execute programs; and
- Maintain an orderly system of files on the disk.

Computer memory has one basic drawback. The area of memory in which your programs and data are stored, called *random-access memory (RAM)*, cannot store information after the electricity has been turned off, even for a fraction of a second. To store information in the computer, you must have some means of recording it. The most common devices for this task are *disk drives,* which are devices that can read or write to magnetic disks.

Magnetic disks divide generally into two categories: *hard disks* and *floppy disks,* or *diskettes.* On a hard disk the magnetic storage medium is rigid, or hard. Hard disks are called *fixed* or *nonremovable* disks if they are built into the drive itself; they are called *removable cartridges* if they can be inserted into and removed from the disk drive. Information is stored on a disk as a collection of characters. Hard disks usually hold at least 10 million characters, and larger models that hold 70 million characters are now available on the newest IBM Personal

System/2 line of microcomputers. Each 10Mb is roughly equivalent to 5000 pages of typed text.

Diskettes usually store less information. The most flexible and common type, the 5¼" diskette, can store several hundred thousand characters of information, depending on the density of the magnetic material on the disk's surface. A high-capacity 5¼" diskette can actually store 1.2 million characters. A less common but increasingly popular type, the 3½" diskette, is often called a *microfloppy* diskette. It owes its growing popularity to higher storage densities, holding as many as 1.44 million characters. This is the largest storage capacity of any diskette; in addition, the microfloppy's small size makes it easier to store and transport.

By now you understand that different types of disks store different amounts of information. However, all disks share information in the same way—as a collection of characters. You may have heard the term *byte;* it is interchangeable with the term *character.* Any keyboard character can be stored and represented by DOS as a series of eight bits (of binary 0's and 1's), which together make a byte. Approximately one thousand (actually 1024, or 2^{10}) of these bytes are together called a *kilobyte,* while approximately one million (actually 1,048,576, or 2^{10}) of them are known as a *megabyte.* The eight bits can be arranged in 256 different ways, thereby representing 256 different characters. Some of these characters are the ones you can type in (A–Z, 0–9, and so on), and others are simply interpreted by DOS as *control* characters. This classification includes all special character codes that control special operations, like sounding a bell on a video monitor or performing a carriage return on a printer. See Appendix C for more details on character sets and numbering methods.

Each complete collection of related characters is called a *file.* A disk can have many files that contain either instructions for the computer (*program files*) or data stored by the user (*data files*). A disk can contain both program files and data files. Each file must be given a unique name so that the computer can later refer to the file and load it from the disk into the computer's memory again.

DOS is responsible for managing this flow of information. As you will learn, DOS contains a host of commands and programs that enable it to store information on any disks connected to your computer. It also has full responsibility for arranging your files on these disks in ways that will contribute to easy and efficient retrieval.

WHAT YOU NEED TO KNOW ABOUT DOS

What does the average user need to know about DOS? This is a hotly debated question. Some people contend that as little time as possible should be spent on DOS. However, since DOS defines the basic structure of the computer system, you must be able to command DOS effectively to exercise full control over the computer. Knowing DOS is especially useful when something goes wrong. In this book, you will learn much about DOS that will help you to deal with both the expected and the unexpected.

THE FUNDAMENTAL HARDWARE

DOS is designed to manage the details of a variety of hardware connections and combinations. You should understand a bit about the hardware before you ever open up the DOS box and use the diskettes.

A microcomputer system is composed of a *central system unit* and a variety of *peripheral devices* (see Figure 1.1). The central system unit usually contains the primary processing chip (the *CPU,* or *central processing unit*), the main system memory (RAM), and usually one or more disk drives. The CPU is the brain of the computer. It performs the various arithmetic operations, as well as controlling the flow of data to and from the additional peripheral devices. The main memory of the computer is the place in which instructions and data are stored during program execution. Keep in mind that the amount of available and required RAM always increases as the sophistication of the programs that are run on your computer increases.

The disk drives in the minimum *configuration* (the arrangement of system components) are usually diskette drives, although a hard-disk drive is included more and more often as hardware prices continue to drop. As Figure 1.1 shows, systems that use diskettes refer to the drives as A: and B:. Systems that use one diskette drive and one hard-disk drive refer to them as A: and C:. This book will refer to these drives simply as A, B, and C.

The peripheral devices in the minimum configuration are the video monitor and the keyboard. The keyboard usually has one of

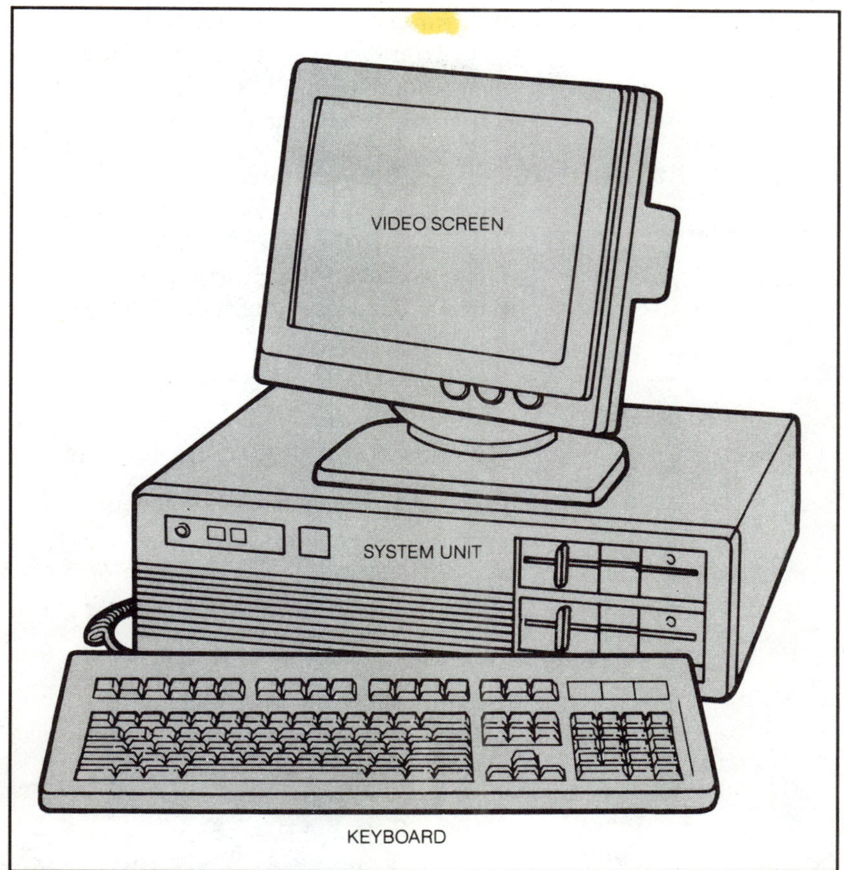

Figure 1.1: A minimum microcomputer system

four layouts, depending upon whether it is designed to be compatible with an IBM PC-XT, the IBM PC-AT, the IBM Personal System/2, or the IBM Convertible. There are several possible choices for a video monitor—monochrome, color graphics, or enhanced graphics are the most common. Higher-resolution monitors, although more expensive, are becoming more common in businesses using desktop-publishing and computer-aided design (CAD) software.

There is virtually no limit to the range of additional devices that can be connected to a microcomputer. Most business microcomputer systems contain more than the minimum, as Figure 1.2 shows. The various *connector ports* in the back of the computer, such as the *parallel* and *serial* ports, allow the straightforward (although not necessarily easy) connection of printers, plotters, digitizers, extra disk drives, and so on. The task of starting DOS so that it manages this hardware is consistent, no matter what hardware configuration you have.

INPUT AND OUTPUT DEVICES

As you have seen, the computer you are working on is really not one machine but a group of related devices. Devices can be attached to the

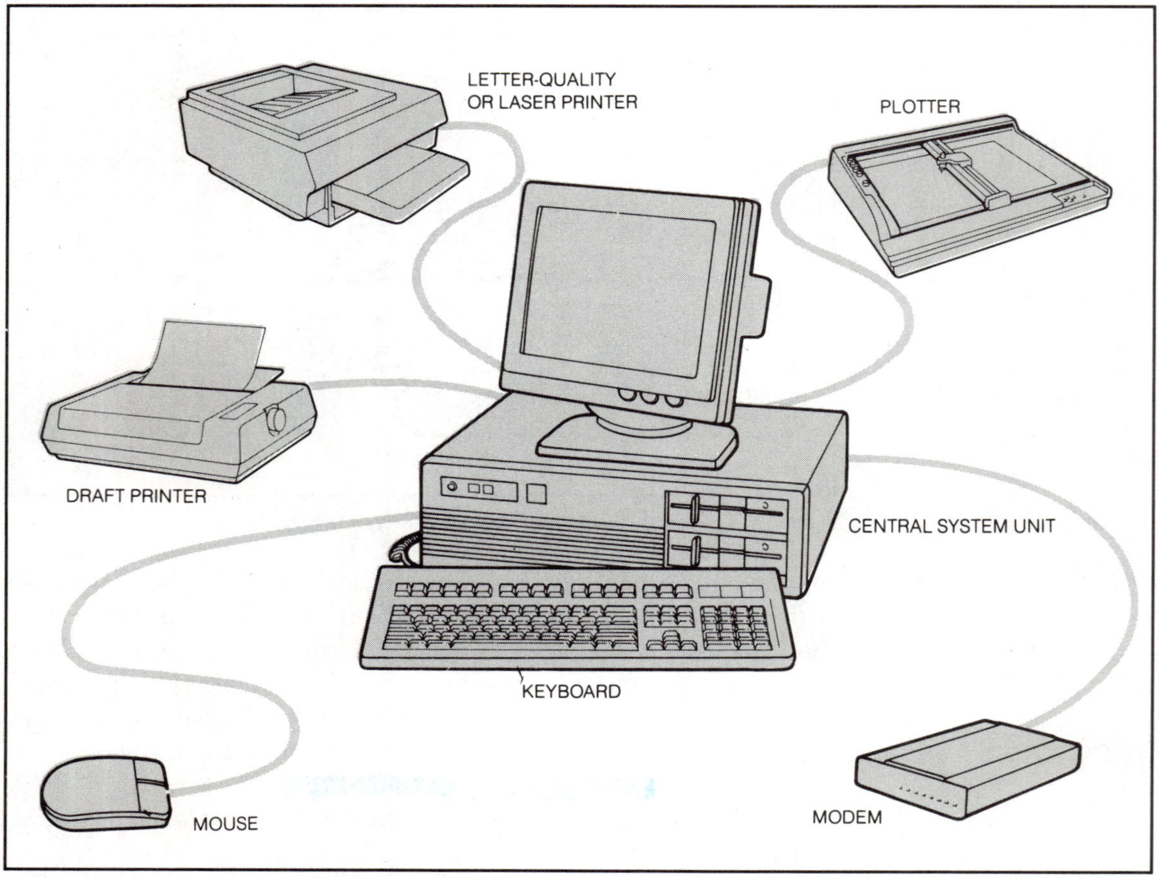

Figure 1.2: A more standard microcomputer system

Disk drives can be both input and output devices. Most DOS commands deal with the complex process of input from and output to the disk drives.

computer internally (inside the system unit) or externally (in separate boxes attached by cables). Some of these devices deal with the information that is input into the computer system, while other devices manage the output of information from the computer system. Some devices do both (see Table 1.1).

HOW DISKS ARE SET UP

When you buy a box of diskettes, the diskettes in that box are *not* ready to be used with your computer. In order to use them, you must prepare the diskettes with some of the special programs provided with your disk operating system. Even hard disks must be prepared. Most people never get a chance to format and set up their hard-disk drives because the dealers usually do this for them. This is not altogether an advantage, since you never learn the basics of disk setup.

This section explains how and why disk-preparation programs are used. The ideas and techniques presented here are some of the first actions you take with a new computer system. The section not only shows you what to do, it also helps you understand what is really going on when you issue these commands.

THE DISK COMMANDS

The concept of DOS is confusing for two reasons:

1. A large part of DOS is invisible to the user. DOS has two parts, one of which (the *hidden files* part) is stored on the disk but does not appear on the disk directory. The other part is a

DEVICE	FUNCTION
Keyboard	Input only
Screen	Output only
Printer	Output only
Disks	Input and output

Table 1.1: Typical purposes of DOS devices

file called COMMAND.COM, which is visible on every diskette used to start up (or *boot*) the system. In DOS 3.3, COMMAND.COM occupies 25,307 bytes, while the two hidden system files together occupy another 52,259 bytes. This 50K (kilobytes) is a price you will pay on every system (boot) disk you create.

2. The actions performed by DOS are divided into two types. *Resident commands* are actions that DOS can always perform, no matter what disk happens to be in the computer. These commands are always resident in memory, and so they execute immediately when you want. *Transient commands* are really small programs for special purposes. If you want to perform any of these actions, you must have the correct disk in the computer, or (as you'll see in Chapter 4) you must tell DOS where these programs are located on your disks. Since transient commands are only brought into memory from a disk when you request them, it is your responsibility to ensure that they are available when needed.

On floppy-diskette systems, the DOS command files must be accessible through one of the drives. Otherwise, DOS will display an error message indicating that it can't find the requested command.

Table 1.2 shows the resident and transient DOS commands. You will learn more about these commands throughout this book. For now, you will be concerned only with the fundamental disk structure that stores these commands for you and makes them available whenever you need them.

DISK ORGANIZATION

When a floppy diskette is taken out of the box, it is totally blank. So, too, is a hard disk. The primary difference between diskettes and hard disks lies only in the arrangement of the magnetic material. This material can be arranged on one or both sides of a diskette, depending on whether the diskette is single-sided or double-sided. Diskettes can also have differing densities. The more densely the magnetic material is written onto a diskette, the more information it can hold. Hard disks, on the other hand, can have several layers of magnetic material, each with two sides, which means they can store even more information.

In order for the computer system to use any disk as a medium for storing information, the entire disk must be divided into sections organized so that every physical location on the disk has a

Resident Commands		
BREAK	DEL	RMDIR
CHCP	DIR	SET
CHDIR	ERASE	TIME
CLS	MKDIR	TYPE
COPY	PATH	VER
CTTY	PROMPT	VERIFY
DATE	RENAME	VOL
Transient Commands		
APPEND	FIND	RECOVER
ASSIGN	FORMAT	REPLACE
ATTRIB	GRAFTABL	RESTORE
BACKUP	GRAPHICS	SELECT
CHKDSK	JOIN	SHARE
COMP	KEYB	SORT
DISKCOMP	LABEL	SUBST
DISKCOPY	MODE	SYS
EXE2BIN	MORE	TREE
FASTOPEN	NLSFUNC	XCOPY
FDISK	PRINT	

Table 1.2: Classification of DOS commands

unique address. This is the same concept as assigning ZIP code numbers to various towns and cities. When DOS assigns addresses, it then has an orderly way in which to store and then find various pieces of information.

The system of magnetic storage used by DOS is one of concentric rings (see Figure 1.3). Each ring is called a *track*. For example, there are 40 tracks (numbered 0 to 39) on each double-sided, double-density diskette, while there are twice as many tracks (numbered 0

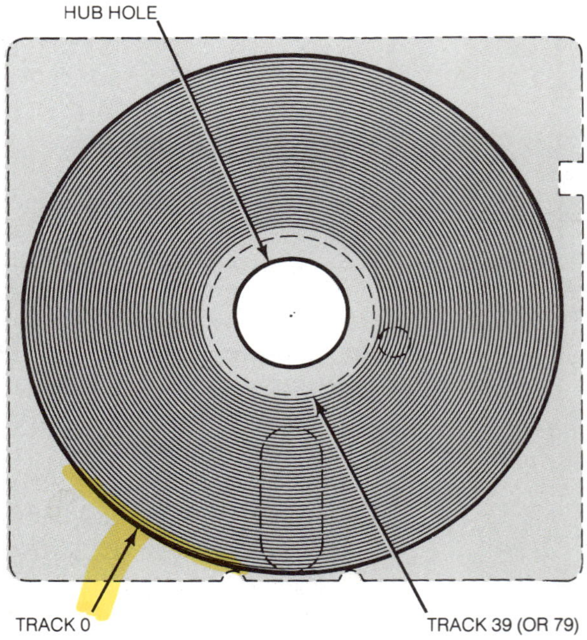

The "hub hole" in Figure 1.3 is merely the center hole in a disk or diskette, which fits onto the spindle of a disk drive. Like the hole in a record and the spindle on a turntable, this hole and spindle ensure that the disk spins in a true circular path. Data can then be read from and written to consistent places on the tracks of the disk.

Figure 1.3: Tracks laid out on a disk

to 79) on a high-capacity diskette. Each track is divided into smaller parts called *sectors*. Tracks and sectors are created when a disk is formatted. It is DOS's job to assign the necessary addresses for each track and sector. You needn't be concerned about this addressing mechanism, since it is really only for DOS's benefit. DOS needs to know the actual disk location of your files; you only have to know their names. That's what makes the operating system such a valuable ally in running application software.

The exact number of sectors depends on what type of diskette is being formatted (see Table 1.3). Standard double-sided, double-density diskettes have 9 sectors per track, while the high-capacity

DISK STRUCTURE	5¼" DOUBLE DENSITY	5¼" HIGH DENSITY	3½" DOUBLE DENSITY	3½" HIGH DENSITY
Number of tracks	40	80	80	80
Sectors per track	9	15	9	18
Characters per sector	512	512	512	512
Total number of sectors	720	2400	1440	2880
Total number of characters	360 K	1.2 M	720 K	1.44 M

Table 1.3: Diskette organization

Standard double-density diskettes can have a maximum of 112 uniquely named files, while high-capacity diskettes can store 224 files. Hard disks can store significantly more individual files, depending on their size (10Mb, 20Mb, and so on).

diskettes available for the IBM PC-AT and compatibles have 15 sectors per track. Each sector can hold 512 bytes. The newest 3½" diskettes containing 1.44Mb have 80 tracks per side, each track holding 18 standard 512-byte sectors.

Some of the formatted disk space is not available to you for storing data—about 6K on a 5¼" diskette to about 18K on a 3½" diskette. When a disk is formatted, some of the sectors are set aside for keeping track of the information stored on that disk. Every formatted disk has these areas. Together, they serve as a catalog of the contents of that disk. These areas are called the *file allocation table* (*FAT*), the *boot record,* and the *directory table.* The details of their use are beyond the scope of this book, but their impact on disk-space usage should be considered.

TAKING CARE OF YOUR DISKETTES

If you have never dealt with diskettes before, they may look and feel flimsy. They are not as flimsy as they appear, but they are also not as durable as many users believe. In many offices, computer users seem to use their diskettes as paperweights on their desks. Sometimes people don't even keep the diskettes in the jackets they originally came in. These are usually the ones who complain most vocally about their diskettes failing several times a year.

A well-maintained diskette can easily last for years. Mishandling diskettes can have serious consequences. An accident can destroy the contents of a diskette in only seconds.

Here are some suggestions for diskette handling. Keep in mind that experience and knowledge lie behind every one of them:

- Keep your diskettes in their jackets when not in use. You never know when they may fall on the floor or when something might fall or spill on them. It's simple risk reduction.
- Don't leave your diskettes in the disk drives, especially if the computer is going to be moved. Remember, others who clean around your computer may move it to clean the table tops.
- Don't leave your diskettes in your car, where the temperature often gets high enough to warp them, making them unreadable for your computer. Also keep them away from any sources of magnetic fields, such as motors, telephone bells, and magnetic card keys.
- Don't touch the magnetic surface of the diskettes—hold them by their jackets. Fingerprints have their place, but it's not on a diskette.
- Make backup copies of all original diskettes, and keep current copies of all diskettes with important, newly created program or data files.
- Keep your backup diskette copies in a different location from the original diskette (for example, at home if your computer is at the office; at work if your computer is at home).
- Label all your diskettes, both electronically with a DOS command and with a printed, gummed label. Write on the label before you attach it to the diskette, or use a soft felt-tipped pen to write carefully on an existing label.
- Don't squeeze the last bit of space out of your diskettes. Always leave them a little empty. In the first place, you may later want to add some new files to that very diskette. Later, you may also want to expand the size of some of the files on the diskette.

SUMMARY

This chapter introduced you to DOS—what it is, what it does, and how it is used. The chapter included the following topics:

- You learned about the fundamental pieces of hardware that make up a typical microcomputer system. This hardware constitutes the environment within which the disk operating system and all of your selected application software perform their tasks. The components are

  The central processing unit, or CPU, which performs analytic or computational tasks.

  The disk drives, which work with disks to store your data and program files.

  Disks and diskettes. There are two types of hard disks, fixed and removable, each storing from 10 to 70 megabytes of data. There are two classes of floppy diskettes, 5¼'' (which can store from 180K to 1.2Mb of data) and 3½'' microfloppy diskettes (which can store from 720K to 1.44Mb of data).

  The system console, consisting of a video monitor for output displays and a keyboard for the input of data and commands.

  Other devices such as modems, mice, digitizers, plotters, and a wide range of printers.

- You learned that the primary means of communicating with your computer is with input and output devices. The principal input device is your keyboard, and the principal output device is the video screen. Most printed copy (hard copy) is generated on a printing device, such as a dot-matrix, letter-quality, or laser printer.
- You learned that DOS has two types of commands, resident and transient. Resident commands reside in a portion of memory reserved by DOS and are always available. Transient commands reside in files on your system disk and must be read into memory before being executed.

- You learned that information is stored on a disk in circular patterns called tracks, which are broken up into easily addressable, 512-byte portions called sectors.
- You learned that DOS arranges and maintains the physical and logical arrangement of information stored on the disks. Your programs and data are stored on the disk in collections of bytes called files.
- You learned that you must treat your diskettes with care.

Now that you've learned the fundamentals of DOS, Chapter 2 will help you begin to actually use your computer. Get ready to take those important first steps with DOS disks and DOS commands.

YOUR FIRST STEPS WITH DOS

CHAPTER 2

YOUR FIRST ACTUAL STEPS WITH DOS HAVE LITTLE to do with the software itself. They involve acquiring the right pieces of hardware, turning the computer on, and preparing the disks for use. Your individual application programs may require additional preparation of certain system parts, such as printers and plotters.

Virtually every piece of peripheral hardware that can be connected to your computer can be initialized, configured, or set up in a way that will be helpful for individual application programs. Such possibilities will be discussed later in this book, but for now, you will concentrate on the basic hardware that goes into a typical microcomputer system.

You will learn in this chapter how to get your DOS system going, and, consequently, how to get going with any application program you will be running. You'll learn how to set the time and date correctly if your system doesn't have a built-in clock/calendar. When Daylight Savings Time comes around, you'll know how to make the necessary adjustments to your system.

In this chapter you'll also begin to learn more and more DOS commands. You'll learn how to correct the errors you'll make quickly and efficiently. Since you may change your mind about a command you've given to DOS, you'll learn how to let DOS know about your changes.

You'll also learn to prepare disks for storing your valuable data and file information, as well as for booting up your system. Backing up your disks and exploring the status of a disk are necessary skills you'll also acquire here. In short, this chapter will start "teaching you the ropes" of DOS.

GETTING STARTED

Your first task after turning on the power is to load DOS into the computer. Place your DOS system diskette into drive A and close the door. (This drive is usually on the left side of most computers; however, some computers place it at the top when the drives are located one on top of the other.) If you have already loaded DOS onto a hard disk, all you need to do is turn the power on at this point. If you haven't prepared your hard disk or loaded DOS onto it, you should refer to your individual disk and DOS manuals for the proper procedure on your computer. Appendix C also offers instructions for this task.

The computer will go through a process called *booting* or *bootstrapping*. This process loads DOS into the memory of the computer and is necessary before the computer can actually be used. Once DOS is in memory, you can begin to work.

SETTING THE DATE AND TIME AT STARTUP

Regardless of whether you have hard disks or floppy diskettes, you should begin by placing the DOS system diskette in drive A. Then turn on the power to the computer. After the computer tests its internal hardware, it will display the following message:

```
Current date is Tue 1-01-1980
Enter new date (mm-dd-yy):_
```

January 1, 1980, is the default startup date each time you bring DOS up on your system. Assuming you do not have an automatic clock in your system, you will see this message each time DOS starts up. You'll be expected to enter the correct date at this point. However, if your system is configured with additional hardware that includes a battery-backed clock, you won't have to enter this date each time. The additional hardware will come with instructions on avoiding the standard DOS request for correcting the date, as well as on dealing with the subsequent request for the time of day:

```
Current time is 0:02:47.82
Enter new time:_
```

DOS keeps track of time in standard military format, so if you wanted to enter a time of 10:30 A.M., you could simply enter 10:30. However, if you wanted to enter 3:30 P.M., you would have to enter 15:30.

After you've entered the correct date and time, you're on your way. DOS will display a version of the following prompt, although the actual wording will vary slightly from computer to computer. In some versions of DOS, you will receive these copyright notices *before* the date and time request:

```
DOS version 3.3
Copyright Matsushita Electric Industrial Co., Ltd 1987
Copyright Microsoft Corporation 1981, 1987
A>_
```

Since in this example the system diskette has been loaded in drive A, the DOS A> prompt now appears. As you will see through much of the rest of the book, when DOS is installed on a hard disk, the typical "DOS is ready" prompt is C>, indicating that DOS is installed and operative on drive C and is waiting for your instructions.

HOW THE DOS SYSTEM GETS GOING

You may wonder how DOS gets into the computer. A small part of it is already in the computer memory. Intelligent bootstrapping logic ensures that the rest of the disk operating system is loaded automatically from the disk when you turn on the computer. That is why *a diskette must always be present in drive A before you turn on the computer.* If you have a hard disk, then that disk is always ready and takes the place of the diskette in drive A. After loading, DOS shares the computer memory with the programs you run and the data those programs use (see Figure 2.1).

To let you know that DOS is active, the computer displays a prompt that looks like this:

```
A>
```

This DOS prompt (usually A> or C>) is a simple way of asking you for your instructions. Unless you deliberately change this prompt (as you will see in Chapter 5), it always has two characters: a letter and a

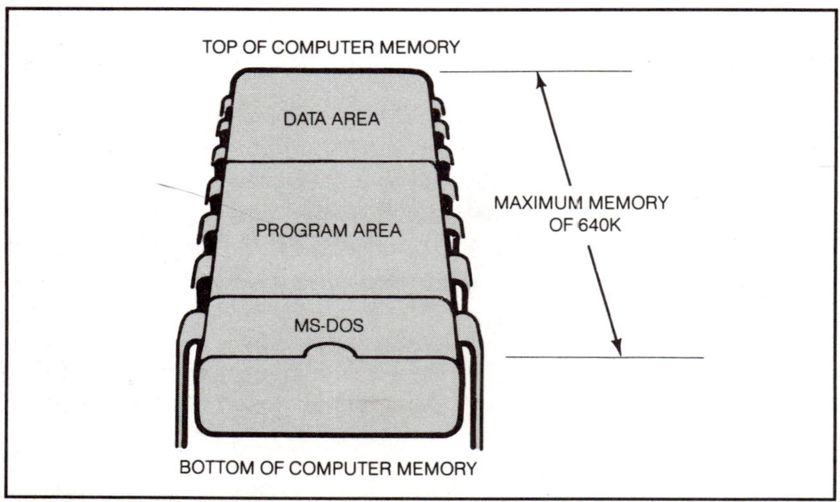

Figure 2.1: Memory map

greater-than sign (>). The letter indicates the current active drive; unless otherwise specified, all commands will affect data on that drive only. If you are using a two-drive system, the letter will be A (for the left drive) or B (for the right drive). Hard-disk users will usually see the letter C, indicating a standard hard-disk drive.

Whenever you see the A> (or C> for hard-disk users), it means that DOS is ready to accept a command from you. It also tells you that you are not working in any other program. Later, you will learn how to change an A to a B or a C.

GIVING COMMANDS TO DOS

You can exercise complete control over what DOS will do for you and when DOS will do it. In this book, you will learn many instructions—commands—that you can give to DOS. Nearly all of the commands must be entered at the DOS prompt. Unless DOS is prompting you for a command entry, you will be unable to enter any commands.

When the blinking cursor is positioned at the DOS prompt, all you need to do is type in a valid DOS command and press the Return key. (The cursor always indicates the position of the next character to be typed.) Some DOS computers label the Return key RETURN;

You must press the Return key after almost every command in DOS. This book will not specify so after each command; instead, you should learn to use the key as an automatic end to each of your commands. Should you *not* be required to press Return for a command, this book will clearly state so at the appropriate point.

others label it ENTER; still others only label it with the ⟵ symbol. All are equivalent. This book will use the term *Return key* to indicate the key that you should press on your keyboard to do this job.

Pressing the Return key is necessary because some DOS commands require more entry information than the command word itself. Simple commands like DIR (to obtain a directory listing) require only that you type the letters (D, I, and R) followed by the Return key. Since even this simple command may be followed by additional specifications, such as the format of the resultant listing or the disk drive you're interested in, DOS does not process your request until it determines that you have actually pressed the Return key. Only then can it assume that you have completed your request.

The additional qualifications for command requests are called *parameters* or *arguments*. (We'll use the term *parameter* in this book.) In general, parameters can be thought of as placeholders for the data that will be typed in when you execute the actual command. The specific data is called the *value* of the parameter. Later, when you actually run those commands, you'll be expected to supply the values for the variable parameters. Parameters in this book will be represented as descriptive terms in italic type—for example, *FileName*. You'll learn the most important examples of all of these modifiers in the context of the appropriate commands.

Modifying a DOS command with a parameter or a switch is analogous to modifying a verb in a sentence with an adverb. By learning to use these modifiers well in the DOS environment, you can produce results that are as aesthetically pleasing as a well-formed turn of phrase in your native language.

Many DOS commands permit the specification of *switches*. A switch slightly changes how the command executes. *What* the command does remains the same; only *how* the command executes its task changes because of the addition of a switch. As you learn new commands in this book, you'll also learn the most important and useful switches available with each command. In some cases, other switches exist, but their purpose is either obscure or not frequently needed. Your DOS user's manual can provide you with an exhaustive list of additional switches.

EDITING CONTROLS

Several keys on the keyboard perform special tasks. The location of these keys differs, depending on whether you are using a keyboard that is compatible with the IBM PC-XT, the PC-AT, the Personal System/2, or the PC Convertible. Figures 2.2 through 2.5 show the complete layouts of these keyboards. Several key combinations also are interpreted in special ways by programs like DOS. The following sections show you how to save energy and time by using these keys.

CORRECTING MISTAKES

What happens if you make a mistake? There are a few editing controls in DOS that you may find handy. The most common one is the Backspace key, often seen as a large ⟵ on your keyboard just above the Return key. If you type

DIR B:*.COM

Figure 2.2: Keyboard layout for the IBM PC-XT and compatible computers

Figure 2.3: Keyboard layout for the IBM PC-AT and compatible computers

but do not press Return, your cursor will be on the space just beyond the last character you typed. To erase that character, you press the Backspace key. The M disappears and the cursor moves one space to the left. To erase the next character, the O, you would again press the Backspace key. Continuing to press this key would remove the entire command, keystroke by keystroke.

Figure 2.4: Keyboard layout for the IBM Personal System/2 and compatible computers

Figure 2.5: Keyboard layout for the IBM PC Convertible and compatible computers

CANCELING A COMMAND

Suppose that you entered a command and decided before you pressed the Return key that you wanted to cancel it. You may have changed your mind, or you may have realized that you simply entered the wrong request; you may even have become confused and need to reconstruct the request completely. One way would be to use the Backspace key to remove all the characters.

A better way, however, is to use the Esc key (short for Escape) to cancel the entire line with a single keystroke. If you entered a typical command like

```
DIR B:*.EXE
```

you could cancel the entire command by pressing Esc. A backslash mark (\) appears on the line you typed, and the cursor moves to the next line. This indicates that the entire command will be ignored:

```
DIR B:*.EXE\
_
```

Note that the command is not erased from the screen—it is only ignored. The cursor moves to the next line, awaiting entry of your next DOS command.

REPEATING A COMMAND

DOS holds the last command you issued in a special place in its memory. If you press one of the special function keys, located usually on the left side or top of your keyboard, your last command will automatically be retyped for you.

Suppose you needed to locate a particular file called 88BUDGET.WK1 on one of several diskettes. You could place the first possible diskette in drive A or B and enter the command

```
DIR 88BUDGET.WK1
```

If you don't see the file listed, you could remove the first diskette, place the second possible diskette in the drive, and press function key number 3, referred to as F3. Your original DIR command is retyped for you on the line. Pressing Return again will execute this DOS request for the second diskette.

Whenever you have to perform the same DOS request multiple times (whether for several diskettes, several files, or several directories), using the F3 key can often save you much time by retyping the command line for you.

CORRECTING PART OF A COMMAND

Suppose you have entered the command

```
DOR B:*.COM
```

DOS responds with the message "Bad command or file name." This makes sense—the command should have been entered as DIR, not DOR. You might think that the only way to correct this mistake is to retype the entire command. However, DOS provides a better way to edit the most recently entered command. The F1 key will recall one letter at a time from the previous command. With this example, pressing F1 will make the D appear. Now you can type the correct letter, I. To recall the rest of the command line, which was entered correctly, you press F3. The entire corrected command is then ready to be executed. Pressing Return will execute the line as if you had retyped the entire line.

The F1 and F3 keys are handy tools to learn how to use. Although other function-key capabilities exist, you won't use them very often; you can later explore their usage on your own. Table 2.1 summarizes the editing keys and their functions for DOS.

CLEARING THE DISPLAY

As you proceed with various DOS commands, you may at times want to clear the current screen display and begin again with a clean screen. DOS contains a command to do this. Entering

```
CLS
```

and pressing Return will clear the screen and then redisplay the current DOS prompt at the top of the screen with the cursor beside it,

KEY NAME	FUNCTION
F1	Retypes one character at a time from the last command entry
F2	Retypes all characters from the last command entry up to the one identical to your next keystroke
F3	Retypes all remaining characters from the last command entry
F4	Retypes all characters beginning at the first match with your next keystroke, and ending with the last character from the last command entry
F5	Permits direct editing of all the characters from the entire last command
F6	Places a special end-of-file code at the end of the currently open file; sometimes referred to as a CTRL-Z or ^Z end-of-file code
Ins	Permits insertion of characters at the cursor
Del	Permits deletion of the character to the left of the cursor
Esc	Abandons the currently constructed command without executing it

Table 2.1: DOS editing keys

awaiting your next command. Note that clearing the screen has no effect on either disk files or programs in computer memory. It simply clears the display of text or output left over from previous commands.

CHANGING THE SYSTEM DATE AND TIME

If your system does not have a built-in, battery-backed clock, you will automatically be prompted by DOS to enter the correct date and time each time you power up. However, even if your system does have the hardware for keeping track of the date and time, there may be times when you need to correct one or the other. For instance, twice a year in most of the United States, Daylight Savings Time requires you to adjust all clocks by one hour. You can enter the TIME command at the DOS prompt anytime you want to see the current system time or change it:

```
C>TIME
Current time is 11:09:14.05
Enter new time:_
```

At this point, you could press Return, which would make no changes to the current time, or you could enter a corrected time in the standard format of hours:minutes:seconds.

Unless you are running DOS 3.3, the changed time of day or date is only retained until DOS is rebooted or the system shuts down. DOS 3.3 improved the TIME and DATE commands so that they change the actual time on almost any permanent system clock calendar whenever they are used. Earlier versions of DOS require the Diagnostics program from the Utilities disk to do so. Systems containing add-on clock/calendar cards or boards also require you to run special utility programs supplied with the card or board.

Occasionally, you may want to run a program that is date-stamped for some day other than the actual day it is run. As an example, consider the case of the paymaster of a large computer company who wanted to run an end-of-quarter report two days early. The quarter ended on Sunday, and he wanted to be off skiing that weekend. He changed the system date with the DATE command like this:

```
C>DATE
Current date is Wed 4-08-1987
Enter new date (mm-dd-yy):
```

Then, after running the report dated for that coming Sunday, he changed the date back for the remainder of the Friday work. (His assumption was that no other transactions would be received and processed in the remaining days of the quarter.) Although his approach is not necessarily advisable, having the command around does give you this capability.

In a more serious vein, the testing of newly developed financial programs, for example, often requires data to be 30, 60, or more than 90 days old. In lieu of creating different data all the time, you could use the same test data and change the system date. This would allow you to make your data *appear to be* 30, 60, and more than 90 days old so you could test the program.

PREPARING YOUR DISKS FOR USE

As you learned in Chapter 1, all disks must be prepared correctly before you can use them. This goes for hard disks, regular and high-density diskettes, and microfloppy diskettes. All disks, once formatted, can store any information you like. If you also want a disk to be able to start your system (in other words, boot it), then you must include on that disk special DOS files, and you must prepare the disk in a special way. Once you've done these steps, the disk is called a *system disk*. However, there is now less room remaining on the disk to store data for or from your application programs.

If you don't need to boot your system from a disk, make your disk a *data disk*. All possible disk space is then available for your program and data storage, and none is consumed for DOS purposes.

There are three main types of disk preparations:

- *Formatting a diskette*. This process is used to create a diskette that will operate in the computer but contain no information initially. Such diskettes are used to receive and store data.
- *Creating a blank system diskette*. This process is most often used when you receive a new software package. Most programs are not ready to run when purchased; you must usually perform this process in order to get a working copy of the program.
- *Backing up an existing diskette*. This process makes an exact copy of another diskette. The DISKCOPY command is used; it is the fastest way for DOS to copy a complete diskette.

The next sections will teach you how to perform these three processes. The FORMAT command is the primary means of preparing disks. As you'll see, you simply use different switches to tell DOS whether you want to create a blank data diskette or a system diskette. A number of other switches allow you to specify different diskette densities and layouts, as you will see in Chapter 18. They are less frequently needed, so you won't go over them here.

FORMATTING A DISKETTE

Use a *scratch diskette* to try the following preparation commands—that is, a diskette that is fresh out of the box from your local computer store, or any old diskette that contains information you don't care about. If you do not have one, you should get one before you continue.

Your computer screen should have the A> prompt on the screen (or C> if you are a hard-disk user); as you learned before, this

When you format a disk, any information that might have been stored on that disk is destroyed. Make sure that the disk you format does not contain any valuable information.

If a number of beginning users have access to your computer system, you might consider renaming your FORMAT command (see Chapter 3) so that unauthorized users can't accidentally do any disk formatting. This helps guarantee that disks with valid data will not accidentally be formatted (and zapped) by beginners who are experimenting with DOS commands for the first time.

prompt is the computer's way of telling you that it is ready to accept a valid DOS command. Place the scratch diskette into drive B (or drive A, often the only diskette drive on a typical hard-disk system). Now you are ready to format the diskette. Enter the command

```
FORMAT B:
```

for a dual-diskette system, or enter

```
FORMAT A:
```

for a hard-disk system.

The computer will then ask you to place a diskette in the drive you've specified. If you had not done so already, you could place the diskette in at this point. When you are ready to begin the formatting process, you press Return. DOS will take over and wipe your diskette completely clean of any data. It electronically lays down a pattern of marks, which makes up the tracks and sectors you learned about in Chapter 1.

Diskettes can be formatted as many times as you like. You can even format some diskettes that were used previously by another computer. Of course, any information stored by the other computer on that diskette will be wiped out.

The number of seconds it takes to format the diskette is variable, depending on the size of the diskette (double-density, high-capacity, or otherwise). When the process is done, the diskette is ready to accept information. The computer will then show you how much room for your files is available on the diskette you have just formatted. This will be 362,496 bytes on a double-sided, double-density diskette or 1,213,952 bytes on a high-capacity diskette.

The computer will then ask you if you want to format another diskette. If you enter a Y, the process will begin again, and you will have a chance to insert another diskette into your selected drive. If you are done, you enter an N. The FORMAT command will end, returning you to the DOS prompt. DOS is now ready for your next command.

MAKING A SYSTEM DISKETTE

You come now to the last type of disk setup procedure. This technique requires you to understand the difference between a system disk and a nonsystem disk. A system disk is one that contains three special files. Their most common names are listed in Table 2.2. If you want to boot up the DOS system with a disk, that disk must have these system files stored in reserved sectors at the beginning of the first track. Only if this is true can the DOS bootup program find them, load them, and bring up DOS properly.

Only COMMAND.COM is visible to the user; the other two files, IO.SYS and MSDOS.SYS, are hidden. This does not mean that they do not take up space on the disk—they do. It means that their names do not appear on any directory listing. These hidden files contain most of the information that you have been calling DOS. When you turn on the computer, one of the first things it does is seek the information in these files and read it into memory. The A> or C> prompt is an indicator that these files have been read and stored in the internal memory of the computer.

The IO.SYS file contains the software programs that understand how to send data to and receive data from peripheral devices like printers and disks. The MSDOS.SYS file contains the logic and routines for managing the data organization itself. In essence, the file system is controlled by logic in MSDOS.SYS, and the more nitty-gritty signal and data communications are handled by routines in IO.SYS.

What would happen if you turned on the computer and the diskette in drive A did not contain these system files? The computer would not load DOS and would therefore not be capable of using the disk drives. You would then receive a message requesting that a DOS system diskette be placed in the boot drive. To correct the situation, you would need to restart the system with the diskette that had the DOS files on it.

You can see that having DOS on a disk is important. When you used the FORMAT command previously, you created a totally blank diskette. This was not a system diskette, because it did not have the three DOS files on it. Now you will learn how to format a diskette and copy the system's files onto it at the same time.

If you enter the following command:

```
FORMAT B:/S
```

MS-DOS Systems	**PC-DOS Systems**
IO.SYS MSDOS.SYS COMMAND.COM	IBMBIO.COM IBMDOS.COM COMMAND.COM

Table 2.2: DOS system file names

the /S (the System switch) tells the computer to add the DOS files to the diskette in drive B when the formatting process completes. To begin this formatting process, you simply press Return after making sure you have the right diskette in drive B.

When the process is done, the computer tells you how much space is used by the DOS system and how much remains available for your use. The diskette in B is now a system disk. It is capable of getting the computer started.

Why bother to set up a diskette with only the DOS files? The answer is that you can now transfer files from another disk onto this one. This is usually what you must do when you buy a new software program; most programs do not come on a system diskette. Although you can sometimes put a DOS system onto your newly purchased application program diskette, it is usually preferable to follow these steps:

1. Format a system disk.
2. Transfer your new program files onto that disk.
3. Use the resulting disk both to boot the computer and to run the application program itself.
4. Put your application software's original diskettes in a safe place.

Here's an example of a situation in which you might need to prepare a system disk. Imagine that you want to place BASICA.COM from your DOS supplementary diskette onto a self-booting disk. The ultimate goal will be to automatically initiate the BASICA program when the system powers up (see Chapter 13). Feel free to follow the steps below, substituting an alternate application program, if you wish, for BASICA.COM. First, select a scratch diskette and format it. Next, follow the appropriate steps for your own system's needs:

FOR DUAL-DISKETTE SYSTEMS

1. Place the scratch diskette in drive B and use the command

```
FORMAT B:/S
```

2. Then copy the BASICA.COM file from drive A to the new system diskette in drive B by using the COPY command:

```
COPY BASICA.COM B:
```

Your diskette is now prepared to receive any other application programs (through the COPY command) as well as to boot the DOS system at power-up time.

FOR HARD-DISK SYSTEMS

1. Place the scratch diskette in drive A and use the command

```
FORMAT A:/S
```

2. Then copy the BASICA.COM file from drive C to the new system diskette in drive A by using the COPY command:

```
COPY BASICA.COM A:
```

Your diskette is now prepared to receive any other application programs (through the COPY command) as well as to boot the DOS system at power-up time.

In the preceding example, you were only concerned with preparing a diskette that could both hold files and be used to boot up the system. At the beginning of Chapter 4, you'll learn how you can give the entire diskette a name, or label, during this formatting process. You'll also learn how to display this label and change it when the diskette's contents change.

BACKING UP AN EXISTING DISKETTE

The FORMAT command prepares a disk with tracks and sectors laid out in precise patterns. This is required for DOS to be able to store files of information on that disk. Now you will see how the DISKCOPY command can be used to precisely duplicate the contents of one diskette on another.

The DISKCOPY command does not require you to format the "target" diskette before using it—DISKCOPY automatically formats the target diskette if necessary. This is the only time that you can use an unformatted diskette for any DOS operation.

COPY-PROTECTED DISKETTES Diskettes that are *copy-protected* cannot be copied by DOS accurately. DOS expects all diskettes to have the same basic setup in terms of tracks, sectors, directories, and so on. If a diskette is organized at all differently, then the DISKCOPY command will not work.

Copy protection was originally designed to prevent users from making inexpensive copies of expensive software. These cheap copies often prevented original manufacturers from receiving all the income from sales that they were due. However, after several legal battles (over the right of users to make legitimate backup copies for themselves) and several marketing battles (over large corporate accounts refusing to buy copy-protected products that could not be placed on hard disks without continued diskette handling), the current trend has been away from copy-protected programs.

It is possible to purchase special programs like COPY II PC, from Central Point Software. These programs can decipher most of the special codes used by copy-protected software, allowing purchasers of protected software to make backup or archival copies of their disks. Since DOS can't do this, such a package is a good investment if your software collection includes copy-protected software.

BACKING UP YOUR DOS DISKETTES

In this section you'll see how to make duplicate (backup) copies of both of the DOS diskettes so that you can employ the backup diskettes, carefully storing and protecting the originals.

The procedure is slightly different if you have a one-diskette or two-diskette system. You may have one diskette drive in your system because that is all you have, or you may have one diskette drive because your system has a hard disk. In either case, you will use the DISKCOPY command to create an exact copy of each DOS diskette. You will need two double-sided, double-density blank diskettes for this purpose.

This section refers to the startup and operating diskettes contained in DOS 3.3. If you are using an earlier version of DOS, your two diskettes are labelled "System" and "Supplementary." The instructions in this section will apply regardless of the DOS version you are using.

DOS produces several prompting messages during the disk-copying operation, in which your original diskette (which you are copying) is referred to as the *source* diskette, and the new blank diskette (onto which you are making your copies) is referred to as the *target* or *destination* diskette (see Figure 2.6).

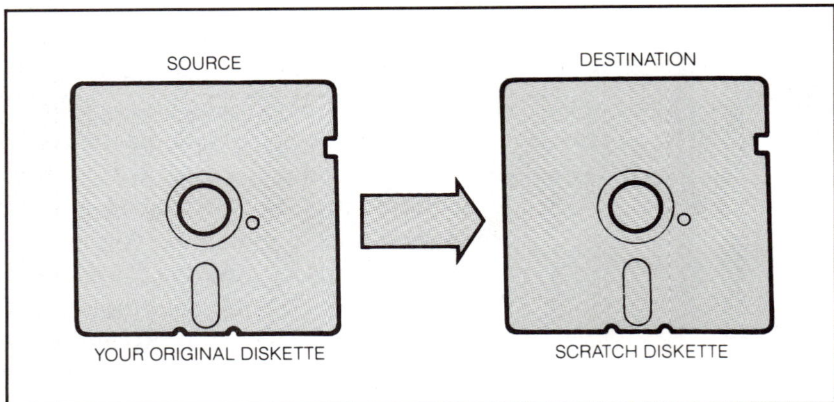

Figure 2.6: Making diskette replicas with DISKCOPY

FOR ONE-DISKETTE SYSTEMS Assuming you are using drive A, the single diskette drive of your system, you should type the following command:

```
DISKCOPY
```

When the DISKCOPY command executes, DOS will prompt you like this:

```
Insert source diskette in drive A:
Press any key when ready...
```

In this single-diskette environment, DOS will actually ask you to place both source and destination diskettes, successively, into drive A (see Figure 2.7).

Assuming your DOS diskette is still in drive A, press the Return key to begin the DISKCOPY operation. DOS will give you an informative message as it is copying your diskette. This message will vary according to the diskette's storage density and its number of sides:

```
Copying 40 tracks
9 Sectors/Track,2 Side(s)
```

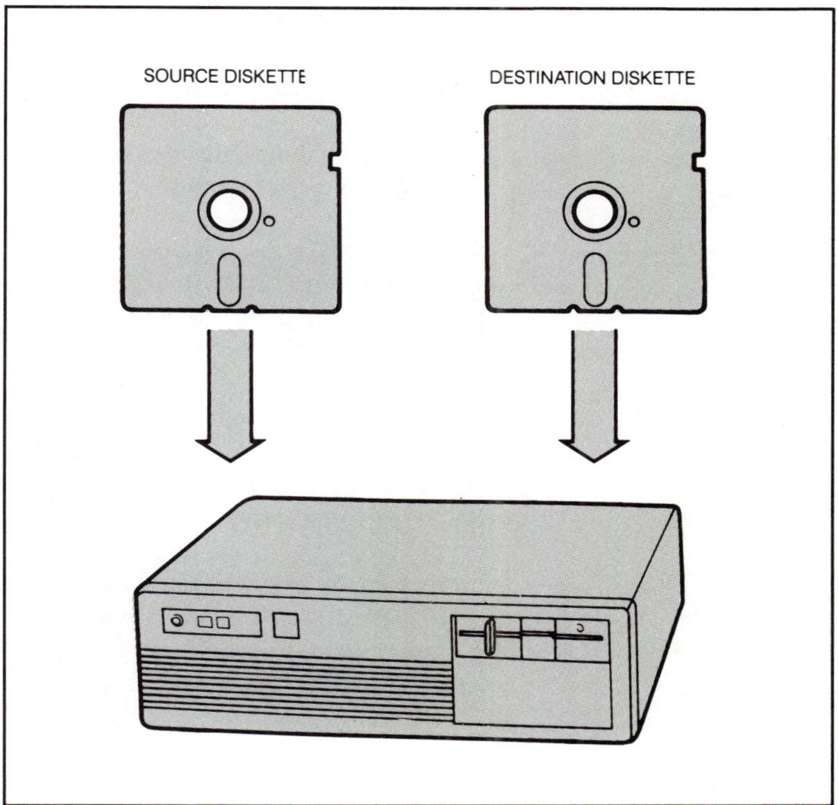

Figure 2.7: Copying diskettes using only one disk drive

When DOS has read as much as it can from the diskette, it will prompt you to

```
Insert target diskette in drive A:
Press any key when ready...
```

At this point, take a label and print "DOS Startup Diskette" on it and then place the label on one of the blank diskettes. Place this blank diskette in drive A and press Return. DOS will then copy onto the blank diskette whatever part of the DOS system diskette it was able to read in its first pass. When it has finished copying this information onto your new diskette, it may prompt you to again place the original DOS system diskette in drive A. This will depend on the total size (in bytes) of your source diskette, and whether it can be completely read into memory and then copied in only one pass. If it can't, DOS will prompt you to

```
Insert source diskette in drive A:
Press any key when ready...
```

If you receive this message, you should remove your blank diskette and put the original DOS diskette in, so that DOS can continue reading information from the source diskette. At some point it will prompt you to again insert the destination diskette in drive A. This is your cue to take out the original diskette and place your newly labeled diskette in drive A. Depending on the amount of memory you have on your computer and the version of DOS you are using, this juggling of diskettes will continue until all of the information from the original diskette is read, and all of it can be written onto the destination diskette.

At the end of this cycle, DOS asks if you would like to copy another diskette. Since you've just copied the first of the DOS diskettes, you should answer with the letter Y (for Yes), since you now intend to go through the entire cycle a second time for your DOS operating diskette.

Prepare a label that says "DOS Operating Diskette" and place it on your second blank diskette. After answering Y to DOS's question, you will again be prompted to insert a source diskette in drive A. At this point, place your DOS supplementary diskette in drive A and begin the entire process again, this time using your newly labeled "DOS Operating Diskette" blank diskette as the target of the DISKCOPY procedure.

FOR DUAL-DISKETTE SYSTEMS If your system has two diskette drives, the diskette-copying procedure can go much faster because no juggling is required. Assuming you have your DOS startup diskette in drive A, place your blank diskette, which you should label "DOS Startup Diskette," in drive B. Then type the following command at the DOS prompt:

```
DISKCOPY A: B:
```

This tells DOS to read everything from drive A and write it onto the diskette in drive B (see Figure 2.8). DOS will prompt you as follows:

```
Insert source diskette in drive A:
Insert target diskette in drive B:
Press any key when ready . . .
```

You should ensure that your DOS startup diskette is in drive A at this point, before you press the Return key, and that your blank diskette, which is to become the copy of the DOS system diskette, is in drive B. Pressing Return will then initiate the operation to completely copy the contents of one diskette onto the other. While DOS makes the copy you will be informed as to what type of diskette it believes it is copying

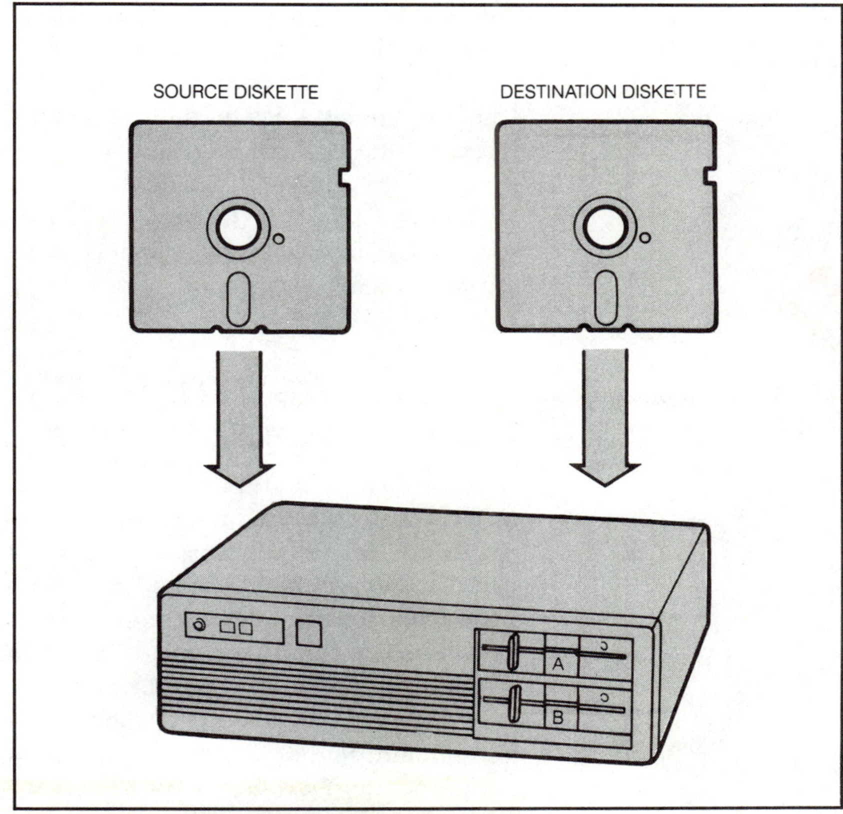

Figure 2.8: Copying disks using two disk drives

(single- or double-sided, the number of sectors to a track, and so on):

```
Copying 40 tracks
9 Sectors/Track,2 Side(s)
```

At the end, DOS will ask you if you want to copy another diskette:

```
Copy another diskette (Y/N)?
```

At this point you should answer Y, indicating that you would like to copy another diskette. You will get the same message, indicating that you should place the source diskette (your DOS operating diskette) in drive A and that you should insert the target diskette (your blank, newly labeled operating diskette) in drive B. Then—and only then—should you press the Return key to initiate the new process of copying the operating programs onto your backup diskette.

You can now answer N (for No) to the question about copying another diskette. When the DOS prompt returns, you are ready to begin using DOS in earnest.

The procedure you have just followed to back up the DOS diskettes can also be used to safely back up copies of most of your application software. However, certain copy-protected programs cannot be backed up in this fashion.

CHECKING THE DISK FOR AVAILABLE SPACE

Your DOS system provides a very useful command called CHKDSK. It is used frequently to check the amount of space, both used and unused, on a particular disk. One of DOS's drawbacks is that it does not pack information as densely on the disk as is possible. Files that contain large amounts of information will take up a significant amount of disk space. The CHKDSK command also gives detailed information about the files on your disk.

There are other uses you should know about for the CHKDSK command: finding and fixing file allocation errors. Both have to do with the way DOS stores file information on the disk. DOS actually allocates space for files in groups of sectors called *clusters*. The number of sectors in a cluster varies according to the type of disk and the version of DOS you are using. This explains why you might run out of disk space, even though the sum of all your file sizes is much smaller than the disk you are using.

If the cluster size is four sectors, then any data from 1 byte to 2K will be allocated all four sectors (2048 bytes) on your disk. If the cluster size is eight sectors, then all files will always require at least 4096 bytes. Even larger files may waste a number of bytes, since the last portion of these files will be allocated an entire cluster, even if only one additional byte is needed.

DOS 3.2 reduced the cluster size for hard disks. If you're still using an earlier version of DOS, this feature in itself may be sufficient reason to upgrade to the latest version. And if you're going to do that, get DOS 3.3; it's faster, offers a number of improved commands, and contains many efficiency features discussed throughout this book. It supports the Personal System/2 series of computers as well.

The CHKDSK command will give you a summary of the amount of space available on each disk. For instance, CHKDSK by itself will give you information about the current default disk drive (as shown by the prompt). Typically, this is drive A in a dual-diskette system and C in a hard-disk system, as shown in Figures 2.9 and 2.10. The same results could have been obtained by explicitly telling DOS which drives to check:

```
CHKDSK A:
```

or

```
CHKDSK C:
```

You might notice after entering the CHKDSK command that the red light on the drive you specified turned on, indicating that the device was activated. Whenever you see the red light, you can assume that the system is reading from or writing to the disk. Unless you are instructed to, you should *never* remove a disk from a drive when the light is on.

```
A>CHKDSK

   362496 bytes total disk space
    45056 bytes in 3 hidden files
   274432 bytes in 43 user files
    43008 bytes available on disk

   524288 bytes total memory
   443136 bytes free

A>_
```

Figure 2.9: CHKDSK output for a diskette (no volume label)

CHKDSK gives you the following information about disk space:

- *Bytes total disk space.* This tells you the number of original bytes of storage available on the disk before any files were added.
- *Bytes in hidden files.* This tells you the number of bytes in the special files used by DOS that are usually hidden from the user's view when a directory is listed.
- *Bytes in user files.* This tells you the number of bytes in the files created by you, which appear on a directory listing.
- *Bytes in bad sectors.* This indicates the number of bytes in bad sectors, which are usually sectors that have been blocked off from use because of some defect detected by the computer system. If all sectors are good, then no "bad sector" display will appear.
- *Bytes available on disk.* This tells you the amount of space left for adding new files to the disk.

The last two lines on the CHKDSK display do not deal with the disk drive. They tell you about the internal memory of the computer: how much total memory is installed in your system and how much is still free

```
C>CHKDSK
Volume ROBBINS      created Mar 22, 1987 4:43p

 21204992 bytes total disk space
    45056 bytes in 3 hidden files
   124928 bytes in 45 directories
 18618368 bytes in 1778 user files
  2416640 bytes available on disk

   524288 bytes total memory
   121920 bytes free

C>
```

Figure 2.10: CHKDSK output for a hard disk (volume label ROBBINS)

for use. This is usually only an issue to consider if you are using many programs at once, or if you don't have the maximum physical memory available on your machine.

Programs can occasionally create problems in DOS's management area, called the *file allocation table* (*FAT*). This is often the result of programs that begin to create files but stop because of some problem.

A special form of the CHKDSK command will list all FAT errors and also tell you if the files are stored in contiguous clusters:

CHKDSK *.*

Contiguous, or adjacent, clusters are desirable since it means the disk heads will travel less distance to read or write the desired sector data; all disk operations will occur faster. The symbol *.* represents a *wild-card* specification. Using the asterisk (*) tells DOS to check all files on the disk. (You'll learn more about wild-card symbols in Chapter 3.) The results of this command might appear as in Figure 2.11, which lets you know that on this disk, at this moment in time, there is only one file, SKN.COM, which is not stored in contiguous sectors.

There is nothing inherently wrong with files in noncontiguous sectors. However, large files in noncontiguous sectors are processed

```
A>CHKDSK *.*

   362496 bytes total disk space
    45056 bytes in 3 hidden files
   309248 bytes in 44 user files
     8192 bytes available on disk

   524288 bytes total memory
   443136 bytes free

A:\SKN.COM
   Contains 3 non-contiguous blocks.

A>_
```

Figure 2.11: CHKDSK request for file-contiguity information

more slowly than are files in contiguous sectors. When possible, it is best not to allow your disk to contain noncontiguous files.

If a CHKDSK command does list file allocation errors, you need to enter a special version of the CHKDSK command to *fix* the errors. The CHKDSK/F command will collect lost or misallocated sectors into a series of files named FILE0000.CHK, FILE0001.CHK, FILE0002.CHK, and so on. These are ASCII text files; you can type their contents from DOS to see the data, or you can use your word processor to try to change the data. (See Appendix B for a more complete description of ASCII codes and files.) You are usually best advised to simply be pleased at recovering the disk space and to erase the "recovered" files. However, if the data they contain represents simple textual data that does not exist any longer in any other form (perhaps it was lost during a power failure), you may use your word processor to try to recover as much as possible. This sometimes saves a good deal of reentry time, especially if the lost data is straight text and there was a good deal of it.

SUMMARY

This chapter contained specific information to guide your first steps with your new operating system. You discovered many important facts about DOS.

- The DOS system actually gets going automatically at power-up time. The startup procedure reads the first sectors on a system disk to bring the DOS hidden files into memory. This loading process ends with the DOS prompt, which indicates that DOS is waiting for your command request.
- You can set the system date and time at startup with the DATE and TIME commands. If you have a built-in clock/calendar, these commands also allow you to update the date and time values whenever you wish.
- Entering and editing commands at the DOS prompt is as simple as typing the command itself, along with any

necessary parameters or switches, and pressing Return. Parameters are merely placeholders for the actual entry values you will type when you give the command. Switches modify the operation of a DOS command, giving you the same sophisticated control over DOS commands as adjectives give you over nouns when you construct a sentence.

- The function keys can provide simple one-keystroke tools to make all your command formulations easier and less time-consuming. DOS uses function keys F1 through F6 for specific command-line editing purposes. The most commonly used function keys are F1, which retypes one character at a time from the last command, and F3, which retypes the entire last command.
- You can correct mistakes immediately by pressing the Backspace key, or cancel a command completely with the Esc key.
- You can erase the entire screen with the CLS command.
- All disks, whether hard, floppy, or microfloppy, must be prepared for use with a required formatting procedure. Disks are set up for different purposes, and you've seen how to prepare a scratch or blank diskette with the FORMAT command. This diskette can be used to boot the system or not, depending on whether you use the /S switch. Using the switch gives the diskette the ability to boot the system, as well as to store files. On the other hand, this does cost you storage space on the diskette; less space is available for your files.
- A working system disk can be created for most software packages by a simple procedure. First, a blank system disk can be prepared; then the appropriate files from your required software can be copied onto it to create a self-booting and complete system disk that contains your application software.
- The DISKCOPY command allows you to make copies of your DOS diskettes. In fact, it can be used to make replicas of any disk that is important enough to back up.
- The CHKDSK command obtains information about how both memory and disk storage are being used. This command can be applied to any disk on your system, and with

the /F switch can be used to fix file information (recover lost data) that has gone bad.

In Chapter 3, you'll learn new commands and skills that will enable you to organize your programs and files.

PART 2

MAKING DOS DO MORE

In Part 2, you will learn how to make DOS do much more for you. Chapter 3 will teach you the commands and features you need to manipulate files in a variety of ways. These include listing directories of files, copying files, typing out the contents of text files, renaming files, and erasing files. In Chapter 4, you will then learn how to create and maintain directory structures on floppy diskettes. You will discover how to create, use, and delete directories and subdirectories.

Chapter 5 is a special look at using directory structures on a hard disk. First you will practice formatting your hard disk. You will then set it up for three types of application programs—a spreadsheet, a word processor, and a database management system, or any other programs you plan to use regularly.

Chapter 6 prepares you to create and modify text files using the DOS line editor, EDLIN. You will use EDLIN throughout the rest of the book to generate and update system files, as well as to write your own simple programs (called batch files). Lastly, in Chapter 7, you will learn how to produce printed output of your work with your system.

MANIPULATING FILES

CHAPTER 3

BY NOW, YOU'VE LEARNED THE FUNDAMENTALS OF DOS, and you've seen what it can do. You've investigated simple command entry and disk preparation. In this chapter, you will learn to manipulate files.

When you work with DOS, you will always deal with files of one sort or another. Program files you purchase must be stored in some portion of your disk; data files you create must be stored in another portion. The more practiced you become at defining these disk portions, or directories, the more success you will have with DOS.

You will learn in this chapter how to access files on a disk in a variety of ways. You will also learn how to make backup and secondary copies of these files for your protection and convenience in making changes. You will see how DOS deals with external hardware devices in a manner similar to data files, and how the same commands, once learned, are doubly valuable.

Manipulating all of your files will give you more confidence and control over your system. You will learn how to type out the contents of text files, erase old files that you no longer need or that are occupying too much space, and how to make copies of any files onto 5¼'' or 3½'' diskettes so you can free disk space for new work.

In order for you to gain the upper hand in the ongoing struggle with confusion and disorganization, you will see how to easily rename files in place. And, if simple renaming isn't enough, you will learn to rapidly copy and regroup files between disk drives with the advanced XCOPY command.

THE DISK DIRECTORY

How can you tell what files are stored on a disk? On diskettes, at least, you could read the printed disk label, although the label may or may not have the correct information on it. Also, it rarely contains all the information available electronically in DOS. The only way to be sure of what is really on a disk is to have DOS display a *directory* of the files on that disk.

Just before storing each diskette you use, print out a directory listing of its contents using the techniques described in Chapter 7. To add a touch of class, use the techniques in Chapter 12 to print out a sorted listing.

The DIR (Directory) command will display on the screen a listing of all the files stored on a disk. If you enter the command

```
DIR
```

the computer will display a listing of all the files on the current active drive. Figure 3.1 shows a sample directory listing. Because the A> prompt was shown, this directory is for a diskette in drive A. The list of files is scrolled automatically on the screen, since the list has too many lines to be seen at one time on a standard 25-line screen. The bottom of the display shows the amount of space left on the diskette for new files.

To control the listing of files on the screen, use a *Ctrl-key combination.* The easiest way to do this is to hold the Ctrl key down and then press another key at the same time. For example, the key combination Ctrl-S, or ^S, freezes the screen and stops the scrolling. The same combination will start the screen output going again. This type of key combination is called a *toggle.*

Each line that appears in the directory represents a file that is stored on the disk. DOS displays four pieces of information about each file: the file name, the file size, and the date and time of its creation or last update:

```
BACKUP    COM    6234  12-30-85 2:00p
   (File Name)   (Size) (Date)   (Time)
```

Try the DIR command now on each of the drives in your own system:

```
DIR A:
DIR B:
DIR C:
```

If you have other drives, try the command on them. If you accidentally try the command with a drive letter that doesn't exist, DOS will tell you so. You'll receive the error message "Invalid drive specification" and then a new DOS prompt will be displayed. However, if

```
 Volume in drive A has no label
 Directory of  A:\

ANSI     SYS     1651  12-30-85  12:00p
ASSIGN   COM     1536  12-30-85  12:00p
ATTRIB   EXE     8247  12-30-85  12:00p
BACKUP   COM     6234  12-30-85  12:00p
BASIC    COM    19298  12-30-85  12:00p
BASICA   COM    36396  12-30-85  12:00p
CHKDSK   COM     9832  12-30-85  12:00p
COMMAND  COM    23791  12-30-85  12:00p
COMP     COM     4184  12-30-85  12:00p
DISKCOMP COM     5792  12-30-85  12:00p
DISKCOPY COM     6224  12-30-85  12:00p
DRIVER   SYS     1115  12-30-85  12:00p
EDLIN    COM     7508  12-30-85  12:00p
FDISK    COM     8173  12-30-85  12:00p
FIND     EXE     6416  12-30-85  12:00p
FORMAT   COM    11135  12-30-85  12:00p
GRAFTABL COM     1169  12-30-85  12:00p
GRAPHICS COM     3220  12-30-85  12:00p
JOIN     EXE     8955  12-30-85  12:00p
KEYBFR   COM     3291  12-30-85  12:00p
KEYBGR   COM     3274  12-30-85  12:00p
KEYBIT   COM     3060  12-30-85  12:00p
KEYBSP   COM     3187  12-30-85  12:00p
KEYBUK   COM     3036  12-30-85  12:00p
LABEL    COM     2346  12-30-85  12:00p
MODE     COM     6864  12-30-85  12:00p
MORE     COM      295  12-30-85  12:00p
PRINT    COM     8976  12-30-85  12:00p
RECOVER  COM     4297  12-30-85  12:00p
REPLACE  EXE    11650  12-30-85  12:00p
RESTORE  COM     6012  12-30-85  12:00p
SELECT   COM     3826  12-30-85  12:00p
SHARE    EXE     8580  12-30-85  12:00p
SORT     EXE     1911  12-30-85  12:00p
SUBST    EXE     9911  12-30-85  12:00p
SYS      COM     4620  12-30-85  12:00p
TREE     COM     3357  12-30-85  12:00p
VDISK    SYS     3307  12-30-85  12:00p
XCOPY    EXE    11200  12-30-85  12:00p
       39 File(s)     22528 bytes free
```

Figure 3.1: Sample directory listing

you ask for a directory listing on a drive letter that *does* exist on your system, but the drive isn't ready (the drive door isn't closed or the diskette hasn't been inserted), you'll receive the "Abort, Retry, Fail" error message (or "Abort, Retry, Ignore" in versions of DOS earlier than 3.3). If you've really made a mistake, simply type the letter A to abort the request; if the diskette wasn't ready, just prepare it and then type R to retry the DIR request. Only select the FAIL option if you are a DOS programmer and understand the nature of the internal system call that has failed, and how to proceed in the program.

The most important aspect of the resulting directory display is the listing of files. Each entry can have three parts:

1. A drive name (optional)
2. A base name
3. An extension (optional)

The general form of every DOS file name is as follows:

D:BaseName.Ext

where *D* represents an optional one-letter drive identifier (A, B, C, and so on), *BaseName* represents the base name, and *Ext* represents an optional three-character file-name extension. Figure 3.2 illustrates the general form.

The drive name can be any letter from A to Z. However, you must have a device connected to the computer to correspond to the drive designation. For example, two drives allow you to use A or B. Hard disks usually default to a drive identifier of C. The drive name is separated from the base name by a colon.

When you enter a file name, you enter it in a manner different from that in which DOS displays it. In the example line

```
BACKUP    COM    6234   12-30-85  2:00p
```

from a directory listing, the name appears as BACKUP   COM, but when you use this name, you must enter it as BACKUP.COM, with a period between the name and the three-character extension.

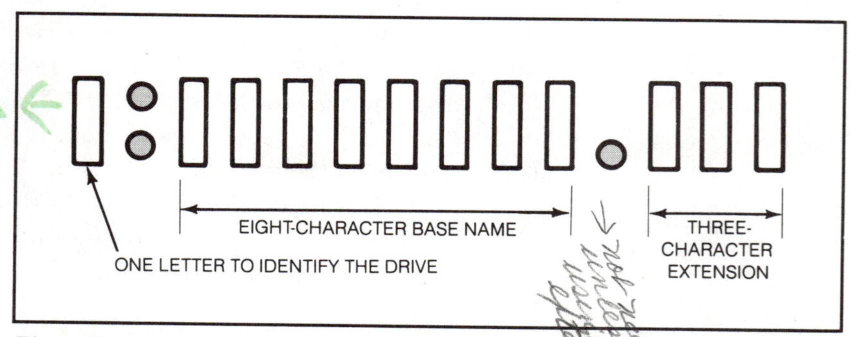

Figure 3.2: File-name structure in DOS

Note that DOS does not care if the letters are upper- or lowercase. However, you cannot enter spaces as part of a file name, even though that is the way they appear in the directory listing.

A file's base name can be between one and eight characters long. Since DOS checks for invalid characters when you enter a base name, you can use any sequence of characters except the following invalid ones:

. " / \ [ ] ¦ < > + : = ; ,

In addition, all DOS control codes (see Appendix B) are also invalid. For the sake of readability as well as typeability, keep your file names to alphabetic and numeric characters.

The following base name would not be acceptable to DOS because it contains a space:

```
MY FILE
```

However, this would be acceptable:

```
MY_FILE
```

The space has been replaced with an underscore, which is a legal character. Many people use this character to simulate a space, since it is visually unobtrusive. Use it if you like, but it always slows down the typing of the name; using the name MYFILE with neither a space nor an underscore would be quicker and easier.

An extension is limited to three characters. The same rules on invalid characters in the base name apply to an extension as well. The extension is separated from the base name by a period.

Take a look at the following list of file names:

- A:LETTER.TXT
- SAMPLE DAT
- X
- MY:FILE
- msdos.les
- Sample.File

- C.test.doc
- b:user.fil

Do you know which of these are valid and which are not? If not, reread the preceding sections before going on. The valid file names are A:LETTER.TXT, X, msdos.les, and b:user.fil. The others are all constructed incorrectly.

SAMPLE DAT is not acceptable because it contains a space. MY:FILE is unacceptable because two characters precede the colon. Colons cannot appear in a base name; they can *precede* the base name if a drive identifier begins the file name. However, a drive identifier can only be a single letter. The file name Sample.File is invalid because a file extension can contain only three characters. (In fact, DOS will accept this entry and treat it as if Sample.Fil had been typed; the ending "e" will be ignored.) The last invalid example, C.test.doc, will not work because a drive specification must be followed by a colon. Also, only one period can appear in a file name.

As stated earlier, drive specifications and extensions are optional. The usual purpose of an extension is to group together files with different names of the same type. Traditionally, file extensions such as .BAS (for BASIC language programs), .COM (machine-language command files), and .DAT (data files) have been used to identify the type of information contained within certain files.

Tradition is not the only reason for following conventions—they also make it easier to see, group, and access all files of the same type. When you look at the files contained in any new application package, you can easily understand the usage of many of them simply by noting the extension names (.HLP for help files, .TXT for text files, .OVL or .OVR for overlay files, and so on). See Table 3.1 for commonly used extensions.

LONG DIRECTORY LISTS

There are two alternative ways to list a directory if it is too long to be displayed on a single screen at one time. Enter

```
DIR/W
```

The directory might look something like the one in Figure 3.3. This is called a *wide directory,* because the files are listed across instead of

FILE EXTENSION	TYPE OF FILE
.BAK	Backup copies of files
.BAS	BASIC programs
.BAT	Batch files
.BIN	Binary object files
.COM	Simple executable programs (like DOS commands)
.DAT or .DTA	Data files
.DBF	Database files
.DRV	Device driver files
.EXE	Executable programs, usually larger than 64K and more sophisticated than .COM programs
.NDX	Index files
.OVL or .OVR	Overlay files
.PRG	dBASE III PLUS program files
.SYS	DOS device drivers
.TXT	Plain ASCII text files
.WKS or .WK1	Worksheet (spreadsheet) files

Table 3.1: Commonly used file-name extensions

vertically, which means that more names can fit on a single screen. Note that DOS no longer displays the size, date, and time of each file, which saves space on the display. The /W is an example of a switch; it modifies the way the DIR command executes.

Here's another variation on the DIR command. In this case /P is the switch, and it modifies the result of the command in a different way. If you enter

```
DIR/P
```

the screen fills and the list pauses until you press another key. If you then press Return again, the next screenful of file names is displayed.

```
A>DIR/W

 Volume in drive A has no label
 Directory of  A:\

ANSI     SYS    ASSIGN   COM    ATTRIB   EXE    BACKUP   COM    BASIC    COM
BASICA   COM    CHKDSK   COM    COMMAND  COM    COMP     COM    DISKCOMP COM
DISKCOPY COM    DRIVER   SYS    EDLIN    COM    FDISK    COM    FIND     EXE
FORMAT   COM    GRAFTABL COM    GRAPHICS COM    JOIN     EXE    KEYBFR   COM
KEYBGR   COM    KEYBIT   COM    KEYBSP   COM    KEYBUK   COM    LABEL    COM
MODE     COM    MORE     COM    PRINT    COM    RECOVER  COM    REPLACE  EXE
RESTORE  COM    SELECT   COM    SHARE    EXE    SORT     EXE    SUBST    EXE
SYS      COM    TREE     COM    VDISK    SYS    XCOPY    EXE
       39 File(s)      22528 bytes free

A>
```

Figure 3.3: Wide directory listing

This is somewhat akin to the ^S combination you saw earlier, except the listing breaks at precise places depending on how many directory entries it takes to fill the screen.

In summary, there are three styles of directory listings:

DIR	Full listing of all files, including size, date, and time
DIR/W	Wide directory; file size, date, and time not shown
DIR/P	Directory listing pauses when one screen is filled; size, date, and time shown

REFERRING TO FILES ON OTHER DRIVES

You can specify another drive's directory by following the DIR command with the letter that indicates the drive. On a dual-diskette system with a diskette in the second drive, if you typed

DIR B:

the computer would display the list of files on the diskette in drive B. You could also get a wide display of the list for drive B by entering

DIR B: /W

CHANGING THE DEFAULT DRIVE

The A> prompt indicates that DOS will work with the diskette in drive A unless you specify otherwise. Thus, drive A is considered the *default* drive for all commands. All commands will act on files located on the default drive unless you specifically include another drive name as part of the command or file-name specification. You can change the default drive simply by typing in the letter for the desired new default drive. Entering

B:

would change the A> prompt to B>. (Note that drive names are always followed by a colon.) Entering the DIR command now would cause the red light on drive B to light, since it is now the default drive; DOS would also tell you this by changing its prompt to B>. At this point, you could still get a listing of drive A by entering

DIR A:

LIMITING THE DIRECTORY DISPLAY

While the DIR command is useful in displaying the names of files, some practical problems require other techniques. For example, you might want to know if the disk in the current drive contains a file called ASSIGN.COM. If you simply entered the DIR command, you might be hard pressed to locate visually the file you were interested in, especially if you had scores of files (or hundreds of files, as you might on a hard disk). It might be better to narrow down the display to just the files that begin with the letter A. This would make it much easier to find out whether the file you wanted was on the disk.

DOS allows you a certain degree of ambiguity in asking for files. This means that there are ways to ask for a directory of files that meet certain criteria. The asterisk is used as a wild-card symbol to indicate your criteria. For example, if you want a list of all files that begin with the letter A, you enter

DIR A*

DOS will display a listing that looks something like this:

```
Volume in drive A has no label
Directory of A:\
     ASSIGN       COM     1536  12-30-85 12:00p
     AUTOEXEC     BAT     34     4-01-87  6:27p
                2 File(s) 124928 bytes free
```

It is now a much simpler matter to determine if ASSIGN.COM is on the disk, because DOS has displayed only a couple of specific files.

Suppose you want to see if the disk in drive A contains a file called WS.COM. You can enter

```
DIR W*
```

DOS will display a listing that looks like this:

```
Volume in drive A has no label
Directory of A:\

File not found
```

This tells you that there are no files beginning with the letter W on the disk in drive A; therefore, the file WS.COM is not on the disk.

Wild cards can be used to select listings of files by their extensions as well as by their file names. Suppose you wanted to list all of the files on the disk in drive A that end with a .DAT extension. Since you do not care what the file name is, an asterisk can be used. If you enter

```
DIR *.DAT
```

DOS will list all the files that have the extension .DAT.

Another way to search for names is to use the ? symbol. The question mark is a wild-card symbol for one character, as opposed to the asterisk symbol, which can stand for a number of characters. For example,

```
DIR ????.COM
```

will produce the display seen in Figure 3.4. The ????.COM

```
A>DIR ????.COM

 Volume in drive A has no label
 Directory of  A:\

COMP     COM     4184  12-30-85  12:00p
MODE     COM     6864  12-30-85  12:00p
MORE     COM      295  12-30-85  12:00p
SYS      COM     4620  12-30-85  12:00p
TREE     COM     3357  12-30-85  12:00p
        5 File(s)     22528 bytes free

A>
```

Figure 3.4: Directory searching with wild cards

specification told DOS to include any files that have names of four characters or less and also have a .COM extension.

The next two commands combine the * and ? wild cards:

```
DIR ??S?????.*
DIR ??S*.*
```

Both of these commands have the same effect: they tell DOS to list only those files that contain the letter S as the third character in their names. (Remember that a DOS base name is limited to a maximum of eight characters plus an extension.)

You can direct DOS to search the disk in drive B by adding B: to the wild card. For example, to list all files on the disk in drive B that begin with F, you would enter

```
DIR B:F*
```

Look at the following command. What type of files will it list?

```
DIR S???.COM
```

Try this command on your DOS master disk. See if your prediction is correct.

Figure out and enter the commands that would elicit the following lists of files:

1. All files on the active drive that begin with M
2. All files on the active drive that end in .COM
3. All files on drive B that begin with S

The solutions are as follows:

1. DIR M*
2. DIR *.COM
3. DIR B:S*

MAKING COPIES OF FILES

Making copies of files is an important ability to have in a computer system, especially a floppy-diskette system. Although a double-density diskette holds about 360 kilobytes and a high-capacity diskette holds 1.2 megabytes, it is often necessary to transfer files from one diskette to another for organizational or backup purposes.

The COPY command will copy files from one device onto another. COPY has many uses. The first one you will learn is how COPY can copy files from one disk to another. (A disk is only one type of device, but it is the most important and commonly used one.)

The general form of the COPY command is

COPY *Source Destination*

or

COPY *OldFile(s) NewFile(s)*

The first name is the name of the file(s) to copy. The second name is the name of the new file(s) to be created. When complete, both files (or sets of files) will contain the same information.

You will find many uses for the COPY command. You might want to make a secondary copy of a file you are working on, or you might want to make a backup copy of a file on another disk for precautionary reasons. You might want to make a replica of several files at the same time, perhaps from someone else's disk to yours. The following sections explore these and other uses of the COPY command.

MAKING SECONDARY COPIES

A second working copy of a file can be made easily with the COPY command. You can retain the original while working on and modifying the copy by entering

```
COPY BUDGET.TXT BUDGET.BAK
```

In this situation, a DIR of your disk would show two files where there had previously been only one, as you can see in Figure 3.5.

MAKING BACKUP COPIES

With COPY, you can make a backup copy on another disk. Suppose that you want to place a copy of your PHONES.DAT file onto the diskette in drive B. You could do this by entering

```
COPY PHONES.DAT B:
```

```
B>DIR

 Volume in drive B has no label
 Directory of  B:\

BUDGET86 TXT     15999    5-19-86   12:00p
BUDGET   TXT     13888    4-02-87    4:42p
        2 File(s)     286720 bytes free

B>COPY   BUDGET.TXT  BUDGET.BAK
        1 File(s) copied

B>DIR

 Volume in drive B has no label
 Directory of  B:\

BUDGET86 TXT     15999    5-19-86   12:00p
BUDGET   TXT     13888    4-02-87    4:42p
BUDGET   BAK     13888    4-02-87    4:42p
        3 File(s)     272384 bytes free

B>_
```

Figure 3.5: Making a secondary copy of a file

The command will create a copy of PHONES.DAT on the diskette in drive B with the same name. Put this backup diskette away to protect yourself against the time when your original file or disk is inadvertently lost.

MAKING MULTIPLE COPIES

Multiple files can be simultaneously copied by using wild cards with the COPY command. If you needed to copy all files with an .SYM extension to a diskette in drive B, you could enter

```
COPY *.SYM B:
```

New users frequently ask if there can be two copies of the same file on a disk if a file is copied twice to the same drive. The answer is no—there is only one copy. DOS will not allow two files to have exactly the same name on the same disk. If a file is copied to a disk that already has a file with that name, DOS erases the old file and then writes the copy of the new file. You receive no warning of this. Thus, it is possible to erase all the information contained in a file by accidentally copying another file of the same name to that disk. When this happens the old file is said to be *overwritten* by the new file, and you are said to be *in big trouble!* (However, as you will see in Chapter 4, when you learn about the possibility of different directories on a disk, there can be two similarly named files on the same disk if the two files are located in different directories.)

When you're not completely confident that a wild-card COPY command will copy over only the files you intend, use a DIR command first with the same wild-card specification. This will ensure that no unexpected duplicate file names will be accidentally overwritten. If you discover this possibility, either change the file name on the destination drive or give a unique name as the destination for the COPY command (COPY *OldFile* B:*NewName*).

Take a moment to practice with the COPY command. If a colleague or friend has some spreadsheet or database files or even games that you've been wanting to take a look at, now's the time. Of course, you should only make copies if there will be no copyright violation involved.

Format a blank diskette, and carefully copy the desired files from the original diskette to your new one. If your system has two diskette drives, you can specify a transfer from A to B by typing

COPY A:*FileNames* B:*FileNames*

If you only have one diskette, you may have to first transfer the files to drive C by typing

COPY A:*FileNames* C:*FileNames*

Then you can switch diskettes and transfer the files onto the new (destination) diskette by entering

```
COPY C:FileNames A:FileNames
```

MAKING COMPLETE DISK COPIES

One of the most common uses of the COPY command is to copy all the files from one diskette to another. This is necessary because diskettes can become worn out from use over a long period of time. Copying the files onto a new diskette will solve this problem. Also, keeping multiple copies of important files protects you against computer problems, human errors, or accidents such as fires.

You've already been introduced to the DISKCOPY command for making a complete copy of all the files from one disk onto another disk. Why should you consider using a version of the COPY command? The answer is subtle. DISKCOPY copies the original disk exactly, *retaining all noncontiguity*. The following version of the COPY command will usually rewrite files onto contiguous tracks and sectors on the new disk, improving future disk-access speed. The net result is that the performance or responsiveness of all your programs may improve.

To copy all the files from the diskette in drive A to that in drive B, you should enter

```
COPY *.* B:
```

If the destination diskette (in drive B in this example) already contains some files, you may find that there is not enough space to hold all the existing files on B as well as the new files from A. If this occurs, however, DOS will display the message "Insufficient Space." The best solution is to use a freshly formatted diskette or to erase files in advance on the destination diskette to ensure that enough space exists to receive the source diskette's files.

COPYING DATA TO OTHER DEVICES

The COPY command can exchange information between the disk and other devices such as the screen and keyboard (CON) or the printer (LPT1). The following command will send the contents of a file named PHONES.DAT to the screen. The destination device CON stands for console device (the monitor):

```
COPY PHONES.DAT CON:
```

COPY also allows the user to enter text into a file. If you use CON as the source device, you can use the keyboard to transfer information from the keyboard through the computer to a disk file.

If you enter the following command:

```
COPY CON: TEXT1.DAT
```

nothing seems to happen, except that the DOS A> prompt does not appear. This is an indication that you are no longer at the system level. DOS will now allow you to enter text directly from the keyboard, and anything that you type will eventually be stored in the file TEXT1.DAT. You could enter

```
This is an example of keyboard entry into a text file.
```

or any other text lines, pressing Return after each line. You would then need to enter the character that DOS uses to mark the end of a file, a Ctrl-Z, which is sometimes shown as ^Z. You obtain this unusual character by holding down the Ctrl key and pressing the letter Z. The symbol ^Z will then appear on the screen.

The colon (:) after a device name (as in CON:) is not strictly necessary, since DOS will figure out what you mean. However, it's good form to enter the colon, if only for consistency with the way you enter drive identifiers (such as A: and C:).

To complete the file, press Return. The disk drive will spin and all the lines of text that you typed at the keyboard will be saved as a file. To see the data, you can simply reverse the items in the COPY command and enter

```
COPY TEXT1.DAT CON:
```

followed by Return. The text will be displayed just as it was typed in. This is a convenient method for creating small text files quickly. Your alternative is to use a line editor (like EDLIN, which is contained in your DOS software and is described in Chapter 6) or a word processor (which offers much more in the way of text manipulation).

COMBINING FILE COPIES

COPY can also be used to join two or more files together, which allows you to gather up small data files into a single large file. This is sometimes useful when several small documents were created, all of which need to be word processed. To see how this is done, you could enter

```
COPY CON: TEXT2.DAT
This is additional text that is stored in another text file
^Z
```

and press Return after each line. You would then use the COPY command to join these two files. This is sometimes called *concatenation*. The general form of the command is shown below. The + sign is used to indicate the joining of text from two or more files:

COPY *SourceFile(s) DestinationFile(s)*

or

COPY *FirstFile* + *SecondFile* + *etc. CombinationFile*

If you want to combine two existing files like TEXT1.DAT and TEXT2.DAT, you would enter the following command:

```
COPY TEXT1.DAT + TEXT2.DAT COMBO.DAT
```

To see the results, you could enter

```
COPY COMBO.DAT CON:
```

The resultant file, COMBO.DAT, would contain all the text lines from both of the two source files:

```
This is an example of keyboard entry into a text file.
This is additional text that is stored in another text file.
```

You can even use the wild-card commands to join text files. For example, if you wanted to join together all the text files with a .DAT extension into one file, you would use a command like

```
COPY *.DAT ALL.TXT
```

This form is simpler than typing "*file1* + *file2* + *file3* + ..." if all the files have the same extension. It is another example of how wild cards can be helpful; it's also a good example of how to save time and effort by intelligently naming similar files with consistent extensions.

VERIFYING ACCURATE DATA TRANSFERS

Another useful switch is the /V switch. If this switch is specified for disk COPY operations, the entire data transfer is verified for accuracy. With normal, unverified transfers, this validation is not guaranteed.

Figure 3.6 shows the normal COPY mechanism, in which COPY reads data from a source disk file into memory and then writes it into the destination disk file. As the figure shows, a portion of memory acts as a *buffer* between the original source of the data (perhaps a disk file) and the eventual destination of the data (perhaps another disk file). In Chapter 8, you'll learn about DOS buffers in more detail. It's enough to know now that a portion of memory is reserved for the temporary storage of file information on its way to or from disk files.

Normally, DOS will copy file information from a source file to a destination file by successively reading one buffer's worth of data into memory and then writing it to the destination drive. Usually, there's no problem. But if the destination drive has a hardware malfunction (unrecognized bad sectors, for example), the resulting destination file may not be the expected replica of the original source file.

The /V switch will take care of the problem. Adding a /V at the end of the COPY command line will cause DOS to perform the sequence depicted in Figure 3.7. In this verified COPY operation, an extra step is undertaken. Each buffer's worth of information that is written to the destination file is also read back into memory. It is then reread to check for errors that may have occurred; if no errors

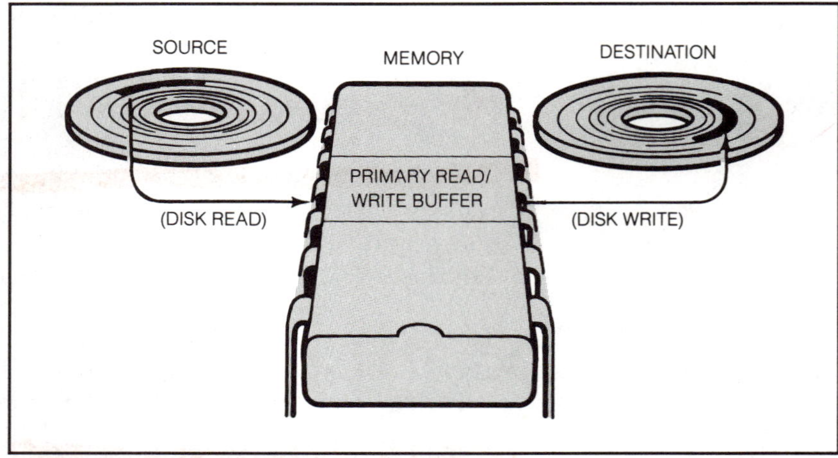

Figure 3.6: Unverified COPY operation

are discovered, DOS assumes that the destination file has received the source file's data accurately. If it is different, DOS can try to rewrite the data again or simply report an error.

Since this procedure adds an additional burden on your system, and since hardware malfunctions do not occur very often, you probably don't need to add the /V switch very often. The tradeoff is time versus security. However, if you want the security but don't want the bother of specifying /V all the time, DOS allows you a special command. Entering VERIFY at the DOS prompt with a parameter of ON (or OFF) will have the effect of appending (or not appending) a /V switch on all copies.

```
VERIFY ON
```

followed by Return will guarantee that all future COPY commands act like the one in Figure 3.7, with what is sometimes called *read-after-write* verification.

USING THE XCOPY COMMAND TO TRANSFER FILES

A special command called XCOPY (available only in DOS 3.2 or 3.3) allows more sophisticated file transfers between disks and directories. It is preferable for multifile transfers because it is usually faster

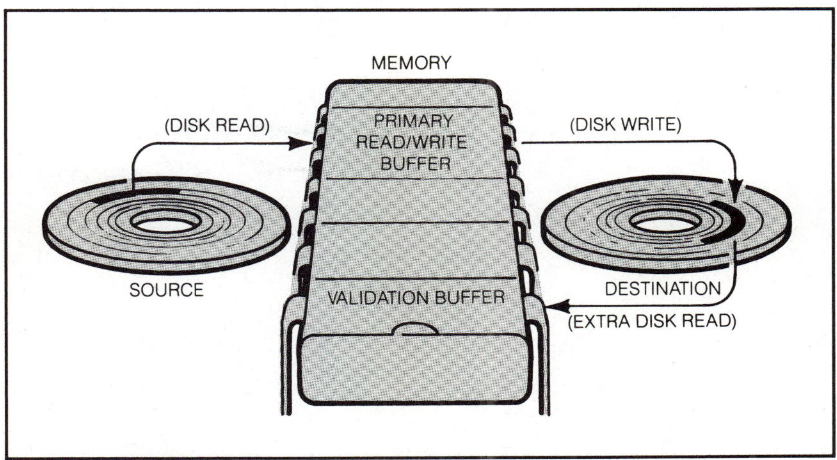

Figure 3.7: Verified COPY operation

than COPY. It is also preferable for transferring files that exist in multiple directories, because XCOPY understands better than COPY how to select files located in remote sections of the disk. You'll learn more about these remote sections, called *subdirectories,* in Chapter 4; they are subdivisions of existing directories on a disk.

XCOPY cannot be used to transfer multiple files to a printer. It is designed for disk transfers only.

The general format of the XCOPY command is

XCOPY *SourceFile(s) DestinationFile(s) /Switches*

where *SourceFile(s)* and *DestinationFile(s)* are specified as they are with the COPY command. Using */Switches* properly can greatly expand the range of files encompassed. Try performing some sample operations using the files contained in three sections of a disk, as shown in Figure 3.8. Conventional directory listings of the files involved are shown in Figures 3.9 and 3.10.

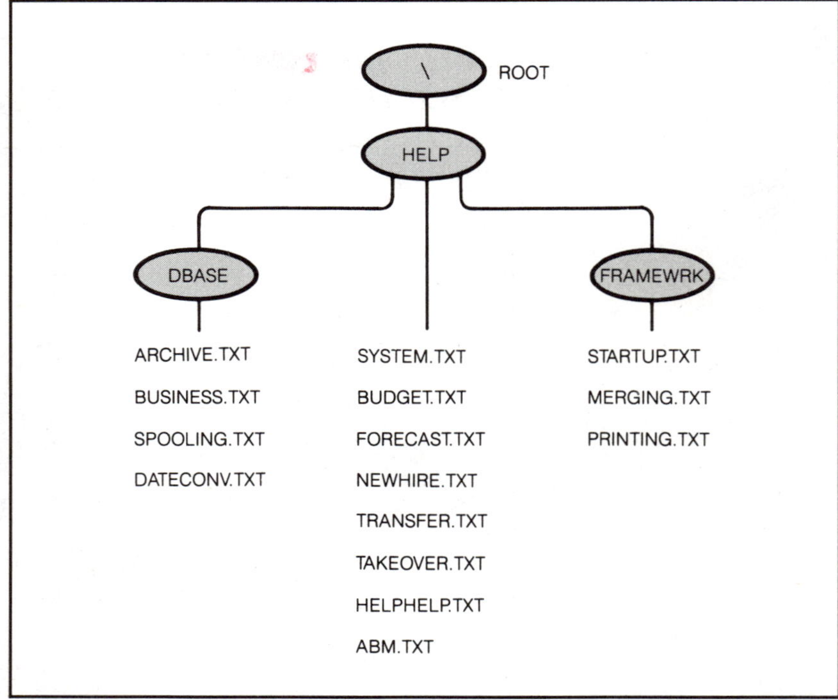

Figure 3.8: Sample directory structure

The simplest example of using the XCOPY command is the following:

XCOPY \HELP*.* A:

will copy all files in the HELP directory to the disk in drive A. As you can see in Figure 3.11, DOS echoes the file names to the screen as they are copied.

```
C>DIR \HELP

 Volume in drive C is ROBBINS
 Directory of  C:\HELP

.            <DIR>        5-03-87    8:16a
..           <DIR>        5-03-87    8:16a
SYSTEM   TXT       328    1-13-87    7:50p
BUDGET   TXT      2186    1-22-87    6:08p
FORECAST TXT       256    1-02-87   12:25p
NEWHIRE  TXT      1781    2-26-87    6:39p
TRANSFER TXT      4429    1-19-87    2:55p
TAKEOVER TXT       621    1-01-87   12:16p
HELPHELP TXT       258    1-14-87    2:41p
ABM      TXT       383    1-13-87    6:33p
DBASE        <DIR>        5-03-87    8:24a
FRAMEWRK     <DIR>        5-03-87    8:24a
       12 File(s)    1130496 bytes free

C>_
```

Figure 3.9: The HELP directory

```
 Volume in drive C is ROBBINS
 Directory of  C:\HELP\DBASE

.            <DIR>        5-03-87    8:24a
..           <DIR>        5-03-87    8:24a
ARCHIVE  TXT      1152   10-25-85    6:46p
BUSINESS TXT       561    4-16-87   10:04p
SPOOLING TXT      2816   10-25-85    6:38p
DATECONV TXT      1536   10-25-85    6:41p
        6 File(s)    1124352 bytes free

C>DIR \HELP\FRAMEWRK

 Volume in drive C is ROBBINS
 Directory of  C:\HELP\FRAMEWRK

.            <DIR>        5-03-87    8:24a
..           <DIR>        5-03-87    8:24a
STARTUP  TXT       195    3-05-86    9:25a
MERGING  TXT       638    2-19-86   10:56a
PRINTING TXT       147    2-19-86   10:58a
        5 File(s)    1124352 bytes free

C>_
```

Figure 3.10: The HELP\DBASE and HELP\FRAMEWRK directories

```
C>XCOPY  \HELP\*.*  A:

Reading source file(s)...
\HELP\SYSTEM.TXT
\HELP\BUDGET.TXT
\HELP\FORECAST.TXT
\HELP\NEWHIRE.TXT
\HELP\TRANSFER.TXT
\HELP\TAKEOVER.TXT
\HELP\HELPHELP.TXT
\HELP\ABM.TXT
        8 File(s) copied

C>_
```

Figure 3.11: XCOPY reading files into memory and writing destination files

The unique aspect of this command is hidden behind the message "Reading source file(s)," which appears first on the screen. The COPY command reads a source file and then writes a destination file. The XCOPY command first reads as many source files as possible into available memory. Only then does it stop to write the destination files. Since memory operations occur much more rapidly than disk operations, the overall operation speed is increased. Simply said, less disk work and more memory work means the entire file is transferred faster.

SWITCHES FOR THE XCOPY COMMAND You should now take a look at the XCOPY command's switches, in the order of their importance. The most powerful switch is /S, which gives you the ability to select files located in the subdirectory structure. Notice in Figure 3.11 that the expected eight .TXT files in HELP were copied. That's the same result as would have been obtained by using the COPY command, but the operation went a little faster.

In Figure 3.12, you can see the direct effect of using the /S switch. It directs DOS to look in all subdirectories of HELP for file names that match the specified *.TXT wild card. As simply as that, the additional four .TXT files in the HELP\DBASE subdirectory are copied, along with the additional three .TXT files in the

```
C>XCOPY  \HELP\*.*  A: /S

Reading source file(s)...
\HELP\SYSTEM.TXT
\HELP\BUDGET.TXT
\HELP\FORECAST.TXT
\HELP\NEWHIRE.TXT
\HELP\TRANSFER.TXT
\HELP\TAKEOVER.TXT
\HELP\HELPHELP.TXT
\HELP\ABM.TXT
\HELP\DBASE\ARCHIVE.TXT
\HELP\DBASE\BUSINESS.TXT
\HELP\DBASE\SPOOLING.TXT
\HELP\DBASE\DATECONV.TXT
\HELP\FRAMEWRK\STARTUP.TXT
\HELP\FRAMEWRK\MERGING.TXT
\HELP\FRAMEWRK\PRINTING.TXT
       15 File(s) copied

C>
```

Figure 3.12: The /S switch searching all subdirectories for wild-card matches

HELP\FRAMEWRK subdirectory. If the respective directories do not already exist on the destination disk, DOS automatically creates them for you and then copies the files into them.

You can exercise further control over the copying operation by employing the /P switch, which offers another improvement. It asks DOS to prompt you (hence /P) for each file name that matches the wild-card specification, giving you control over whether each file name will be included in the actual copying operation.

Look at the example XCOPY transfer in Figure 3.13, which uses the same /S switch as in the last example but asks you to answer a prompt for each file. In the figure's example, the prompt was answered affirmatively (Y) only four times. The destination drive consequently received copies of the four selected files only. These files were

- HELP\BUDGET.TXT
- HELP\FORECAST.TXT
- HELP\DBASE\BUSINESS.TXT
- HELP\FRAMEWRK\MERGING.TXT

It's important to notice that two of these files are in subdirectories of the HELP directory. The /S switch also ensures that the same

```
C>XCOPY  \HELP\*.*  B: /S /P
\HELP\SYSTEM.TXT (Y/N)? N
\HELP\BUDGET.TXT (Y/N)? Y
\HELP\FORECAST.TXT (Y/N)? Y
\HELP\NEWHIRE.TXT (Y/N)? N
\HELP\TRANSFER.TXT (Y/N)? N
\HELP\TAKEOVER.TXT (Y/N)? N
\HELP\HELPHELP.TXT (Y/N)? N
\HELP\ABM.TXT (Y/N)? N
\HELP\DBASE\ARCHIVE.TXT (Y/N)? N
\HELP\DBASE\BUSINESS.TXT (Y/N)? Y
\HELP\DBASE\SPOOLING.TXT (Y/N)? N
\HELP\DBASE\DATECONV.TXT (Y/N)? N
\HELP\FRAMEWRK\STARTUP.TXT (Y/N)? N
\HELP\FRAMEWRK\MERGING.TXT (Y/N)? Y
\HELP\FRAMEWRK\PRINTING.TXT (Y/N)? N
        4 File(s) copied

C>_
```

Figure 3.13: The /P switch prompt before copying

subdirectory structure is recreated on the destination disk (if it is not there already), as you can see in Figure 3.14. Figure 3.15 verifies that the specified files are also copied over accurately and into the proper subdirectories.

Another important switch, /D, allows you to specify that all files should be copied if their creation dates are the same as or later than the date specified. The form required is /D:mm-dd-yy unless you have installed a DOS version with a different international date format (see Chapter 11). In that case, you can specify the date in whatever format your system recognizes. As an example, Figure 3.16 demonstrates how all files in the HELP directory that were created on or after January 19, 1987, are copied to drive A.

Remaining switches are of less practical importance. The /A switch selects files that are marked for backup (see Chapter 9 for a discussion of backups). The archive attribute is not changed by this switch. The /M switch copies the same files that are marked for backup, but it does change the archive attribute to indicate that the files have been backed up.

The /V switch performs the same task as it does on the COPY command, requesting the extra read-after-write verification step. The /W switch is hardly worth mentioning, since its only job is to pause briefly, asking you to press any key to begin copying files.

```
C>DIR B:

 Volume in drive B has no label
 Directory of  B:\

BUDGET   TXT      2186   1-22-87   6:08p
FORECAST TXT       256   1-02-87  12:25p
DBASE        <DIR>       5-03-87   9:20a
FRAMEWRK     <DIR>       5-03-87   9:20a
        4 File(s)    173568 bytes free

C>_
```

Figure 3.14: Destination drive after using /S and /P

```
C>DIR B:\DBASE

 Volume in drive B has no label
 Directory of  B:\DBASE

.            <DIR>       5-03-87   9:20a
..           <DIR>       5-03-87   9:20a
BUSINESS TXT       561   4-16-87  10:04p
        3 File(s)    173568 bytes free

C>DIR B:\FRAMEWRK

 Volume in drive B has no label
 Directory of  B:\FRAMEWRK

.            <DIR>       5-03-87   9:20a
..           <DIR>       5-03-87   9:20a
MERGING  TXT       638   2-19-86  10:56a
        3 File(s)    173568 bytes free

C>_
```

Figure 3.15: Accurately created destination subdirectories

OTHER FUNDAMENTAL ACTIVITIES

There are just a few more commands that you should know about to aid your activities at this point. Of course, many other commands do exist, but you'll only need them in more advanced situations, covered later in this book. You should now become comfortable with typing out text files, renaming files, and deleting files.

```
C>XCOPY  \HELP\*.*  A:  /D:1/19/87

Reading source file(s)...
\HELP\BUDGET.TXT
\HELP\NEWHIRE.TXT
\HELP\TRANSFER.TXT
        3 File(s) copied

C>_
```

Figure 3.16: Specifying dates with XCOPY and /D

TYPING OUT A TEXT FILE

The TYPE command is similar to the COPY CON command. It can show the contents of any standard text or ASCII file. TYPE is also the best way to view the contents of *batch files,* which are only simple ASCII text files. In both cases, these files consist solely of letters, numbers, and symbols that can be typed on a standard keyboard. Although you won't learn about DOS batch files in depth until Chapter 13, you should take note of the TYPE command now.

Remember to use the Ctrl-S key combination to stop and start the display of the contents of the README.TXT file. In Chapter 12 you'll learn how to use the MORE command at the DOS prompt to display one screenful of information at a time.

Many business application programs are purchased on diskette. Whether you eventually use the software on diskette or on a hard disk, the manufacturer usually provides a special file called README.TXT or some similar name. Special usage information that arrived too late to be included in the printed user manual usually is included in this file. The TYPE command is the easiest way to read the file. To use it, enter

```
TYPE README.TXT
```

CHANGING THE NAME OF A FILE

You can change the name of a file without affecting the contents of that file. There may be times when you want to change some file names so that you can take advantage of the ? or * wild card to deal with blocks of files.

During the writing of this book, many screen images were captured and a number of text-file figures were created. When screen images are captured, they are given names like SCREEN##.CAP. It is more convenient to rename them according to the chapter and figure name, since then all figures can be managed together using wild-card expressions.

You can only use the RENAME command for a single file on a single disk. You *cannot* use the RENAME command to simultaneously copy a file from one disk to another while renaming it—use the COPY command to do that particular chore. RENAME only changes the name of the file, whereas COPY creates a new file entirely. With COPY, you begin with one file and end up with two; with RENAME, you begin with one file and end up with the same file.

Figure 3.17 shows a wide directory listing of a group of figures prepared for this book. At the bottom of the figure, the listing shows the file containing the most recently captured screen image, SCREEN03.CAP. Using DOS's RENAME command, you can change the SCREEN03 file name without changing the data inside the file, and still retain the extension (see Figure 3.18):

```
RENAME SCREEN03.CAP FIG8-12.CAP
```

The command has changed SCREEN03.CAP to FIG8-12.CAP. Notice in Figure 3.18 that DIR SCREEN*.CAP doesn't find any screen files, since the only previously existing .CAP had its name changed to FIG8-12.CAP.

The general form of this command is

RENAME ***OldName NewName***

The first file name is the old name you want to change. The file name that follows is the new name the file will receive.

You can also use the * and ? wild cards with the RENAME command. For example, if you want to change all files that have an extension of .CMD to files that end in .PRG, you can do so with one command:

```
RENAME *.CMD *.PRG
```

This sort of operation often is required when you switch from one system to another, or when a software manufacturer makes a major change in its naming conventions. For example, if you need to run programs written in Ashton-Tate's dBASE II under the auspices of your dBASE III PLUS, this is exactly the type of renaming task you would perform.

```
C>DIR/W  FIG*.CAP

 Volume in drive C is ROBBINS
 Directory of  C:\PROGRAMS\FW\SYBEX

FIG11-1  CAP    FIG11-2  CAP    FIG11-3  CAP    FIG11-5  CAP    FIG11-6B CAP
FIG2-10  CAP    FIG2-11  CAP    FIG2-12  CAP    FIG2-6   CAP    FIG2-7   CAP
FIG2-8A  CAP    FIG2-8B  CAP    FIG4-10A CAP    FIG4-10B CAP    FIG4-10C CAP
FIG4-14  CAP    FIG4-15  CAP    FIG4-2   CAP    FIG4-3   CAP    FIG4-4   CAP
FIG4-5   CAP    FIG4-6   CAP    FIG4-7   CAP    FIG4-8   CAP    FIG4-9   CAP
FIG7-3   CAP    FIG7-4   CAP    FIG7-5   CAP
       28 File(s)   2293760 bytes free

C>DIR SCREEN*.CAP

 Volume in drive C is ROBBINS
 Directory of  C:\PROGRAMS\FW\SYBEX

SCREEN03 CAP      4256   3-30-87   9:38a
        1 File(s)   2287616 bytes free

C>_
```

Figure 3.17: Listing of figure and screen files

```
C>RENAME  SCREEN03.CAP  FIG8-12.CAP

C>DIR/W FIG*.CAP

 Volume in drive C is ROBBINS
 Directory of  C:\PROGRAMS\FW\SYBEX

FIG11-1  CAP    FIG11-2  CAP    FIG11-3  CAP    FIG11-5  CAP    FIG11-6B CAP
FIG2-10  CAP    FIG2-11  CAP    FIG2-12  CAP    FIG2-6   CAP    FIG2-7   CAP
FIG2-8A  CAP    FIG2-8B  CAP    FIG4-10A CAP    FIG4-10B CAP    FIG4-10C CAP
FIG4-14  CAP    FIG4-15  CAP    FIG4-2   CAP    FIG4-3   CAP    FIG4-4   CAP
FIG4-5   CAP    FIG4-6   CAP    FIG4-7   CAP    FIG4-8   CAP    FIG4-9   CAP
FIG7-3   CAP    FIG7-4   CAP    FIG7-5   CAP    FIG8-12  CAP
       29 File(s)   2281472 bytes free

C>DIR SCREEN*.CAP

 Volume in drive C is ROBBINS
 Directory of  C:\PROGRAMS\FW\SYBEX

File not found

C>_
```

Figure 3.18: Using the RENAME command

The RENAME command also offers a limited degree of protection. You may not be the only person with access to your computer and disks. In that case, you may desire a measure of security for some of your data files. You can rename an obvious file like BUDGET.WK1 to TEMP.NDX, a clearly misleading name. Prying eyes are not as likely to come to rest on the renamed file.

Take a moment now to try this renaming technique on any files for which you'd like to restrict access. But be careful: first, don't forget the new file name you choose; second, don't select a dispensable name (like TEMP.NDX) if anyone else using your disk is at all likely to delete files.

ERASING A FILE

From time to time you will want to get rid of a file on a disk. The ERASE command will do this for you. The general form of the command is

```
ERASE FileName(s)
```

The following command will erase the file PHONES.DAT from drive A:

```
ERASE phones.dat
```

The ? and * wild-card operators also work with ERASE, so you can erase groups of related files with a single command. Be careful with ERASE—it will erase files without asking for confirmation. The following command will erase all .TXT files:

```
ERASE *.TXT
```

As you were advised in the section on the COPY command, *be certain* when you issue a command with wild cards that it will affect only the files you intend.

The only time DOS will ask you if you really meant what you said is when you specify

```
ERASE *.*
```

This command includes all files. Be sure of yourself if you answer yes to that question. If you make a mistake and accidentally erase any files you didn't mean to—or all of them—stop immediately. Do nothing else until you buy a file recovery program.

Another command exists that works exactly the same as ERASE: the DEL command. However, this command should be avoided—it's much closer in appearance to the commonly used DIR command, but devastatingly different in its effect. Too many people have typed DEL *.* when they intended to type DIR *.*; you don't have to make the same mistake. Use the ERASE command when you want to remove files from your disks.

You should always precede an ERASE request that uses wild cards with a DIR command, using the same wild-card specification, to ensure that you know which files will be picked up by the command.

The most common use for the ERASE command is to clean up disks that have been in use for a while. Old versions of data files often proliferate; early copies of memos and other word-processed documents always seem to expand to fill any available space on your disk. If you have a disk that fits this description, now is a good time to use ERASE and clean it up.

SUMMARY

To use your computer effectively, you need to understand how data, programs, and information of any sort are stored in files and how to properly manage these files. This chapter presented the principal commands and mechanisms in DOS for file management. You learned the following:

- The DOS disk directory contains a listing of all base names and extensions for each separate file in it. It also contains the sizes, as well as the dates and times of creation of these files.
- The DIR (Directory) command permits you to obtain listings of each directory's contents.
- Certain switches modify the DIR command request. More files can be listed on the screen with the /W (Wide) switch, and information can be presented one screenful at a time with the /P switch.
- DOS references files only on the current default drive. However, by preceding the file name with a drive identifier, like A: or C:, you can reference files on different drives.
- The DIR listing can be restricted to only some of the files in the directory by using placeholding wild-card symbols. The * and ? symbols can be used to ask DOS to manipulate multiple files at the same time. These symbols can take the place of part or all of a file's base name and extension.
- The powerful COPY command can be used to make secondary copies or backup copies of files by specifying the desired file name as the source file, and the new file name as the destination file.

- COPY can also copy multiple files at a time if you carefully use wild cards as the source and destination file names.
- COPY can transfer data between several different physical devices if you simply specify a device identifier (for example, PRN: for a printer) as either the source or destination for the COPY file transfer.
- Files can be combined if you combine their names with a plus sign as the source specification for a COPY command.
- The XCOPY command, available in DOS 3.2 or 3.3, can provide extended capabilities for transferring files between disks and directories.
- Several other useful and fundamental commands exist for typing out the contents of text files (TYPE), for changing the name of a file (RENAME), and for completely deleting a file (ERASE). In each case, these commands require you to specify the file names you want to use as parameters on the command line.

In the next chapter, you'll take a closer look at what goes on behind the scenes when you make any of these file management requests. You'll see how the disk directory can be organized in special ways for efficiency and clarity. You'll learn how to set up your disk in the best way for your application plans, and you'll see how to quickly maneuver around your sophisticated organizational design.

UNDERSTANDING THE DOS DIRECTORY STRUCTURE

CHAPTER 4

CHAPTER 3 TAUGHT YOU HOW TO MANAGE AND manipulate your files and introduced the concepts of directories and subdirectories. In this chapter, you'll explore what subdirectories are and how you can use them to organize your data and program files efficiently. If you have DOS version 2.X or higher, every disk in your system can be logically split up into directories and subdirectories. This ability to create and maintain purposeful groupings of files is the most powerful organizational tool in DOS.

Directories are like separate drawers in a file cabinet. Subdirectories are like the further labeled categories within each drawer. Files are stored in subdirectories and isolated from other files. Just as a well-organized file cabinet promotes efficiency in the office, a well-organized set of DOS directories and subdirectories enables you to quickly and easily store and retrieve your program and data files.

The words *directory* and *subdirectory* are often used interchangeably in DOS. Both are correct. *Subdirectory* is a relative term; any directory is a subdirectory of another directory, with the exception of the root directory. In this book, the word *subdirectory* refers to any directory on a disk other than the *root* (main) directory. The word *directory* refers to either the root or any one of the many possible subdirectories extending from it.

As Table 4.1 shows, a hard disk will store many times the amount of data or number of files that can be stored on a floppy diskette. For example, if the average size of your files is 20,000 bytes, then a 10-megabyte hard disk would hold approximately 500 uniquely named files. If the average file is smaller (say, 10,000 bytes), then you could have 1000 different files on the disk. This raises the problem of keeping order among a huge list of files. DOS allows you to create subdirectories—units of organization that divide the hard disk into sections—to solve this problem.

While subdirectories are usually associated with hard disks, DOS can just as easily create subdirectories on floppy diskettes. They will function exactly the same on diskettes as they do on hard disks, and they will differ only in the volume of data they are capable of holding.

TYPE OF DISK	TOTAL STORAGE (BYTES)	NUMBER OF 20K FILES
5¼" floppy	360K	18
High-capacity 5¼" floppy	1.2Mb	60
Double-sided 3½" floppy	1.44Mb	72
Hard disk	10Mb	500
Hard disk	20Mb	1000

Table 4.1: Potential files on differently sized disks

In this chapter, you'll explore the directory commands in the context of a diskette. In Chapter 5, you'll apply what you learn to the more spacious realm of the hard disk. Read this chapter even if you have a hard-disk system—it presents many concepts and techniques you'll need for hard disks as well.

A FIRST LOOK AT A DISK'S DIRECTORY STRUCTURE

Figure 4.1 shows the directory listing for a sample user diskette placed in drive B. (Hard-disk users can try these methods on any diskette placed in drive A.) As the directory shows, there are five files stored on the diskette.

Look at the first line of the directory display:

```
Volume in drive B has no label
```

This line refers to the *volume label,* an 11-character name. If you have a label for your disk or diskette, it will appear at the top of the directory listing whenever you enter the DIR command. (The disk will also have an additional hidden file entry, which is inaccessible to you, to store the 11 characters in the label.)

The sample diskette in Figure 4.1 has no label because it was prepared according to the instructions in Chapter 2. Unfortunately, most

Always label your disks when formatting them. Use a name that is indicative of the kind of data or files you intend to place on the disk. You can go back with DOS's LABEL command (available on version 3.0 and higher) to modify the volume label whenever you wish.

```
B>DIR

 Volume in drive B has no label
 Directory of  B:\

IMCAP     COM     6114   6-20-85    1:09p
IMSHOW    EXE    20090   6-20-85   10:09a
QD2       EXE    74752  11-14-86   12:00p
SKN       COM    34009   8-05-85    6:14p
SR        COM     5356   1-01-85
        5 File(s)    175104 bytes free

B>
```

Figure 4.1: Directory listing of sample diskette

users don't bother with labels, which were designed for the user's benefit. Labels are a simple but effective method of categorizing the files on a disk. Anyone using that disk can quickly ascertain the nature or purpose of the disk's contents. When no label is entered, DOS displays the message "Volume in drive B has no label."

To prepare a diskette for a volume label, you can use the /V switch with the FORMAT command, which allows you to enter an 11-character name. Spaces are allowed in this label, even though file names do not permit spaces. Figure 4.2 shows a typical sequence used to prepare a completely different diskette, which will be able to boot up the DOS system (/S) with a volume label (/V) that says SYBEX BOOK.

If you decide after you have formatted a diskette to add a volume label, or if you wish to modify an existing volume label, you should use the LABEL command, available on DOS version 3.0 and higher. Figure 4.3 shows how the label BOOK SAMPLE has been placed on the previously unlabeled diskette.

The second line of the initial directory display shown in Figure 4.1 indicates which directory is being listed. It reads

Directory of B:\

A disk with no subdirectories has only a single directory. The backslash symbol (\) is used to indicate a directory name. When DOS

```
A>FORMAT B: /S /V
Insert new diskette for drive B:
and strike ENTER when ready

Format complete
System transferred

Volume label (11 characters, ENTER for none)? SYBEX BOOK


    362496 bytes total disk space
     69632 bytes used by system
    292864 bytes available on disk

Format another (Y/N)?N
A>
```

Figure 4.2: Formatting a diskette with a volume label

```
A>LABEL B:

Volume in drive B has no label

Volume label (11 characters, ENTER for none)? BOOK SAMPLE


A>DIR  B:

 Volume in drive B is BOOK SAMPLE
 Directory of  B:\

IMCAP    COM     6114   6-2Ø-85    1:Ø9p
IMSHOW   EXE    2ØØ9Ø   6-2Ø-85   1Ø:Ø9a
QD2      EXE    74752  11-14-86   12:ØØp
SKN      COM    34ØØ9   8-Ø5-85    6:14p
SR       COM     5356   1-Ø1-85
        5 File(s)    22Ø16Ø bytes free

A>
```

Figure 4.3: DOS's LABEL command

shows B:\, it indicates that you are looking at the main or root directory of the disk. This root directory is created when a disk is formatted. Every disk has one—and only one—root directory. In the next section, you'll see how to subdivide the root directory into smaller but more refined groupings: subdirectories.

CREATING A SUBDIRECTORY

In this section you will create a subdirectory called UTIL to store a group of related files. The UTIL subdirectory will hold some DOS utility programs selected from a DOS master disk. Without subdirectories, you would have to store all the files in the single unorganized root directory.

Before you create this first subdirectory, you should log on to the disk drive with the sample diskette. If your machine has a hard-disk drive and one floppy-diskette drive, your sample diskette should be in drive A and you should log on to that drive by simply typing A: at the DOS C> prompt:

```
C>A:
```

For dual-diskette systems, switch to drive B by typing B: at the DOS A> prompt:

```
A>B:
```

To create a subdirectory you can use the Make Directory command—either MKDIR or MD. Both versions have the same effect, but the MD command is easier to type. The command to create the UTIL subdirectory on your sample diskette is as follows:

```
MD \UTIL
```

This command produces the new directory display seen in Figure 4.4. Note that you use the left-slanting backslash character, not the right-slanting slash character usually used to indicate arithmetic division. This backslash symbol is used in DOS to clarify the hierarchical directory structure. A backslash is a *delimiter* that precedes any subdirectory's name, in part to specify the name as representing a subdirectory, and in part to separate its name from the directory in which it can be found.

The directory in Figure 4.4 has a new type of entry. It is marked with the <DIR> symbol, which tells you that UTIL is not a file but the name of a subdirectory. Remember, directories just contain files (or other directories, as you'll soon see); files actually contain data or programs.

```
B>MD \UTIL

B>DIR

 Volume in drive B is BOOK SAMPLE
 Directory of  B:\

IMCAP    COM      6114   6-2Ø-85   1:Ø9p
IMSHOW   EXE     2ØØ9Ø   6-2Ø-85  1Ø:Ø9a
QD2      EXE     74752  11-14-86  12:ØØp
SKN      COM     34ØØ9   8-Ø5-85   6:14p
SR       COM      5356   1-Ø1-85
UTIL         <DIR>       1-Ø1-8Ø  12:46a
        6 File(s)    219136 bytes free

B>▪
```

Figure 4.4: Listing of root directory containing new subdirectory

ACCESSING FILES IN A SUBDIRECTORY

You can indicate that a command should work with a subdirectory by using the name of the subdirectory preceded by the \ symbol. Entering the DIR command with a first argument of \UTIL produces the directory listing shown in Figure 4.5. This figure shows the directory of the files stored in the new subdirectory UTIL. There are no files listed because you have not created or copied any files into this subdirectory.

You may wonder about the two entries that do appear, the one-dot and two-dot entries. Ignore them! These obscure references to the "current directory" and the "parent directory" are used so infrequently that they are practically useless to the typical DOS user.

What happened to the two files you had before? They are still on the disk, but they are in the root directory. To see them, you can always explicitly request a directory listing of the root directory like this:

```
DIR \
```

```
B>DIR  \UTIL

 Volume in drive B is BOOK SAMPLE
 Directory of  B:\UTIL

.            <DIR>      1-01-80  12:46a
..           <DIR>      1-01-80  12:46a
        2 File(s)    219136 bytes free

B>_
```

Figure 4.5: Directory listing of new subdirectory

CHANGING THE DEFAULT DIRECTORY

Just as DOS allows you to select a default drive, it also allows you to select a default directory for a disk. Once you've created a new directory, you can tell the operating system that you want it, rather than the root, to be the default directory. This allows you to work with only the files contained within that subdirectory. Then you won't have to enter the subdirectory name before each DOS command in order to reference files tucked away in some other subdirectory.

The command used to change directories is the CHDIR or CD command. (Again, CD is easier to type.) If you simply enter a DIR command, you see a listing of the root directory; if you enter a DIR command followed by the backslash and a subdirectory name, you see a listing of that subdirectory. The CD command, on the other hand, allows you to enter DOS commands that will then assume that the new default area of the disk (the subdirectory) is the specified one. For example, entering

```
CD \UTIL
```

makes the UTIL subdirectory the current DOS default whenever you make references to files on the current disk drive.

Notice in Figure 4.6 that the same DIR command produces a listing of the current default directory, which is different before and after the CD \UTIL command. The directory listing at the bottom of the figure is for the UTIL subdirectory. The CD command has reset the default directory to UTIL, so the DIR command lists only the files contained within that subdirectory.

COPYING FILES INTO A SUBDIRECTORY

Now that you have created a subdirectory, you can use it to store files. The basic DOS commands (COPY, ERASE, RENAME, and so on) will work with subdirectories. Since the default drive is the one you're working with, you'll need to specify the source drive for the files you're going to copy into the new UTIL subdirectory. First copy FORMAT.COM from drive A into this subdirectory by entering

```
COPY A:FORMAT.COM
```

Notice there is no second argument to indicate the destination. When you don't specify a destination, the COPY command assumes that the current drive and the current subdirectory (UTIL) are the defaults, using the same file name for this default destination file name. Copying another file into the UTIL subdirectory with

```
COPY A:CHKDSK.COM
```

and then entering a directory listing request will result in the listing shown in Figure 4.7. This confirms that the files have been copied successfully from your source diskette to the UTIL subdirectory of your sample diskette.

RETURNING TO THE ROOT DIRECTORY

You can reset the default to the root directory at any time by entering the CD command and using the root directory symbol (\)

```
B>DIR

 Volume in drive B is BOOK SAMPLE
 Directory of  B:\

IMCAP    COM      6114   6-20-85   1:09p
IMSHOW   EXE     20090   6-20-85  10:09a
QD2      EXE     74752  11-14-86  12:00p
SKN      COM     34009   8-05-85   6:14p
SR       COM      5356   1-01-85
UTIL         <DIR>       1-01-80  12:46a
        6 File(s)    219136 bytes free

B>CD \UTIL

B>DIR

 Volume in drive B is BOOK SAMPLE
 Directory of  B:\UTIL

.            <DIR>       1-01-80  12:46a
..           <DIR>       1-01-80  12:46a
        2 File(s)    219136 bytes free

B>_
```

Figure 4.6: Changing the current default directory

```
B>COPY  A:FORMAT.COM
        1 File(s) copied

B>COPY A:CHKDSK.COM
        1 File(s) copied

B>DIR

 Volume in drive B is BOOK SAMPLE
 Directory of  B:\UTIL

.            <DIR>       1-01-80  12:46a
..           <DIR>       1-01-80  12:46a
FORMAT   COM     11135  12-30-85  12:00p
CHKDSK   COM      9832  12-30-85  12:00p
        4 File(s)    197632 bytes free

B>_
```

Figure 4.7: Organizing files in a subdirectory

all by itself:

CD \

There can only be one active directory at a time. If you use the CD command to make a directory active, it is implicit that all the other directories are inactive.

Entering the DIR command now would produce the same results as you saw in Figure 4.4, before you switched defaults to the UTIL subdirectory. Note that the files copied into UTIL do not appear in this directory. They can only be seen now by specifically referring to the UTIL subdirectory.

HOW SUBDIRECTORIES WORK

DOS keeps track of the unique groupings of subdirectories by attaching a prefix or *path name* to every file that is stored in a subdirectory. Normally, the prefix is not displayed when you use the DIR command. However, there is a special form of the CHKDSK command that reveals the prefixes attached to files. Entering

A:CHKDSK/V

results in a detailed display like that in Figure 4.8. This is necessary for discovering the hierarchical grouping of any disk. Once you've created a number of directories and placed various files in them, it becomes harder and harder to remember where everything is. This command can help you to stay in control of your files and the disk structure you've created for them.

Full path-name referencing of this type is a convenience available to DOS 3.X users. DOS 2.X can only access commands on the active directory of a particular drive.

Remember that CHKDSK is not a resident DOS command, so if it's not on the current default drive (B), you must specify where it can be found. That explains why you need to preface the name CHKDSK

```
B>A:CHKDSK /V
Volume BOOK SAMPLE created Jan 1, 1980 12:06a
Directory B:\
      B:\IMCAP.COM
      B:\IMSHOW.EXE
      B:\QD2.EXE
      B:\SKN.COM
      B:\SR.COM
      B:\BOOK SAM.PLE
Directory B:\UTIL
      B:\UTIL\FORMAT.COM
      B:\UTIL\CHKDSK.COM
      B:\UTIL\FIG4-8.CAP

   362496 bytes total disk space
        0 bytes in 1 hidden files
     1024 bytes in 1 directories
   168960 bytes in 8 user files
   192512 bytes available on disk

   524288 bytes total memory
   435136 bytes free

B>_
```

Figure 4.8: Verbose output from the CHKDSK command

with A:, since in this simple dual-diskette configuration, the DOS master files are on the disk in drive A. The /V switch requests a *verbose* listing, which includes complete file names (see Figure 4.8).

The display reveals first the disk-drive prefix, then the directory prefix for every file. The FORMAT.COM file in the UTIL subdirectory may be accessed by using the path name of B:\UTIL, while the SKN.COM in the root may be accessed by preceding its name with the path-name prefix of B:\.

MULTILEVEL DIRECTORIES

The path system in DOS subdirectories allows you to create ever more complex yet organized groupings. Taking advantage of this system, you can create subdirectories of subdirectories. You could create a subdirectory of UTIL called SPECIAL with the following command:

```
MD \UTIL\SPECIAL
```

However, if you used the DIR command to look at the entries in the root directory, you would see only the original files and the UTIL subdirectory (see Figure 4.9). Where is the new subdirectory? It does not appear on this listing because it is a subdirectory of UTIL. In order to see a listing of the new subdirectory, you must first log into UTIL with the CD command, as shown in Figure 4.10.

APPLYING DOS COMMANDS TO SUBDIRECTORIES

Many DOS commands allow you to specify the subdirectory in which the files are to be found or placed. The COPY command can accept this type of parameter. For example, suppose that you wanted to copy all the files from drive A that begin with the letter M into the subdirectory UTIL\SPECIAL. You would enter the following:

```
COPY A:M*.* \UTIL\SPECIAL
```

However, a directory listing now would not list the resulting files unless you first changed the default directory to the new SPECIAL subdirectory, or unless you specified the complete path name to the desired subdirectory (see Figure 4.11).

UNDERSTANDING THE CONCEPT OF PATHS

In order to get through to the SPECIAL subdirectory, you must first go through the UTIL subdirectory. This requirement to follow a

```
B>MD \UTIL\SPECIAL

B>DIR \

 Volume in drive B is BOOK SAMPLE
 Directory of  B:\

IMCAP     COM      6114   6-20-85   1:09p
IMSHOW    EXE     20090   6-20-85  10:09a
QD2       EXE     74752  11-14-86  12:00p
SKN       COM     34009   8-05-85   6:14p
SR        COM      5356   1-01-85
UTIL          <DIR>       1-01-80  12:46a
        6 File(s)    196608 bytes free

B>_
```

Figure 4.9: Current root directory

```
B>CD \UTIL

B>DIR

 Volume in drive B is BOOK SAMPLE
 Directory of  B:\UTIL

.             <DIR>       1-01-80  12:46a
..            <DIR>       1-01-80  12:46a
FORMAT    COM     11135  12-30-85  12:00p
CHKDSK    COM      9832  12-30-85  12:00p
SPECIAL       <DIR>       1-01-80   4:19a
        5 File(s)    191488 bytes free

B>_
```

Figure 4.10: Display of a subdirectory within a subdirectory

path to any particular file can be compared to climbing a tree. All trees have roots, but to get to any particular branch, you have to first climb past the larger branches leading to it. Any branch on the tree is analogous to a DOS directory or subdirectory.

Each branch of a tree can have new branches growing from it. Similarly, each subdirectory can have new subdirectories defined within it. And just as each branch may also have fruit or leaves on it, each subdirectory may have program or data files stored in it.

The series of subdirectories that you link together is the path. You can see by the way the tree is structured that each subdirectory, and each file within it, has a unique path from the root directory. The large arrows shown in Figures 4.12, 4.13, and 4.14 represent the current default directory in each of the three situations that were presented in Figures 4.9, 4.10, and 4.11, respectively. Use these figures to help you understand the concept of paths.

It's helpful to always keep in mind which directory is the DOS default on the disk drive you're using. Otherwise, you could end up like the tree surgeon who forgot where he was while working on a tree. Figure 4.15 shows you what could happen!

Let's make one last subdirectory. Enter the command

```
MD \UTIL\SPECIAL\FINAL
```

```
B>COPY  A:M*.*  \UTIL\SPECIAL
A:MODE.COM
A:MORE.COM
        2 File(s) copied

B>DIR \UTIL\SPECIAL

 Volume in drive B is BOOK SAMPLE
 Directory of  B:\UTIL\SPECIAL

.            <DIR>        1-01-80    4:19a
..           <DIR>        1-01-80    4:19a
MODE     COM       6864  12-30-85   12:00p
MORE     COM        295  12-30-85   12:00p
        4 File(s)    178176 bytes free

B>_
```

Figure 4.11: Listing of the SPECIAL subdirectory

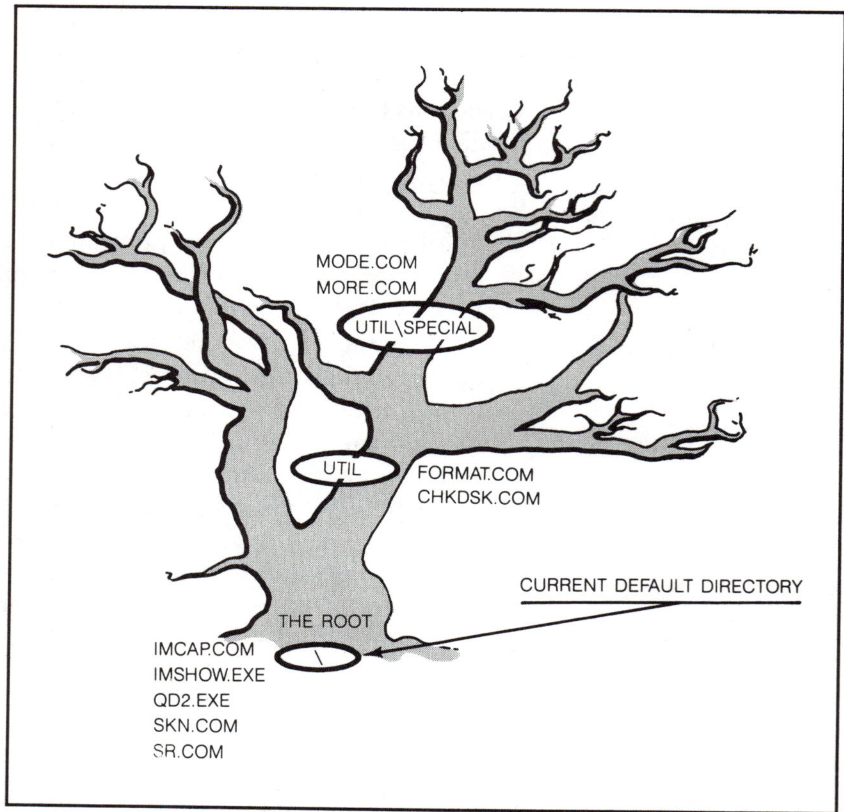

Figure 4.12: Root (\) as the current default directory

You have now extended the tree another level. To see how well you've understood the methods and concepts of directories and subdirectories, create the tree of directories described so far in this chapter, ending with the SPECIAL directory. Then copy all the .EXE files from your DOS master disk to the SPECIAL directory.

Verify that your creation and transfer worked properly by listing the contents of the SPECIAL directory. It should list the one- and two-dot entries, along with all the .EXE files from your DOS master disk.

MOVING FILES BETWEEN DIRECTORIES

So far, you've copied files from drive A into subdirectories on drive B. But what if you want to transfer files from one subdirectory to another

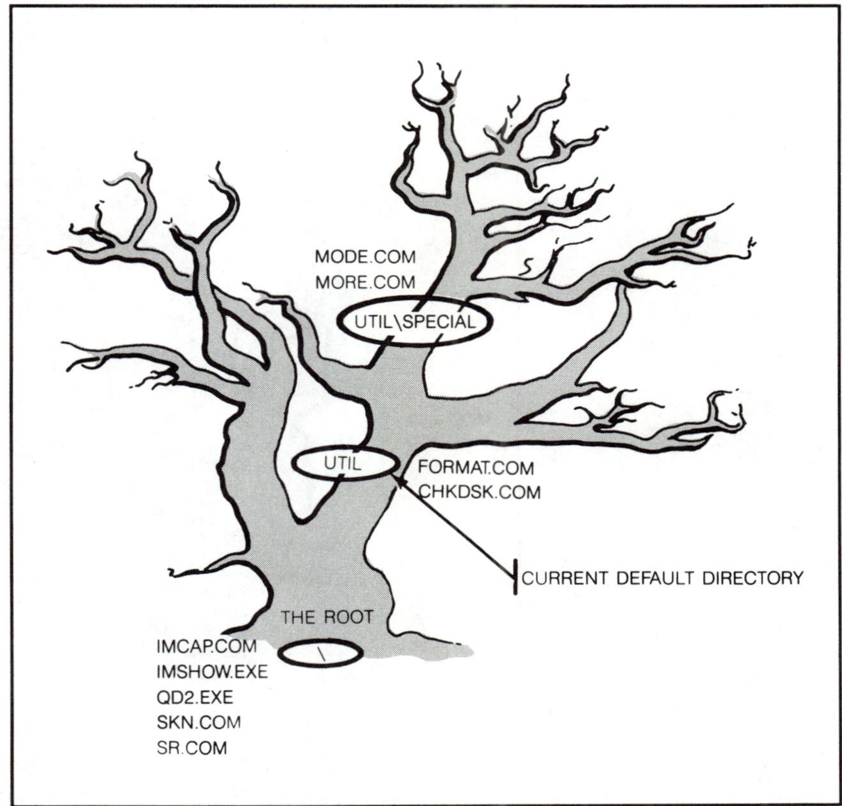

Figure 4.13: UTIL as the current default directory

on the same diskette? For example, you might want to move the two utility programs in the root, IMCAP.COM and IMSHOW.EXE (see Figure 4.1), into the newly created SPECIAL directory. This will require two steps:

1. Use COPY to make a copy of each of the files in the new directory.
2. Use ERASE to erase the original copies of the files after verifying that the transfer took place correctly.

The key is to specify the correct path name when you enter the commands. Remember that you want to copy a file in the root (path

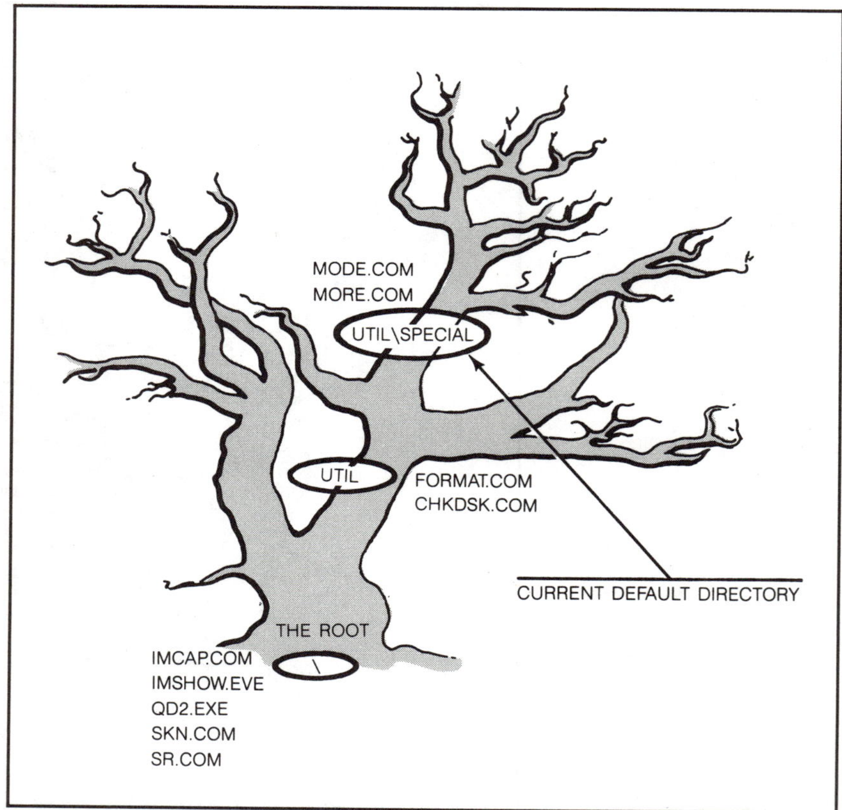

Figure 4.14: UTIL\SPECIAL as the current default directory

name \) to a directory with the full path name \UTIL\SPECIAL. Type

```
COPY \IMSHOW.EXE \UTIL\SPECIAL
COPY \IMCAP.COM \UTIL\SPECIAL
```

and press Return after each command. Figure 4.16 shows this sequence followed by a DIR command to verify the transfer and an ERASE command to delete the old files from the root.

SOME FINE POINTS ABOUT COPYING FILES In all of the cases so far, the new file created in the destination directory received the same name as the original file. When necessary, you can direct DOS to assign new names as part of the COPY procedure. For

Figure 4.15: Forgetting where you are in the directory tree

example, the command

```
COPY *.DBF \BACKUPS\*.BAK
```

will make backup copies of all .DBF (database) files in the current directory. The new copies will appear in the BACKUP directory with the extension .BAK.

Note that in having a first argument of *.DBF, you are assuming that all the .DBF files are on the current drive and in the current directory. In the second argument, since you specify the desired directory, BACKUPS, you are only making an assumption about the current drive. For anything other than the default, you must specify either the drive, the directory, or both.

```
B>COPY \IMSHOW.EXE  \UTIL\SPECIAL
        1 File(s) copied

B>COPY \IMCAP.COM  \UTIL\SPECIAL
        1 File(s) copied

B>DIR   \UTIL\SPECIAL

 Volume in drive B is BOOK SAMPLE
 Directory of  B:\UTIL\SPECIAL

.            <DIR>      1-Ø1-8Ø   4:19a
..           <DIR>      1-Ø1-8Ø   4:19a
MODE     COM     6864  12-3Ø-85  12:ØØp
MORE     COM      295  12-3Ø-85  12:ØØp
IMSHOW   EXE    2ØØ9Ø   6-2Ø-85  1Ø:Ø9a
IMCAP    COM     6114   6-2Ø-85   1:Ø9p
        6 File(s)   151552 bytes free

B>ERASE \IMSHOW.EXE

B>ERASE \IMCAP.COM

B>_
```

Figure 4.16: Copying files between directories on the same disk

MANEUVERING AROUND THE DOS DIRECTORY STRUCTURE

While subdirectories are essential for good organization, they can become confusing very quickly. DOS has some commands that help you navigate through the complex tangle of directories.

VIEWING THE STRUCTURE

The TREE command enables you to get a summary of the directories and subdirectories on a disk. TREE is not a resident command. This means that it will not work at all times or in every circumstance. TREE, like CHKDSK, is really a program file provided in DOS. This file, TREE.COM, must be present on one of the disks in your system, or you cannot execute the TREE command.

Since TREE.COM is in drive A of the dual-diskette example, entering

```
A:TREE
```

will list the volume label of the diskette in the current default drive (BOOK SAMPLE) as well as all the directories created on that diskette and any subdirectories created within them. See Figure 4.17.

```
B>A:TREE

DIRECTORY PATH LISTING FOR VOLUME BOOK SAMPLE

Path: \UTIL

Sub-directories:  SPECIAL


Path: \UTIL\SPECIAL

Sub-directories:  None


B>_
```

Figure 4.17: DOS's TREE command

You can also get a more detailed tree display that lists the specific files in each subdirectory. Entering

A:TREE/F

produces the output seen in Figure 4.18. The /F switch asks DOS to include the file names found in each directory.

It's hard to display a TREE listing on the screen, because it is usually too long for one screen. If you have a printer, you can get a printed copy of the screen display by entering

A:TREE /F > PRN

This command uses a special feature called *redirection,* which will be presented in much more depth in Chapter 12.

SEARCHING PATHS

The main purpose of the subdirectory system is to separate groups of files. However, there may be instances when you will need to reach a file in a directory other than the one you happen to be in (that is, the default directory). For example, the sample diskette used so far now has some files located in the root directory, others in the UTIL directory,

```
DIRECTORY PATH LISTING FOR VOLUME BOOK SAMPLE

Files:              QD2     .EXE
                    SKN     .COM
                    SR      .COM

Path: \UTIL

Sub-directories:    SPECIAL

Files:              FORMAT  .COM
                    CHKDSK  .COM


Path: \UTIL\SPECIAL

Sub-directories:    None

Files:              MODE    .COM
                    MORE    .COM
                    IMSHOW  .EXE
                    IMCAP   .COM


C>■
```

Figure 4.18: Detailed TREE listing (/F switch)

and still others in UTIL\SPECIAL. A copy of CHKDSK, for example, is located in the UTIL directory.

Assume you are currently back in the root directory (CD \). If you try to execute the CHKDSK command by typing

    CHKDSK

and pressing Return, the computer will tell you that you have entered a bad command or file name. Why? The answer is simple. You are currently logged into the root directory, and the CHKDSK file is located in UTIL.

DOS has a command that you can enter to specify where to look for files that are not located in the default directory. When this path is opened, the computer will search the directories to find the command file you are looking for. To create a path from the current working directory to the UTIL directory, you would enter

    PATH \UTIL

This command opens a path between the current working directory and the directory containing the desired file. Entering CHKDSK now will produce the desired result; the CHKDSK program will execute because DOS was able to find it along the specified search path in the UTIL directory.

The PATH command does not change the active directory. It simply tells DOS to search another directory if the program requested is not to be found in the active directory.

Test your understanding of the PATH command now. If you have a directory structure set up with a program you normally use, purposely change the current directory (CD) to some other directory. Then set the path properly so you can run the desired program, even though it is not available in the current directory. Also, try setting up the path with multiple directory entries, so you can run several different programs without having to change directories.

If your own system is not set up yet with any usable utility or application programs, look at the structure shown in Figure 4.18. You can see that there is a file named IMSHOW.EXE in the UTIL\SPECIAL directory. How would you set the path in DOS to run this program if your current default directory is still the root? For example, which of these commands would you use?

1. PATH \UTIL;\SPECIAL;\FINAL
2. PATH \UTIL
3. PATH \UTIL\SPECIAL
4. PATH UTIL\SPECIAL

Many people are uncertain about the use of delimiters, which are simply characters that separate one computer term from another. How and when they are used is always very critical. In this example, three delimiters must all be used correctly. The backslash symbol, as you know, separates directory names in a single path. The space symbol separates the PATH command from the list of directory names. The semicolon separates different directory names in the same path listing.

Choice 3 is the correct one. PATH \UTIL\SPECIAL is the full path name from the root to the directory containing the desired program. The semicolons make choice 1 incorrect, since this path specifies the UTIL directory and the nonexistent SPECIAL directory. It does not exist in the root; it exists in the UTIL branch of the directory tree. Choice 2 is wrong, since UTIL is the branch of the directory tree that contains the subdirectory SPECIAL, and not the desired program IMSHOW.EXE.

Choice 4 is going to be wrong *most* of the time. It will be correct only when you try to execute the IMSHOW.EXE program while your current default directory is the root. At all other times, the lack of a leading backslash means that the path branches off the current directory.

SETTING UP A COMPLEX PATH

You can open a path to several directories at once by entering a series of path names separated by semicolons. For example, if DOS can't find the program you ask for in the current default directory, you could ask it to search the UTIL directory first and then UTIL\SPECIAL by entering

```
PATH \UTIL;\UTIL\SPECIAL
```

Each directory to be successively searched should be separated by a semicolon (and no space). Multiple paths allow you to access programs in several directories without having to constantly revise the PATH command declaration.

WHEN THE PATH COMMAND ISN'T ENOUGH

The PATH command can only be used to search a directory for files with the extensions .COM, .EXE, and .BAT. The first two types are executable programs, and the last is a DOS batch file. (Batch files are presented in depth in Chapters 13 through 15; they are simple DOS programs that contain sets of DOS commands.) DOS will not search the path directories for files with other extensions, nor will it search those drives for data files not found in the active drive.

Some programs require special *overlay* or *driver* files in order to load properly. These files have extensions like .OVR, .OVL, and .DRV and contain additional program information that usually won't fit into memory all at the same time. The PATH command enables DOS to locate and load the main program, like WS.COM, it but may fail to locate WSOVLY1.OVR, the required overlay program.

Some of the newest programs requiring overlays are able to run because they are smart enough to use DOS's path information themselves to locate any required overlay files. Older programs that need overlay files often cannot be run simply by opening a path to the directory in which they are stored. If you are using one of the older programs, you may have to use the Change Directory command to run the program from within the directory that contains the main and overlay files. DOS 3.3 contains a new command, APPEND, which also provides a solution. This command is presented in depth in Chapter 16. In essence, APPEND provides you with the ability to set up a path to overlay files and data files, effectively closing up the former gap in DOS's ability to locate these files. You'll look at this issue again in the next chapter.

CHECKING THE PATH

There will be times when you have worked in different directories of your hard disk and may not be sure which is the current directory. You may also not be sure which path DOS will take to search for files not found in the current directory. If this is the case, you can make DOS show you the current path. To see what the current defined path is, you can enter

```
PATH
```

To close the path, enter the PATH command with the semicolon (;) alone. This indicates that the path is once again reset to the current working directory:

```
PATH;
```

After you've entered this, asking DOS for the current path will produce the message "No Path."

PRUNING THE TREE

There comes a time on many disks, as on many trees, when a branch must be cut back or cut off. It's a good idea to use the ERASE command regularly to limit uncontrolled use of space on your diskette. Once in a while, you may also want to put files together and collapse two directories into one. Or, if all the files in a directory are no longer needed, you may want to completely remove the directory they're in.

Performing the following sequence will move all the files from UTIL\SPECIAL into the UTIL directory. Keep in mind that the directory tree looks somewhat like Figure 4.19.

```
Directory B:\

        B:\QD2.EXE
        B:\SKN.COM
        B:\SR.COM
        B:\BOOK SAM.PLE

Directory B:\UTIL

        B:\UTIL\FORMAT.COM
        B:\UTIL\CHKDSK.COM

Directory B:\UTIL\SPECIAL

        B:\UTIL\SPECIAL\MODE.COM
        B:\UTIL\SPECIAL\MORE.COM
        B:\UTIL\SPECIAL\IMSHOW.EXE
        B:\UTIL\SPECIAL\IMCAP.COM


C>_
```

Figure 4.19: Current directory tree

First you need to copy the files from UTIL\SPECIAL to the UTIL directory:

```
COPY \UTIL\SPECIAL\*.* \UTIL
```

DOS will display the file names as they are copied:

```
B:\UTIL\SPECIAL\MODE.COM
B:\UTIL\SPECIAL\MORE.COM
B:\UTIL\SPECIAL\IMSHOW.EXE
B:\UTIL\SPECIAL\IMCAP.COM
        4 File(s) copied
```

You should always verify that your new copies are in place before erasing the old copies (see Figure 4.20).

Since the files have been copied successfully, you can now use the RD (Remove Directory) command to remove the old directory:

```
RD \UTIL\SPECIAL
```

DOS will immediately respond with

```
Invalid path, not directory, or directory not empty
```

```
DIR \UTIL

Volume in drive B is BOOK SAMPLE
Directory of  B:\UTIL

.            <DIR>       1-01-80   12:46a
..           <DIR>       1-01-80   12:46a
FORMAT   COM     11135  12-30-85   12:00p
CHKDSK   COM      9832  12-30-85   12:00p
SPECIAL      <DIR>       1-01-80    4:19a
MODE     COM      6864  12-30-85   12:00p
MORE     COM       295  12-30-85   12:00p
IMSHOW   EXE     20090   6-20-85   10:09a
IMCAP    COM      6114   6-20-85    1:09p
        9 File(s)    149504 bytes free




C>_
```

Figure 4.20: Directory status of UTIL

This is DOS's way of protecting you from a major catastrophe—namely, the removal of an entire directory when there may still be useful but forgotten programs stored within it. In this case, you haven't made a mistake. You just need to erase the old files before removing the directory from the DOS tree with the RD command:

```
ERASE \UTIL\SPECIAL\*.*
Are you sure (Y/N)?Y

RD \UTIL\SPECIAL
```

Figure 4.21 reveals the new directory structure.

SUMMARY

In this chapter you have examined the treelike directory structure of DOS and worked with directories and subdirectories on floppy diskettes. You learned the following things:

- Each diskette can be given a unique name, called a volume label, with the LABEL command. This name can be as long as 11 characters. It is used to identify either the contents or the ownership of a disk.

```
Directory B:\

        B:\JUNK1.TXT
        B:\QD2.EXE
        B:\SKN.COM
        B:\SR.COM
        B:\BOOK SAM.PLE

Directory B:\UTIL

        B:\UTIL\FORMAT.COM
        B:\UTIL\CHKDSK.COM
        B:\UTIL\MODE.COM
        B:\UTIL\MORE.COM
        B:\UTIL\IMSHOW.EXE
        B:\UTIL\IMCAP.COM




C>_
```

Figure 4.21: Revised directory tree structure

- The MD (Make Directory) command creates new areas on your disk. Each new area becomes a separately named portion of your disk, and can be used to effectively group your files for easy storage and retrieval.
- Files can be easily moved into and among various disk directories with the COPY command.
- You can make any disk directory into the current working directory with the CD (Change Directory) command. All program or DOS command references to files will look in this default directory first, before looking elsewhere.
- The CHKDSK/V and the TREE/F commands offer two ways to list all the files by directory group. CHKDSK/V is more concise, more readable, and therefore more desirable.
- The PATH command allows you to specify a list of other directories on your disk where you want DOS to look whenever you or your programs refer to .EXE (executable), .COM (command), or .BAT (batch) files. The APPEND command allows you to direct DOS to look in directories beyond the current working one for any other type of file. This includes overlay files, data files, and all possible application files.

- DOS commands apply to files in the current directory unless you have set up a PATH or APPEND sequence. However, even if these are not set up, you can still refer to files or commands in other directories by simply using the full path name as a prefix in front of the file name.
- The RD (Remove Directory) command removes empty directories from your hierarchical structure. However, DOS will only do this if there are no other directories or files of any sort remaining in the directory you are trying to remove.

In the next chapter you will continue your study of DOS directories, but in the context of the more complex and eminently more useful environment of a hard disk.

WORKING WITH HARD-DISK DIRECTORY STRUCTURES

CHAPTER 5

WORKING WITH HARD DISKS REQUIRES GOOD organization and planning. This chapter takes you through some pragmatic examples that will give you that organizational ability. In Chapter 4, you learned about the DOS directory structure and the commands necessary to set up and use that structure on your floppy diskettes. This chapter focuses on the directory structure of hard disks.

As the price of hard disks decreases, their availability on typical computer systems increases. Knowledge of DOS directory structures becomes even more important as the amount of hardware under your control grows. Knowing how to successfully manage all that disk space will make you more efficient and save you time; the manipulation of diskettes to run your application programs can then be replaced by the knowledgeable manipulation of DOS directories.

In this chapter, you'll format your hard disk, or review the formatting process if your disk is already formatted. Then you'll use the appropriate directory commands to set up the hard disk for three common and very popular types of programs: a spreadsheet, a word processor, and a database management system. The techniques you learn will be directly applicable to setting up a hard disk for using any application software.

This chapter describes how to create new directories, copy files between disks and directories, list subdirectories, and change the active directory. It also tells you how to include directory information in the DOS prompt and how to view the hard-disk structure.

FORMATTING THE DISK

Just like floppy diskettes, hard disks must be prepared or formatted before information can be stored on them. If your machine is brand new, you should follow any instructions from the manufacturer to prepare it (this usually involves running an FDISK program; see your DOS user's manual).

Place the DOS master diskette into drive A and close the door. Then enter the proper format command at the A> prompt. Remember that you want to create a system disk out of the hard disk; therefore, you must use the following form of the FORMAT command. It will format the disk and copy the system information files at the same time. Since the hard-disk drive is usually drive C, type

```
A>FORMAT C: /S
```

Follow these formatting instructions only if your hard disk is totally unprepared, or if you purposely intend to erase everything on it.

When the formatting is complete, change the active drive to C:

```
A>C:
```

For the rest of this chapter, the default drive will be C, and you'll be moving around the directory tree on the hard disk.

A PLACE FOR THE DOS FILES

The DOS prompt on your screen now indicates that drive C is the active drive. The first command you should enter is the Directory command, DIR. Entering it reveals that you have one file on your drive, COMMAND.COM, and that you have over 10 million bytes of free space (or 20 or 30 million bytes, depending on the size of your hard disk). The display also tells you that COMMAND.COM is in the root directory, indicated by the backslash (C:\). The COMMAND.COM file is part of the computer's basic operating system and must always appear in the root directory.

The DOS system has a number of special utility programs that will be helpful to the proper operation of your system. Right now these programs are stored on the DOS master diskettes, but they can be copied to your hard disk. If you have 5¼'' floppy-diskette drives, these utility files are separated on two 360K floppies; if you have the appropriate 3½'' microfloppy drive, all the DOS utility files are included on one diskette also included with your DOS 3.3 package. These files include all of the disk-resident DOS commands, from CHKDSK, to FORMAT, to support for international-type keyboards. Performing any of these utility operations requires that the appropriate DOS support files be available on your hard disk. However, before the copies are made, you need to take an organizational step.

CREATING NEW DIRECTORIES

When adding files to a hard disk, it is always a good idea to create a special directory for all files that are related to one another. Having similar and related files together will make it easier and faster to find them and use them later. In this example, all of the DOS files will be copied to a directory called DOS so that they are all grouped together.

To create the directory, you enter the Make Directory command, MD:

```
MD \DOS
```

You can see that on the screen, nothing has happened, but in fact the computer has recorded a change. Entering a DIR request produces this information:

```
Volume in drive C is JUDDROBBINS
Directory of C:\

COMMAND COM 23791 12-30-85 12:00p
DOS        <DIR>        1-01-80 12:05a
        1 File(s) 10565240 bytes free
```

The <DIR> symbol next to the name DOS indicates that DOS is not a file, but a directory. You can now store information in that directory.

COPYING FILES BETWEEN DISKS AND DIRECTORIES

The COPY command transfers copies of files from one disk to another and to subdirectories on the same or different disks. The next step will transfer the DOS support files from the source diskette in drive A to the destination hard disk directory, C:\DOS (drive C, subdirectory DOS). Enter

When entering commands, remember that you should always follow drive names with a colon, as in A:, B:, or C:, while subdirectory names should always be preceded by a backslash character, such as \DOS, \LOTUS, or \DBASE.

```
COPY A:*.* C:\DOS
```

DOS will list the files as they are copied. However, a directory listing now will still show only one file, COMMAND.COM. This is because the current directory listing is for the root directory; the files that were just copied were stored in the DOS directory.

To see the contents of this subdirectory, one of two methods can be used:

1. Specify the subdirectory name in the DIR command.
2. Change the default directory to the desired directory and enter the DIR command.

The following sections employ both methods.

LISTING A SUBDIRECTORY

To list the contents of a directory other than the current default directory, you can add the name of the subdirectory to the DIR command:

```
DIR \DOS
```

If your current default disk were in a drive other than C, you could even explicitly ask for the DOS directory on drive C by typing

```
DIR C:\DOS
```

CHANGING THE ACTIVE DIRECTORY

The second method used to list the contents of a subdirectory requires you to tell the operating system that you want to work in a directory other than the root. When you issue a command to change the directory, you are telling the computer to assume that all succeeding commands should affect the files in that directory, and not in the root directory.

If you enter a command that tells the computer to change the directory to DOS, and then enter DIR, only the files in the DOS subdirectory will be listed. The advantage of changing the directory is that you do not have to bother to type the prefix \DOS after each command and before each file name.

As you saw in Chapter 4, entering the Change Directory command (CD) allows you to ask for a DIR operation without specifying any directory. Type

```
CD \DOS
DIR
```

and press Return after each line. The desired directory is now the current default directory. All names for files in the DOS subdirectory will now be listed.

RETURNING TO THE ROOT DIRECTORY

The CD command can be used to return the default to the root directory. If you enter the backslash character alone as

```
CD \
```

the default directory will be reset to the root directory. A request for a directory listing will now produce a listing for the root directory.

You may need to use the CD command often. Each time you switch directories in order to run a special program like 1-2-3 or dBASE, it's a good idea to reset to the root directory afterward. This will avoid trouble—it's good hard-disk management.

CHANGING THE PROMPT

As you know, the DOS prompt usually consists of two characters: a letter indicating the active drive and the > character. The > character is not required, but it makes the display easier to read by separating the drive letter from any command you might type in.

When you are working on a disk with more than one directory, it is useful to expand the prompt to include the directory name along with the drive identifier. The PROMPT command can be used to change the prompt displayed whenever DOS is active.

To change the prompt, you should enter

```
PROMPT $p$g
```

after the > character. PROMPT recognizes the argument $p as a command to display the directory and the argument $g as a command to tell DOS to display the > character. (The letters p and g can be entered in either upper- or lowercase.) This command changes the DOS prompt from the default C> to C:\>, which shows both the drive identifier (C:) and the current directory (the root \) followed by the > character. The DOS prompt will now always reflect the current default directory. For example, entering a Change Directory command like

```
CD \DOS
```

after the C:\ prompt will cause DOS to change the prompt to

```
C:\DOS>
```

The prompt tells you that the active directory is now C:\DOS.

You can ask DOS to return to its normal prompt at any time by reentering the PROMPT command by itself:

```
C:\DOS>PROMPT
```

The prompt will return to

```
C>
```

You will explore more advanced uses of the PROMPT command in Chapter 10.

LOADING YOUR WORD PROCESSOR ONTO THE HARD DISK

In this section, you'll set up your hard disk to store all your word-processing files in a particular directory. To do this, you must have a copy of the program already on a floppy diskette. It is assumed that your word processor is *not* copy-protected. If it is, you'll need to follow the special instructions in its user's manual.

Although your word processor may be different from the example given here, the process of setting up your hard disk will be similar. You'll still need to take the following steps:

1. Create a subdirectory for word processing.
2. Copy the word-processing files from the floppy diskette onto the correct subdirectory of the hard disk.
3. Change the default directory to the word-processing directory.
4. Run the program.

CREATING YOUR WORD-PROCESSING DIRECTORY

To create a word-processing directory, enter the MD (Make Directory) command:

```
MD \WP
```

To check that all went well, you could enter a DIR command. The root directory would show two entries with the <DIR> indicator, DOS and WP. There are now two directories branching off from the root directory (see Figure 5.1). The next step is to copy the files from your word-processing diskette(s) to the new WP directory.

COPYING WORD-PROCESSING PROGRAMS TO THE NEW DIRECTORY

Sometimes, your new word-processing program diskette will have a prewritten installation program to do all of the following steps. Use it. You can always redo things in your own way later, after you've become more comfortable with directory structures. In any case, the next step that either you or the installation program should follow is to place the word-processing master diskette into drive A and use the COPY command:

```
COPY A:*.* C:\WP
```

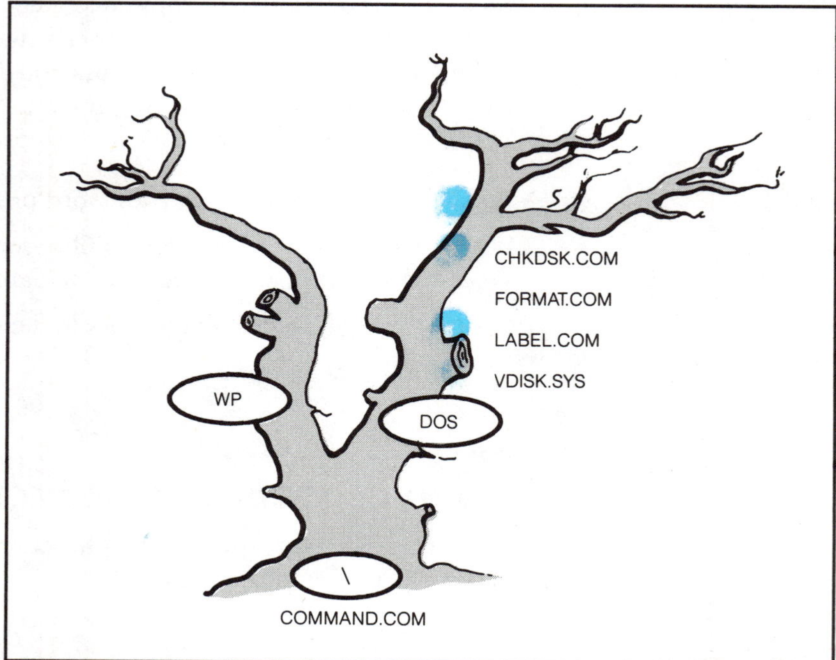

Figure 5.1: DOS and WP directory structure

When you press Return, the computer lists the names of the files as they are copied. If your word processor is on more than one diskette, repeat this step for each diskette.

RUNNING YOUR WORD PROCESSOR FROM THE NEW DIRECTORY

If you want to run your word processor, you must change the default directory to WP and type the name of the main program. To do so, you enter

CD \WP

Then enter

WS

for WordStar,

WP

for WordPerfect, or the name of whatever other program you use.

The opening screen of your word processor will appear. Now it's time to open up your word processor's user's manual and proceed to create and edit documents. When you finally exit the program, remember to return to the root directory with

```
CD \
```

Now that your word processor has been copied to the hard disk, remember that you must change the default to the WP directory each time you want to run the program again. The root directory now only lists the COMMAND.COM file and the primary DOS and WP directories, which themselves contain the bulk of your files. Keeping the root directory uncluttered makes finding your way around the hard disk much easier. If you did not have subdirectories, the root directory would be a virtually unreadable list of hundreds of files.

LOADING YOUR SPREADSHEET PROGRAM ONTO THE HARD DISK

When entering commands, remember that you should always follow drive names with a colon, as in A:, B:, or C:, while subdirectory names should always be preceded by a backslash character, such as \DOS, \LOTUS, or \DBASE.

Loading a popular spreadsheet like Lotus 1-2-3 onto a hard disk is not much different from working with a word processor like WordStar or WordPerfect. Although the procedure will be similar if you have a different spreadsheet program, the example presented here uses 1-2-3 because it contains a copy-protection mechanism (unlike the word-processing example of the previous section). This special situation requires some discussion.

All the information necessary to run some copy-protected programs like 1-2-3 cannot be straightforwardly transferred to the hard disk. Lotus employs a copy-protection scheme on its program disks; thus, if you simply transfer all the Lotus files to the hard disk with the COPY command, 1-2-3 still needs to access the original floppy diskette in order to run.

The most recent versions of 1-2-3 allow you to install the software onto the hard disk permanently. Even though the program is copy protected, it is still worthwhile to copy the files to the hard disk for two reasons:

- The program will load more quickly.
- All of the Lotus 1-2-3 system files can be placed in a single subdirectory, thus requiring no future juggling of all the Lotus diskettes.

SUBDIRECTORIES FOR DATA

Most newer software packages like 1-2-3 allow you to store work and access files in one of several directories. With earlier and still popular versions of programs like WordStar, all of the data files you create occupy the same subdirectory as the program.

1-2-3 can switch from one data subdirectory to another while the program is operating. This allows you to group together related 1-2-3 program files and separate them from worksheet files. As you'll soon see, you can use the DOS directory structure more effectively by maintaining directories for groups of worksheets, separate from the main LOTUS directory of program files.

The first step is to create a directory for all of the Lotus system files. Enter

```
MD \LOTUS
```

Then, for each of the original diskettes in the Lotus package, copy the necessary programs into that directory by entering

```
COPY A:*.* C:\LOTUS
```

Now that the 1-2-3 files have been copied, you can run the program. First change the default directory to the LOTUS directory and then enter the name of the main program, pressing Return after each command:

```
CD \LOTUS
LOTUS
```

The screen will then prompt you to select a program. If you select the main 1-2-3 spreadsheet program, 1-2-3 will spin the diskette in drive

A to check the copy-protection scheme if you have not installed it permanently according to the manufacturer's instructions. In either case, you no longer need to have the floppy diskette in drive A.

CONFIGURING PROGRAMS

When you copy a program to a hard disk from a floppy diskette, the program is not necessarily *configured.* Configuration refers to those special settings in the software that give the program all of the information unique to your system, such as what type of screen display and printer are being used. In addition, some programs require you to specify the default data drive and directory. 1-2-3 is one of those programs.

Just because the program was copied to the hard disk, it does not follow that 1-2-3 knows what actual drive you want to use for data. Many times when 1-2-3 is copied onto a hard-disk drive, it still attempts to store data on drive B. To change the default disk and directory for any program like this, there is usually some command in the software that can be invoked. You should refer to your application software's user's guide to discover it. In 1-2-3, it is the /wgdd command.

CREATING MULTIPLE SUBDIRECTORIES FOR YOUR DATA FILES

Since 1-2-3 allows you to change the subdirectory used to store program data, you can create a separate directory for your spreadsheet files. In fact, if you work in an office where more than one person uses the computer, each person's work can be stored in a different subdirectory. The same concept can be used to store work related to different projects in separate subdirectories.

To see how this works, you must return to the operating system level. As you know, subdirectories are organized in a hierarchical order. The root directory is the parent of all subdirectories. Each directory created in the root can in turn have its own children; for example, LOTUS is a subdirectory of the root. LOTUS can also have subdirectories of its own.

Suppose that in your office, three people, Sue, Harry, and Alice, will be working with 1-2-3. To keep their work from getting confused, it might be useful to separate and store their files into unique subdirectories. Create individual directories for each of these people by entering the following:

```
MD \LOTUS\SUE
MD \LOTUS\HARRY
MD \LOTUS\ALICE
```

Drive C will then be structured as shown in Figure 5.2. Figure 5.3 shows another way to visualize the directory structure. In the remainder of this chapter, you'll use this line view.

Figure 5.2: DOS directory structure (tree view)

RUNNING PROGRAMS FROM WITHIN SUBDIRECTORIES

At this point you have set up a directory that contains the main program files (the Lotus programs in this example, but it could just as well be the word-processing programs of the last section). To run the program, you would change the main directory to LOTUS with CD, bring up the program, and then tell the program in which subdirectory you wish it to work. This type of request from within a program varies with each program, but the concept remains the same.

In 1-2-3, the command to change default subdirectories is the File Directory command (/FD). The program will first display the current directory setting. Because you started 1-2-3 when you were in the main LOTUS directory, 1-2-3 automatically sets the default to C:\LOTUS. To change directories, you would enter the full path name of the subdirectory that you want to use. If you were Alice, for instance, you would specify to 1-2-3 that you want it to use your specific directory. Including the drive as well, you would enter

Because every program has different assumptions about default directories, you may at times try to retrieve a file and not find it. Check the default directory. The solution is often as easy as resetting it to the directory that you usually use for file work.

```
C:\LOTUS\ALICE
```

All files would be saved in or retrieved from the subdirectory LOTUS\ALICE. In this way, Alice can have her work separated

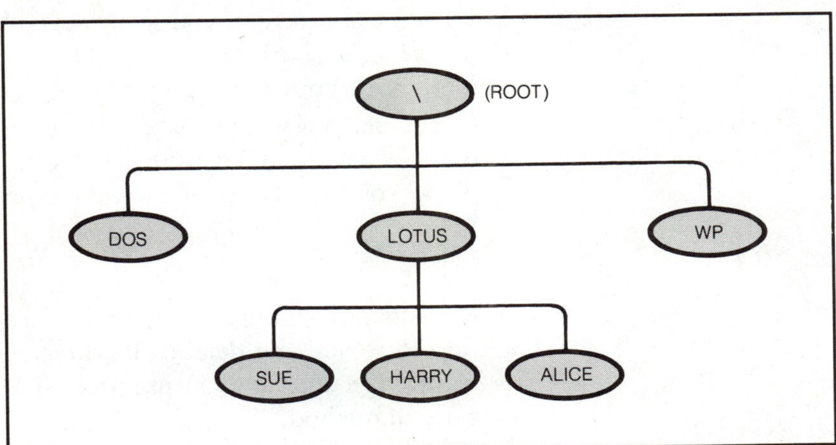

Figure 5.3: DOS directory structure (line view)

from Harry's and Sue's. If Harry or Sue later logged on, they could go through the same sequence to ensure that they had access to the files in their different subdirectories.

RUNNING YOUR DATABASE MANAGEMENT SYSTEM

As a last example, let's create a directory for a DBMS (database management system). Suppose you intend to use a package like dBASE III PLUS for several purposes. You may plan to write your own custom accounting program to manage your entire inventory system; you may even plan to manage your company's personnel records with the software.

With the following commands you can quickly visualize and then create the new directory structure:

```
MD \DBMS
MD \DBMS\ACCOUNTS
MD \DBMS\INVNTORY
MD \DBMS\PRSONNEL
```

The results are shown in Figure 5.4. As you can see, you've set up a directory structure that is organized by application purpose. Similarly, in the last section, you set up several subdirectories, one for the data files for each user of the spreadsheet program. It's always up to you to decide on the grouping of your files.

Of course, now you probably want to run your DBMS program. If you are a dBASE III PLUS user, you could simply use the CD \DBMS command and then enter the program name:

```
DBASE
```

You could then change the default directory from within the program. However, the default file directory can be conveniently set *before* you execute the main program. The next section will describe this useful method.

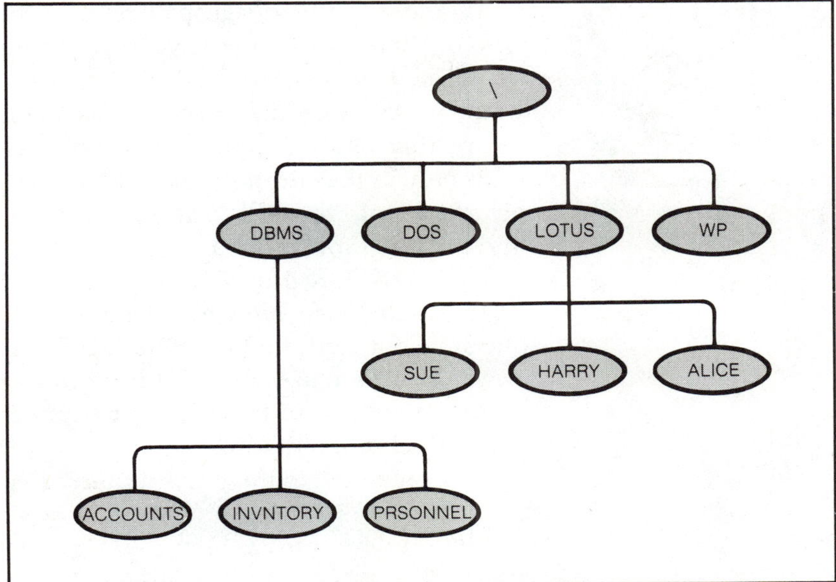

Figure 5.4: Directory structure for DBMS applications

RUNNING ANY PROGRAM ON YOUR HARD DISK

There will be many times when you have set the working directory to the one you want to be in; related files will be read from and written into that directory. Sometimes, you will then want to run a utility program that is in another directory. For instance, you may want to run the CHKDSK program in the DOS directory, or a special hard-disk management program like QDOS II, located in the UTILITY\MISC directory.

Most of the time, you do not want to leave the current directory and go through the hassle of resetting to another directory. In fact, since more and more programs are allowing you to run other programs while they are still active, you will purposely want to maintain the current working directory. The PATH and APPEND commands are your best solution. (APPEND, however, is only available to DOS 3.3 users.)

Assuming that you've copied all the necessary database programs onto the hard disk, suppose you wanted to see how much space was left on it. If you entered CHKDSK now to analyze the disk, you would probably get the message "Bad command or file name." This means that DOS is unable to run the CHKDSK program. DOS looks only in the current directory for that program. You are probably logged into the DBMS directory, so DOS reports that it cannot find the program you requested.

The CHKDSK program *is* on the hard disk, but it is stored in the DOS subdirectory. How can you tell DOS to check the DOS subdirectory if it can't find the requested program in the current directory? You can use the PATH command. It tells DOS what subdirectories, in addition to the current one, it should check when you enter a program to run.

To open a path to the DOS subdirectory, you would enter

```
PATH \DOS
```

The CHKDSK command would now execute properly, because the path to the correct subdirectory is open.

As you saw in Chapter 4, you can open a more complex path by using a semicolon to separate a list of directory names. For this example, enter

Do not leave any spaces between the entries on the path list. DOS stops reading the line when it comes across the first space on the list.

```
PATH \DOS;\WP;\LOTUS;\DBMS
```

If the program name you enter can't be found in the current default directory, DOS will first look for that program in the DOS subdirectory. If it isn't there, DOS will then successively look in the WP, LOTUS, and DBMS subdirectories. Only if it doesn't find it in any of these directories will it return the "Bad command or file name" message to you.

What this all means to you is that you can anticipate setting the default directory before you start up your main program. You can have the path set to enable DOS to find the requested program. Whenever your program reads or writes files, it will use the default directory. To do database work with the accounting files, you could set the DOS default to the DBMS\ACCOUNTS directory and the path to DBMS, and then invoke the database management program (in this case, dBASE III PLUS) by entering

```
CD \DBMS\ACCOUNTS
PATH \DBMS
DBASE
```

Preface all entries in a path with a drive designator for that directory. Then you can execute the program in that directory from any logged drive.

and pressing Return after each line. The default directory is now ACCOUNTS, so dBASE will expect to find all databases and program (.PRG) files in that directory. It will hunt for its own management programs along the directories specified on the path, and it will find them in DBMS.

LIMITATIONS OF THE PATH COMMAND

PATH opens a searching channel for programs and batch files only—it can't be used to access data files in other subdirectories. In fact, some main programs like WordStar (through version 3.3) can't even run properly if you use the PATH command. The reason is that WordStar, dBASE, 1-2-3, and most other sophisticated microcomputer programs need to occasionally load overlay files in addition to the main .COM or .EXE file. (Remember, overlay files contain additional program information that usually just can't fit into memory all at the same time as the main .COM or .EXE file.) The PATH command will only search the designated directories for files that end with .COM, .EXE, or .BAT. The result is that while DOS may find WS.COM in the WP subdirectory, WordStar can't find the .OVR files that it needs to run.

The SMARTPATH program is only one of many utility programs you can buy to significantly extend the power of DOS. In the likely event you begin to collect these add-on tools, it is a good idea to place them in their own utility directory. You can create this directory once and then copy your new utility programs to it. You can then add the UTIL directory name to the main path so that DOS can find the SMARTPATH program and any other utility programs when you ask for them.

Some programs like dBASE III PLUS are smart enough to search the operating system path themselves. In such cases, you can set up a useful partitioned directory structure like the one seen in Figure 5.4. However, when the main program is *not* smart enough to use path information, you may have to put up with the limitation, placing all your data files along with the main program files in one large directory.

There is a better solution that still allows you the flexibility of using DOS's directory organization. If your DOS is version 3.2 or earlier, you can use a separately purchasable utility program called SMARTPATH, which extends the path concept to include other types of files besides .EXE, .COM, and .BAT files.

should seriously consider acquiring to enable you to both extend and more easily harness the capabilities of your operating system.

For now, you should consider using a single PATH command that enables DOS to hunt for and find all of your main programs:

```
PATH \DOS;\UTIL;\LOTUS;\DBMS;\WP
```

Consider redefining the directory path for certain applications. The more often DOS has to resort to the path to find files, the longer it will take and the slower the system's response time will be. In addition, since DOS searches the path in the order in which you list directory names, you should list the directories in the order most likely to succeed.

As an alternative, DOS 3.3 users can use the APPEND command, whose syntax is similar to PATH. Just list the directory names containing the files you want DOS to find, after the command name itself. For instance,

```
APPEND \WP;\DBMS\DATA
```

will establish another searching path that DOS will follow when the need arises to locate overlay files for a word processor or command and database files for your database management system.

MAPPING YOUR HARD DISK

When you work with floppy diskettes, the DIR command is usually a sufficient way to get a map of each diskette. That's because you probably don't have anything but a root directory on most or all of your floppy diskettes. When you are working with a hard disk that contains many directories, however, DIR is no longer adequate—it will operate only on one directory at a time. The TREE and CHKDSK commands will allow you to get information about the hard disk as a whole.

As you saw in Chapter 4, TREE is used to list all the directories and subdirectories on a disk. Figure 5.5 shows a TREE listing for the hard-disk directory structure created in this chapter. In Chapter 4, you also saw another option—the CHKDSK/V command. This command will list not only all directories but the file names within them, as well as information about disk and memory usage. If this information is unneeded, you should stick to the TREE command. If you like the format of the TREE command but also want the file names listed (but not the disk and memory status information), you can use the /F switch with TREE.

```
DIRECTORY PATH LISTING FOR VOLUME SYBEX_BOOK

Path: \DBMS
Sub-directories:  ACCOUNTS
                  INVNTORY
                  PRSONNEL

Path: \DBMS\ACCOUNTS
Sub-directories:  None

Path: \DBMS\INVNTORY
Sub-directories:  None

Path: \DBMS\PRSONNEL
Sub-directories:  None

Path: \DOS
Sub-directories:  None

Path: \LOTUS
Sub-directories:  SUE
                  HARRY
                  ALICE

Path: \LOTUS\SUE
Sub-directories:  None

Path: \LOTUS\HARRY
Sub-directories:  None

Path: \LOTUS\ALICE
Sub-directories:  None

Path: \WP
Sub-directories:  None
```

***Figure** 5.5:* Output from the TREE command

With either CHKDSK/V or TREE/F, the resultant listing is usually much longer than one screenful of data. Since the information displayed by TREE is very valuable to have, you might want to print the TREE display. You can do this by using the >PRN redirection command with the TREE command:

```
TREE/F > PRN
```

You will now get a complete printed listing of all the files on your hard disk. (You will learn more about this interesting redirection capability in Chapter 12.) Like the TREE/F command, the CHKDSK/V command can also generate a printed copy if you use the redirection command:

```
CHKDSK/V > PRN
```

You have now seen two methods by which you can produce a complete listing of all the files on the hard disk. With these lists, you can figure out where on the hard disk various programs and files are stored. They can also help you to find lost files and identify which files should be erased.

SUMMARY

In this chapter, you have explored the DOS capability for setting up a complex but highly usable structure of directories on any hard disk. You learned how to set up your hard disk for a word processor, a spreadsheet, and a database management system. Using these examples, you should be able to set up a functioning directory structure for any application software system.

The chapter has presented a number of commands that allow you to create and maneuver around any desired hard-disk structure:

- You can use the Make Directory (MD) command to create a new subdirectory in any existing directory.
- You can use the Change Directory (CD) command to reset the default directory pointer to any chosen disk directory.
- You can use the PROMPT command to automatically display the current default directory when you enter DOS commands for your hard-disk system.
- You can use the PATH command to direct DOS to search through a specified series of selected directories for .EXE, .COM, and .BAT files that are not located in the current working directory.
- With DOS 3.3, you can use the APPEND command to tell DOS to search through a specified series of directories for data and overlay files not located in the current working directory.
- You can use the TREE/F or CHKDSK/V command to view the hard-disk map or structure.

The next two chapters, on the DOS editor and DOS printing, will teach you how to manage the output of information created and manipulated by your particular applications. You will be able to make textual changes to standard text files, which will be crucial to effective management of certain DOS configuration and control features to be discussed later in this book. You will soon learn how to control the flow of information to the screen (Chapter 6), to the printed page (Chapter 7), and even to other devices through the DOS communications ports (Chapter 8).

USING THE DOS EDITOR

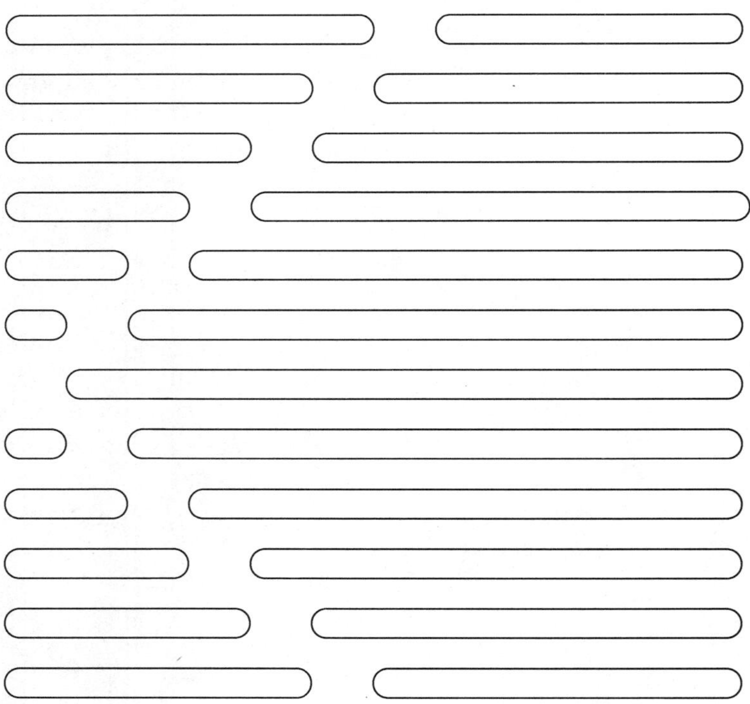

CHAPTER 6

IN ADDITION TO THEIR ABILITY TO PROCESS NUMBERS and large amounts of data, computers are exceptionally good at manipulating text. It comes as no surprise, then, that there are so many different programs available to do this.

The advantages of using a computer instead of a typewriter are many. Text can be manipulated on the screen, changed, and corrected before it is printed out. Also, whole documents and reports can be stored on disk for later use. This means you can type in half a report, go away for a week, and then come back and finish it. You can also create a rough draft and later make corrections to it in minutes, without having to retype everything.

There are two primary kinds of programs that allow you to create and manipulate text. The first kind is a line editor like the DOS EDLIN editor. With a line editor, you work with a line of text at a time. Line editors number each line and reference each line by these numbers. You can make corrections to only one line at a time.

The second kind of program, a word processor, shows you a full screen of text. You can move the screen cursor to any character position on any line and make changes anywhere on the screen. Word processors usually support such features as multiple fonts, boldfacing, and underlining.

Naturally, it's up to you to choose the kind of program you want. You may want to use both, at different times. The DOS line editor is very small (only 7526 bytes), and it can comfortably fit on most application diskettes in diskette-based systems. This means that you won't need to juggle diskettes often. On the other hand, you may feel much more comfortable using the more extensive set of commands available with most word processors. You might also prefer to edit any character on any line in the full-screen mode of a typical word processor. However, word processors usually require tens of thousands of bytes of disk space merely to contain them, and they have more extensive RAM requirements than line editors. In addition, you must usually purchase them, whereas EDLIN is available in your DOS system at no additional charge.

The EDLIN program is so small that you can keep a copy of it on each of several diskettes for rapid and easy file editing. Most advanced word processors are too large to fit on diskettes that contain any other sophisticated software.

DOS provides the EDLIN.COM program as part of your system. It is disk-resident and acts like any other transient command. You can use EDLIN to create and edit text files, which are files that contain standard letters, numbers, and punctuation symbols. Except for the special codes indicating carriage returns, line feeds, and the end of a file (Ctrl-Z), these files have no control codes for such features as underlining on a printer or high intensity on a display. (A text file can be displayed easily onscreen with the TYPE command.) In short, EDLIN works with whole lines of text, but you cannot use it to change fonts or to produce boldface or underlined text. EDLIN can, however, manipulate text files, and it contains search and replace functions and standard text-editing features.

GETTING EDLIN STARTED

EDLIN is started from the DOS prompt with the command

```
EDLIN FileSpec
```

The optional /B switch (short for Binary) can be used with this EDLIN command when the file you will be working on contains Ctrl-Z markers other than the end-of-file marker. As you'll learn later in this chapter, you can use EDLIN to incorporate and then edit control characters in a text file.

where *FileSpec* is the drive, path, file name, and extension of the file to be edited. You must use the full file name, including any extension. As always, EDLIN must either be resident on the disk you are using, in the current default directory, or on the path to be searched by DOS.

STARTING A NEW FILE

If EDLIN is invoked with a *FileSpec* value for a file that does not currently exist, it will respond with the following message and prompt:

```
New file
*_
```

EDLIN is giving you a clean slate, awaiting your commands. Table 6.1 summarizes the commands you can use with EDLIN, their actions, and their general formats. You will learn about each of these as you work through this chapter.

CHANGING AN EXISTING FILE

Invoking EDLIN with the *FileSpec* of an existing file will yield the following:

```
End of input file
*_
```

EDLIN tries to load your entire text file into available memory

COMMAND	ACTION	GENERAL FORMAT
A	Appends lines	[*Num*]A
C	Copies lines	[*Line*],[*Line*],*Line*[,*Count*] C
D	Deletes lines	[*Line*][,*Line*] D
—	Edits line	[*Line*]
E	Updates and exits	E
I	Inserts lines	[*Line*]I
L	Lists lines	[*Line*][,*Line*] L
M	Moves lines	[*Line*],[*Line*],*Line*M
P	Displays full page	[*Line*][,*Line*] P
Q	Aborts and exits	Q
R	Replaces globally	[*Line*][,*Line*] [?] R[*String*][^Z*NewString*]
S	Searches globally	[*Line*][,*Line*] [?] S[*String*]
T	Merges files	[*Line*] T [*FileSpec*]
W	Writes lines	[*Num*] W

Table 6.1: Summary of EDLIN commands

(RAM). When it tries to load a file that is longer than 75 percent of the currently available RAM, it will load only the first part of that file and will use only 75 percent of the available memory. The message just shown will not appear, but the prompt will. You may then edit the lines that were loaded. When you are done editing these lines, you can use EDLIN commands to write the edited lines out to a diskette and then bring in additional text lines to edit.

BRINGING NEW TEXT INTO MEMORY

The command needed to add new, unedited lines of text from a disk file is the Append command, abbreviated as the single character A. This command is only used when you have loaded a file that is larger than 75 percent of current memory. Entered at the EDLIN * prompt, its general format is

[*Num*]A

The brackets around parameters in this chapter indicate that these EDLIN parameters are optional for a command. The brackets themselves are not entered as part of the command.

This command loads *Num* lines from the rest of the file (where *Num* is the number of lines to load), provided there is room. If there is insufficient room to load any more lines from your file, the command will not load anything. You must then use the W command (described shortly) to write some of your edited lines from EDLIN to disk.

If you successfully load the rest of the file into memory, the following message will appear:

```
End of input file
```

You can then continue editing using any of the EDLIN commands.

COMBINING SEPARATE TEXT FILES

The Transfer command (T) is used to combine two text files: one in memory and another somewhere else. When you specify the file to be transferred into the middle of your current file (*FileSpec*), the whole file is read in and inserted before the line number specified by *Line:*

[*Line*] T *FileSpec*

If *Line* is not specified, the file's contents are inserted before the current line.

This command can be quite useful. For example, suppose you have the following two files:

```
File1                File2
1: Line 1, File 1    1: Line 1, File 2
2: Line 2, File 1    2: Line 2, File 2
3: Line 3, File 1    3: Line 3, File 2
4: Line 4, File 1    4: Line 4, File 2
```

If File1 is the current file being edited in memory, and you enter the following command:

```
3 T FILE2
```

the result is a new combined file, which looks like this:

```
1:  Line 1, File 1
2:  Line 2, File 1
3:*Line 1, File 2
4:  Line 2, File 2
5:  Line 3, File 2
6:  Line 4, File 2
7:  Line 3, File 1
8:  Line 4, File 1
```

Note that the current line is now the first line of the transferred file, as indicated by the EDLIN * prompt.

MAKING SPACE FOR LARGE FILES

The Write command (W), like the Append command, is only needed when your file is too large to fit in 75 percent of available memory. In that situation, only 75 percent of your file will have been loaded. If you want to edit the rest of the file, you need to make some room. You must transfer lines from the file in memory to disk, thus freeing up enough space to let more if not all of the rest of the file be loaded. The general format of this command is

[*Num*] W

where *Num* is the number of lines to be written. After you execute this command, you can load the rest of the file with the A command.

If you do not specify the number of lines to be written, the W command will keep writing lines to the disk, starting with line 1, until 75 percent of available memory is free. If there is already 75 percent of available RAM freed for EDLIN text lines, then no lines will be written to disk. If, for example, the first 200 lines were written to disk, then line 201 of the total file would become line 1 of the memory portion being worked on by EDLIN. For example, the command

```
200 W
```

would cause the first 200 lines of the current file to be transferred to disk, and line 201 would be numbered line 1. You could then read in additional text lines from the disk file with the A command.

DISPLAYING EDLIN FILES

Perhaps the most common activity you'll ask your line editor to perform will be to show you the text in your file. EDLIN offers two commands for this purpose: the L command for listing any range of lines, and the P command for rapidly looking at complete screenfuls of your file.

LISTING YOUR TEXT FILE

Since line numbers change each time you add or delete a line, the List command (L) will probably be your most frequently used command. You will always want to see the new numbers assigned to each of your text lines before you execute new line-oriented commands.

You can list a block of lines in a variety of ways. If you don't provide explicit line numbers for starting and stopping, EDLIN will attempt to display 23 text lines—a screenful. The size of the display range can extend from 11 lines before the current line to 11 lines after the current line.

Perhaps the most common format for this command is to specify the precise line numbers at which to begin and end the listing. For example,

```
6,19L
```

displays lines 6 through 19 on your screen and then redisplays EDLIN's prompt.

Simply typing L with no line-number specification will display the 11 lines preceding the current line, then the current line, and then the 11 lines after the current line. If your file does not have 23 lines, the entire file will be listed.

LISTING YOUR TEXT FILE RAPIDLY

The Page command (P) is like the L command, except that it redefines the current line number to whatever line has been displayed last on the screen. This command provides you with a rapid way to list all the lines in your text file, a screenful at a time.

Entering a line number alone, as in

```
17 P
```

will display up to 23 lines starting with line 17. The last line listed becomes the current line. You can also display a specified range of lines and make the last line the current line, as in

```
14,28 P
```

If you simply enter P, EDLIN will make its standard assumptions, giving you a 23-line display, starting with the line after the current line and making the last line displayed the new current line.

EDITING EDLIN FILES

As you have worked through the previous sections on getting EDLIN started, you have seen that EDLIN is *command-oriented;* that is, it does not display menus, but rather expects you to enter individual commands, just as DOS does. Because of this, you can move around and do things in EDLIN much more quickly than you could with a menu system, but you must know the commands in order to execute them quickly.

You have also seen the EDLIN prompt, the asterisk symbol. Whenever you see this on the screen with a blinking cursor next to it, EDLIN is prompting you for a command. This prompt also shows you the current line of the file being edited, which is the default line being worked on. Any EDLIN command you enter will deal with the text on this particular line (and possibly others as well). You can move a certain number of lines forward or backward from the current line, and you can insert, edit, or delete in relation to it.

Here are some useful tips to keep in mind as you work with EDLIN:

- Most commands can be entered using just the first letter of the command. When you are performing an operation on a specific line or group of lines, specify the line numbers first.
- The EDLIN letter commands can be entered in uppercase, lowercase, or a combination of the two.
- Line numbers can be specified in a number of ways; however, they must be whole numbers between 1 and 65529. When you enter more than one line number, you must separate them with commas. If you enter a line number higher than the highest line number in memory and you are going to add a line, the line will be added after the highest line number.
- You can use the number sign (#) to refer to the as-yet-nonexistent line following the highest line number in memory.
- You can use a period to specify the current line.
- The Plus and Minus keys can be used to specify lines *relative* to the current line number. For example,

  ```
  -20,+5D
  ```

  will delete the 20 lines preceding the current line number, the current line number, and 5 lines after the current line number. If the current line number was 50, lines 30 through 55 would be deleted.
- You can enter more than one command on a line. If you do this, separate each complete command by a semicolon (;).
- It is possible (although not often necessary) to enter a control character into your file. To do this, you must press Ctrl-V first and then the desired control character (in uppercase).

- If you are displaying a lot of data, you can pause the screen output by pressing the Break key, Ctrl-ScrollLock. Press Ctrl-ScrollLock again to restart the output. Note that the processing of the command will have stopped also.

Now let's take a look at the editing tasks you'll want to do with EDLIN, and the commands that perform these tasks.

INSERTING NEW LINES

The Insert command (I) is used to insert lines. Its general format is

[*Line*]I

Inserting lines will change all line numbers after the insertion. For example, if you insert new text at line 3, remember that all line numbers after 3 have been changed. It's best to do a new listing (L) to discover the new numbering before issuing any new commands.

Again, *Line* may be specified as either a specific or a relative line number. Not including *Line* will result in lines being added before the current line. If you created a new file called LINCOLN.TXT by calling up EDLIN, you would use the I command to insert text for the first time at line 1. Entering 1I at the EDLIN * prompt like this:

```
*1I
```

would yield

```
1:*_
```

which places you in insert mode. As you can see in Figure 6.1, EDLIN shows you each line number as you type it.

Notice the ^C on line 4. This is EDLIN's response when you press Ctrl-C during text insertion. Use the Ctrl-C key combination to exit from text insertion and return to the EDLIN prompt.

The I command can also be used to insert new text before any existing text line in the file. Simply specify the line number in the file before which you want the new text to be placed.

CHANGING EXISTING LINES

Editing a line merely means that you are changing the information on the line, *not* adding or deleting a line. If no line number is specified (in other words, you have simply pressed Return), then you will start editing the line after the current line. If the current line is the last line in the file, pressing Return will do nothing but produce another * prompt. Usually, however, you can enter any line number to put you into edit mode for that line. You may also use relative line numbers to edit a line.

When you are put into edit mode (for example, by entering 3 and pressing Return), the display looks something like this:

```
3:*a new operating system (more or less).
3:*_
```

The arrow keys or any of the function keys will work as they do at the DOS prompt. For example, pressing F3 will do the following:

```
3:*a new operating system (more or less).
3:*a new operating system (more or less)._
```

The original line 3 is completely retyped, with the cursor waiting at the end of the line for additional input.

While editing any line, pressing the Right Arrow key will move the cursor one character to the right and display the character it was on (or under). Pressing Esc-Return or the Break key combination anywhere on the line will take you out of edit mode and leave the line unchanged.

If you want to add something to the end of the line, simply press F3 and start typing. You will automatically be put into insert mode. If your cursor is located anywhere else on the line, you must press the Ins key to enter insert mode, and press it again to leave that mode. In Figure 6.2, you can see how line 3 of our example was changed. F3 was pressed, the Backspace key was used to erase the period, and then the new characters ", dedicated" were typed. Both before and after the change, the L command was used to list the current contents of the file.

The edit to line 3 is only the first step in a common sequence, as shown in Figure 6.3. A change is made, followed by a listing of the file. Then another editing command follows (in this case, a new text insertion at the end of the file), and yet another L command is used to verify the results of the last edit. Continuing this process and adding still more text (with a correction to line 10 along the way) results in the 12-line text file shown in Figure 6.4.

```
C>EDLIN  LINCOLN.TXT
New file
*1I
        1:*Four score and seven months ago (approximately),
        2:*DOS's forefathers brought forth upon this nation
        3:*a new operating system (more or less).
        4:*^C

*-
```

Figure 6.1: Inserting text for the first time

```
C>EDLIN LINCOLN.TXT
End of input file
*L
        1:*Four score and seven months ago (approximately),
        2: DOS's forefathers brought forth upon this nation
        3: a new operating system (more or less).
*3
        3:*a new operating system (more or less).
        3:*a new operating system (more or less), dedicated
*L
        1: Four score and seven months ago (approximately),
        2: DOS's forefathers brought forth upon this nation
        3:*a new operating system (more or less), dedicated
*-
```

Figure 6.2: Making corrections to a line

MOVING LINES (CUTTING AND PASTING)

The Move command (M) allows you to move one line or a body of lines in a file to a new location in the file. (A group of lines to be moved is called a *block*.) For example, entering

```
9,12,6M
L
```

```
C>EDLIN LINCOLN.TXT
End of input file
*L
         1:*Four score and seven months ago (approximately),
         2: DOS's forefathers brought forth upon this nation
         3: a new operating system (more or less).
*3
         3:*a new operating system (more or less).
         3:*a new operating system (more or less), dedicated
*L
         1: Four score and seven months ago (approximately),
         2: DOS's forefathers brought forth upon this nation
         3:*a new operating system (more or less), dedicated
*4I
         4:*to the proposition that all computers (with the same
         5:*microcomputer chip) are created equal.
         6:*^C

*L
         1: Four score and seven months ago (approximately),
         2: DOS's forefathers brought forth upon this nation
         3: a new operating system (more or less), dedicated
         4: to the proposition that all computers (with the same
         5: microcomputer chip) are created equal.
*_
```

Figure 6.3: Adding new lines at the end of a file

```
         5: microcomputer chip) are created equal.
         6: We are met today to chronicle a part of these DOS
         7: wars.  It is altogether fitting and proper (some may
         8: disagree) that we should do this.
         9: Now, we are engaged in a great computer war (more
        10: have fallen than have risen), testing whether this DOS
        11: or any other DOS so conceived and so dedicated, can
        12: long endure.
*10
        10:*have fallen than have risen), testing whether this DOS
        10:*have fallen than have risen), testing whether this DOS,
*L
         1: Four score and seven months ago (approximately),
         2: DOS's forefathers brought forth upon this nation
         3: a new operating system (more or less), dedicated
         4: to the proposition that all computers (with the same
         5: microcomputer chip) are created equal.
         6: We are met today to chronicle a part of these DOS
         7: wars.  It is altogether fitting and proper (some may
         8: disagree) that we should do this.
         9: Now, we are engaged in a great computer war (more
        10:*have fallen than have risen), testing whether this DOS,
        11: or any other DOS so conceived and so dedicated, can
        12: long endure.
*_
```

Figure 6.4: Intermediate version of the text file

at the EDLIN prompt will move lines 9 through 12 in the file shown in Figure 6.4 to a new position—in front of line 6, as shown in Figure 6.5. This is commonly called *cutting and pasting*. Naturally, when the operation is completed, all affected lines are renumbered. Notice that the current line has moved to the new sixth line, since this was the first line in the block that was moved.

```
        3: a new operating system (more or less), dedicated
        4: to the proposition that all computers (with the same
        5: microcomputer chip) are created equal.
        6: We are met today to chronicle a part of these DOS
        7: wars.  It is altogether fitting and proper (some may
        8: disagree) that we should do this.
        9: Now, we are engaged in a great computer war (more
       10:*have fallen than have risen), testing whether this DOS,
       11: or any other DOS so conceived and so dedicated, can
       12: long endure.
*9,12,6M
*L
        1: Four score and seven months ago (approximately),
        2: DOS's forefathers brought forth upon this nation
        3: a new operating system (more or less), dedicated
        4: to the proposition that all computers (with the same
        5: microcomputer chip) are created equal.
        6:*Now, we are engaged in a great computer war (more
        7: have fallen than have risen), testing whether this DOS,
        8: or any other DOS so conceived and so dedicated, can
        9: long endure.
       10: We are met today to chronicle a part of these DOS
       11: wars.  It is altogether fitting and proper (some may
       12: disagree) that we should do this.
*_
```

Figure 6.5: Cutting and pasting text

COPYING LINES

The Copy command (C) is used to copy blocks of lines to other places in a file. It is similar to the M command, although not as frequently used. When you use the C command, the original lines are not bodily moved to a new place in the file; instead, they are replicated in the new place, leaving the original lines intact. After the copy has been made, all line numbers will be recalculated, and the first line that was copied will become the new current line.

There are three versions of the C command. In the first, you can make a replica of the current text line anywhere else in the file. The copy of the current line will be inserted in front of the line specified by *Line:*

,,*Line*[,*Count*] C

The commas represent placeholders for values that haven't been entered by you; the default (that is, the current line) is used. The optional *Count* parameter can be used to specify the number of times the operations should be repeated.

You can also copy multiple lines at once using the C command. The following format causes all of the lines from *Line1* through the current line to be copied to the position before *Line2:*

Line1,,*Line2*[,*Count*] C

In any EDLIN command that allows the specification of multiple lines, the beginning line number must be less than or equal to the ending line number. EDLIN cannot work backwards.

The third possible format of the C command allows you to explicitly specify the range to be copied:

Range,*Line3*[,*count*] C

Range represents a pair of delimited line numbers. This version of the C command is similar to the previous version, except that in *Range* you specify the last line number to be copied, instead of defaulting to the current line number.

Here's an example of using the *Count* parameter with the C command. If you were editing any text file of at least five lines and executed the following:

*1,4,5,3 C

you would be telling EDLIN to make a copy of lines 1 through 4 in your file at a point just before line 5, and then to repeat this operation twice more (a total of 3 for *Count*).

SEARCHING FOR TEXT STRINGS

The Search command (S) locates lines. You can ask EDLIN to carry out the search over a variety of ranges. The general format of this command is

[*Scope*] [?] S[*String*]

Scope can be defined as any of the following parameters:

- *Line* causes the search to start at *Line* and stop at the end of the file;
- ,*Line* causes the search to start at the line after the current line and end at *Line;*
- *Line1*,*Line2* causes the search to cover only the lines within the block between *Line1* and *Line2*.

- Not using the *Scope* parameter results in the search starting at the line after the current line and ending at the last line in the file.

The *String* parameter specifies the text that you are looking for. The first character of this text should immediately follow the S. If *String* is not included on the command line, the search string last used in a Search or Replace command is used. If no Search or Replace command has yet been used in the session, then the message "Not found" will be displayed.

If you specify ? in this command, EDLIN will stop each time it locates the specified string, and it will ask you for confirmation that the string is the correct one.

The Search and Replace commands are case-sensitive—they will look for *exactly* what you type. For example, the S command will consider *Judd* and *judd* to be two different words because of the different capitalization.

As an example of using the Search command, let's look for all occurrences of the word *is* in the following file:

```
1: This is the first line
2: of a test file to demonstrate
3: the use of the Search command.
4: It is included for your own
5: information.
```

You would enter the following command:

```
*1,5 ? Sis
```

You would then see

```
 1: This is the first line
O.K.? n
 4: It is included for your own
O.K.? n
 Not found
 *_
```

You can see that line 4 has become the current line, as it was the last line to contain a match with *String*. Notice that line 1 only came up once in the search. This is because the search finds a whole line with a match on it. If there is more than one match, it's a waste of time to successively redisplay the same line.

SEARCH AND REPLACE CAPABILITIES

R is the Replace command. It gives you the ability to search through any specified range of lines and replace every occurrence of specific text (*String*) with new replacement text (*NewString*).

The general format for the R command is

[*Scope*] [?] R[*String*][Ctrl-Z*NewString*]

The *Scope* and *String* parameters are the same as those for the Search command. If you are going to enter replacement text (*NewString*), end *String* by pressing Ctrl-Z. (This is optional, since you may only want to search for and remove the specified string wherever it is found.)

NewString is the text that will replace *String*. It does not need to be the same size as *String,* since it will be inserted after *String* has been deleted. If *NewString* is left out, then *String* will be deleted in the specified block. If *String* is left out as well, EDLIN will use the *String* value from the last Search or Replace command, and the *NewString* value from the last Replace command. If Search and Replace have not been used during the current session, you will get the message "Not found."

When ? is specified in this command, EDLIN will display the replaced or modified line and ask whether you wish to confirm the changes that were made ("O.K.?"). You should answer Y or press Return if you want the changes to become permanent.

Once an occurrence of *String* has been found and you have accepted or not accepted the change, the search will continue in the specified block. Multiple occurrences on the same line are included in the replacements.

Let's try this command with the example you worked with earlier in this chapter. You can quickly ask EDLIN to search in the file for each occurrence of the text string *DOS.* When found, the command will replace *DOS* with *MS-DOS* (see Figure 6.6).

In this example, you specified that all occurrences in lines 1 through 12 are to be acted upon. You can see by the EDLIN prompt that line 10 has become the current line, since it was the last line changed. Notice also that each line that contained the sought-after string of characters was displayed after the change was made (lines 2, 7, 8, and 10). As shown in the figure, you usually execute the L command to verify the results of your command request.

```
         7: have fallen than have risen), testing whether this DOS,
         8: or any other DOS so conceived and so dedicated, can
         9: long endure.
        10: We are met today to chronicle a part of these DOS
        11: wars.  It is altogether fitting and proper (some may
        12:*disagree) that we should do this.
*1,12RDOS^ZMS-DOS
         2: MS-DOS's forefathers brought forth upon this nation
         7: have fallen than have risen), testing whether this MS-DOS,
         8: or any other MS-DOS so conceived and so dedicated, can
        10: We are met today to chronicle a part of these MS-DOS
*L
         1: Four score and seven months ago (approximately),
         2: MS-DOS's forefathers brought forth upon this nation
         3: a new operating system (more or less), dedicated
         4: to the proposition that all computers (with the same
         5: microcomputer chip) are created equal.
         6: Now, we are engaged in a great computer war (more
         7: have fallen than have risen), testing whether this MS-DOS,
         8: or any other MS-DOS so conceived and so dedicated, can
         9: long endure.
        10:*We are met today to chronicle a part of these MS-DOS
        11: wars.  It is altogether fitting and proper (some may
        12: disagree) that we should do this.
*_
```

Figure 6.6: Search and replace operation

DELETING LINES

Deleting lines causes all lines after the deletion to be renumbered. Even if you do not request a listing of the lines (with L), they are still renumbered. For example, if you execute the command 1D twice, you will have deleted lines 1 and 2.

The Delete command (D) is used to delete one or more lines from the file. Its general format is

[*Line*],[*Line*]D

The *Line* parameters specify the line or lines that you want to delete.

Suppose you had written some new text and added it to the current file beginning at line 13 (see Figure 6.7). Then you decided (either immediately or later) that this new text was not appropriate, so you needed to delete it with the D command. Figure 6.8 shows the results of deleting the lines and then listing the remaining file.

ENDING THE EDITING SESSION

There are two ways to exit EDLIN, depending on whether you want to save the changes you've made to the file or not. You can abort the entire editing operation and restore the file to its original condition, or you can save all your edits to the disk file, permanently engraving those changes in the original file.

QUITTING THE EDITING SESSION WITHOUT SAVING

Entering the Quit command (Q) all by itself is one way of getting out of EDLIN and back to DOS without saving all of the work you have just done. EDLIN will ask you if you are sure you wish to leave without saving your file. Anything other than an answer of Y will abort the Q command, and you will be back at the EDLIN prompt.

```
        8: or any other MS-DOS so conceived and so dedicated, can
        9: long endure.
       10: We are met today to chronicle a part of these MS-DOS
       11: wars.  It is altogether fitting and proper (some may
       12: disagree) that we should do this.
*13I
       13:*The world will little note (not counting book reviewers,
       14:*of course) nor long remember what we say here, but you
       15:*can never forget what you learn here (who could possibly
       16:*forget such drama, not to mention irreverence?).
       17:*^C
*L
        6: Now, we are engaged in a great computer war (more
        7: have fallen than have risen), testing whether this MS-DOS,
        8: or any other MS-DOS so conceived and so dedicated, can
        9: long endure.
       10: We are met today to chronicle a part of these MS-DOS
       11: wars.  It is altogether fitting and proper (some may
       12: disagree) that we should do this.
       13: The world will little note (not counting book reviewers,
       14: of course) nor long remember what we say here, but you
       15: can never forget what you learn here (who could possibly
       16: forget such drama, not to mention irreverence?).
*_
```

Figure 6.7: Additional text entries

```
        7: have fallen than have risen), testing whether this MS-DOS,
        8: or any other MS-DOS so conceived and so dedicated, can
        9: long endure.
       10: We are met today to chronicle a part of these MS-DOS
       11: wars.  It is altogether fitting and proper (some may
       12: disagree) that we should do this.
       13: The world will little note (not counting book reviewers,
       14: of course) nor long remember what we say here, but you
       15: can never forget what you learn here (who could possibly
       16: forget such drama, not to mention irreverence?).
*13,16D
*1L
        1: Four score and seven months ago (approximately),
        2: MS-DOS's forefathers brought forth upon this nation
        3: a new operating system (more or less), dedicated
        4: to the proposition that all computers (with the same
        5: microcomputer chip) are created equal.
        6: Now, we are engaged in a great computer war (more
        7: have fallen than have risen), testing whether this MS-DOS,
        8: or any other MS-DOS so conceived and so dedicated, can
        9: long endure.
       10: We are met today to chronicle a part of these MS-DOS
       11: wars.  It is altogether fitting and proper (some may
       12: disagree) that we should do this.
*_
```

Figure 6.8: Multiple lines deleted

This exit path usually is used when you have made a mistake. Suppose, for example, that you changed your mind about the deletion of lines 13 to 16 done in the last section. You've decided to keep those lines in the text after all. You could type them in all over again; or, if there are no other edits at stake, you could abort the entire editing process, go back to DOS, and then call up the text file for editing once again. Figure 6.9 demonstrates this process. Using Q to abort the editing process, returning to DOS, and then immediately recalling the LINCOLN.TXT file returns the unchanged text file to you.

SAVING YOUR WORK AND EXITING TO DOS

Make sure that there is enough room on your disk for the file to be saved. If there is not, the part of the file that *can* fit will be saved with an extension of .$$$. The original file will be retained on the disk, no new .BAK file will be created, and the part of the edited file not saved will be lost.

The usual way to exit EDLIN and save your changes is to use the End command (E). With this command, the file you originally named when you started EDLIN will be given a .BAK extension; the edited file will retain the original extension. If you created a completely new file, no .BAK file would be created.

At the end of the file, EDLIN will insert a carriage return and line feed if they are not already there. It will also insert a Ctrl-Z code to be used for an end-of-file marker.

EDLIN will *not* prompt you to make sure you want to leave. Entering E followed by a press of the Return key is all you need to save all of your editing changes and return to DOS (see Figure 6.10).

```
        10: We are met today to chronicle a part of these MS-DOS
        11: wars.  It is altogether fitting and proper (some may
        12: disagree) that we should do this.
*Q
Abort edit (Y/N)? Y
C>EDLIN LINCOLN.TXT
End of input file
*L
         1:*Four score and seven months ago (approximately),
         2: MS-DOS's forefathers brought forth upon this nation
         3: a new operating system (more or less), dedicated
         4: to the proposition that all computers (with the same
         5: microcomputer chip) are created equal.
         6: Now, we are engaged in a great computer war (more
         7: have fallen than have risen), testing whether this MS-DOS,
         8: or any other MS-DOS so conceived and so dedicated, can
         9: long endure.
        10: We are met today to chronicle a part of these MS-DOS
        11: wars.  It is altogether fitting and proper (some may
        12: disagree) that we should do this.
        13: The world will little note (not counting book reviewers,
        14: of course) nor long remember what we say here, but you
        15: can never forget what you learn here (who could possibly
        16: forget such drama, not to mention irreverence?).
*
```

Figure 6.9: Aborting the editing process

```
        12: disagree) that we should do this.
*Q
Abort edit (Y/N)? Y
C>EDLIN LINCOLN.TXT
End of input file
*L
          1:*Four score and seven months ago (approximately),
          2: MS-DOS's forefathers brought forth upon this nation
          3: a new operating system (more or less), dedicated
          4: to the proposition that all computers (with the same
          5: microcomputer chip) are created equal.
          6: Now, we are engaged in a great computer war (more
          7: have fallen than have risen), testing whether this MS-DOS,
          8: or any other MS-DOS so conceived and so dedicated, can
          9: long endure.
         10: We are met today to chronicle a part of these MS-DOS
         11: wars.  It is altogether fitting and proper (some may
         12: disagree) that we should do this.
         13: The world will little note (not counting book reviewers,
         14: of course) nor long remember what we say here, but you
         15: can never forget what you learn here (who could possibly
         16: forget such drama, not to mention irreverence?).
*E

C>_
```

Figure 6.10: Normal EDLIN termination sequence

SUMMARY

In this chapter, you've learned about the commands available in DOS's line editor, EDLIN, for creating and manipulating text files, as well as for modifying the text within them. Here is a brief review:

- All of EDLIN's capabilities are accessible with simple one-letter commands. These commands act on one or more lines within the text file, and act on the text within those lines.
- You can create a new file simply by typing EDLIN *FileName*. The file will be created and you can execute any of EDLIN's editing commands by typing in the appropriate command at the asterisk prompt.
- If the available memory in your system is not sufficient to hold your entire text file, you can use the Write command with the Append command to write edited lines to disk and then add unedited lines to memory.
- You can enter new text with the Insert command. The Break key allows you to terminate the data entry.

- You can list any or all text lines with the Line command. You can also list the entire file, a screenful at a time, with the Page command.
- Once entered, text can be modified in a variety of ways. The DOS function keys can be used to modify any line once you've brought up that line by typing its number.
- You can move one or more lines around in the file with the Move command. You can also leave those lines in place, while making a complete copy of them elsewhere with the Copy command.
- Besides the Move and Copy commands, which manipulate large blocks of text, the Transfer command can insert one complete text file into another.
- What goes in can always come out. The Delete command can remove one or more text lines—permanently.
- Any text string can be searched for with the Search command. The even more powerful Replace command can search for any text string and replace it with another string. If you like, the Replace command can be used to replace one string with *nothing,* effectively creating a large-scale (global) deletion capability.
- You can end your EDLIN editing session with the End command, which saves your edited work under the original file name and then returns you to the DOS prompt. Or you can abort the entire editing session with the Quit command, which, after confirming that you really mean to do it, restores your file to its original condition.

Now that you know how to create and modify text files with EDLIN, you should turn to Chapter 7. Having beautifully sculpted text on a disk may be satisfying, but printing it out on paper is even better. You will find that it's much better to read the entire file from a printed manuscript than from one 23-line display at a time.

PRINTING

CHAPTER 7

COMPUTERS CAN DO MANY MARVELOUS THINGS, AND do them all at lightning speeds. Cardiac simulations, missile interception analyses, genetic and chemical modeling are just a few of the tasks that would be tedious or even impossible without computers. However, the magic of the computer would be all for naught if there were no way to see the results.

We often take output for granted. Yet, you know by now that without a DIR, TYPE, or COPY command, you'd never be able to see the results of your work. In this chapter, you'll learn a wide range of output capabilities in DOS. You'll discover some easy methods, some "quick-and-dirty" techniques, and some sophisticated commands for controlling when output will occur, where it will go, and what it will look like. You'll also learn why these alternatives work as they do.

Printing simple screen images of both text and graphics screens is the easiest kind of output to master quickly, so you'll learn that right away. Since printing onto paper is unquestionably the standard method for obtaining hard-copy results from programs, the principal focus of this chapter will be on producing printed output.

Indirect printing plays a very important role in more and more systems. The last section in this chapter will take an in-depth look at this feature. With indirect printing, you can continue to work on your computer while it sends output to a printer. This is DOS's first step into the world of multitasking and multiprocessing, where more than one program can execute at one time and more than one user can share the system's capabilities. The full potential of this power will not be realized until the next generation of hardware and software becomes available. For now, however, it can provide a significant improvement in system performance, allowing printing to occur simultaneously with other computing tasks.

PRINTING SCREEN IMAGES

It's often easier to generate results on the video screen than on any other output device. However, as you'll learn in this chapter, anything that can be displayed on your video screen can also be transferred to your printer.

A Color Graphics Adapter (CGA) monitor can generate graphics images using an array of pixels (dots) that is 640 pixels wide by 200 high. This density—128,000 pixels—is acceptable for most applications, although many programs produce more pleasing and detailed results using denser output screens. An Enhanced Graphics Adapter (EGA) monitor has a density that is twice that of the CGA. Its graphics mode produces an array of 640 × 350 pixels, while its successors, the Professional Graphics Adapter (PGA) and the Video Graphics Array (VGA), produce 640 × 480. The VGA has several additional display modes, a popular one being 720 × 400 resolution for increasing the number of text lines displayed. The top of the line in graphics capabilities on the new Personal System/2 machines features a 1024 × 768 pixel addressability.

All printers can create an exact replica of any text that appears on a screen. With DOS commands, you can easily obtain hard copies of any important data that is being displayed on your monitor. This may be all you ever need to be satisfied with printed output from your computer system. In fact, many users never need to print anything with DOS commands—their application programs have built-in commands for managing output printing. To accurately replicate an image on the screen that was created in graphics mode instead of text mode, however, you must have a printer capable of creating graphics.

If neither you nor your dealer has yet connected your printer, you should do so now. If you need to do more than simply connect your printer and cable to the appropriate ports, consult Chapter 8, which covers communications in detail.

DOS requires you to press the keystroke combination Shift-PrtSc to print a copy of whatever is on the screen. The Shift-PrtSc key combination will work on any video monitor if the information being displayed is in standard text characters. To see how it works, turn on your computer and bring up any program at all; or just try a simple DOS directory command. Turn on your printer, and press Shift-PrtSc. It's as simple as that to obtain hard copy.

Assuming you have a printer capable of generating graphics images, you can also create printed images of graphics by following a simple preparatory procedure. The GRAPHICS command in DOS is a disk-resident program that enables the same Shift-PrtSc combination to capture a graphics screen image for printing if you have an IBM- or Epson-compatible printer. You must invoke this command *before* attempting to print a graphics screen.

The simplest form of the command is invoked by typing

GRAPHICS

This causes future presses of the Shift-PrtSc combination to reproduce on your printer all screen images, including graphics images. Graphics images cannot be printed without taking this crucial step.

If you have a graphics program or an integrated package that includes graphics, try running it now and printing one of the resulting graphics images. First try it without executing GRAPHICS. Then go back to DOS and run the GRAPHICS command. Return to your program, and try Shift-PrtSc with the same graphics image.

The GRAPHICS command has some flexibility when it comes to output appearance. Its general form is

GRAPHICS *PrinterType* /R /B

where *PrinterType* is one of the possible parameter values defining printer type, as shown in Table 7.1. /R and /B are switches you can use for background color and reverse video, as you will see shortly. As always, if the GRAPHICS.COM file is not in the current directory,

PARAMETER	PRINTER TYPE
COLOR1	For a color printer with a black ribbon (prints up to four shades of grey)
COLOR4	For a color printer with a red/green/blue ribbon
COLOR8	For a color printer with a cyan/magenta/yellow ribbon
COMPACT	For the IBM Personal Computer Compact printer
GRAPHICS	For the IBM Personal Graphics printer, or the IBM Proprinter (this is the default)
THERMAL	For the IBM PC Convertible printer

Table 7.1: *PrinterType* parameters for the GRAPHICS command

you should precede the GRAPHICS command with the drive and directory where it can be found.

Figure 7.1 shows a typical graphics screen. If you do not run the GRAPHICS command, and simply try to print this screen with the Shift-PrtSc combination, the result will be unsatisfactory, as you see in Figure 7.2. However, if you use the GRAPHICS command with the default graphics *PrinterType* by first typing

```
GRAPHICS
```

then pressing Return, and *then* using Shift-PrtSc, the printed result will be what you want to see, as shown in Figure 7.3.

Printing a screen that contains only text with Shift-PrtSc is reasonably quick (under a minute for most microcomputer printers). Printing a screen containing graphics will take several minutes, depending on the graphics resolution and screen contents, as well as the speed of your printer.

If you specify *PrinterType* as COLOR4 or COLOR8, you have the option of printing the background screen color. You then use the /B switch when you invoke the command by typing, for example,

```
GRAPHICS  COLOR4  /B
```

As an alternative, the /R switch with this command produces a striking *reverse-video* image (white letters on a black background). For example, typing

```
GRAPHICS  COLOR4  /R
```

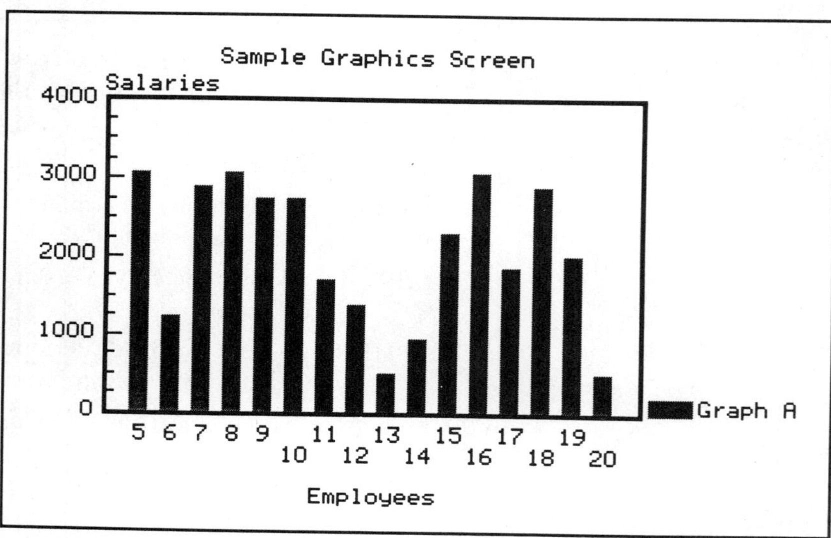

Figure 7.1: A typical graphics screen on a video display

would produce the reverse-video printing shown in Figure 7.4.

Finally, you should know that the graphics mode of your video display will affect the printed image. If your screen is in high-resolution

Figure 7.2: Figure 7.1 printed with the Shift-PrtSc combination

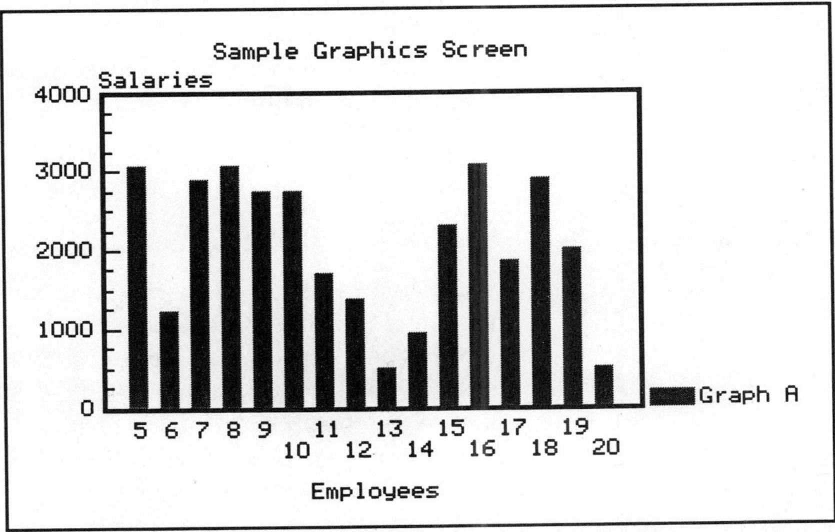

Figure 7.3: Figure 7.1 printed with the GRAPHICS command and Shift-PrtSc

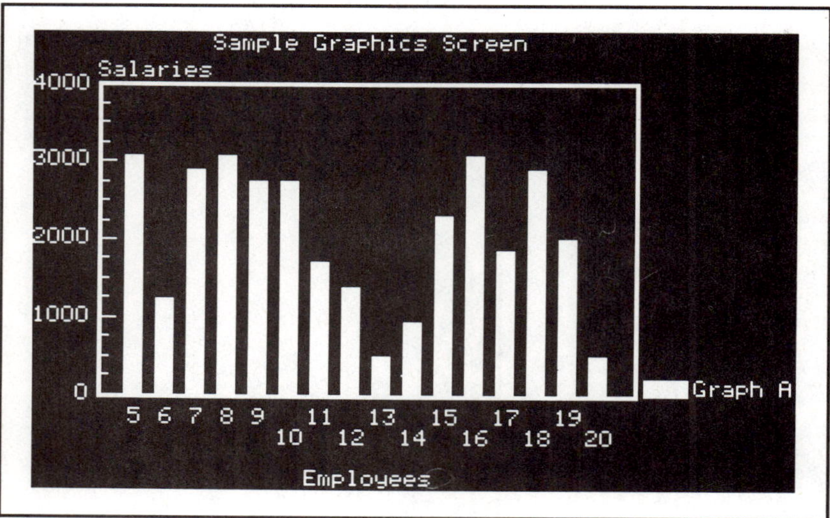

Figure 7.4: Reverse-video printout of Figure 7.1

mode (640 columns by 200 rows), then the printed image will be rotated 90 degrees on the paper. This is often called a *horizontal landscape* image. If the screen is in medium-resolution mode (320 columns by 200 rows), the printed image will be printed as you see it. This is called a *vertical portrait* image. The resolution affects color printouts as well as displays; it is possible to obtain four colors in medium-resolution mode, but only two different colors in high-resolution mode.

PRINTING FILES

Creating exact replicas of displayed data with the Shift-PrtSc command and the GRAPHICS command is easy, but it is limited to one screenful of information at a time. There will be many times when you need a printed copy of an entire data file. Most files are created as standard ASCII files, which usually contain standard letters, numbers, and punctuation. In addition, each line of an ASCII file has a carriage return and line feed (CR/LF) at the end of it, but no other special control characters are embedded within the file. An ASCII file can be printed in several ways, as you will see in the following sections.

PRINTING FILES WITH THE COPY COMMAND

Keep in mind that if a file is stored in some special format (as it is for spreadsheet programs, database programs, and many word-processing programs), you will need to use a special output printing sequence for the appropriate program to obtain a printed copy.

The most straightforward way to print one or more data files is to use the COPY command. The general form of the COPY command is

```
COPY FileName(s) DeviceName
```

where *FileName(s)* is the name of the file (or files) and the destination, *DeviceName,* is the printer's *reserved device name.* (You will learn about these names in Chapter 8.) DOS reserves several special names like LPT1 or COM1 for the hardware ports to which printers are connected.

If the file you want to print is called KEYS.DTA, then it can be printed simply by specifying either of the following two commands:

```
COPY KEYS.DTA LPT1:
COPY KEYS.DTA PRN:
```

In these commands, LPT1 is a name for the first parallel printer port (see Chapter 8) and PRN is the standard default device name for the first connected printer. The printer will be engaged immediately, and the entire file will be printed. You will now have to wait until the printout is completed before the DOS prompt will return. Nothing else can be done by your DOS system or by you until the printing terminates.

As you learned in Chapter 3, you can copy multiple files with one command by using a wild-card specification. In this situation, you can also initiate the printing of multiple text files with one statement. For instance, you could initiate the printing of all the .TXT files in the HELP directory by entering

```
COPY \HELP\*.TXT PRN:
```

DOS will respond to this request by successively echoing on the screen the name of each .TXT file. After echoing a name, it will transmit all the contents of that file to the printer and move on to the next file in the HELP directory that meets the .TXT file specification. Once again, you will not regain control at the DOS prompt until all of the specified files have been printed.

INDIRECT PRINTING AND SPOOLING

In the previous section, the COPY command allowed you to transfer files to a printer. However, COPY will not relinquish control of the system until the print transfer is complete. Since the DOS prompt does not reappear, you are unable to enter any other DOS command or do anything else while the printing proceeds.

The PRINT command is DOS's solution. Unlike the COPY command, which directly prints to your printer, the PRINT command causes printing to occur indirectly. PRINT sends information out to a disk file to indicate which data files are to be printed. Then, later, while you are doing other work, DOS will independently read this disk file to discover which data files should be printed. The printing will occur simultaneously with other work you may then be doing with DOS and your computer system.

Indirect printing is often called *spooling*, an acronym for "*s*imultaneous *p*eripheral *o*perations *o*n-*l*ine." Spooling is the only form of limited multitasking available in the current DOS operating system. (Multitasking is the apparent simultaneous operation of different programs or computer tasks.)

Switches and wild cards, when used intelligently, can also help you control the flow of information and files from one place to another—in this case, from a disk to a printer. The biggest complaint about system performance centers is the long waiting time for slow peripheral devices like printers and plotters, and the PRINT command and switches help to address that complaint.

Use the directory of .PRG text files seen in the DBASE\ADMIN\EXPERT directory of Figure 7.5 as you work through the following sections.

PRINTING FILES WITH THE PRINT COMMAND

The PRINT command is functionally similar to COPY. You could enter the following to print a file name or names on a standard system printer:

COPY *FileName(s)* PRN:

You could also enter just

PRINT *FileName(s)*

```
C>DIR/W \DBASE\ADMIN\EXPERT\*.PRG

 Volume in drive C is ROBBINS
 Directory of  C:\DBASE\ADMIN\EXPERT

ARCHIVE  PRG    COLPRINT PRG    COMM     PRG    DATE     PRG    DELAY    PRG
DIR      PRG    DISKRPT  PRG    DUPLICAT PRG    GETSPACE PRG    LOWER    PRG
MAIL     PRG    MENU     PRG    MESSAGE  PRG    MODIFY   PRG    PRINT    PRG
PRINTER1 PRG    PRINTER2 PRG    PRINTER3 PRG    RUNDIR   PRG    SBENTRY  PRG
SBREPORT PRG    SBUPDAT2 PRG    SBUPDATE PRG    SNAP     PRG    STATS    PRG
STRIP    PRG    TIME     PRG    VALIDATE PRG    WASH     PRG    WINDEMO  PRG
WINDOW   PRG
       31 File(s)   1212416 bytes free

C>_
```

***Figure** 7.5:* The DBASE\ADMIN\EXPERT directory

Unlike the COPY command, which has to be told a printing destination such as PRN, PRINT *knows* that its job is to send the specified file names to a printer. You can use one of the special switches, discussed later in this section, to indicate which printing device the files are to be printed on, but it's not really necessary. If you haven't specified the switch, DOS will ask you for a destination the very first time you invoke the PRINT command:

Name of list device [PRN]:

At this point, you could just press Return to accept the displayed default device name of PRN, or you could enter a specific reserved device name (like COM2) for your system.

Stop now briefly and try the PRINT command to print any text files (.TXT, .BAT, .DTA, and so on) you have on your system. Just enter the PRINT command at the DOS prompt, followed by a list of the file names you want to print. Use two or three names the first time; then, when DOS asks you for the name of the list device (the destination), just press Return.

DUAL TASKING WITH PRINT

The major difference between PRINT and COPY is apparent immediately after you specify the file names to print and answer any questions PRINT may ask you the first time you use it. The DOS prompt returns right after PRINT begins its work. You can invoke other programs or commands while PRINT prints your files. The effect is apparently simultaneous action: the CPU seems to be managing the printing job at the same time it is responding to your new requests at the DOS prompt for nonprinting work. The indirect printing, or spooling, is called a *background task,* while your principal new work (if any) is called the *foreground task.*

This dual-tasking technique is actually electronic chicanery—a silicon sleight-of-hand. A DOS computer has only one central processing chip (CPU), and it can really only do one thing at a time. However, it *can* do things very quickly. In any given period of time, a CPU can rapidly shift its processing attention from a slow printer to a slow typist to a not-really-so-fast disk drive.

If an operating system were advanced enough to manage all this shifting of attention from one operation to another and from one device to another, you would see a true multitasking environment. However, DOS is only advanced enough to play this juggling game between two things: printing and, at most, one other activity.

Figure 7.6 shows a request for the printing of a single text file, MAIL.PRG, as a background task. In this example the PRINT command has been invoked for the first time since DOS was brought

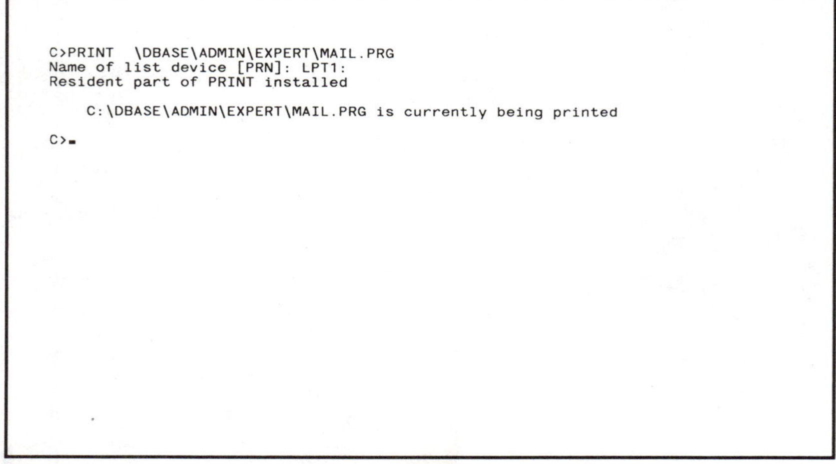

```
C>PRINT  \DBASE\ADMIN\EXPERT\MAIL.PRG
Name of list device [PRN]: LPT1:
Resident part of PRINT installed

    C:\DBASE\ADMIN\EXPERT\MAIL.PRG is currently being printed

C>_
```

Figure 7.6: First use of PRINT for background printing

up. The name of the desired printer was solicited (with DOS using the formal specification "list device"), and LPT1 was explicitly entered.

Notice that a message appears informing you that the resident part of PRINT has been installed. PRINT expands the resident memory requirements of DOS when it runs. Although the extra memory requirement reduces the memory remaining for your primary application program, this cost is a small price to pay for the ability to continue using your computer while printing proceeds. PRINT also displays a message stating that the requested file is currently being printed. Then the standard DOS prompt reappears. If you now initiate any other command or program, DOS will simply shift its processing power back and forth between the new job and the currently running print job.

Depending on how much slack time exists in your new program (for example, keyboard or disk waiting), the new program may not get held up to any noticeable extent. Usually, however, the print job can never run as fast as it could if it were not contending with a foreground task for the processor's attention. DOS will do its best to efficiently juggle the time-sharing between tasks.

USING SWITCHES WITH PRINT

DOS provides you with certain switches that give you performance controls for indirect printing. Detailed analysis of these switches is beyond the scope of this book. In fact, using these switches at all may be unnecessary for the average user. When future versions of DOS permit multitasking, these parameters will be more useful for fine-tuning advanced DOS.

In the example seen in Figure 7.6, no switches were specified. DOS set its own intelligent initial values for the performance parameters. However, you can specify other values for these parameters. The memory-resident setup will follow defaults unless you specify other values by switches. Some of these switches can only be used the first time PRINT is invoked. These switches and their parameters are shown in Table 7.2.

The only one of the six initialization switches that you might want to consider setting consistently is /Q, the Queue switch, which indicates how many separately named files can be managed by the

PRINT command. A *queue* is just a waiting line, like a line of people waiting for a bus or bank service. In this context, a queue is a list of files to be printed. DOS allows ten file names in the queue as a default

SWITCH AND PARAMETER	EFFECT
/D:*Device*	Specifies the device to which print output is to be sent (COM1, LPT2, and so on)
/Q:*QueueSize*	Specifies how many files can be accepted by the PRINT command at one time for background printing. Maximum number is 32, and the default value is 10
/M:*MaxTicks*	Specifies the maximum of CPU clock ticks to be used by the PRINT command each time it is given control by the CPU. Range of allowable values is 1 to 255, with a default value of 2
/B:*BufferSize*	Specifies the number of bytes in memory to be used for data to be printed. 512 bytes is standard, but it can be increased in 512-byte increments
/U:*BusyTicks*	Specifies how many clock ticks to wait for a printer that is still busy with earlier printing. Allowable range is 1 to 255, with a default value of 1
/S:*TimeSlice*	Specifies how long PRINT waits prior to getting its share of the CPU. Range is 1 to 255, with a default value of 8

Table 7.2: Switches and parameters for the first PRINT command

maximum, but you can adjust that value with the /Q switch.

Figure 7.7 shows what will happen if you try to ask DOS to queue more than 10 files under normal conditions. Even though there are 31 files that match the wild-card specification (*.PRG), only the first 10 are accepted for printing into the queue. Since the /Q switch has not been used, the default assumption of ten slots was taken by PRINT.

In this situation, DOS displays several messages. It first indicates that the PRINT queue is full. Next, it indicates that the first file, ARCHIVE.PRG, is currently being printed. Messages also appear indicating that each of the other nine files is currently in the queue. Figure 7.8 portrays how this queueing works.

The remaining 21 .PRG files that were not accepted into the queue for printing will have to be queued up with other PRINT commands after these 10 finish printing. At best, other PRINT commands that are issued when some of the ten slots open up will fill the open slots. However, the total number of queued files can never exceed the maximum queue size. If you know that you will frequently need to queue up more than ten files at a time, you can type your very first PRINT request as

PRINT ***FileName(s)*** **/Q:32**

```
C>PRINT  \DBASE\ADMIN\EXPERT\*.PRG
PRINT queue is full

     C:\DBASE\ADMIN\EXPERT\ARCHIVE.PRG is currently being printed
     C:\DBASE\ADMIN\EXPERT\COLPRINT.PRG is in queue
     C:\DBASE\ADMIN\EXPERT\COMM.PRG is in queue
     C:\DBASE\ADMIN\EXPERT\DATE.PRG is in queue
     C:\DBASE\ADMIN\EXPERT\DELAY.PRG is in queue
     C:\DBASE\ADMIN\EXPERT\DIR.PRG is in queue
     C:\DBASE\ADMIN\EXPERT\DISKRPT.PRG is in queue
     C:\DBASE\ADMIN\EXPERT\DUPLICAT.PRG is in queue
     C:\DBASE\ADMIN\EXPERT\GETSPACE.PRG is in queue
     C:\DBASE\ADMIN\EXPERT\LOWER.PRG is in queue

C>PRINT /T
PRINT queue is empty

C>_
```

***Figure** 7.7:* Partial PRINT queue

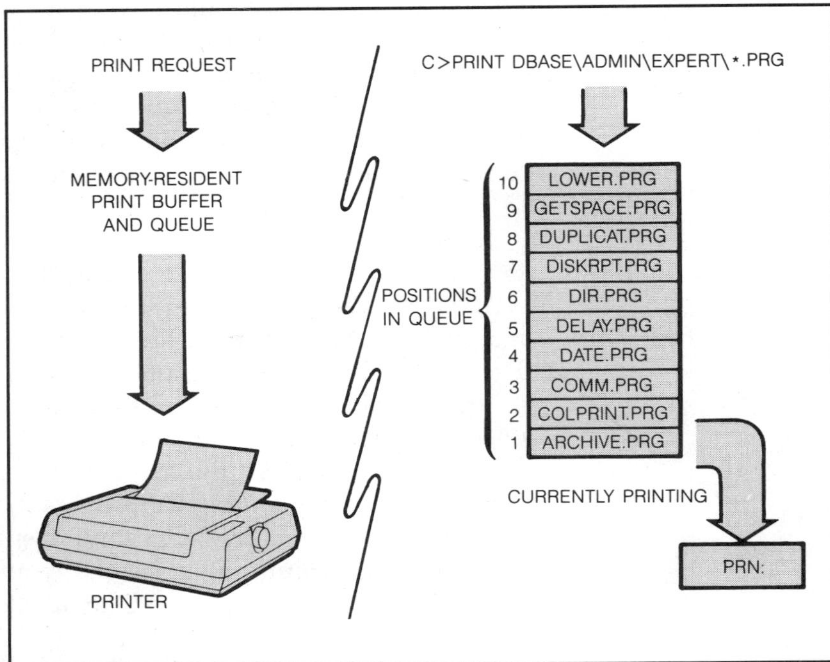

Figure 7.8: How the PRINT queue works

Although each increase in queue size takes up additional memory, you should use this command if you frequently need to print many files.

Three other switches are always available to you for management of the queue and its entries. As you can see in Table 7.3, they are /P (Print), /C, (Cancel printing), and /T (Terminate all spooling). These can be used each time PRINT is invoked, although you'll usually prefer to simply list the files you want to print.

You'll probably use /P least often, since it is already the system default. If you enter

```
CD \DBASE\ADMIN\EXPERT
PRINT STRIP.PRG SNAP.PRG WASH.PRG
```

DOS will queue the three text files specified, assuming that there are at least three available slots in the queue. The /P switch was assumed by DOS; it was not necessary to enter it specifically. You will only need to use it when you construct more complicated PRINT requests.

SWITCH AND PARAMETER	EFFECT
/P:*FileName(s)*	Prints the file(s) specified; this is the default
/C:*FileName(s)*	Cancels the printing of the file(s) specified
/T:*FileName(s)*	Terminates the printing of all specified file(s) in the PRINT queue

Table 7.3: Switches and parameters for any PRINT command

When specifying file names in a PRINT command, you can list several separately named files on the same PRINT request line.

If you want to cancel the printing of one or more files already in the queue, you can do so with the /C switch. For instance, to remove the DIR.PRG and DATE.PRG entries from the queue, effectively canceling the former print request for those two files, enter

```
PRINT DIR.PRG /C DATE.PRG
```

Notice that the /C switch applies to the file name immediately preceding the switch in the command line and all files listed after it (up until the next switch). This allows a complex but useful construction in which you simultaneously add and remove queue entries. In the next example, LOWER.PRG and DUPLICAT.PRG are removed from the queue with /C, while STATS.PRG is added with /P:

```
PRINT LOWER.PRG /C DUPLICAT.PRG STATS.PRG /P
```

Like the /C switch, the /P switch applies to the file name immediately preceding it on the command line.

If the file you wish to cancel is currently printing, the printing will stop and you will receive a message to that effect. If the file you cancel is elsewhere in the queue, it will be removed, and the new status of the PRINT queue will be displayed on your monitor. In fact, you can always see the current queue status by simply entering the PRINT command at the DOS prompt with no parameters or switches. Figure 7.9 demonstrates a status request issued partway through the printing of the .PRG files.

```
C>PRINT

    C:\DBASE\ADMIN\EXPERT\DISKRPT.PRG is currently being printed
    C:\DBASE\ADMIN\EXPERT\DUPLICAT.PRG is in queue
    C:\DBASE\ADMIN\EXPERT\GETSPACE.PRG is in queue
    C:\DBASE\ADMIN\EXPERT\LOWER.PRG is in queue

C>
```

Figure 7.9: Current status of the PRINT queue

If you use a plotter and your software allows off-line plotting (that is, the software doesn't have to control the plotting process directly), you can use the PRINT command to queue several plots at once. Refer to your plotting program's documentation for further details.

Finally, the /T switch will cancel all file names in the queue. Perhaps the paper has jammed, or an ink-jet cartridge has run dry while the printing continues. In these cases, you may like to cancel all outstanding print requests and then restart the output spool, naming specific files in your desired order. Simply enter the command

PRINT /T

DOS will print the message "All files canceled by operator" on the printer. It will also display on the screen a message stating that the PRINT queue is empty.

SUMMARY

Printed output from your system is fundamental for nearly all software applications. This chapter has presented a variety of methods for obtaining printed output for both simple screen images and files:

- You can easily obtain hard-copy printouts of screen images consisting solely of text characters by using the Shift-PrtSc key combination.

- You can generate printed images of graphics screen images with the same Shift-PrtSc combination, provided that you first run the GRAPHICS command.
- You can use the GRAPHICS command with two useful switches for "special effects." The /B switch prints a separate background screen color if you are using multicolor printer ribbons. The /R switch produces the dramatic effect of white letters on a solid black background.
- You can use COPY to print larger text files that don't fit on one screen, by simply copying the files to a printer instead of to another file.
- You can use PRINT to print files indirectly while you work at the same time with other DOS programs or commands. This works for plotters as well as printers.
- You can control the files placed into the PRINT queue for output spooling by means of switches. You can initially configure the queue to hold up to 32 files with the /Q switch, and you can control how much time and memory DOS will reserve for spooling operations with the /M, /B, /U, and /S switches.
- You can add more files to the PRINT queue with the /P switch, remove files from the queue with the /C switch, and terminate all spooling operations by removing all files from the queue with the /T switch.

Now that you've learned several methods of printing with DOS, you can extend these techniques with the information in the next chapter. Printing is only one form of data communications. Chapter 8 will take you on an extended tour of other DOS communications capabilities, which permit information to be transferred to many other output devices besides printers.

This concludes the second major section of this book, "Making DOS Do More." You have acquired all the principal skills necessary to use DOS effectively, both on its own and with other application programs. The next section of this book, "Revving It Up," will speed you on your way to becoming a DOS power user. It will address the more advanced techniques available in DOS.

PART 3

REVVING IT UP

In Part 3, you will learn advanced techniques that are normally overlooked by beginning and by many intermediate DOS users. Chapter 8 describes communications terminology and technology, and shows you how to control data transmission with DOS commands. Chapter 9 tells you how to protect your files by backing them up and how to restore backed-up files if the originals are lost.

In Chapter 10, you will start learning how to customize your disk operating system. You will find out how to specify the number of active files and buffers, create and use a RAM disk, control the screen display, and redefine keys. Chapter 11 describes specialized customization methods for using your computer in a foreign country or for working with a foreign language. These include adapting your keyboard, screen display, and printer.

Finally, Chapter 12 teaches you how to use pipes, filters, and redirection to control input and ouput in your computer system.

COMMUNICATIONS

APTER 8

PRINTING IS ONE FORM OF SYSTEM COMMUNICATIONS; you learned about it first in Chapter 7 because of its central role in any computer system. This chapter concentrates on the speaking and listening that goes on between computer devices. As you'll see, there are many other devices to understand besides printers in any complete computer system. Beyond simply connecting these devices, you will learn in this chapter how to get them started and how to transfer information to and from them. Learn this information well, and you will no longer be at anybody else's mercy when it comes to buying and hooking up new equipment.

This chapter will help you understand the differences between parallel and serial communications, so you can make intelligent decisions about which is right for you. You will also learn enough about the various aspects of these two kinds of communications to use the DOS communications setup commands properly.

One major DOS command in particular, the MODE command, is central to an understanding of data transfer to printers, serial ports, and the video display. You'll learn what it can do for you and when to use it. It will give you control over

- Your printer (for improving the appearance of your hardcopy output),
- Your video screen (for enhancing all displayed information),
- Your keyboard (for getting more out of each key than simply what is printed on the key), and

- Just about any additional device at all that connects t
the communications ports (plugs) in the back of you
puter. This includes such devices as plotters, moder
digitizers.

SYSTEM COMMUNICATIONS IN GENERAL

To understand computer communications, you need to
stand the concept of data structure and storage. When you ent
board characters into programs, either as data or instructio
enter them as numbers, letters, or punctuation marks, as repr
on the face of the key. Each of these keystrokes is interpreted
computer as a well-defined string of *binary digits*, the 0's and
may already know about.

A computer and all its connected devices (*peripheral* devices)
thought of simply as a large collection of very tiny electroni
Each of those parts can receive—or *not* receive—a small v
according to the logic built into the computer. The voltages af
bits of magnetic material that store data for you or store instr
for the computer itself. If a bit is energized with a small vol
has a value of 1. If it receives no voltage, it has a value of
word *binary* means two; as you see, a single bit has two possi
ues, 0 or 1.

You may not realize it, but in communicating with others, you usually perform a variety of tasks based on simple yes/no answers or simple directives. Everything can be broken down into smaller and smaller components, from hitting a baseball properly, to conducting an interview, to carrying out a superior's orders. Similarly, in a computer system, everything can be broken down into component bits. Complex logic and decision making are broken down into sequences of bits that either receive voltage or do not receive voltage—values of 1 or 0. Perhaps this is not as rich an alphabet as A through Z, but it serves the same purpose.

Communication between people is a sequence of sentences, which consist of a sequence of words, which in turn consist of a sequence of letters. These sequences are broken up by verbal pauses or inflections, or written punctuation marks, intended to help the listener (or reader) better understand the speaker (or writer). Pauses and punctuation, therefore, help to *synchronize* the communication of information. To synchronize computer communications, a sequence of 0's and 1's is grouped into seven or eight data bits, each group representing a character. Characters can be letters (A–Z), numbers (0–9), or special symbols or codes (* # % " : > ? and so on).

To understand why some communications use seven data bits while others use eight, let's briefly look at the binary number system. One bit can have the value 0 or 1. Therefore, two bits in a row have four possible combinations of values, since each bit has two possible values:

- 0 followed by 0, or 00
- 0 followed by 1, or 01
- 1 followed by 0, or 10
- 1 followed by 1, or 11

Taking this a step further, three bits in a row can have eight possibilities:

- 0 followed by 00, or 000
- 0 followed by 01, or 001
- 0 followed by 10, or 010
- 0 followed by 11, or 011
- 1 followed by 00, or 100
- 1 followed by 01, or 101
- 1 followed by 10, or 110
- 1 followed by 11, or 111

As you can see, the binary system is based on powers of the number 2. With one data bit, there are two possibilities (2^1); with two data bits, there are four possibilities (2^2); and with three data bits, there are eight possibilities (2^3). Continuing this progression will result in the following:

- Four data bits = 16 possibilities (2^4)
- Five data bits = 32 possibilities (2^5)

- Six data bits = 64 possibilities (2^6)
- Seven data bits = 128 possibilities (2^7)
- Eight data bits = 256 possibilities (2^8)

The standard keyboard and ASCII character set is more than covered by the 128 possibilities contained in seven data bits. However, there are additional characters (graphics characters, foreign-language characters, and so on) that constitute what is called the *extended ASCII set.* When these additional characters must be transmitted, the eight-bit form of data communications is used. Appendix C covers this issue more fully. You will usually see characters represented as eight bits, and communicated as such. This conventional eight-bit unit is a byte, the fundamental storage and data unit you deal with throughout DOS.

The groups of bits we have been examining represent either data or controlling information. In a conversation, you gain someone's attention by saying their name or saying something like "Hey, you." Computer communications use special groups of bits to gain the attention of another device. Once the attention is obtained with this *control code,* or special sequence of bits, the actual data transmission can begin.

Computers also use additional bits to ensure synchronization. *Stop bits* follow each unique character code (string of bits) to set it off from other transmitted information. In order to minimize sending or receiving errors, a *parity bit* is also sent after the data bits. This bit is used by both the transmitting and receiving equipment, but how it is computed and used is beyond the scope of this book.

PARALLEL VERSUS SERIAL COMMUNICATIONS

When you type a capital J from the keyboard, a code is sent to the computer's input routines, which translate it into the binary digits 01001010. The letter itself is echoed back to the video screen to confirm what you typed (see Figure 8.1). Remember that the video screen is part of what the system calls its console; the keyboard is the input part of the console and the video screen is the output part.

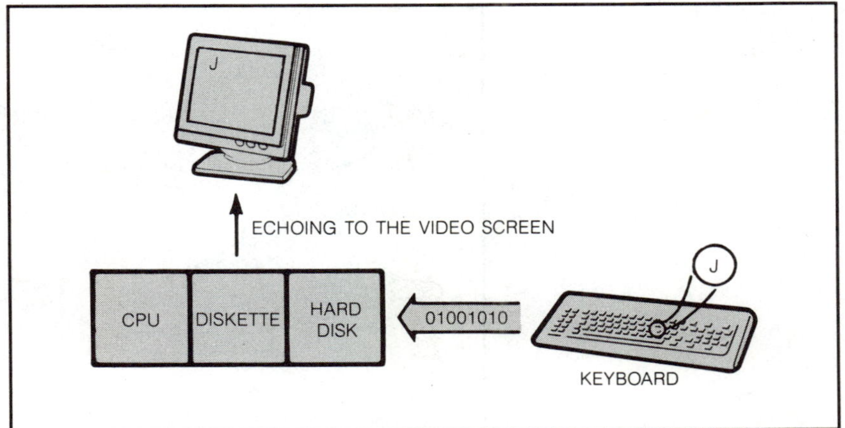

Figure 8.1: Keyboard echoing—a simple data transmission

The passing of information between these parts is called data transmission.

There are two methods of data transmission: parallel and serial. Nearly all DOS microcomputers are connected with peripheral devices using one of these two communication techniques. Although most printers use the parallel method of data transmission, some use the serial method. Other peripheral devices like plotters, digitizers, modems, and mice usually transmit data serially.

If a peripheral device is connected to a serial port and is designed for serial transmission, each bit will be sent to or received from the central processing unit one bit at a time, and only one transmission wire will be used. If the peripheral device is connected to a parallel port and is designed for parallel transmission, then eight separate bits will be transmitted simultaneously over eight separate wires. (In both cases, other wires are used for additional purposes, such as the synchronization of signals or grounding; however, it's sufficient in this context to understand the concept in terms of one wire versus eight.)

Consider a simple analogy. In Figure 8.2 an airport's baggage terminal has eight conveyor belts, and passengers' suitcases are unloaded from eight flights simultaneously. In Figure 8.3, however, the airport has only one conveyor belt. The baggage from all eight flights is unloaded onto it. The passengers in this situation have to wait eight times as long as those in the first airport, and they probably

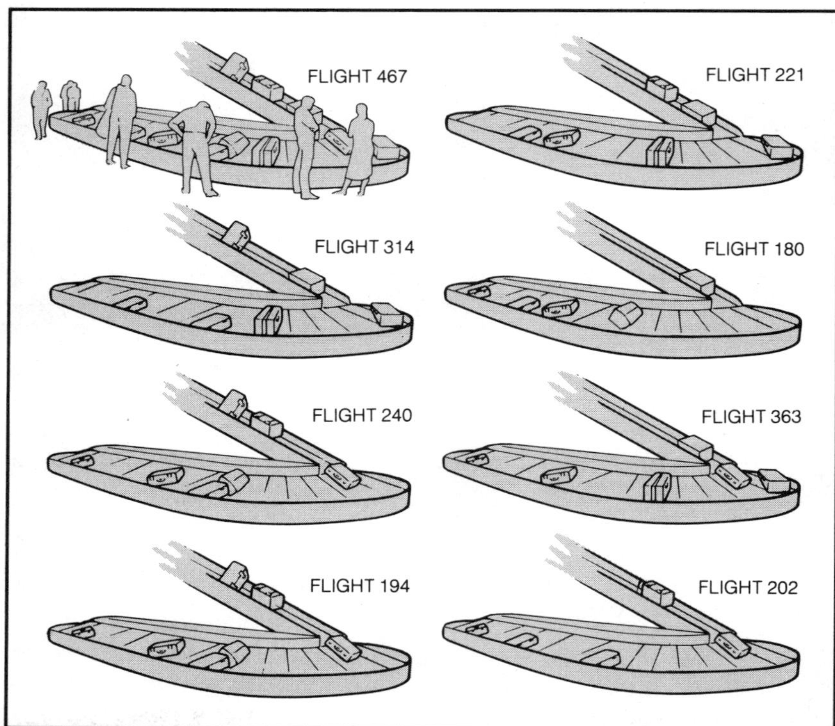

Figure 8.2: Unloading luggage with multiple conveyor belts

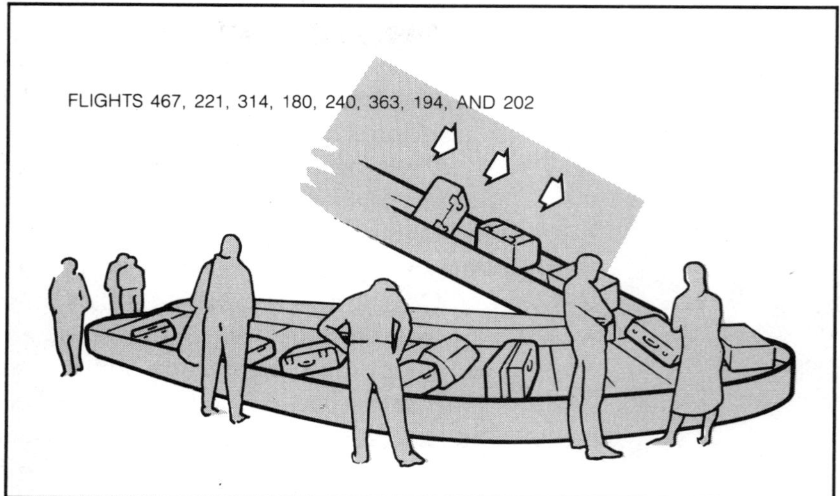

Figure 8.3: Unloading luggage with one conveyor belt

won't be happy about it. Then again, the airline officials may not mind, since they spent one-eighth the amount of money on the conveyor mechanism and the ongoing expenses for maintenance and terminal space rental. It's a tradeoff of time versus money. In this analogy, you are the airline officials. You make the decision about what equipment you buy and use, deciding whether to spend more money on parallel connections or less money on serial connections, which require more waiting time for certain peripheral devices.

Serial communications are often referred to as *asynchronous communications*, because the sending and receiving devices do not send and receive simultaneously, or synchronously. Instead, each uses an agreed set of electrical signals to indicate when to stop and start actual data transmission (see the MODE command later in this chapter).

Let's return to the example of keyboard data transmission. Say you type in the word JUDD and you want the CPU to send it to a peripheral device. Your keystrokes will be translated into the ASCII character codes shown in Table 8.1.

Figure 8.4 shows a parallel transmission of these characters. As you can see, eight wires are used. A serial transmission of the same characters would require only one wire, as you can see in Figure 8.5. However, the transmission of data would be much slower. This explains why virtually all printers that print faster than several hundred characters per second *must* use parallel transmission and be connected to a computer correctly for parallel transmission.

DOS DEVICES VERSUS FILES

Operating systems treat devices that represent either the source of data or the destination for data in a consistent manner. As you've seen many times already, you specify the source and destination of the data in your software commands. The consistency with which you can reference hardware devices (like the console) or software

LETTER	BINARY DIGITS
J	01001010
U	01010101
D	01000100
D	01000100

Table 8.1: ASCII codes for the letters J, U, D, and D

"devices" (like a disk file) makes it easy to learn both new commands and new concepts. As you saw in Chapter 3, commands like COPY work in precisely the same way for a data transfer from a CPU to a disk file or a data transfer from a CPU to a peripheral device (a printer).

DOS is designed to understand and permit the referencing of certain typical peripheral devices. Unlike file names, which you can make up yourself (as long as you obey certain rules), device names

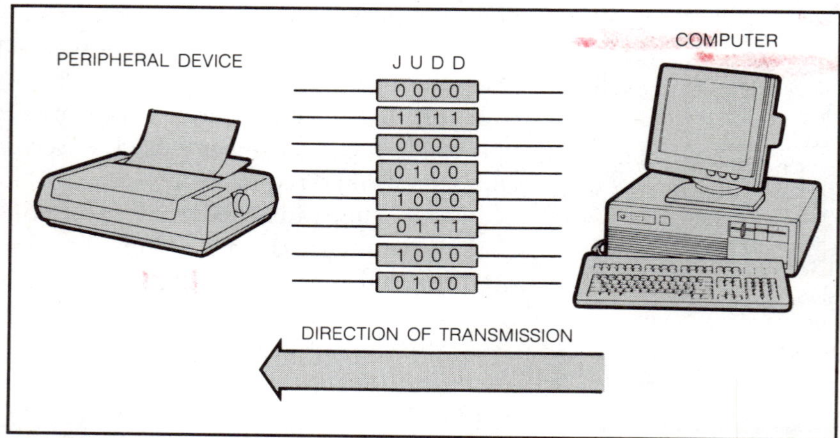

Figure 8.4: Parallel data transmission

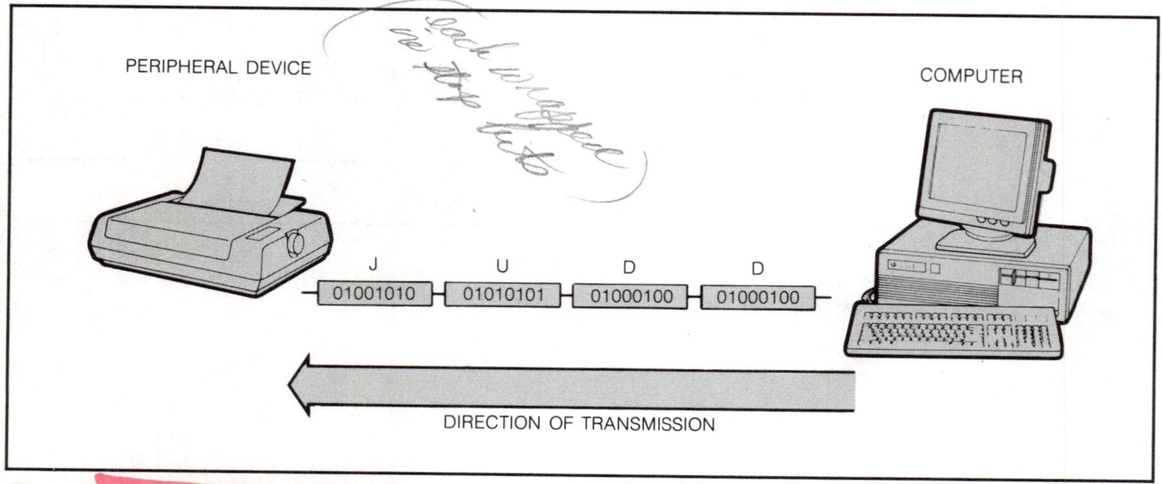

Figure 8.5: Serial data transmission

are restricted to certain reserved names, shown in Figure 8.6. DOS allows only three specific parallel device names (LPT1, LPT2, and LPT3) and four serial device names (COM1, COM2, COM3, and COM4). Versions of DOS earlier than 3.3 only allowed two serial device names, COM1 and COM2.

Like the drive names in previous chapters (A, B, C, and so on), reserved device names should be followed by a colon in your commands. This lets DOS know when the device name ends and the sequence of parameter values begins.

The additional device names in Figure 8.6, AUX and PRN, are called standard device names. They are used to communicate with the first connected serial and parallel ports, respectively. You can use these nonspecific device names if you don't want to be bothered with the details of which communications port is connected to your printer or device. Programs don't necessarily have to know which device is connected to which port. They can simply reference PRN, and the output will be routed to the first connected parallel port; or they can reference AUX, and the output will be routed to the first connected auxiliary communications (serial) port.

You can improve the flexibility of your system design by using PRN and AUX as port device names. AUX can refer to any one of the four serial ports, COM1 to COM4. Later, you can easily change your hardware connections without having to make any changes to your software references.

Keep in mind that you must purchase the actual hardware to make the proper connections. In other words, DOS may understand what it means to send data to a serial port called COM1, but you must have a serial connector on your system, and it must be connected to a serial device, or the request is meaningless.

Even if you have purchased various pieces of peripheral equipment and sufficient add-in boards to connect them, DOS may not be able to address all of them. For instance, if your setup is like that in Table 8.2, there are no more reserved names available if you decide

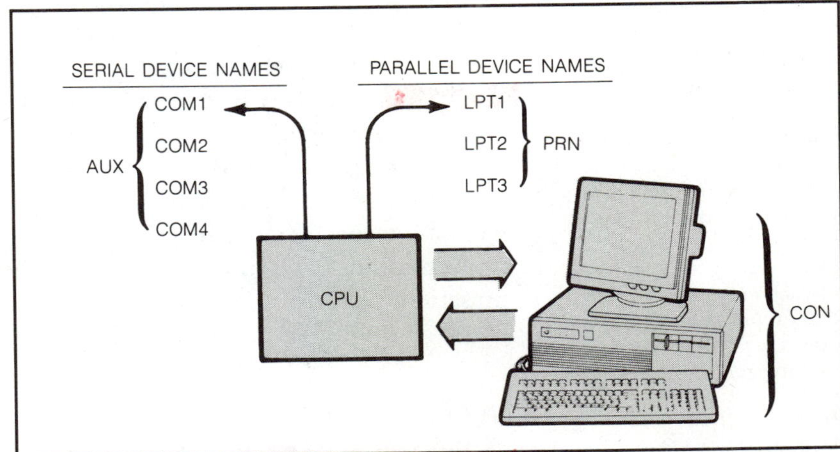

Figure 8.6: Reserved device names in DOS

DOS RESERVED NAME	DEFINITION	EXAMPLE CONNECTION
LPT1	First parallel port	Fast draft printer
LPT2	Second parallel port	Letter-quality printer
LPT3	Third parallel port	Laser printer
COM1	First serial port	Modem
COM2	Second serial port	Plotter
COM3	Third serial port	Mouse
COM4	Fourth serial port	Digitizer

Table 8.2: An example port configuration

to buy another serial device (perhaps an inexpensive networking alternative). In this case, you would have to buy some form of switch. You would need to connect the switch to one port (say, COM1) and then connect the two peripherals (the mouse and the modem, for example) to the switch.

When you are using the same serial line for two purposes, one operation must wait for the other to finish. If you are plotting, you cannot throw the switch to activate the mouse until all the plotting data has been transmitted to the plotter. When you are using the mouse to control cursor movement and menu selections, you cannot switch over to the plotter for output until all mouse movements have been completed.

Once all this hardware has been connected, you still must exercise great care to ensure that your software will work. The key to this is to make sure that two or more devices connected to the same switch do not try to transmit data at the same time. Your first reaction may be that this isn't a complication you expect to run into very often. On the other hand, you may have a computer with only one serial port (COM1), and you might want to use a graphics package that requires a mouse for input and a plotter for output. In this case, short of buying another serial-port connector, you can run your software by using a switch for the two devices. You might not think that there will be any problem with both devices trying to use the same serial line simultaneously, but what actually happens is that you become impatient with the slowness of the plotter, and long to regain control of the computer while the plot progresses independently.

INITIALIZING DEVICES AND PORTS

Different peripheral devices, when connected to the computer, require special setup sequences. The MODE command permits you to initialize aspects of your printers and your serial-port devices, as well as to redirect output between parallel and serial ports, and even to control some features of your video display. Other capabilities of MODE for the support of foreign-language characters will be discussed in Chapter 10. Figure 8.7 depicts the four capabilities of the MODE command that you'll explore in this section.

In all four situations, the MODE command is invoked like any other disk-resident external DOS command. Simply typing MODE at the DOS prompt, preceded by any drive or path-name specification, will initiate the MODE operations. Assuming MODE is either in the current drive and directory or on the path you have specified, you would enter

MODE *Parameters*

Depending on what parameters you specify, one of the four versions of this command will be activated. The four major versions of this command almost act as four separate commands.

CONTROLLING THE PRINTER

An operation that is often desired by users is to turn on *compressed print.* Wide spreadsheets and database records are often hard to read when the number of characters per line exceeds the standard 80 characters. Most printers assume a normal default of 80 characters, because most programs generate data using an 80-column video screen. Printers also assume a default value of 6 lines per vertical inch, but you can control that as well.

This version of the MODE command assumes you are using the most common kind of printer: an EPSON MX series, an IBM graphics printer, or a compatible. Any other printer may require different control codes, making this DOS command useless to you.

Programs that can scroll left and right, like spreadsheets and database management programs, can generate more than 80 columns on a line. The following version of MODE gives you a simple way to instruct DOS to send the printer the necessary control codes requesting it to squeeze up to 132 characters on a line, or to squeeze up to 8 lines of output per vertical inch on the paper. The general form of this MODE command is

MODE *PrinterPort CharsPerLine LinesPerInch*

Filling in the parameters with values, you could issue the following command to initialize the printer port to LPT1, the characters per

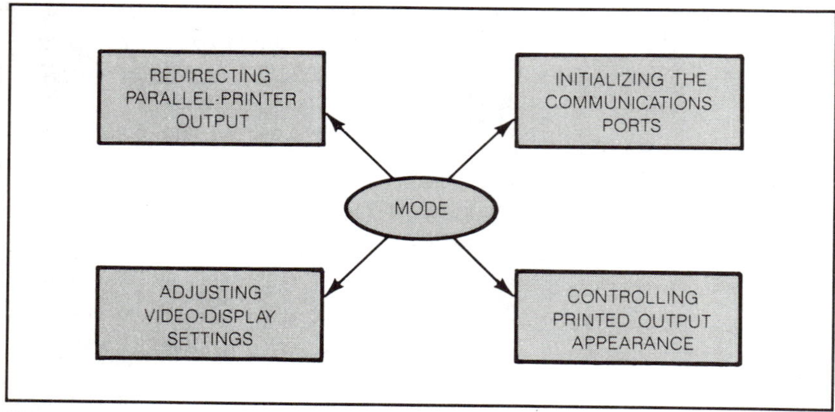

Figure 8.7: Four capabilities of the MODE command

line to 132, and the lines per inch to 8:

```
MODE LPT1: 132, 8
```

Figure 8.8 demonstrates what a sample text file would look like if it were printed after this command was executed. Figures 8.9 through 8.11 show the other variations on the two parameters controlling characters per line and lines per inch.

With these MODE commands for compressed print, DOS will respond to your command entry with statements similar to the following:

```
LPT1: not rerouted
LPT1: set for 132
Printer lines per inch set
No retry on parallel printer time-out
```

The first and fourth lines of these DOS messages refer to other versions of the MODE command, which you'll see shortly. The second and third lines indicate the horizontal and vertical printer settings, respectively.

Dot-matrix printers make the horizontal compression occur by printing the dots closer together. Letter-quality printers create the same effect by leaving less space between characters. Compressing the print on letter-quality printers usually requires you to change the print wheel or thimble so the resulting squeezed printout is readable.

The MODE command has limited capability for sending control codes to printers. Some applications like Lotus 1-2-3 and Framework II offer you the convenience of sending control codes directly to a printer. In fact, you can use EDLIN or your own word processor to include a sequence of control codes in a file (say, CTRLCODE.TXT), and then send the file and the control codes directly to a printer with the simple instruction COPY CTRLCODE.TXT PRN.

```
This line and the next are limited to 80 characters or less.
........10........20........30........40........50........60........70........80
This next line typifies wide spreadsheet rows or data base records (and 'wraps around' in 80 column mode)
........10........20........30........40........50........60........70........80........90.......100.......120.......132..
These next four lines take up 1/2" vertically
when lines per inch (LPI) is set to 8,
and take up 2/3" when LPI = 6,
regardless of how the characters per line is set.
```

Figure 8.8: Output of MODE LPT1: 132,8

```
This line and the next are limited to 80 characters or less.
........10........20........30........40........50........60........70........80
This next line typifies wide spreadsheet rows or data base records (and 'wraps a
round' in 80 column mode)
........10........20........30........40........50........60........70........80
........90.......100.......120.......132..
These next four lines take up 1/2" vertically
when lines per inch (LPI) is set to 8,
and take up 2/3" when LPI = 6,
regardless of how the characters per line is set.
```

Figure 8.9: Output of MODE LPT1: 80,6 (the DOS default)

```
This line and the next are limited to 80 characters or less.
........10........20........30........40........50........60........70........80
This next line typifies wide spreadsheet rows or data base records (and 'wraps around' in 80 column mode)
........10........20........30........40........50........60........70........80........90.......100.......120.......132..
These next four lines take up 1/2" vertically
when lines per inch (LPI) is set to 8,
and take up 2/3" when LPI = 6,
regardless of how the characters per line is set.
```

Figure 8.10: Output of MODE LPT1: 132,6

```
This line and the next are limited to 80 characters or less.
........10........20........30........40........50........60........70........80
This next line typifies wide spreadsheet rows or data base records (and 'wraps a
round' in 80 column mode)
........10........20........30........40........50........60........70........80
........90.......100.......120.......132..
These next four lines take up 1/2" vertically
when lines per inch (LPI) is set to 8,
and take up 2/3" when LPI = 6,
regardless of how the characters per line is set.
```

Figure 8.11: Output of MODE LPT1: 80,8

INITIALIZING THE SERIAL COMMUNICATIONS PORT

Synchronization is a difficult problem when serial devices are connected to computers. For example, if a computer sends data out to the serial port at a rate of 1200 bits per second, any printer connected

Don't bother initially with this version of the MODE command; follow the initialization instructions in your software program's manual or in your serial device's instruction book. This usually is all you need for success—only if this fails will you need to understand these MODE parameters more fully.

to that port must be set (by means of hardware switches or software initialization) to receive this information at the same rate. This requirement also works in reverse.

A second version of the MODE command allows you to correctly set a number of parameters for this and other aspects of serial communications. The general form of this MODE command is

MODE *SerialPort BaudRate, Parity, DataBits, StopBits, DeviceType*

The parameters have the following meanings:

- *SerialPort* indicates which one of the four possible peripheral connectors is being used by DOS for a particular device.
- *BaudRate* sets the speed at which data bits will be transmitted through the serial port.
- *Parity* represents the number of binary 1's, if any, that are used in a data transmission; this is used for error detection.
- *DataBits* specifies the number of bits used to represent actual transmitted data.
- *StopBits* represents the one or two bits used at the end of the data bits to indicate that end.
- *DeviceType* indicates whether or not the port is being used by a serial printer.

Table 8.3 contains the allowable values for these parameters.

As an example, the following command issued at the DOS prompt would set the second serial port to transmit at 1200 baud, with no parity, using eight data bits with one stop bit:

```
MODE COM2: 1200, N, 8, 1, P
```

The last parameter value, P, requests that DOS automatically try again to send data to a busy communications port. This is necessary when the first request is met by a control signal indicating that the device is still busy processing the last transmission. The P value is particularly useful with printers, which process data significantly slower than the computer's central processing unit.

PARAMETER	POSSIBLE VALUES
SerialPort	COM1, COM2, COM3, or COM4
BaudRate	110, 150, 300, 600, 1200, 2400, 4800, 9600, or 19200
Parity	N, O, or E (none, odd, or even)
DataBits	7 or 8
StopBits	1 or 2
DeviceType	P (if a serial printer); otherwise blank

Table 8.3: Allowable parameter values for serial communications

This version of the MODE command is disk-resident, but it does require that a permanent part of physical memory be reserved for its processing and buffering chores. This means that when you run the command for the first time, it will take up a small additional amount of memory, extending the memory requirements of your DOS's memory-resident portion. A message to that effect is issued by DOS at the same time as confirmation is made of the port settings:

```
Resident portion of MODE loaded
COM2: 1200,n,8,1,p
```

Normally, serial devices are accompanied by instruction manuals that describe the required settings. The best advice is to follow scrupulously the suggested settings for connection. Switches often have to be set on or in the printer, as well as on the board that is controlling your serial port itself. In addition, the software product you are using might need to be initialized as well, since it may send its data directly to the port.

All of these locations and parameters are opportunities for error or frustration in connecting serial devices to computers. Unfortunately, there is no consistent standard for serial communications as there is for parallel communications. You must determine the characteristics of your serial device and issue the proper MODE command *before* using the port in any way. Good luck!

CONNECTING A SERIAL PRINTER TO A COM PORT

In the specific case where the serial device you have connected to a COM port is a printer, an additional version of the MODE command is required. Printed output usually goes to a PRN device (usually a parallel port like LPT1), so you must redirect that output to a COM port with the command

```
MODE LPTNumber: = COMNumber
```

The *Number* parameter should hold the specific number of your chosen port.

Assuming that you have first initialized the communications parameters for the port so that the device and the CPU are synchronized, as in the last section, you can redirect the LPT1 port to the COM2 port with

```
MODE LPT1: = COM2
```

DOS will confirm the redirection for all succeeding print output requests with the following:

```
LPT1: rerouted to COM2:
```

CONTROLLING THE MODE OF THE VIDEO DISPLAY

Certain video characteristics can be controlled with the final version of the MODE command. This version is used most often when you purchase nonstandard equipment and when you connect multiple monitors to your computer. The command is used to tell DOS which monitor is receiving the video-display request; it also allows you to adjust the video image in a horizontal direction.

The command has at most three parameters, of which the first is the most often used:

```
MODE VideoType, Direction, TestPattern
```

The three parameters can take on the values shown in Table 8.4.

PARAMETER	POSSIBLE VALUES
VideoType	MONO (for IBM monochrome display)
	CO80 (for color 80-column display)
	CO40 (for color 40-column display)
	BW80 (for black-and-white, 80-column display; this disables color on a normal color monitor)
	BW40 (for black-and-white, 40-column display)
	80 (adjusts to 80-column display; does not change the color status)
	40 (adjusts to 40-column display; does not change the color status)
Direction	R or L (for right or left)
TestPattern	T (if a test pattern is to be shown)

Table 8.4: Video-display values for MODE parameters

The simplest form of this version of the MODE command only involves the *VideoType* parameter. Setting the display mode to 40 or 80 characters is as simple as entering

```
MODE 80
```

or

```
MODE 40
```

80-column mode is the standard for business applications, although some games reset the mode to 40 columns. Naturally, 40-column mode produces larger, more legible characters on the video monitor. Figures 8.12 and 8.13 demonstrate the same directory display in 80- and 40-column modes.

Entering a parameter value of 40 or 80 for *VideoType* will not affect the current status of the monitor's color. Assuming the monitor is controlled by a CGA (color graphics adapter) or an EGA (extended graphics adapter), you can explicitly enable or disable color by preceding the column number by CO (to enable color) or BW (to disable color, leaving a black-and-white image). If you have an IBM monochrome display, the proper parameter value is MONO. In fact, if your system has both a monochrome *and* a color graphics monitor, you can switch output between them by simply entering

MODE MONO

```
C>DIR

 Volume in drive C is ROBBINS
 Directory of  C:\UTILITY\XENO

.            <DIR>       5-02-86    1:17p
..           <DIR>       5-02-86    1:17p
XENOCOPY EXE    83968    8-17-87    6:18p
README           5067    8-21-87   12:35p
XDEF     OPT     1221    8-25-87   10:06a
SYBEX    OPT     1221    8-25-87   10:07a
        6 File(s)    634880 bytes free

C>_
```

Figure 8.12: Directory display after a MODE 80 command

```
C>DIR

 Volume in drive C is ROBBINS
 Directory of  C:\UTILITY\XENO

.            <DIR>       5-02-86    1:17p
..           <DIR>       5-02-86    1:17p
XENOCOPY EXE    83968    8-17-87    6:18p
README           5067    8-21-87   12:35p
XDEF     OPT     1221    8-25-87   10:06a
SYBEX    OPT     1221    8-25-87   10:07a
        6 File(s)    634880 bytes free

C>_
```

Figure 8.13: Directory display after a MODE 40 command

to switch output to the monochrome monitor, or

```
MODE CO80
```

to switch output to the color monitor, using 80 columns with color enabled.

Some monitors need a certain amount of horizontal adjustment. You may not need to adjust yours very often, but if you do, the *Direction* and *TestPattern* parameters will come in handy. You can shift the display to the right or to the left by entering an R or an L as the *Direction* parameter. In either case, you can display a test pattern on the screen to help with the adjustments by entering a T as the *TestPattern* parameter. Entering

```
MODE 80, L, T
```

produces the screen shown in Figure 8.14.

If you answer N (for No) to the question on seeing the rightmost 9, DOS will shift the entire screen image to the left by one character (if the display mode is 40 columns) or by two characters (if it is 80 columns). You will then be asked the same question, and you can shift the display until all 80 characters are visible—when the rightmost 9 can be seen.

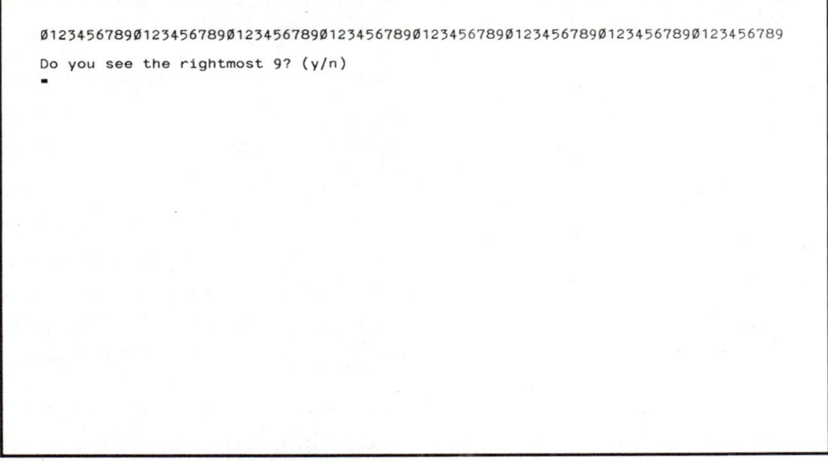

Figure 8.14: Shifting the video image left with MODE

SUMMARY

This chapter covered important communications aspects of DOS. Output from your system is fundamental to effectiveness, and in this chapter, you learned quite a bit about data transfer and system output in general. Here is a brief review:

- Files and hardware devices share certain similarities, which permits you to use them interchangeably in a number of commands.
- Devices communicate with the central processing unit of your computer in one of two ways: by parallel or serial data transmission. Parallel communications send data bits out to a device on separate wires simultaneously. Serial communications send the same data bits out to a device on a single wire successively, using additional control characters and bits to help distinguish when and where the transmission and characters begin and end.
- Each bit of magnetic memory—data bit—can be either energized with a voltage or not energized, with a value of 1 or 0, respectively. Eight bits make up the proverbial byte, and each byte can represent up to 256 different codes. These codes can represent either standard letters, numbers, and punctuation, or special control codes, foreign-language characters, and graphics characters.
- DOS can send and receive bytes of information to and from three parallel devices connected to hardware ports. These devices and their parts are addressed by programs as LPT1, LPT2, and LPT3.
- DOS 3.3 also can send data to and accept data from as many as four separate devices connected to four communications ports. These serial ports are addressed by the names COM1, COM2, COM3, and COM4. Earlier versions of DOS only allowed the first two COM ports to be referenced.
- The MODE command is the principal DOS command for controlling serial communications. It handles both the setup and status of certain serial and parallel output devices. It is

also required to properly initialize the communications between a computer and a printer or plotter. Several parameters defining the command must be carefully set in order to synchronize the CPU and the device, or the data transfer may not work at all. The parameters include the baud rate, the parity of the transmission, the number of data bits and stop bits, and the type of device.

- Other versions of the MODE command allow you to control multiple display monitors, which can be either color or black-and-white and can display either 40 or 80 columns across.

By now you've certainly learned many new things about DOS and have no doubt begun to use your disk and hardware capabilities more efficiently. This is a good time to step back and consider the work invested in your system. The next chapter emphasizes the protection of this investment—it shows you how to make copies of any and all of your important files.

BACKUPS AND RESTORATIONS

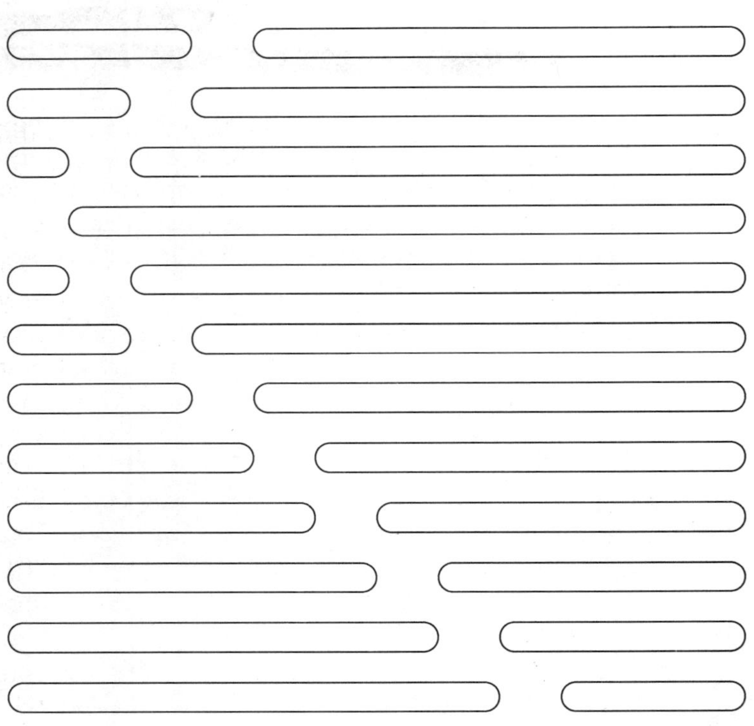

CHAPTER 9

ONE OF THE DISADVANTAGES OF HARD DISKS IS THAT when and if they fail, or crash, all the information stored on them can be lost. Much more is at stake than just one floppy diskette's worth of contents. Back up your hard disk regularly or run the constant risk of losing your data!

Of course, you can also rewrite backed-up versions of files back onto your hard disk; this is usually done when the hard-disk version has been deleted, destroyed, or corrupted. You may never need to restore a file, but your backup files will provide you with some inexpensive protection against either hardware or software failure.

Experience seems to be the best teacher in all things, and most people who back up files regularly do so because they have experienced an uncomfortable loss of data at some point. The more data they lost, the more frequently they now back up.

This chapter describes in depth how to protect your programs—and more importantly, your data—from loss due to operator error or hardware failure. However, you must remember to back up your files on a regular basis to keep the backup floppy diskettes up-to-date with the changes you've made on your hard disk. Depending on how frequently you generate new data files or update old ones, you may want to back up your disk every week or every month (or more or less frequently).

In fact, other than the regular backups you are going to make, there are three times when you should back up your hard disk:

1. Your computer is going to be moved. Especially if your computer will be traveling long distances in airplane cargo holds or in shipper's trucks, you should back up your data before the trip. Your hard disk may not survive the physical handling (or occasional abuse).

2. You are running out of space on your hard disk, and you decide to take an hour or two to delete some files, consolidate some directories, and create new branches in your directory tree since you now feel much more comfortable using the DOS directory structure. With such a massive project, you should protect yourself against your own enthusiasm and fatigue by doing a backup.
3. You are going to run a fragmentation elimination program like Hard Disk Tuneup. If you run such a program, your entire hard-disk contents are liable to loss in the event of a power failure. Do a complete disk backup just prior to running such a program.

SPECIAL COMMANDS FOR YOUR DISKS

If you're using a dual-diskette system, you can easily use DISKCOPY, COPY, or XCOPY to back up diskette files onto another diskette. Protecting yourself from the major trauma of losing an entire hard disk, however, requires more effort than that. DISKCOPY is designed for diskette copies, and the COPY and XCOPY commands have a fundamental weakness: the destination for your copied files is limited to what can be stored on that one drive. If the directory you're in contains more files than can fit on one destination diskette, or even if it contains one extremely large file that exceeds the capacity of the backup floppy, the COPY and XCOPY commands simply can't handle the job.

The BACKUP command does not work for copy-protected diskettes.

In order to allow you to back up files onto a series of floppy diskettes or another fixed (hard) disk, DOS provides a special command called BACKUP. With BACKUP you can make copies of the files on any of your disks. This command is usually used to back up the files from a hard disk and spread them, if necessary, over a series of floppy diskettes.

HOW BACKUP FILES ARE STORED

The files placed on a diskette by the BACKUP command are not stored as standard DOS files. Figure 9.1 shows the directory listing of the original files from the hard disk. Figure 9.2 shows the directory listing of the first backup diskette in drive A after the backup procedure has been completed. Compare these two figures. You'll see that

```
 Volume in drive C is ROBBINS
 Directory of  C:\DBASE\ADMIN

DB3BOOK  PRG      449  11-26-86   2:41a
START    PRG     2532  11-26-86   2:21a
INVOICE  PRG     3010   3-12-86   7:40a
CERTIF   PRG     1981  11-26-86   2:38a
RECOMM1  PRG      463  11-26-86   2:40a
RECOMM2  PRG      422  11-26-86   2:42a
PAYROLL  PRG     4224   4-28-86  12:57p
PAYROLL2 PRG     1792   3-12-86   9:17p
EXPERT   PRG     2432  10-24-85   6:48p
EXPERT1  PRG     2146   6-13-85   9:57p
EXPERT2  PRG     2944  10-18-85   8:11p
EXPERT3  PRG     3689  10-25-85  10:59a
EXPERT4  PRG     2176   7-30-86   9:08p
MESSAGE  PRG     1280   4-09-85   3:41p
LEDGER   PRG     2688  11-26-86  10:53a
INVOICE2 PRG     3200  11-26-86  11:16a
BOOKS2   PRG     2048  11-26-86  11:20a
DISKPREP PRG      905  11-26-86   2:00a
       18 File(s)    8806400 bytes free

C>_
```

Figure 9.1: Directory of original files before backup

```
C>DIR A:

 Volume in drive A is BACKUP   001
 Directory of  A:\

BACKUP   001    38381   7-09-87  10:23a
CONTROL  001      821   7-09-87  10:23a
        2 File(s)    322560 bytes free

C>_
```

Figure 9.2: First backup diskette after completion

your original files have not been backed up in their original format.

Figure 9.3 shows you the manner in which your files have been backed up. Your original files have been combined efficiently into one single file, called BACKUP.001, which contains only the original data. A separate control file, called CONTROL.001, contains the actual file names and their lengths, as well as the source directory from which these files were obtained. You could add up the file lengths seen in Figure 9.3 to verify that BACKUP.001 has efficiently combined all the bytes from each of the original files.

The DOS 3.3 version of BACKUP is faster than previous versions, while requiring less disk space to store the original files. The primary reason for this is that each file does not waste extra disk cluster space during the storage process. The compaction technique uses both space and time more efficiently.

This procedure is new with DOS 3.3. If you have an earlier DOS version, your backup diskette will be quite different. It will have *file versions* (not replicas) of each of your original files, as well as an additional entry in the directory listing called BACKUP.@@@, with a length of 128 bytes. If you have a disk with this entry, it indicates that the files stored on that disk have been put there with an earlier DOS version of the BACKUP command.

Files stored with earlier versions of BACKUP *appear* to be independently accessible, but they cannot be read meaningfully with any of DOS's other commands, like the COPY command. In earlier versions of DOS, BACKUP changes the actual file contents, whereas in Version 3.3, it compacts the files into one file. You can only use these

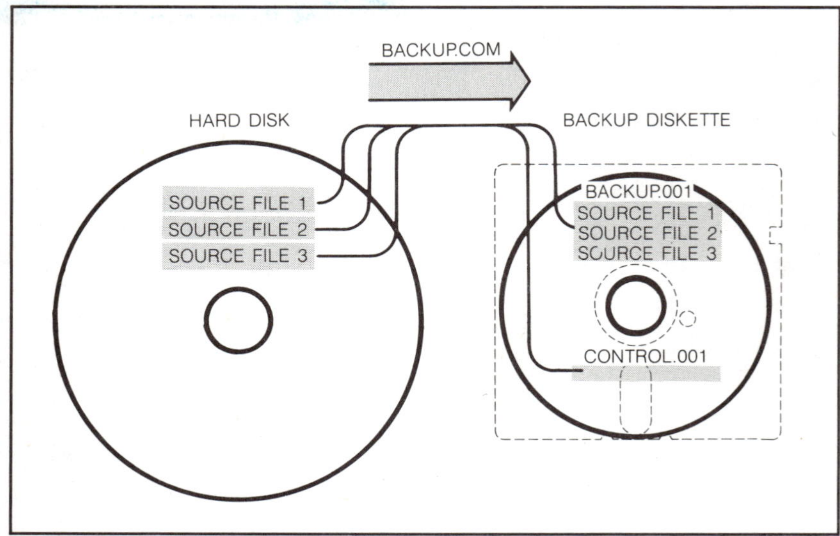

Figure 9.3: The BACKUP command compacts files

files again by restoring them to their original condition with the RESTORE command.

MAKING BACKUP COPIES OF YOUR FILES

You can back up a hard disk either onto diskettes or onto another hard disk. When you back up a hard disk onto diskettes, you also need to format enough diskettes before you begin. If you are using DOS 3.3, you will be able to format them during the backup process. If you are using an earlier version of DOS, however, you should prepare in advance enough formatted destination diskettes to hold all of your data, since you cannot back up onto unformatted disks. (Only the DISKCOPY command can do that.) You will have to stop the backup process (or borrow someone else's computer) if you run out of formatted disks in the middle of backing up your files.

When you format a diskette for use during the backup process, it is not necessary to use the /S switch. In fact, it is inadvisable: using /S will make less space available for the backup files on floppy diskettes.

Backing up files from one hard disk to another is much faster than backing them up onto a collection of diskettes. It is also easier, since you don't have to insert and remove successive diskettes; the backup process between hard disks can proceed unattended.

If your system has an extra hard disk for backup, make sure that it has enough space to hold all the backup files. If it doesn't, the entire process will terminate, and you'll have to make space on the backup disk by deleting some files.

Before you start backing up files, you should learn how to use the DOS VERIFY command. VERIFY controls the degree of error checking performed by DOS after all disk write operations. When you execute the command

```
VERIFY ON
```

the verification mode is turned on. Each disk write will be followed by a confirmation procedure verifying that the data just written can be read without error. It is a good idea to execute this command just prior to running a backup; it increases the likelihood that your backup files will be written accurately. Although data errors occur infrequently, a backup file is the worst place for such an error to occur. After your backup operation, you can execute VERIFY OFF at the DOS prompt to restore normal read/write operations. When the verification mode is on, overall DOS operations are significantly slowed down.

BACKING UP A COMPLETE DIRECTORY

The general form of the BACKUP command has two parameters:

```
BACKUP SourceFile(s) DestinationDrive
```

SourceFile(s) is the standard path name plus any specific file names you wish to select for backup. *DestinationDrive* is the letter identifier of the disk drive that will receive the file copies.

Suppose that you wanted to back up all the files in your DBASE\ADMIN directory. You would simply specify the name of the desired directory as the first parameter. When you do not specify any specific files, DOS selects and copies all files in the directory to the backup drive (A).

```
BACKUP C:\DBASE\ADMIN A:
```

DOS displays the message

```
Insert backup diskette 01 in drive A:

Warning! Files in the target drive
A:\ root directory will be erased
Strike any key when ready
```

This warning gives you a chance to verify that you put the correct diskette into drive A, before DOS overwrites everything on it. Presumably, you are placing a blank diskette into the destination drive to receive the source files. You could, of course, be reusing a previously used diskette containing files you don't mind writing over.

Pressing Return at this point will begin the backup process. All the files in the named directory will now be copied over to your backup diskette (or your backup hard disk, if your destination drive is another hard disk). DOS will list all the files in this directory as they are being backed up to the specified disk drive.

BACKING UP A PARTIAL DIRECTORY

You can also perform selective backups—for example, backing up only the .PRG files from the DBASE\ADMIN directory. Simply specify the names of the files you wish to back up. To back up all .PRG files in the DBASE\ADMIN directory, enter

```
BACKUP C:\DBASE\ADMIN\*.PRG A:
```

As always, DOS will list the files while it writes the backup copies (see Figure 9.4). You *must* enter the leading drive identifier (in this example, C:). Otherwise, DOS will display the message "Invalid drive specification."

If DOS runs out of room on your first diskette, you will be prompted like this:

Files created by the BACKUP command may not be deleted; they are created with an attribute indicating that they are read-only, which means that you cannot erase them (see the ATTRIB command in Chapter 16). In order to regain the disk space on this diskette, you will have to reformat it with the FORMAT command.

```
Insert backup diskette 02 in drive A:

Warning! Files in the target drive
A:\ root directory will be erased
Strike any key when ready
```

DOS will continue to copy backup versions of your files onto this second diskette. The process will continue with additional diskettes, as necessary, until all your requested files have been copied.

```
Strike any key when ready

*** Backing up files to drive A: ***
Diskette Number: Ø1

\DBASE\ADMIN\DB3BOOK.PRG
\DBASE\ADMIN\START.PRG
\DBASE\ADMIN\INVOICE.PRG
\DBASE\ADMIN\CERTIF.PRG
\DBASE\ADMIN\RECOMM1.PRG
\DBASE\ADMIN\RECOMM2.PRG
\DBASE\ADMIN\PAYROLL.PRG
\DBASE\ADMIN\PAYROLL2.PRG
\DBASE\ADMIN\EXPERT.PRG
\DBASE\ADMIN\EXPERT1.PRG
\DBASE\ADMIN\EXPERT2.PRG
\DBASE\ADMIN\EXPERT3.PRG
\DBASE\ADMIN\EXPERT4.PRG
\DBASE\ADMIN\MESSAGE.PRG
\DBASE\ADMIN\LEDGER.PRG
\DBASE\ADMIN\INVOICE2.PRG
\DBASE\ADMIN\BOOKS2.PRG
\DBASE\ADMIN\DISKPREP.PRG

C>_
```

Figure 9.4: DOS lists file names as files are backed up

OTHER TYPES OF BACKUP PROCESSING

You may often need to do more than back up to a blank diskette all or some of the files in a DOS directory. For example, you might want to add additional files to a backup set to maintain some grouping and organization in your backups. You might also want to include files in the directory tree *below* the main directory you've just specified. Then again, you might want to combine these possibilities with selection criteria that go beyond simple wild-card specifications. You might want to back up files that have changed since your last backup, and not want to spend time backing up unchanged files when they are already on a perfectly good backup disk. Or, you might want to back up only those files created or modified since a certain date or even after a certain time on a certain day.

All of these options can be invoked by using one or more of the DOS switches for the BACKUP command (see Table 9.1). These switches are described in the following sections. You will concentrate in this chapter on the most important ones.

If you already know how to use some advanced commands like SUBST, JOIN, APPEND, or ASSIGN (see Chapter 16), do not have these commands active when you issue the BACKUP command. They're difficult enough to use properly; it would not be possible for DOS to later restore files properly if these commands were active in a different way when you ran the BACKUP command.

ADDING FILES TO AN EXISTING BACKUP

The /A switch tells DOS not to erase (write over) any existing files stored on the floppy diskette, but to add the newly backed-up files to

SWITCH	RESULT
/A	Adds files to a backup disk
/S	Backs up subdirectories
/M	Backs up modified files only
/D	Backs up files by date
/T	Backs up files by time on the date specified by /D
/F	Formats the destination diskette if necessary
/L	Creates a log file for the files contained in the compacted backup file

Table 9.1: Switches for the BACKUP command

that disk. For example, Figure 9.5 shows the selective file backup of all the files in the CHAP07 subdirectory. The resulting backup-diskette directory would look like the one in Figure 9.6, with BACKUP.001 and CONTROL.001 files.

At some point, you might also want to back up the files in another directory (in this example, the CHAP09 directory). Although you could back them up to a separate diskette, you might logically want to

```
C>BACKUP C:\PROGRAMS\FW\CHAP07 A:

Insert backup diskette 01 in drive A:

Warning! Files in the target drive
A:\ root directory will be erased
Strike any key when ready

*** Backing up files to drive A: ***
Diskette Number: 01

\PROGRAMS\FW\CHAP07\CHAP07.FW2
\PROGRAMS\FW\CHAP07\FIG7-14.CAP
\PROGRAMS\FW\CHAP07\FIG7-15.CAP
\PROGRAMS\FW\CHAP07\FIG7-16.CAP
\PROGRAMS\FW\CHAP07\SAMPLE.DTA
\PROGRAMS\FW\CHAP07\TBL7-1.TXT
\PROGRAMS\FW\CHAP07\TBL7-2.TXT
\PROGRAMS\FW\CHAP07\TBL7-3.TXT
\PROGRAMS\FW\CHAP07\TBL7-4.TXT
\PROGRAMS\FW\CHAP07\PART-3.FW2
\PROGRAMS\FW\CHAP07\TOC7.TXT

C>_
```

Figure 9.5: Backup requiring only a partial diskette

```
C>DIR A:

 Volume in drive A is BACKUP   001
 Directory of  A:\

BACKUP   001     52050    7-09-87  12:23p
CONTROL  001       583    7-09-87  12:23p
        2 File(s)     309248 bytes free

C>_
```

Figure 9.6: Resultant directory listing after backup

add these additional files to the same backup set. You could do this—even if more than one diskette is required—by using the /A switch. Figure 9.7 shows the CHAP09 directory and the four files within it. It also shows the necessary form of the BACKUP command:

BACKUP C:\PROGRAMS\FW\CHAP09 A: /A

This adds the new files to the BACKUP.001 file on the diskette in drive A. It also updates the CONTROL.001 file with information about the newly added files. Figure 9.8 portrays this process. Compare it to the original portrayal in Figure 9.3.

The resulting backup diskette (see Figure 9.9) now contains all the originally backed-up files, as well as the newly added ones. Notice the increase in size of the two files. As before, this increase represents the augmentation of the BACKUP.001 file with the contents of the four CHAP09 files, and the addition of information about the files to the CONTROL.001 file.

If the existing backup required multiple diskettes, you would be prompted to insert the last backup diskette before the actual backup copies would be written to the backup set:

Insert last backup diskette in drive A:
Strike any key when ready

```
C>BACKUP C:\PROGRAMS\FW\CHAP09 A: /A

Insert last backup diskette in drive A:
Strike any key when ready

*** Backing up files to drive A: ***
Diskette Number: 01

\PROGRAMS\FW\CHAP09\TBL9-1.TXT
\PROGRAMS\FW\CHAP09\FIG9-1.CAP
\PROGRAMS\FW\CHAP09\FIG9-14.TXT
\PROGRAMS\FW\CHAP09\CHAP09.FW2

C>_
```

Figure 9.7: Adding files to an existing backup set

Let's put some of these skills to work on your system. First, select two separate sets of files on your disk that need to be backed up. Try choosing files in two separate but important directories. Next, prepare several formatted diskettes to receive your selected files.

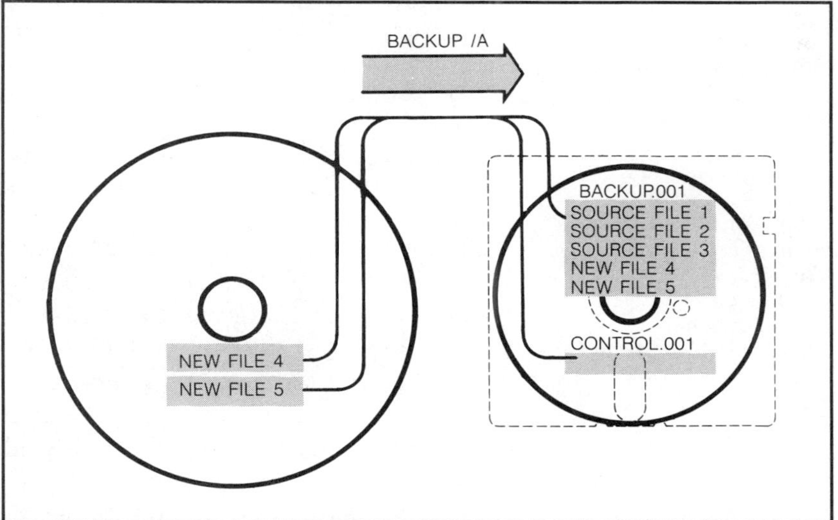

Figure 9.8: Adding files updates BACKUP and CONTROL files

```
C>DIR A:

 Volume in drive A is BACKUP   ØØ1
 Directory of  A:\

BACKUP   ØØ1     77655   7-Ø9-87  12:13p
CONTROL  ØØ1       789   7-Ø9-87  12:13p
        2 File(s)    283648 bytes free

C>_
```

Figure 9.9: Augmented disk directory after successive backups

In order to decide how many diskettes you need, use the DIR command to display the names of all the files you plan to back up. Add up all the file sizes for your selected diskettes, and then divide by the number of bytes on each of your backup diskettes. This number represents how many diskettes you'll need. For example, if you were backing up onto double-density, double-sided diskettes (360K), your calculations might go like this:

DOS 3.3 makes it easy for you to back up a variable amount of file information. If you add an /F switch to a BACKUP command, DOS will automatically format any diskette being used that is not already formatted. This relieves you from the obligations of calculating how many diskettes you'll need and preparing sufficient formatted diskettes. Using this switch requires that the FORMAT.COM command file be available either in the current default directory or somewhere along the DOS path.

1. Total size of all selected files: 3Mb
2. Number of bytes per diskette: 360K
3. 3,000,000 divided by 360,000: 9 diskettes

This calculation is only approximate for two reasons. First, 360K is really not 360,000 bytes. (Since a kilobyte equals 1024 bytes, 360K equals 360 × 1024, or 368,640 bytes.) The approximation is close enough, however, since the CONTROL.001 file takes up a variable number of bytes, depending largely on how many files are backed up. Performing the same type of calculation for the other types of diskettes supported by DOS 3.3 would give the results seen in Table 9.2.

Once you have calculated the correct number of diskettes and formatted them, issue the correct BACKUP command to back up all

Description	**Capacity**	**Required Diskettes To Back Up 10M**
5¼" single-sided	160K	63
5¼" single-sided	180K	56
5¼" double-sided	320K	32
5¼" double-sided	360K	28
5¼" high-capacity	1.2Mb	9
3½" double-sided	720K	14
3½" double-sided	1.44Mb	7

Table 9.2: Calculating the number of required backup diskettes

the files in your first selected directory. Then issue a second BACKUP command to append the files from the second directory you chose onto the first backup-diskette set. Use the /A switch.

Finally, issue one or more DIR commands for the backup diskettes to verify that all the original files were successfully copied. You'll have to add up the sizes of the original files to be sure of the backup diskette's completeness.

BACKING UP SUBDIRECTORIES

The /S switch tells DOS to copy the files contained in any subdirectories of the directory being backed up. This switch is extremely powerful with the BACKUP command, on par with the ability of the XCOPY command to move automatically through the directory tree structure. For example, if you started the backup in the root directory (C:\) and you used the /S option:

```
BACKUP C:\ A: /S
```

DOS would attempt to back up the entire hard disk.

The /S switch tells DOS first to back up all data and program files in the root directory and then to go to each subdirectory in the root. DOS backs up all files in each subdirectory and then proceeds to do the same for each subdirectory of that subdirectory.

If you wanted to back up just a portion of your hard-disk tree structure, you would just specify the main branch to begin with. Assuming a tree structure like the one in Figure 9.10, you could back up all the files in the DBASE branch by entering

```
BACKUP C:\DBASE A: /S
```

DOS would first back up the files in the DBASE directory. Then it would proceed to the next directory in that portion of the tree (DB3PLUS) and copy the files located there. It would then continue on through each of the other subdirectories (CLASSES and ADMIN) in the tree structure, copying all the files in them. DOS will prompt you to enter additional backup diskettes as each one fills up.

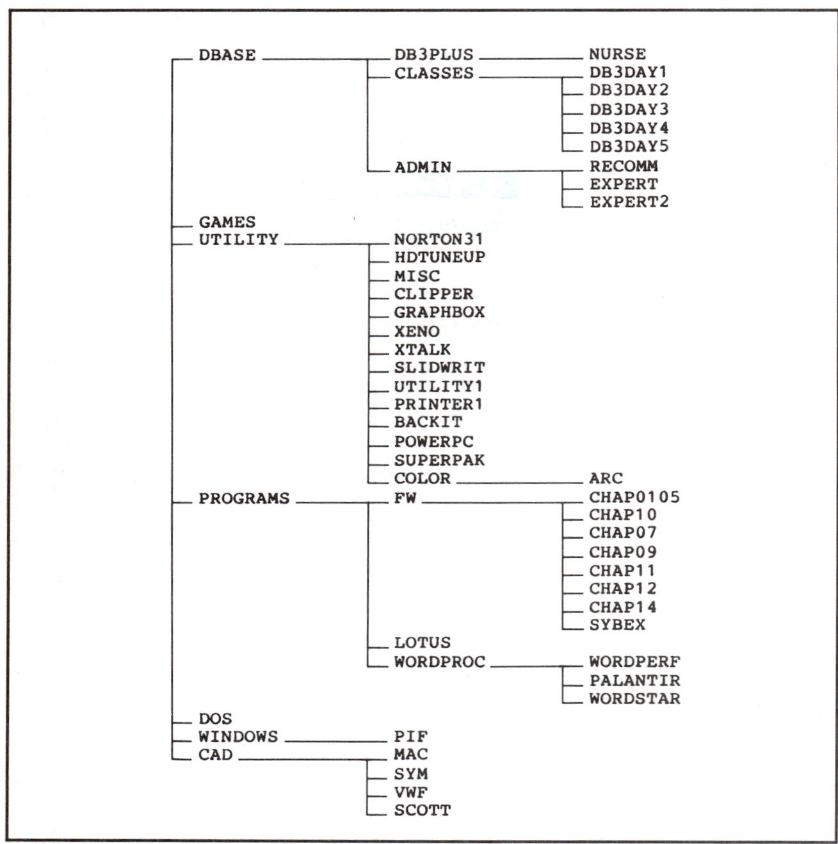

Figure 9.10: Sample directory structure

PERFORMING MULTIPLE OPERATIONS WITH ONE COMMAND

As in most DOS commands, multiple switches can be used simultaneously as long as it makes sense to do so. The /A and /S switches can work together for some useful purposes. You might be interested in locating and backing up all the BASIC program files (*.BAS) on your entire disk. Using the /S switch will allow the BACKUP command to look successively into each subdirectory you specify.

The following command will locate and back up all .BAS files anywhere on the disk:

```
BACKUP C:\*.BAS A: /S
```

This works because you've specified the root directory with which to begin (C:\), the wild card for finding BASIC files only (*.BAS), and the subdirectory search switch (/S).

As you know, changing the starting directory can limit the portion of the directory tree that is searched. The following command will find only .BAS files located in the UTILITY subdirectory and in all subdirectories located below it in the directory structure (see Figure 9.11):

```
BACKUP C:\UTILITY\*.BAS A: /S
```

The addition of an /A switch to the preceding examples will add all the files found to the existing backup disk:

```
BACKUP C:\UTILITY\*.BAS A: /S /A
```

BACKING UP MODIFIED OR NEW FILES

The /M option tells DOS to back up only files that have not already been backed up or that have been modified since the last backup. DOS is able to do this because it marks each file on the disk as it is backed up. This mark—actually a bit stored by DOS for every file—is called the *archive bit*. Whenever a file is modified or a new file is created, DOS changes the mark to indicate that the file will need to be backed up later. This archiving feature allows the backup process to skip files that have not been changed since the last backup. When any file is newly created in DOS, its archive bit is set to indicate that it should be treated like any other existing file that has undergone some changes.

As an example, suppose that you have a GAMES directory in which you keep your children's favorite computer games. Naturally, you need to safeguard your sanity in the event of a disk crash. You may suffer more if all these games are lost than you would if your business files were lost. Of course, neither situation will faze you if you've been conscientiously backing up your files.

Assume that you recently backed up all your files in this example directory. Your children then bring home two new games, HEADROOM.COM and MADMAX.EXE. You can add these to your existing GAMES backup set with the /M and /A switches (see Figure 9.12). The /A switch tells DOS to add all selected files to an existing

```
C>BACKUP C:\UTILITY\*.BAS A: /S

Insert backup diskette Ø1 in drive A:

Warning! Files in the target drive
A:\ root directory will be erased
Strike any key when ready

*** Backing up files to drive A: ***
Diskette Number: Ø1

\UTILITY\MISC\POUNDS.BAS
\UTILITY\MISC\TREETOP.BAS
\UTILITY\MISC\OKIDATA.BAS
\UTILITY\BASMAIN\PARKIT.BAS
\UTILITY\BASMAIN\MENUONE.BAS
\UTILITY\BASMAIN\GAMESMNU.BAS

C>_
```

Figure 9.11: Subdirectory search for files to add to backup

```
C>BACKUP C:\GAMES  A:  /M /A

Insert last backup diskette in drive A:
Strike any key when ready

*** Backing up files to drive A: ***
Diskette Number: Ø1

\GAMES\MADMAX.EXE
\GAMES\HEADROOM.EXE

C>BACKUP C:\GAMES  A:  /M /A

Warning! No files were found to back up

C>_
```

Figure 9.12: Backing up recently created or modified files

backup, while the /M switch selects only the two new files from the much larger collection of unchanged files.

Immediately attempting to back up the very same files again would result in a message stating that no files were found to back up. This is because the archive bit was changed to indicate that the two files had already been backed up. Figure 9.12 also demonstrates this situation.

BACKING UP BY DATE AND TIME

DOS allows you to specify by date, and by time on that date, the files to be backed up. When you enter a date, DOS will back up only files that possess the same date or a more recent date.

If you are using a date format for a different country, as discussed in Chapter 11, you should revise the form of the date used here. For example, European countries usually use dates in the form *day/month/year,* so a selection of files on or after February 4, 1987, would require /D:4/2/87 to be entered for the switch.

Let's look at an example. In the word-processing directory named PALANTIR, there are 37 files (see Figure 9.13). Some of these are the word processor's system files, some are old document files, and others are more recent work. Assume that all the files dated earlier than February 4, 1987, are either on backup disks or on the original system disks. You can selectively back up only the 11 files created in this directory since February 4 by using the /D switch:

```
BACKUP C:\PROGRAMS\WORDPROC\PALANTIR A:
            /D:2/4/87
```

As usual, the first argument selects the directory or the set of desired files, the second argument indicates the destination drive, and the final entry on the line is the switch (see Figure 9.14). Notice that the /D switch is followed by a colon, which is followed immediately by the specific date on or after which you want the new and updated files to be selected for backup.

CREATING A LOG FILE OF THE FILES BACKED UP

Since all the files you back up are compacted into a single backup file, it's a good idea to simultaneously ask DOS to create a log file for you. This file will store the date and time of the backup, as well as the full path and file name of each backed-up file. It will have the extension .LOG. Also, DOS will indicate which of the possible backup diskettes each particular file was stored on.

To use this feature you need to add another switch to your BACKUP command. The /L switch alone will cause DOS to create the log file under the name BACKUP.LOG; it will store this file in the root directory of your source drive. If you would like to give the log file another name, the switch format to use is

/L:*LogFileName*

As an example, if you wanted to generate a log file for the previous presented backup of word-processing files, you would add an /L switch to the complete BACKUP command:

BACKUP C:\PROGRAMS\WORDPROC\PALANTIR A:
/D:2/4/87 /L

```
C>DIR/W \PROGRAMS\WORDPROC\PALANTIR

 Volume in drive C is ROBBINS
 Directory of  C:\PROGRAMS\WORDPROC\PALANTIR

.                ..               STUDY5   WP      PALANTIR WPO     STANDARD WPF
WPINSTAL EXE     SPELL    HLP     WP       COM     LEX      4       LEX      3
SPELL    COM     LEX      1       LEX      2       DEFAULT  WP      STUDY1   WP
STUDY2   WP      CAD2     WP      CAD1     WP      CADBOOK1 WP      CADBOOK2 WP
QUELETT  WP      CADEXERS WP      CADBOOK3 WP      STUDY4   WP      STUDY3   WP
WORK     BLK     VISITYPE BAS     VISITYPE COM     SYBEX    WPB     WKSHPS   WP
NEWBOOK  WPB     LASTPAGE TXT     UCSC     WP      STUFF    WP      SYBEX    WP
NEWBOOK  WP      CHICAGO  WP
       37 File(s)    768000 bytes free

C>_
```

Figure 9.13: All files in the sample PALANTIR directory

```
C>BACKUP C:\PROGRAMS\WORDPROC\PALANTIR A: /D:2/4/87

Insert backup diskette 01 in drive A:

Warning! Files in the target drive
A:\ root directory will be erased
Strike any key when ready

*** Backing up files to drive A: ***
Diskette Number: 01

\PROGRAMS\WORDPROC\PALANTIR\VISITYPE.BAS
\PROGRAMS\WORDPROC\PALANTIR\VISITYPE.COM
\PROGRAMS\WORDPROC\PALANTIR\SYBEX.WP
\PROGRAMS\WORDPROC\PALANTIR\SCREEN04.CAP
\PROGRAMS\WORDPROC\PALANTIR\SCREEN05.CAP
\PROGRAMS\WORDPROC\PALANTIR\WKSHPS.WP
\PROGRAMS\WORDPROC\PALANTIR\NEWBOOK.WP
\PROGRAMS\WORDPROC\PALANTIR\LASTPAGE.TXT
\PROGRAMS\WORDPROC\PALANTIR\UCSC.WP
\PROGRAMS\WORDPROC\PALANTIR\STUFF.WP
\PROGRAMS\WORDPROC\PALANTIR\CHICAGO.WP

C>_
```

Figure 9.14: Backing up files by date of last update

If you preferred to store the log-file information in a file in the original source directory, you could do so by making the /L switch more specific:

```
BACKUP C:\PROGRAMS\WORDPROC\PALANTIR A: /D:2/4/87
                /L:\PROGRAMS\WORDPROC\PALANTIR\FEB4.LOG
```

The results of running this BACKUP command switch can be seen in Figure 9.15, which represents what DOS displays on the screen during the logging operation.

Figure 9.16 shows the contents of the log file (FEB4.LOG) itself. Using logging again during file-adding operations (/A) will add the newly backed-up files, along with their full path names, to this log file. This parallels the adding of file data and controlling information to the BACKUP and CONTROL files on the backup disk.

RESTORING FILES FROM A BACKUP DISK

The RESTORE command is used to bring files from a backup-diskette set (or a fixed disk) back onto a hard drive. It can be the original source hard-disk drive for the files, or it can be another hard-disk drive onto which you want to place the files.

```
Logging to file \PROGRAMS\WORDPROC\PALANTIR\FEB4.LOG

Insert backup diskette Ø1 in drive A:

Warning! Files in the target drive
A:\ root directory will be erased
Strike any key when ready

*** Backing up files to drive A: ***
Diskette Number: Ø1

\PROGRAMS\WORDPROC\PALANTIR\VISITYPE.BAS
\PROGRAMS\WORDPROC\PALANTIR\VISITYPE.COM
\PROGRAMS\WORDPROC\PALANTIR\SYBEX.WPB
\PROGRAMS\WORDPROC\PALANTIR\FEB4.LOG
\PROGRAMS\WORDPROC\PALANTIR\WKSHPS.WP
\PROGRAMS\WORDPROC\PALANTIR\NEWBOOK.WPB
\PROGRAMS\WORDPROC\PALANTIR\LASTPAGE.TXT
\PROGRAMS\WORDPROC\PALANTIR\UCSC.WP
\PROGRAMS\WORDPROC\PALANTIR\STUFF.WP
\PROGRAMS\WORDPROC\PALANTIR\SYBEX.WP
\PROGRAMS\WORDPROC\PALANTIR\NEWBOOK.WP
\PROGRAMS\WORDPROC\PALANTIR\CHICAGO.WP

C>_
```

Figure 9.15: DOS messages during logging operation

```
C>TYPE \PROGRAMS\WORDPROC\PALANTIR\FEB4.LOG

7-9-1987  23:11:13
001   \PROGRAMS\WORDPROC\PALANTIR\VISITYPE.BAS
001   \PROGRAMS\WORDPROC\PALANTIR\VISITYPE.COM
001   \PROGRAMS\WORDPROC\PALANTIR\SYBEX.WPB
001   \PROGRAMS\WORDPROC\PALANTIR\FEB4.LOG
001   \PROGRAMS\WORDPROC\PALANTIR\WKSHPS.WP
001   \PROGRAMS\WORDPROC\PALANTIR\NEWBOOK.WPB
001   \PROGRAMS\WORDPROC\PALANTIR\LASTPAGE.TXT
001   \PROGRAMS\WORDPROC\PALANTIR\UCSC.WP
001   \PROGRAMS\WORDPROC\PALANTIR\STUFF.WP
001   \PROGRAMS\WORDPROC\PALANTIR\SYBEX.WP
001   \PROGRAMS\WORDPROC\PALANTIR\NEWBOOK.WP
001   \PROGRAMS\WORDPROC\PALANTIR\CHICAGO.WP
C>_
```

Figure 9.16: Contents of the FEB4.LOG file

The RESTORE command is the only way to properly copy files from a backup diskette. Neither the COPY nor the XCOPY command will accomplish this task correctly.

The general form of the RESTORE command is

RESTORE *BackupDrive Destination*

Restoring files is almost the reverse of backing them up, with fewer switches and options for restoration. Unfortunately, there is one point of potential confusion. Contrary to what you might expect, RESTORE does not work in exact reverse of the BACKUP command. With BACKUP, you can specify a directory name alone, indicating you want to back up all files in the directory. With RESTORE, it's a little trickier. The second parameter, *Destination,* is the problem. If you do not specify a destination at all, the restoration is made to the current directory. However, in such a case, the current directory must be the same directory as the original source of the files on the backup disk. Otherwise, you'll receive the possibly misleading message "No files were found to restore." And, as Figure 9.17 shows, it isn't even enough to specify the correct directory as an argument to the RESTORE command.

The additional requirement for the *Destination* parameter is that you explicitly specify a file name, as in Figure 9.18, which simply adds the wild-card *.* specifier. Perhaps the simplest way to solve this problem is shown in Figure 9.19, which requires the CD

```
C>RESTORE  A:  \PROGRAMS\WORDPROC\PALANTIR

Insert backup diskette Ø1 in drive A:
Strike any key when ready


*** Files were backed up Ø7-Ø9-1987 ***

*** Restoring files from drive A: ***
Diskette: Ø1

Warning! No files were found to restore

C>_
```

Figure 9.17: Incorrectly formed RESTORE command

```
C>RESTORE  A:  \PROGRAMS\WORDPROC\PALANTIR\*.*

Insert backup diskette Ø1 in drive A:
Strike any key when ready


*** Files were backed up Ø7-Ø9-1987 ***

*** Restoring files from drive A: ***
Diskette: Ø1
\PROGRAMS\WORDPROC\PALANTIR\VISITYPE.BAS
\PROGRAMS\WORDPROC\PALANTIR\VISITYPE.COM
\PROGRAMS\WORDPROC\PALANTIR\SYBEX.WPB
\PROGRAMS\WORDPROC\PALANTIR\FEB4.LOG
\PROGRAMS\WORDPROC\PALANTIR\WKSHPS.WP
\PROGRAMS\WORDPROC\PALANTIR\NEWBOOK.WPB
\PROGRAMS\WORDPROC\PALANTIR\LASTPAGE.TXT
\PROGRAMS\WORDPROC\PALANTIR\UCSC.WP
\PROGRAMS\WORDPROC\PALANTIR\STUFF.WP
\PROGRAMS\WORDPROC\PALANTIR\SYBEX.WP
\PROGRAMS\WORDPROC\PALANTIR\NEWBOOK.WP
\PROGRAMS\WORDPROC\PALANTIR\CHICAGO.WP

C>_
```

Figure 9.18: RESTORE requires a complete path name

command to be issued prior to RESTORE. In that case, specifying only drive C as the destination is sufficient, since the default directory is now the proper one—the one from which the files were originally backed up. Naturally, as with all DOS commands, the drive specifier C: is not strictly necessary since, in its absence, the current directory would be used by default anyway.

```
C>CD  \PROGRAMS\WORDPROC\PALANTIR

C>RESTORE  A:  C:

Insert backup diskette Ø1 in drive A:
Strike any key when ready


*** Files were backed up Ø7-Ø9-1987 ***

*** Restoring files from drive A: ***
Diskette: Ø1
\PROGRAMS\WORDPROC\PALANTIR\VISITYPE.BAS
\PROGRAMS\WORDPROC\PALANTIR\VISITYPE.COM
\PROGRAMS\WORDPROC\PALANTIR\SYBEX.WP
\PROGRAMS\WORDPROC\PALANTIR\SCREENØ4.CAP
\PROGRAMS\WORDPROC\PALANTIR\SCREENØ5.CAP
\PROGRAMS\WORDPROC\PALANTIR\WKSHPS.WP
\PROGRAMS\WORDPROC\PALANTIR\NEWBOOK.WP
\PROGRAMS\WORDPROC\PALANTIR\LASTPAGE.TXT
\PROGRAMS\WORDPROC\PALANTIR\UCSC.WP
\PROGRAMS\WORDPROC\PALANTIR\STUFF.WP
\PROGRAMS\WORDPROC\PALANTIR\CHICAGO.WP

C>_
```

Figure 9.19: Restoring the current directory

RESTORING ONLY SOME OF YOUR BACKED-UP FILES

As always, DOS provides a variety of very useful switches for commands like RESTORE. There are two principal switches presented here that will be quite useful to you at various times. Other possible switches are presented in Part V.

The ability to select the files you want restored can be very useful. It can also cut down on the time required to restore files by restoring only those files you actually need.

If you have backed up an entire directory tree or any subdirectory tree, you will need to use the /S switch to restore the subdirectory tree structure. Also, if you have made changes to any of the previously backed-up files, you should use the /P switch to ensure that the old version does not overwrite the new version.

RESTORING DIRECTORY STRUCTURES The /S switch on the RESTORE command is the exact reverse of the /S switch on the BACKUP command. When used with BACKUP, /S allows you to search through a directory and all of its subdirectories for files to back up. When used with RESTORE, /S ensures that the backed-up files are restored to their proper subdirectories.

In fact, if DOS discovers that a subdirectory is missing during the restoration process, it will automatically recreate that subdirectory before copying the backed-up files to it. Your destination directory may be missing for a variety of reasons. Your entire disk may have crashed or have been erased inadvertently. More likely, you may have erased the directory and file contents, after backing them up, in order to reclaim the disk space for other purposes. Or you may simply be restoring the directory structure and files to a different computer and hard disk.

PROTECTING AGAINST ACCIDENTAL OVERWRITING The /P switch is extremely useful if you're not completely sure of yourself or if a good deal of time has elapsed between the backup and restoration. When this switch is specified, DOS will ask you during the restoration if you really mean to restore an old version and overwrite an existing disk file. It will do this when the existing disk file has been updated since the earlier backup version, or if the disk file has been marked as read-only. (The latter situation almost never occurs, so you needn't worry about it; you will learn about read-only files in Chapter 15.)

As a last example of RESTORE, let's use DOS's selective restoration capability to redo the example shown in Figure 9.13. Instead of restoring all the files from the diskette in drive A, let's select only the document files (.WP):

```
RESTORE A: C:\PROGRAMS\WORDPROC\PALANTIR\*.WP
```

Since the files UCSC.WP and STUFF.WP have been changed since the backup, let's make sure that they aren't accidentally overwritten:

```
RESTORE A: C:\PROGRAMS\WORDPROC\PALANTIR\*.WP /P
```

The resultant protective sequence is shown in Figure 9.20.

The /P switch enabled RESTORE to note that two of the .WP files had been changed since they were backed up. The prompt allows you to inhibit overwriting and protect the changed version. Unfortunately, the display is somewhat confusing, since some but not all of the other restored files are interspersed between the warnings.

Now test your understanding of the RESTORE process. First back up any selected set of text files. If you completed the earlier exercises using BACKUP, you can use the resulting diskette if it contained text files. Otherwise, choose some files from your word processing (or other text-oriented) directory.

```
C>RESTORE  A: \PROGRAMS\WORDPROC\PALANTIR\*.WP /P

Insert backup diskette Ø1 in drive A:
Strike any key when ready


*** Files were backed up Ø7-Ø9-1987 ***

*** Restoring files from drive A: ***
Diskette: Ø1
Warning! File SYBEX.WP
was changed after it was backed up
Replace the file (Y/N)?
N

\PROGRAMS\WORDPROC\PALANTIR\WKSHPS.WP
Warning! File NEWBOOK.WP
was changed after it was backed up
Replace the file (Y/N)?
N

\PROGRAMS\WORDPROC\PALANTIR\UCSC.WP
\PROGRAMS\WORDPROC\PALANTIR\STUFF.WP
\PROGRAMS\WORDPROC\PALANTIR\CHICAGO.WP
-
```

Figure 9.20: Protecting against file overwriting with /P

Make some textual change to one of the text files by using your word processor or DOS's EDLIN (see Chapter 6). Next, restore the backed-up files to their original directory. Use the /P switch so you do not overwrite the newly changed text files. Use your text-editing program to verify that the old versions of the changed files were not rewritten onto your disk.

SUMMARY

This chapter has taught you how to back up your disks. Power failures do occur in businesses, brownouts occur even more frequently, and a multitude of other incidents can cause the intermittent loss or corruption of important files. Therefore, making backups is of critical importance for avoiding disaster. This chapter has presented the following backup information:

- You should back up your files before moving your computer, when you are close to filling up your hard disk, and just before running a fragmentation reduction program.
- The BACKUP command can make a complete copy of all the files in a directory when you simply specify the directory name and the disk drive to receive the backup copies.

- Backup copies of files are written into a compacted file on each backup diskette. The compacted file is called BACKUP.*xxx,* where *xxx* is the number of the backup disk.
- Each BACKUP.*xxx* file is accompanied by a file called CONTROL.*xxx* (again, *xxx* is the disk number). This file contains such controlling information as the names and lengths of the files compacted into the BACKUP.*xxx* file.
- With the BACKUP command you can make selective backups of some of the files in a directory by using appropriate switches. For instance, you can make backups of files that have changed since the last backup was performed by using the /M switch.
- The /D switch permits the backup of files that have changed or that have been created since a certain date.
- The /T switch permits the backup of files based on the time of creation or modification.
- Adding a new set of files to a backup set is easily done by using the /A switch.
- The powerful /S switch allows you to back up files located deep within the directory tree.
- Automatic formatting of the destination diskettes for the BACKUP command will be done by DOS whenever you specify the /F switch.
- All backup processing can be recorded in a log file by using the /L switch. You can specify your own path and file name to receive the logging information; otherwise, a BACKUP.LOG file is created in the root directory of the source drive.
- The RESTORE command allows you to write files and directories from the backup-diskette set back to a hard disk—either the original or a new one. The /S switch permits restoration of the treelike directory structure. The /P switch allows you to complete this process safely in the event that existing disk versions of any files are newer and should not be overwritten.

In the next two chapters, you'll look at more precise control over DOS's internal setup and system configuration. In Chapter 10, you'll learn how to initialize several key DOS parameters and how to exploit the power of DOS drivers. In Chapter 11, you'll revisit the MODE command in yet another one of its significant roles—support for foreign-language characters, graphics characters, and multiple keyboard layouts.

CUSTOM CONFIGURATIONS OF DOS

CHAPTER 10

SO FAR, EVERYTHING YOU'VE SEEN ABOUT DOS HAS been clearly defined. Every feature has had a concrete definition and strict limits on how it could be used and what results you could expect. Behind the scenes, however, there are several additional aspects to DOS itself which have considerable flexibility, and which you can control.

DOS is like your home: you can walk in and accept everything as it is, or you can adjust the environment to your liking. In your home, you can open some windows or close others; you can turn the lights on or off; you can set the thermostat to a different temperature; you can even rearrange the furniture. DOS, too, also has a certain way in which it appears when you "walk in," or start it up. This internal configuration, and how you can adjust it, is the subject of this chapter.

In DOS, you can customize your system in many ways. Chapters 13, 14, and 15 concentrate on the batch-file mechanism for complete on-line adjustments. Here, you'll focus on customizing some of the inner workings of DOS itself.

Two principal mechanisms exist for the internal setups: the CONFIG.SYS file and the PROMPT command. Using the CONFIG.SYS file, you can specify the number of internal DOS buffers. You can also use CONFIG.SYS to load additional drivers such as ANSI.SYS, which enables you to redefine keys and control the display. DOS has another driver you can load to create a RAM disk. In this chapter, you'll learn all these customization methods.

USING THE CONFIG.SYS FILE

When a microcomputer is turned on, it runs through a built-in bootstrap program. The time-consuming part of a typical bootstrap is a memory test. The more memory you have, the longer the test will take; if you ever expand the memory of your system, you will probably notice the difference.

Following the memory test, the bootstrap attempts to find the disk-resident portion of DOS on one of the drives in the system, usually beginning with drive A. That is why the light on drive A comes on before the hard drive is accessed, even if you have a hard disk. It is also why anyone can circumvent a menu system set up on your hard disk—one can always place a DOS system disk in drive A, boot the system from that disk, and then access any files on the hard disk.

When the system drive is found (the one that has a copy of the DOS files on it), the computer reads the information into its memory. The next thing DOS does is to scan the root directory of the drive from which it has read the DOS files for a special file called CONFIG.SYS. If this file is not present, DOS initializes your system according to built-in default values. If a file called AUTOEXEC-.BAT exists (see Chapter 15 for a detailed explanation of this file), DOS then proceeds with the instructions in that file and displays the DOS prompt (usually A> or C>, depending on which drive contained the system files).

If a CONFIG.SYS file is present in the root directory DOS scans, it will contain a list of special statements that define a nonstandard system configuration. Figure 10.1 shows a sample CONFIG.SYS file actually used on a typical 640K DOS system. You'll learn in this chapter what each line of this file represents.

CONFIG.SYS is unique in the following ways:

- It can alter the internal setup of DOS itself.
- It can only be activated by booting or rebooting the computer.

```
FILES=20
BUFFERS=15
DEVICE=C:\DOS\ANSI.SYS
DEVICE=C:\DOS\VDISK.SYS 120
```

Figure 10.1: A typical CONFIG.SYS file

- It can contain only a limited set of commands.

Since the CONFIG.SYS file is a standard ASCII text file, you can create and modify it with a text editor like EDLIN (see Chapter 6) or your own word processor. Each line in this file has the form

Command = *Value*

The commands you'll learn about in this chapter are the most important and useful ones. They are FILES, BUFFERS, and DEVICE.

SPECIFYING THE NUMBER OF ACTIVE FILES

More and more frequently, users are running sophisticated programs like WordStar 4.0, dBASE III PLUS, and Framework II. These programs can work with several files at the same time, so they require the installation of a special CONFIG.SYS file. This usually requires you to change the normal DOS default value for FILES. The default value set by DOS is only eight files. This means there are eight places reserved by DOS inside its own memory space to track information about open files. DOS itself uses three of these, and every running application program, overlay file, RAM-resident program, and so on, may use additional places out of the eight.

Most popular application programs recommend that you set the FILES value to 20 in your CONFIG.SYS file, although some programs recommend higher or lower settings. Unless you're willing to run extensive performance tests in your system environment, just follow the software manufacturer's instructions for setting the value of FILES. However, you might be using several different software application packages. For example, you may be using a computer-aided design package that recommends the setting FILES = 20, and you may also be using a database management package that recommends FILES = 15. Take the larger value. Although it will cost you some additional memory space when DOS boots up, it won't be much (48 bytes per open file), and at least you'll be guaranteed that your software will run.

SPECIFYING THE NUMBER OF INTERNAL DOS BUFFERS

The BUFFERS command refers to the way DOS manages the input and output of data to and from the disk drives. When a command is issued by a program to read information from a file, DOS really serves the role of an intermediary by loading the information into a reserved buffer area. Figure 10.2 presents a visual interpretation of this activity.

Efficiency is the primary reason that operating systems use buffers. Imagine yourself in the role of an operating system. Then imagine that someone (an application program) wants to give you something, while someone else (a disk file) wants to get that same thing. If you act as a buffer by accepting the object with one hand and then hold it until you can locate the receiving person, the transaction will be fairly straightforward. However, if you try to do this procedure without using your hands or moving around, getting the giver together with the receiver in the same room, you've made your job much more difficult. In addition, you would not be able to do much else until the two-person operation was completed. DOS uses buffering to make transactions efficient.

When a disk request is made, DOS checks the information in its buffer before it tries to read the disk. This can sometimes eliminate the need to actually read the disk; DOS may find that the requested

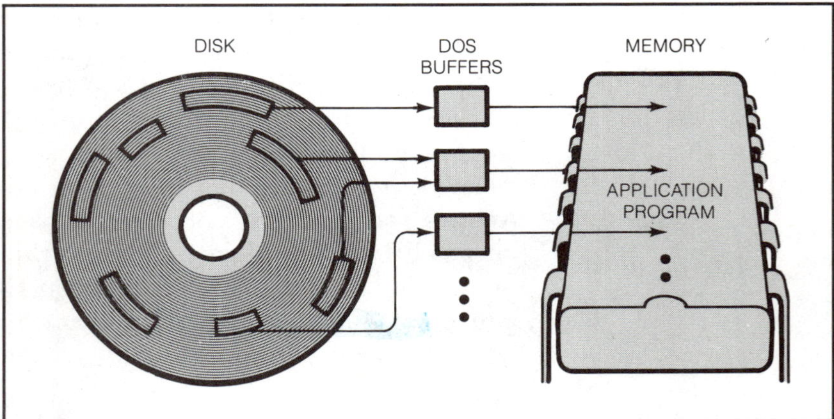

Figure 10.2: Disk data passing through DOS buffers

file data is already in the buffer—if, for instance, the file has recently been called up by another program or DOS request. The result is that some programs will perform certain operations faster.

Each buffer in DOS can hold 528 bytes. If you increase the number of buffers, the memory-resident requirements for DOS itself will increase. This will decrease the available memory for any application program, as well as for any memory-resident program you wish to use during your main program's execution. Sophisticated programs like Framework II, which has its own buffer management and configuration file and therefore uses memory intensively, will suffer greatly from too large of a BUFFERS value.

A law of diminishing returns is at work here. Up to a point, more DOS buffers means faster performance for your system. On the other hand, too many buffers means DOS may spend more time looking through its buffers than it would spend to just go to the disk and read the necessary data. Unless you have a good reason, use the software manufacturer's recommended setting for BUFFERS. A common setting is a value of 15.

USING DEVICE DRIVERS TO CUSTOMIZE DOS

The CONFIG.SYS file is also used to load additional software drivers into DOS. Software drivers are special-purpose programs whose only responsibility is to control specific peripheral devices (see Chapter 11 for an additional discussion of device drivers). DOS can't be responsible for knowing all the control codes for all possible external devices; operating systems in general leave the details of communicating with and controlling these devices to the special driver programs.

Device drivers extend the command range of DOS. Naturally, they also take up more memory, which is one reason why they are optional. A special driver called ANSI.SYS extends the functions of DOS to include reprogramming or redefinition of keys and screen colors in DOS. You'll look at that feature more closely in the following section.

DOS also has a driver that is used to create a *RAM disk* (sometimes called a *virtual disk*). The RAM disk is not really a disk—it is an area in memory that simulates the operations of an additional disk drive. A critical aspect of this mechanism is that any files placed on the RAM disk are really memory-resident. They can therefore be retrieved at the speed of memory, which is usually microseconds or nanoseconds. Files on actual mechanical disk drives are slower, usually in the millisecond range.

Memory reserved for use as a RAM disk is no longer available for internal use by programs like Framework II or Symphony. If you take up too much space with a RAM disk or any other memory-resident software, there may not even be enough remaining memory to load your main application software. You can make more memory space available by using extended or expanded memory, discussed below.

You must do a bit of calculating to figure out how much memory is available for your RAM disk. Simply subtract the memory required by your version of DOS from your total physical memory (640K, 512K, or whatever). Then subtract the memory requirements of your particular application program (for example, 378K for dBASE III PLUS or 512K for CADVANCE) from the remaining number. This tells you the maximum remaining memory that could be allocated for a RAM disk. For example, if the total physical memory of your system is 640K, the space required by your DOS 3.3 is 45K, and the space required by your application program is 384K, you have 211K remaining for your RAM disk (640 – 45 – 384 = 211).

There are a few other things you must consider. The size of your version of DOS varies according to the values of FILES, BUFFERS, and any other CONFIG.SYS parameters. It also varies according to how many additional DOS programs you've run, which requires extra memory (like the MODE command of Chapter 7 and the KEYB command of Chapter 9). Naturally, if you run any memory-resident programs like Sidekick, you need to subtract their memory requirements as well.

Use only as much memory for your RAM disk as you need. You should know in advance how you plan to use this space.

CREATING A RAM DISK

You know that DOS maintains a directory and a file allocation table (a DAT and an FAT) on each disk, along with the actual data and program files. In order to simulate this structure in memory, a special piece of software is required. This software is included in your DOS in a file called either VDISK.SYS (for PC-DOS) or RAMDRIVE.SYS (for MS-DOS).

The simulated RAM disk seen in Figure 10.3 can be implemented simply by including the following values in your DEVICE

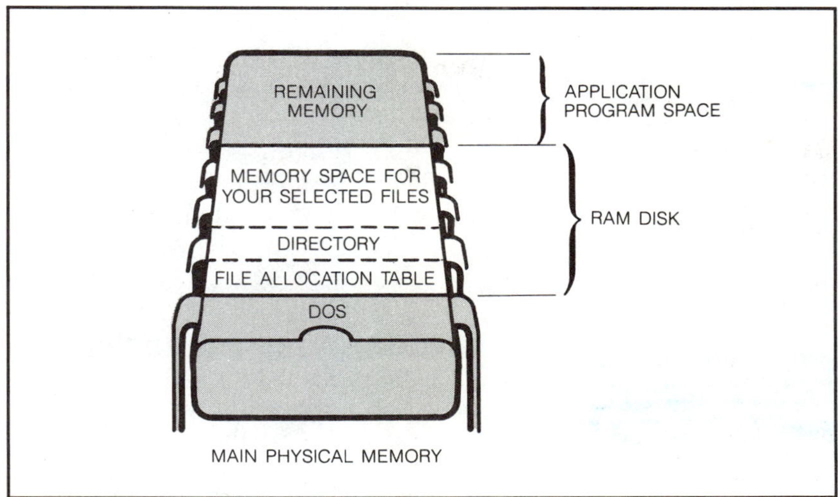

Figure 10.3: RAM disk simulation using physical memory

If you are using a version of DOS for any machine other than an actual IBM computer, you will need to substitute RAMDRIVE.SYS wherever you read VDISK.SYS in this text.

If you don't have AT extended memory, you can place your RAM disk in *expanded* memory, such as Intel's Above Board. Expanded memory, specially configured according to the "LIM standard," works in regular PCs and XTs, as well as ATs. It actually overcomes the DOS 640K limit, so many programs are written to use it for data just like regular memory.

specification:

```
DEVICE=C:\DOS\VDISK.SYS 120
```

This DEVICE setting brings into memory the VDISK (virtual or RAM disk) driver.

In this example, the VDISK.SYS file itself is located on drive C in the DOS directory. The parameter value of 120 indicates that a total simulated disk of size 120K should be created from the available physical memory (640K or whatever you have in your system).

If you have an IBM PC-AT or a compatible computer, you should know about a switch you can use when you set up a RAM disk. The /E switch will use *extended memory*—extra memory above the conventional 1Mb of addressable memory—if your machine has this additional memory installed. The previous example could be modified to generate a 120K RAM disk in extended memory like this:

```
DEVICE=C:\DOS\VDISK.SYS 120 /E
```

DOS also allows you to have multiple RAM disks simultaneously. Just as you can use different physical devices to protect files from one another by separating them on different drives, you can do the same

If you intend to create and use disk drives with drive identifiers beyond the letter E, DOS 3.2 and 3.3 will permit you to do so but will require another statement in your configuration file. This additional statement must be of the form LASTDRIVE = *x*, where *x* is the last valid alphabetic character DOS will use for a drive identifier.

with the much faster RAM disks. Each RAM disk will be given a new single-character drive identifier by DOS.

All you need to do to create multiple RAM disks is have multiple copies of the DEVICE command. DOS knows what physical drives exist in your system, and it creates the additional drives using the next available letters. For instance, if your system had one or two diskette drives and one hard-disk drive, then adding the following two statements to your CONFIG.SYS file would create the RAM disks D and E with sizes of 120K and 184K (see Figure 10.4):

```
DEVICE = C:\DOS\VDISK.SYS 120
DEVICE = C:\DOS\VDISK.SYS 184
```

There are other methods for creating RAM disks. These usually require software that comes with enhancement boards like AST's Six-Pak Plus or Quadram's Quadboard, or they require add-on boards that act as dedicated RAM disks. Some of these have their own power supplies and battery backups, which means no data loss will occur during power outages. Another benefit of this type of add-on is that no system memory is used up by the device driver that manages the RAM disk. Installing a RAM disk with software packages or add-on boards requires a different procedure; you should follow the manufacturer's instructions.

```
C>CHKDSK D:
Volume VDISK  V3.3 created Dec 6, 1984 12:00p

   119168 bytes total disk space
        0 bytes in 1 hidden files
   119168 bytes available on disk

   524288 bytes total memory
   132208 bytes free

C>CHKDSK E:
Volume VDISK  V3.3 created Dec 6, 1984 12:00p

   183936 bytes total disk space
        0 bytes in 1 hidden files
   183936 bytes available on disk

   524288 bytes total memory
   132208 bytes free

C>_
```

Figure 10.4: Multiple RAM disks

None of the CONFIG.SYS file's settings take effect until the DOS system is booted up. Remember this if you make any changes to your CONFIG.SYS file—you must reboot before the changes take effect.

An advantage of these other methods is that the RAM disk doesn't have to be carved out of memory at bootup time. Instead, you can first run your own programs, making use of all available memory. Then, at your convenience, you can run the special software to set up the RAM disk. Only then will you need to confront the problem of memory requirements. In Figure 10.4, the 512K machine with two RAM disks has only 152,912 bytes free in which to run programs. Having consumed so much memory with the two RAM disks, you would have to change the CONFIG.SYS file and reboot before you could reuse that memory space in any other way.

USING A RAM DISK

Now that you know how to create a RAM disk, you should also know how to use what you've created to its best advantage. Here are some suggestions for using your RAM disk.

Place a copy of your DOS system's primary disk-resident program, COMMAND.COM, on your RAM disk. Then employ the following special instructions to inform DOS that all future references to COMMAND.COM can locate it on the RAM disk, not on the boot disk. Assuming your RAM disk is on drive D (substitute the appropriate letter on your system), you should enter the following command at the DOS prompt:

```
SET COMSPEC = D:\COMMAND.COM
```

This will speed up all programs that invoke DOS from within themselves, such as Framework II or QDOS II. These programs work by loading a second copy of the command processor (COMMAND-.COM) from a RAM disk. This command will also speed up application software that overwrites the command-processor portion of DOS and then requires its reloading before the software can restore DOS and its prompt.

Load the files for frequently referenced DOS commands, like CHKDSK.COM and FORMAT.COM, onto your RAM disk; also load EDLIN.COM if you use EDLIN often to edit small text files (see Chapter 6). In fact, load any text files that are run frequently, like batch files.

Load any large support files (like spelling dictionaries or a thesaurus file) that your word processor or integrated software may need. Also place index-type files (generated by many database management systems) on the RAM disk for much more rapid accessing of data records, especially if you must search through many records in large data files.

Place your favorite disk-resident utility programs (shareware, public domain, or purchased, like the Norton Utilities) on the RAM disk if you use them frequently. Also place overlay files on your RAM disk for improved execution of your software. These overlays contain the portion of your application program that couldn't fit into memory and is normally read into a special part of memory only when needed. The overlay features of your software will operate at rapid RAM speeds if you place them on your RAM disk. Note that you will need to make your RAM disk into the default DOS disk before invoking your application program so it will look for the overlay file on the RAM disk and not on the standard drive.

Remember to set your path properly so DOS can find main programs. Set the RAM disk near or at the front of the PATH specification so that the file copies on the RAM drive are accessed first, not the original files that may also be accessible from directories on the path.

Before you follow these suggestions for using your RAM disk effectively, you should learn how to use it safely. As you know, using a RAM disk is much faster than using real disks. Programs that formerly took hours to run may take minutes, minutes can become seconds, and waiting time can disappear. When RAM disks are used improperly, however, hours of work can disappear in seconds.

Since a RAM disk is created in memory, any information stored on it will vanish when the computer is turned off. You gain great advantage by storing and accessing the right files on a RAM disk, but you must remember that these files are destroyed when you turn off the power or a power failure occurs, if there's a brownout in your building, if your computer plug comes out of the wall, or if you reboot your system with Ctrl-Alt-Del.

If you place and update important data files on a RAM disk for the sake of rapid access, save copies of them to a real disk before you turn off the power. Also back up copies of them to a real disk at frequent intervals to avoid losing all your work.

ADDING POWER WITH THE ANSI SYSTEM DRIVER

The ANSI (American National Standards Institute) system allows you to modify the default setup of your screen and keyboard. For example, you can change the characteristics of the screen, including both the cursor position and screen colors (with a color monitor, of course). You can also redefine the expected value of keys on your keyboard, so you can customize the use of your function keys, as well as how the Ctrl, Shift, or Alt key affects them.

In order to obtain any of these customizing capabilities, you must have the ANSI.SYS driver installed in your system. The third line of CONFIG.SYS (see Figure 10.1) does just that:

```
DEVICE=C:\DOS\ANSI.SYS
```

Some special-purpose application programs like PreCursor, a hard-disk management program, and SuperKey, a keyboard redefinition program, require that you include this type of command in your CONFIG.SYS specification. Of course, you should specify the full path name to the ANSI.SYS file; in this example, ANSI.SYS is located in directory DOS on drive C.

Even if you are not yet using application software that requires the ANSI.SYS driver, the possibilities in the next section will probably inspire you to include this line in your CONFIG.SYS specification all the time.

ANSI.SYS AND THE PROMPT COMMAND

The PROMPT command is used to enter ANSI commands. For example, the form of the PROMPT command used to change the color of the screen is

PROMPT $e[*aaaa*m

The letter m in the PROMPT escape sequence signifies the end of your sequence of attribute settings. It must be lowercase.

where *aaaa* represents screen attributes or colors (shown in Table 10.1). Separate these values with semicolons if you use more than one. $e is a special symbol combination (the dollar sign $ followed by the letter e), recognized by DOS as an equivalent of the Esc key. The ANSI driver is invoked when an escape sequence is received, which is any series of keystrokes begun with the Esc key; therefore, $e invokes the ANSI driver. There is no limit to the number of attributes you can enter between the left bracket [and the letter m.

CONTROLLING THE SCREEN DISPLAY

It's up to you to decide if you like the standard white letters on a black background (even if you've bought a color monitor), or if you prefer something flashier. Using the attribute and color codes shown in Table 10.1, along with the PROMPT command, you can customize things as you like.

ATTRIBUTES	
0	All attributes off
1	Bold
4	Underline (on IBM-compatible monochrome monitors only)
5	Blinking
7	Reverse video

COLORS	FOREGROUND	BACKGROUND
Black	30	40
Red	31	41
Green	32	42
Yellow	33	43
Blue	34	44
Magenta	35	45
Cyan	36	46
White	37	47

Table 10.1: Video-screen color and attribute codes

To switch the display to dark letters on a light background (see Figure 10.5), you would use an attribute value of 7 for reverse video:

```
PROMPT $e[7m
```

All future output on your screen will now appear as reverse video—black on white. Notice that in Figure 10.5, the DIR/W itself is displayed in reverse video after the PROMPT command has been executed.

To return to normal video (see Figure 10.6), you would use an attribute value of 0, which turns off all special attributes:

```
PROMPT $e[0m
```

USING META SYMBOLS

Notice that there appears to be no visible prompt at the bottom of the screens just shown. This is because the PROMPT command was used to set video attributes only. Various other possibilities can be combined with these attributes by stringing them together. You can create a wide range of output possibilities by using symbolic replacements, called *meta symbols,* for the desired output result. Table 10.2

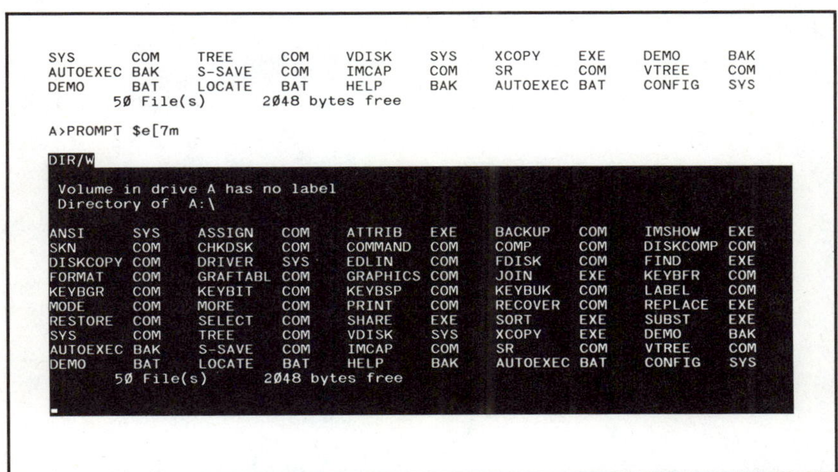

Figure 10.5: Setting reverse video with PROMPT and ANSI.SYS

```
SYS       COM    TREE      COM    VDISK     SYS    XCOPY     EXE    DEMO      BAK
AUTOEXEC  BAK    S-SAVE    COM    IMCAP     COM    SR        COM    VTREE     COM
DEMO      BAT    LOCATE    BAT    HELP      BAK    AUTOEXEC  BAT    CONFIG    SYS
       5Ø File(s)      2Ø48 bytes free

PROMPT $E[Øm

DIR/W

 Volume in drive A has no label
 Directory of  A:\

ANSI      SYS    ASSIGN    COM    ATTRIB    EXE    BACKUP    COM    IMSHOW    EXE
SKN       COM    CHKDSK    COM    COMMAND   COM    COMP      COM    DISKCOMP  COM
DISKCOPY  COM    DRIVER    SYS    EDLIN     COM    FDISK     COM    FIND      EXE
FORMAT    COM    GRAFTABL  COM    GRAPHICS  COM    JOIN      EXE    KEYBFR    COM
KEYBGR    COM    KEYBIT    COM    KEYBSP    COM    KEYBUK    COM    LABEL     COM
MODE      COM    MORE      COM    PRINT     COM    RECOVER   COM    REPLACE   EXE
RESTORE   COM    SELECT    COM    SHARE     EXE    SORT      EXE    SUBST     EXE
SYS       COM    TREE      COM    VDISK     SYS    XCOPY     EXE    DEMO      BAK
AUTOEXEC  BAK    S-SAVE    COM    IMCAP     COM    SR        COM    VTREE     COM
DEMO      BAT    LOCATE    BAT    HELP      BAK    AUTOEXEC  BAT    CONFIG    SYS
       5Ø File(s)      2Ø48 bytes free

-
```

Figure 10.6: Resetting to default video attributes

SYMBOL	MEANING
e	The Esc key
p	Current directory of the default drive
g	The > character
n	Default drive identifier
d	System date
t	System time
v	Version number
l	The < character
b	The ¦ character
q	The = character
h	A backspace
_	The carriage-return/line-feed sequence

Table 10.2: Meta symbols for the PROMPT command

lists the single-character meta symbols that can be used in conjunction with the $ character to influence the output of the PROMPT command.

For instance, to display the current directory, you would enter

```
PROMPT $p
```

To display the current directory and the > symbol, you would enter

```
PROMPT $p$g
```

To display the current directory and the > symbol, *and* to set to boldface all future video output, you would enter

```
PROMPT $p$g$e[1m
```

The results of this command are shown in Figure 10.7.

COMBINING MULTIPLE ATTRIBUTES

All of the preceding possibilities can be combined to create more complex prompt effects. The simplest combinations only involve two attributes at once. For example, to create a reverse-video display that blinks, you can combine the codes for blinking (5) and reverse video (7):

```
PROMPT $e[5;7m
```

Future output will be seen as black characters that blink on a light background. To set things back to normal again, you would enter

```
PROMPT $e[0m
```

You can enter text into your prompt by simply typing it with no special meta symbols; text can also be embedded between any special-purpose meta symbols. For example, you can change the prompting message to "Your Command?" and display it in high intensity with the following:

```
PROMPT $e[1mYour Command?$e[0m
```

The beginning $e[1m turns high intensity on for the phrase "Your Command?" and the ending $e[0m turns it off.

```
SYS       COM   TREE      COM   VDISK     SYS   XCOPY     EXE   DEMO      BAK
AUTOEXEC  BAK   S-SAVE    COM   IMCAP     COM   SR        COM   VTREE     COM
DEMO      BAT   LOCATE    BAT   HELP      BAK   AUTOEXEC  BAT   CONFIG    SYS
       50 File(s)      2048 bytes free

A>PROMPT $P$G$E[1m

A:\>DIR/W

 Volume in drive A has no label
 Directory of  A:\

ANSI      SYS   ASSIGN    COM   ATTRIB    EXE   BACKUP    COM   IMSHOW    EXE
SKN       COM   CHKDSK    COM   COMMAND   COM   COMP      COM   DISKCOMP  COM
DISKCOPY  COM   DRIVER    SYS   EDLIN     COM   FDISK     COM   FIND      EXE
FORMAT    COM   GRAFTABL  COM   GRAPHICS  COM   JOIN      EXE   KEYBFR    COM
KEYBGR    COM   KEYBIT    COM   KEYBSP    COM   KEYBUK    COM   LABEL     COM
MODE      COM   MORE      COM   PRINT     COM   RECOVER   COM   REPLACE   EXE
RESTORE   COM   SELECT    COM   SHARE     EXE   SORT      EXE   SUBST     EXE
SYS       COM   TREE      COM   VDISK     SYS   XCOPY     EXE   DEMO      BAK
AUTOEXEC  BAK   S-SAVE    COM   IMCAP     COM   SR        COM   VTREE     COM
DEMO      BAT   LOCATE    BAT   HELP      BAK   AUTOEXEC  BAT   CONFIG    SYS
       50 File(s)      2048 bytes free

A:\>_
```

Figure 10.7: Combinations in the PROMPT command

Complicated or long screen prompts can wrap around to a second screen line as you type them in, but you should not press the Return key to get to the second line. The Return key terminates your prompt-string input; DOS will wrap a multiple-line command request on its own.

Color monitors present other interesting alternatives. Using the color codes of Table 10.1 and the meta symbols of Table 10.2, it's easy to set any desired combination for foreground and background colors. For example, the following command will set a three-line prompt. The first line will contain the current directory (p). The carriage-return/line-feed sequence (_) ensures that the system date (d) appears on the next line. The time (t) and the > character (g) will be on the third line, and all succeeding text (including the future prompting strings) will be displayed as blue characters on a yellow background:

```
PROMPT $p$_$d$_$t$g$e[34;43m
```

A slight change to this command could give you similar information, while using reverse video for the special information only. In this way, the same PROMPT command could be used for both color and monochrome monitors. Notice in Figure 10.8 that the display of commands and output is in normal video, since the reverse-video code is reset immediately after the > symbol is output:

```
PROMPT $e[7m$p$_$d$_$t$g$e[0m
```

You may not like the multiline appearance of this information. You could just as easily put the same information on one line with the

```
C>PROMPT $e[7m$p$_$d$_$t$g$e[Øm

C:\PROGRAMS\FW\CHAPØ7
Tue  4-21-1987
18:43:Ø5.Ø1>DIR/W

 Volume in drive C is ROBBINS
 Directory of  C:\PROGRAMS\FW\CHAPØ7

.               ..              CHAPØ7   FW2     FIG7-1   TXT     FIG7-4   TXT
FIG7-5   CAP    FIG7-6   CAP    FIG7-7   TXT     FIG7-8   CAP     FIG7-9   TXT
FIG7-3B  TXT    FIG7-1Ø  TXT
       12 File(s)    1591296 bytes free

C:\PROGRAMS\FW\CHAPØ7
Tue  4-21-1987
18:43:13.36>VOL

 Volume in drive C is ROBBINS

C:\PROGRAMS\FW\CHAPØ7
Tue  4-21-1987
18:44:12.35>_
```

Figure 10.8: A three-line, reverse-video prompt

following variation:

```
PROMPT $e[7m$p  $d  $t$g$e[0m
```

The spaces in this command are critical to the separation of the directory name, date, and time. The results are shown in Figure 10.9.

There are many more fanciful things you can do with the PROMPT command to control the video display. The codes required would go well beyond the scope of this book, but you can manipulate the cursor and its location in a variety of ways.

Use the PROMPT command now to redefine your DOS prompt to provide more information. Issue the proper command to display the DOS version number on one line, the system date on the next line, and the current directory on the third line of this multiline prompt. On a fourth line, generate the text string

```
Enter next command, please :
```

If you have a monochrome monitor, have this message appear in reverse video. Remember to reset the video attribute so that the rest of the video display appears in normal video. If you have a color monitor, have this message appear as white letters on a red background.

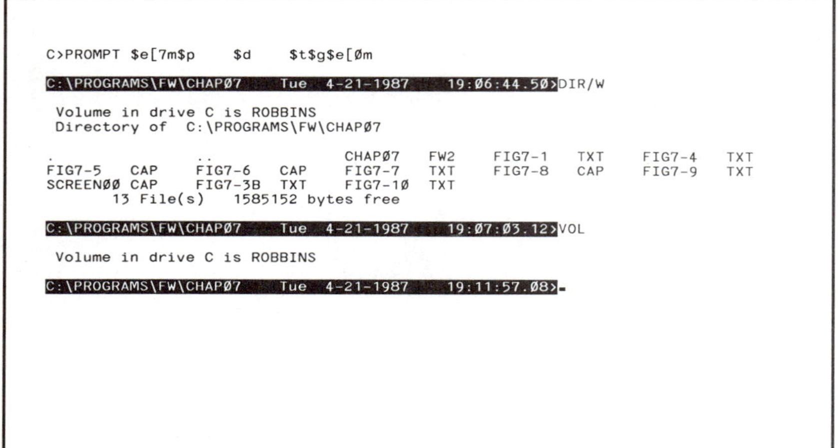

Figure 10.9: A one-line, reverse-video prompt

REDEFINING KEYS

As well as changing screen colors, you can use the ANSI system to reprogram some of your keys to type out commands or phrases. You can define any of the ASCII keys or the extended keyboard keys (F1–F10, Home, End, and so on). Some people have even used this technique to redefine individual keys to represent other individual keys, so that the keyboard assumes a different layout.

Like screen attributes, key reassignment begins with the special symbol for the Esc key ($e) and continues with the left bracket ([). If you want to assign new values to a normal key like the "a" key or the = key, you enter the ASCII value of the key, like 96 for the letter a or 61 for =. However, if you want to reassign values to the special keys on your keyboard (which is a more common goal), you must begin the key assignment with a zero and then follow it with the special code given the key by DOS (see Table 10.3).

For example, F10 has the reassignment code 68. Suppose that you wanted to have the F10 key automatically type the command DIR/W. You would enter

```
PROMPT $e[0;68;"DIR/W";13p
```

First, $e[tells DOS that an ANSI command is being entered. Next, 0

Function Key	**Redefinition Code**	**Function Key**	**Redefinition Code**
F1	59	Ctrl-F1	94
F2	60	Ctrl-F2	95
F3	61	Ctrl-F3	96
F4	62	Ctrl-F4	97
F5	63	Ctrl-F5	98
F6	64	Ctrl-F6	99
F7	65	Ctrl-F7	100
F8	66	Ctrl-F8	101
F9	67	Ctrl-F9	102
F10	68	Ctrl-F10	103
Shift-F1	84	Alt-F1	104
Shift-F2	85	Alt-F2	105
Shift-F3	86	Alt-F3	106
Shift-F4	87	Alt-F4	107
Shift-F5	88	Alt-F5	108
Shift-F6	89	Alt-F6	109
Shift-F7	90	Alt-F7	110
Shift-F8	91	Alt-F8	111
Shift-F9	92	Alt-F9	112
Shift-F10	93	Alt-F10	113

Table 10.3: Function-key redefinition codes

tells DOS that the key to be redefined is part of the extended keyboard. The 68 selects F10 as the key to be redefined. "DIR/W" is the text of the command. (Note that these text characters are enclosed in quotation marks to indicate that they are not codes for ANSI.SYS to interpret.) 13 is the code for the Return key, which is required after the DIR/W command, just as it would be if you typed in DIR/W at the keyboard yourself. The last character in a key redefinition is always p, just as the last character in the video redefinition was an m.

Try out this technique now. Use the ANSI.SYS system to program your F7 function key to perform a CHKDSK command. Don't forget to make sure you have a CONFIG.SYS file in your root directory, and be sure it contains a DEVICE specification that loads the ANSI.SYS driver.

Finally, some very fancy custom menu systems can be set up simply with the PROMPT command and a well-thought-out group of function-key assignments. There are ten function keys (F1–F10), ten shifted function keys, ten Ctrl–function-key combinations, and ten Alt–function-key combinations. These provide 40 assignment possibilities. The extended code numbers for redefining these keys are also shown in Table 10.3.

The following PROMPT commands redefine several keys. The first will cause the shifted F4 key to type FORMAT A:. The second will cause the Ctrl-F6 combination to type CHKDSK, and the third will cause the Alt-F8 combination to type CD \:

```
PROMPT $e[0;87;"FORMAT A:";13p
PROMPT $e[0;99;"CHKDSK";13p
PROMPT $e[0;111;"CD \";13p
```

Some programs reset the function-key definitions when they begin, and you will not be able to use the PROMPT command for key redefinition. When you encounter such a situation, the best solution is to purchase and use a keyboard redefinition program like Keyworks, which will allow you to redefine any key while another program is operating.

You must assign a key its original code value in order to reset it. The following sequence will reset all three of the example function-key sequences:

```
PROMPT $e[0;87;0;87p$e[0;99;0;99p$e[0;111;0;111p
```

The nicest thing about all these possibilities is that they are cumulative—that is, you can issue any number of key redefinition requests and they will accumulate. Until you reset each one, they will retain their new definitions while you are at the DOS prompt level.

SUMMARY

In this chapter, you've learned some very powerful methods in DOS to customize your system for both power and convenience:

- The CONFIG.SYS file permits you to initialize several internal DOS system variables at bootup time.

- The BUFFERS command defines precisely how many internal buffers DOS will use.
- The FILES command specifies the maximum allowable number of open files that DOS will understand and support while DOS and your application programs run.
- The DEVICE command allows you to incorporate any number of specialized peripheral device drivers into your DOS configuration.
- A RAM disk is a memory-resident simulation of a typical mechanical disk. It offers you increased system performance and speed.
- The ANSI.SYS device driver provides extraordinary controls over both the video monitor and the keyboard. It provides a number of special codes, which give you the ability to redefine any keys and to control the video output. Using these codes with the PROMPT command allows you to make your system more intelligent, useful, and fun to operate.

In the next chapter, you'll learn about another type of system configuration: initializing your keyboard and monitor to understand and display international character sets.

INTERNATIONAL SETUP OF DOS

CHAPTER 11

If you're a foreigner in the U.S., you can easily switch between the U.S. default key values and your own. In this way, you can avoid learning the U.S. keyboard layout in order to work on computers here. The same is true in reverse for Americans working abroad. This feature is explained in detail later in this chapter.

DIFFERENT COUNTRIES USE DIFFERENT SYMBOLS TO represent their own systems. For example, currency symbols differ among countries—the $ in the USA, the DM in Germany, and the F in France. Time formats also vary: the separator symbol between the hour and minutes is a colon in the U.S., but a period in Norway. Decimal numbers are also punctuated differently; in the U.S., they contain a period, but in Spain they contain a comma. You'll learn in this chapter how to set up your version of DOS to understand the default values for symbols used in different countries.

Different countries also employ different keyboard layouts. If you learned to type in the U.S. and then tried typing on a French typewriter or keyboard, you would type the letter A each time you meant to type a Q, and vice versa. This is because the key labeled A on an American keyboard is labeled Q on a French keyboard. You'll also learn in this chapter about the differences between keyboard layouts in different countries and how you can easily ask DOS to redefine all the keys properly. In addition, you'll learn how to rapidly switch between the various possible layouts.

This chapter presents the national language-support features found in DOS 3.3 only. You may need to make some adjustments to your system to improve the display and printout of foreign characters; the required steps will be presented later in this chapter.

CHARACTER SETS FOR DIFFERENT COUNTRIES

The group of characters used in a country or on a computer composes the character set of that country or computer. Most countries, like the United States and Great Britain, share a common set of characters. However, some countries have enough different characters and symbols to justify creating a special character set just for them.

Along with the different character sets comes different placement of the characters on a computer keyboard, which makes sense—commonly used elements must be easy to use. For example, on a French keyboard certain keys are reversed, and other keys facilitate the production of accented letters.

ASCII CODES

A computer does not interpret letters as letters per se, but assigns an ASCII code to each letter. These codes range from 0 to 255, representing the 256 possible combinations of binary digits contained in an eight bit byte.

Codes 0 through 31 are usually reserved for control codes, the codes that do not produce a visible character but perform some particular action. For example, printing the code 7 on most computers causes the computer to beep, and code 13 causes a carriage return. These codes control the functions of the hardware.

Codes 32 through 126 are standard characters and symbols (see Table 11.1). The capital alphabet starts at code 65, and the lowercase alphabet starts at code 97. Code 127 represents the deletion symbol. The control codes and the standard character codes together make up an entire set (from 0 to 127) called ASCII codes. The computer translates characters into these codes, and so does any other device using the characters. When a computer sends ASCII 65 to the printer, it expects an A to be printed out, so the printer must also translate from code 65 to A. You can see why it is important for these codes to be standardized; many pieces of equipment rely on the same code.

Codes 128 through 255 are computer/printer specific. IBM uses codes 128 through 255 for some graphics characters, while Epson, on some of its printers, uses them for italics.

The extended ASCII codes also represent certain specialized keys or key combinations, such as Alt-C or F1. These codes are defined by

HEX DIGITS	1st	0-	1-	2-	3-	4-	5-	6-	7-
2nd									
-0					0	@	P	’	p
-1				!	1	A	Q	a	q
-2				”	2	B	R	b	r
-3				#	3	C	S	c	s
-4				$	4	D	T	d	t
-5				%	5	E	U	e	u
-6				&	6	F	V	f	v
-7				‘	7	G	W	g	w
-8				(	8	H	X	h	x
-9				)	9	I	Y	i	y
-A				*	:	J	Z	j	z
-B				+	;	K	[	k	{
-C				,	<	L	\	l	¦
-D				-	=	M	]	m	}
-E				.	>	N	^	n	~
-F				/	?	O	_	o	⌂

Table 11.1: Standard ASCII characters and symbols

first sending an ASCII null character (code 0) to the device, and then another code. For example, sending code 0, then code 59 would have the same effect as pressing the F1 key.

The combinations of all these codes produce the complete visual and printed output you are used to seeing. Depending on where you live and work, however, you may have altogether different characters in your language and keys on your keyboard.

WHAT COUNTRY DO YOU CALL HOME?

When DOS boots up, the system date and time are queried. Everybody agrees that any given date has a month, a day, and a year, but not everyone agrees on that order. In the U.S., dates are shown with the month first, the day next, and the year last. In Europe, the day is shown first, the month next, and the year last. In the Far East, the year is first, the month next, and the day last. Hence, 11/04/07 can mean November 4, 1907; April 11, 1907; or April 7, 1911. It depends on who's writing the date *and* who's reading it. Again, that's why standards are so important.

The DATE function in DOS will display the system date according to the accepted custom in a specific country. Table 11.2 shows the countries currently understood by DOS, along with their country and keyboard codes. You'll learn later in this chapter how to set up your version of DOS to understand which country or keyboard is in use.

The order of the month, day, and year fields is only one of many things that differ among countries. Separator symbols between the month, day, and year values also vary from country to country. In fact, there are a host of special symbols that vary among countries: time separators (a colon or a period), list separators (a semicolon or a comma), decimal separators (a period or a comma), thousands separators (a comma or a period), and currency symbols ($, F, Fr, MK, DKR, and others). The U.S. shows time in 12-hour A.M./P.M. format, while most other countries use a 24-hour display. Most countries show two decimal places of accuracy in currency displays, while Italy shows none.

DOS maintains internal tables of these differing values according to which country has been set up as the system default. If you do nothing, the U.S. will be assumed to be the standard. However, if you wish to customize the system for some other country, you can simply use the proper country code from Table 11.2 to add a line to your CONFIG.SYS file:

```
COUNTRY = Code
```

Figure 11.1 shows the results of DOS date and time requests after the system CONFIG.SYS file was changed to a default of Switzerland (code 041).

Getting the date and time was easy in this example. The real value of the COUNTRY code in CONFIG.SYS can only be realized fully by programmers using specialized assembly-language techniques.

COUNTRY	COUNTRY CODE	KEYBOARD CODE
Arabic	785	
Australia	061	US
Belgium	032	BE
Canada (Eng.)	001	US
Canada (Fr.)	002	CF
Denmark	045	DK
Finland	358	SU
France	033	FR
Germany	049	GR
Hebrew	972	
Italy	039	IT
Latin America	003	LA
Netherlands	031	NL
Norway	047	NO
Portugal	351	PO
Spain	034	SP
Sweden	046	SV
Switzerland (Fr.)	041	SF
Switzerland (Ger.)	041	SG
United Kingdom	044	UK
United States	001	US

Table 11.2: International DOS country and keyboard codes

Thus, only a programmer can really obtain the specialized symbol and separator information necessary to customize an application program to the country it may run in. However, you can make a reasonable amount of adjustment yourself.

UNDERSTANDING CODE PAGES

DOS provides a complex ability to redefine its understanding of the keyboard you use. This is based on the new feature in DOS 3.3

called *code pages*. Code pages represent some complicated concepts, but with a little help and some extra knowledge, they can easily be understood. Let's start with the keyboard.

THE KEYBOARD TRANSLATION TABLE

The keyboard is simply a segregated group of buttons, monitored by a microprocessor that sends a signal to DOS when any key is pressed. The signal that goes to DOS is called a *scan code.* A scan code is not a letter or an ASCII code, but simply a code that tells DOS which key has been pressed. It has nothing to do with what is printed on the physical key, but merely with the physical location of the key.

During the entire process of handling each keyboard interrupt, DOS does not treat a scan code as any particular letter or symbol (such as the letter A), but simply as an ASCII code (such as 65).

At any time, whether DOS is busy or not, something will happen inside the computer when you press a key. This "something" is called an *interrupt.* One kind of interrupt occurs when a hardware device asks for the attention of the CPU. In the case of a keyboard, a small electrical signal—a scan code—is sent to DOS, indicating which key was pressed. The part of DOS that takes in the interrupt and processes it is called a *device driver* (or sometimes an *interrupt handler*).

When the keyboard device driver receives a signal, it processes the scan code to determine which key was pressed *and* to convert the scan code back into an ASCII code. This translation is done through a

```
C>TYPE \CONFIG.SYS
FILES=20
BUFFERS=15
DEVICE=C:\DOS\ANSI.SYS
COUNTRY=041

C>DATE
Current date is Thu  7.05.1987
Enter new date (dd-mm-yy):

C>TIME
Current time is 17.36.46.15
Enter new time:

C>_
```

Figure 11.1: Date and time requests for COUNTRY = Switzerland

table in memory that compares scan codes and ASCII codes. Figure 11.2 diagrams this process.

Take a look at the two different Personal System/2 keyboards used in the United States and France, shown in Figures 11.3 and 11.4. There are more than fifty other keyboard layouts in use on different computers in different countries. All of these are understood by DOS; the complete layouts for these alternatives are displayed in your DOS user's manual.

On a U.S. keyboard, if you press A, its scan code will be translated into ASCII code 65. However, if you hit the same key on a computer with a French keyboard translation routine embedded in the device driver, the same scan code will be converted to ASCII code 81, or the letter Q.

If a key combination such as Alt-Ctrl-2 is pressed with the U.S. translator installed, not much will happen, because the U.S. keyboard translator does not have an entry in its table for this scan code. However, if you press this key combination on a computer with the French keyboard translator in effect, you will get the @ symbol. The French translator understands this scan code and will match it up. The ASCII code generated will be 64, which is the same code

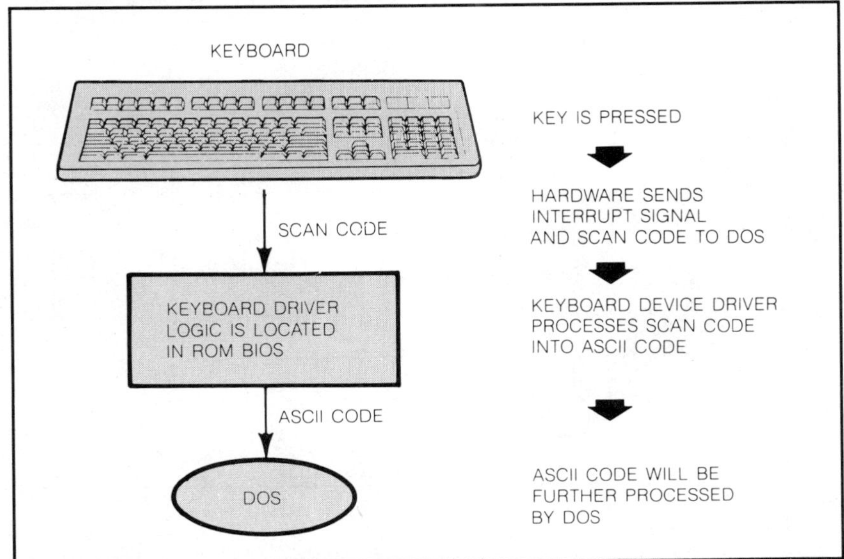

Figure 11.2: Processing keyboard interrupts

generated by pressing Shift-2 with a U.S. keyboard translator. Both yield the same @ symbol. The two keyboard translation tables translate different keyboard scan codes to the same ASCII codes, allowing countries with different keyboards to use all the same characters, even though the keys are labeled differently. Countries that have different keyboard layouts but still use the same character set are grouped into the same code page.

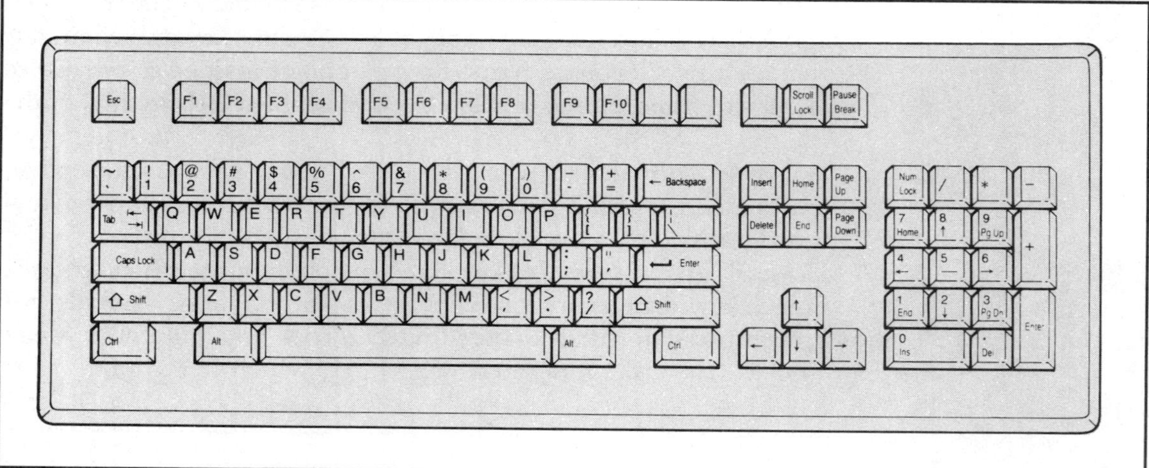

Figure 11.3: U.S. Personal System/2 keyboard

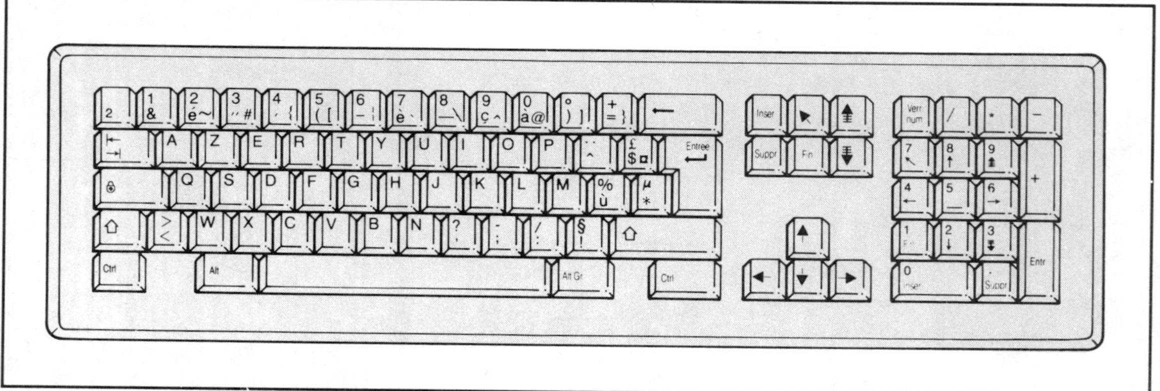

Figure 11.4: French Personal System/2 keyboard

CODE PAGES

After interpreting what key was pressed on the keyboard and converting the scan code into an ASCII code by means of a translation table, DOS next determines where the ASCII code should go. If it goes to a disk drive, it is simply routed there and stored on the disk. If, however, it is destined for a monitor or printer, it is first processed by a code page. A code page is yet another translation table that converts an ASCII code into a printable or displayable character.

There are five code pages available in DOS. The standard code page (numbered 437 in DOS) for the United States can be seen in Table 11.3. (Refer to Appendix C for a complete explanation of the hexadecimal system shown in this table, as well as other number systems.) The other principal code page is the Multilingual code page, numbered 850 (see Table 11.4). It contains a host of international characters.

You'll soon learn how to use and switch between these code pages, as well as the other three code pages also available in DOS (Portuguese, Norwegian, and Canadian French). See your DOS user's

HEX DIGITS 1st / 2nd	0-	1-	2-	3-	4-	5-	6-	7-	8-	9-	A-	B-	C-	D-	E-	F-
0-		►		0	@	P	`	p	Ç	É	á	░	└	╨	α	≡
1-	☺	◄	!	1	A	Q	a	q	ü	æ	í	▒	┴	╤	β	±
2-	☻	↕	"	2	B	R	b	r	é	Æ	ó	▓	┬	╥	Γ	≥
3-	♥	‼	#	3	C	S	c	s	â	ô	ú	│	├	╙	π	≤
4-	♦	¶	$	4	D	T	d	t	ä	ö	ñ	┤	─	╘	Σ	⌠
5-	♣	§	%	5	E	U	e	u	à	ò	Ñ	╡	┼	╒	σ	⌡
6-	♠	▬	&	6	F	V	f	v	å	û	ª	╢	╞	╓	µ	÷
7-	•	↨	'	7	G	W	g	w	ç	ù	º	╖	╟	╫	τ	≈
8-	◘	↑	(	8	H	X	h	x	ê	ÿ	¿	╕	╚	╪	Φ	°
9-	○	↓	)	9	I	Y	i	y	ë	Ö	⌐	╣	╔	┘	Θ	•
A-	◙	→	*	:	J	Z	j	z	è	Ü	¬	║	╩	┌	Ω	·
B-	♂	←	+	;	K	[	k	{	ï	¢	½	╗	╦	█	δ	√
C-	♀	∟	,	<	L	\	l	|	î	£	¼	╝	╠	▄	∞	ⁿ
D-	♪	↔	-	=	M	]	m	}	ì	¥	¡	╜	═	▌	φ	²
E-	♫	▲	.	>	N	^	n	~	Ä	Pt	«	╛	╬	▐	ε	■
F-	☼	▼	/	?	O	_	o	⌂	Å	ƒ	»	┐	╧	▀	∩	

Table 11.3: Code page 437 for the United States

HEX DIGITS 1st / 2nd	0-	1-	2-	3-	4-	5-	6-	7-	8-	9-	A-	B-	C-	D-	E-	F-
0-		►		0	@	P	`	p	Ç	É	á	░	└	ð	Ó	-
1-	☺	◄	!	1	A	Q	a	q	ü	æ	í	▒	┴	Đ	β	±
2-	☻	↕	"	2	B	R	b	r	é	Æ	ó	▓	┬	Ê	Ô	=
3-	♥	‼	#	3	C	S	c	s	â	ô	ú	│	├	Ë	Ò	¾
4-	♦	¶	$	4	D	T	d	t	ä	ö	ñ	┤	─	È	õ	¶
5-	♣	§	%	5	E	U	e	u	à	ò	Ñ	Á	┼	ı	Õ	§
6-	♠	▬	&	6	F	V	f	v	å	û	ª	Â	ã	Í	µ	÷
7-	•	↨	'	7	G	W	g	w	ç	ù	º	À	Ã	Î	þ	¸
8-	◘	↑	(	8	H	X	h	x	ê	ÿ	¿	©	╚	Ï	Þ	°
9-	○	↓	)	9	I	Y	i	y	ë	Ö	®	╣	╔	┘	Ú	¨
A-	◙	→	*	:	J	Z	j	z	è	Ü	¬	║	╩	┌	Û	·
B-	♂	←	+	;	K	[	k	{	ï	ø	½	╗	╦	█	Ù	¹
C-	♀	∟	,	<	L	\	l	|	î	£	¼	╝	╠	▄	ý	³
D-	♪	↔	-	=	M	]	m	}	ì	Ø	¡	¢	═	¦	Ý	²
E-	♫	▲	.	>	N	^	n	~	Ä	×	«	¥	╬	Ì	¯	■
F-	☼	▼	/	?	O	_	o	⌂	Å	ƒ	»	┐	¤	▀	´	

Table 11.4: Code page 850 for multilingual operations

manual for the precise layouts of these remaining code pages.

Code pages are simply character sets. As you saw in the last section, one character set (code page) can satisfy the needs of several different countries. Countries with significantly different character sets and keyboards are grouped into other code pages. The 21 different country codes (shown in Table 11.2) correlate altogether with, at most, five different character sets, so only five different code pages are needed. Remember, a code page has 256 entries, so even if in the U.S. you rarely use an accented e, it is included in one of the extra spaces in the U.S. character set.

After the scan code has been translated into an ASCII code, it is matched to the currently active code-page translation table. Now you're into the output side of DOS management. The device driver responsible for the output device now uses built-in logic to send a sequence of control instructions to the output device. These instructions describe precisely how to display the character that was represented by the ASCII code. The process by which DOS and the output device drivers convert the ASCII code to visual output is shown in Figure 11.5.

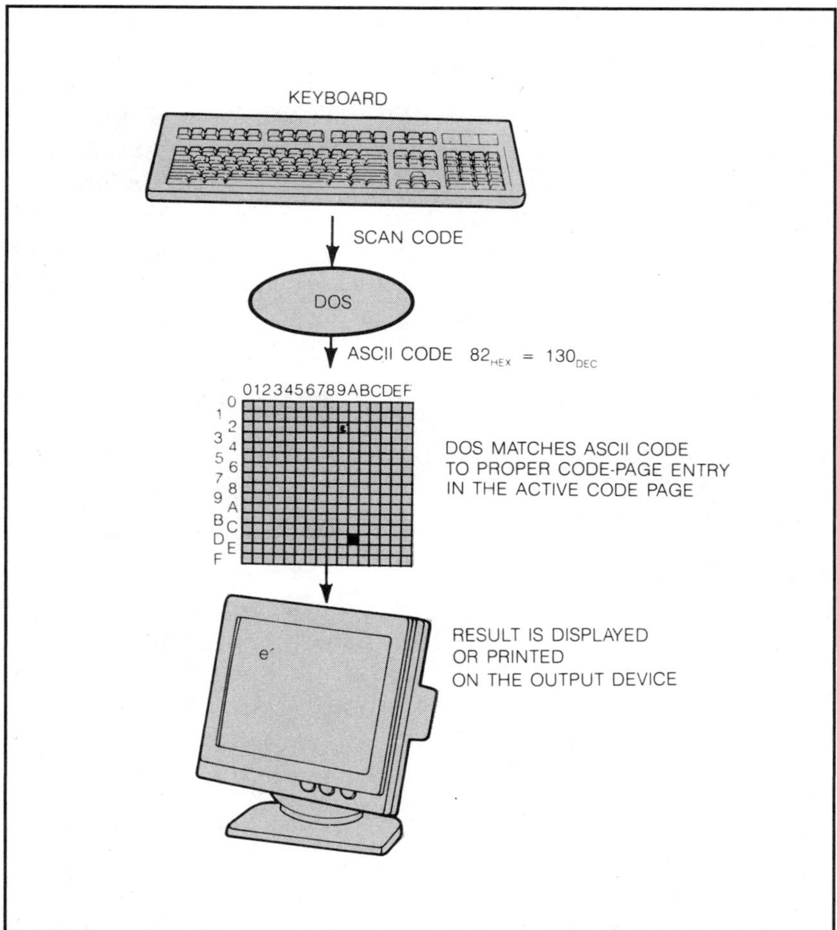

Figure 11.5: Code pages and device drivers control output

DEVICES AND THEIR DRIVERS

All output consists of sequences of codes being sent to an output device like a monitor or printer. Unfortunately, not all monitors or printers act the same, have the same features, or can be controlled by the same device driver. In fact, sometimes the device driver consists of software instructions residing in your computer's main memory, while at other times these instructions reside in special memory built into the output device. Microsoft provides device drivers for two printers, the IBM Proprinter Model 4201 and the IBM Quietwriter III Printer Model 5202, as well as device drivers for the PC Convertible display (LCD) and the Enhanced Graphics Adapter used on the PC-XT, PC-AT, and Personal System/2 displays.

Each output device driver translates the requested output data into the specific commands needed to form the character for each device. Figure 11.6 shows this part of the process. As the figure suggests, you must have one of the special monitors or printers to access any special additional symbols available in DOS 3.3's four code pages other than the U.S. page.

TRANSLATION TABLES AND DEVICE DRIVERS

DOS supports more than 50 different keyboard layouts and 11 languages. Microsoft has supplied all of the necessary keyboard

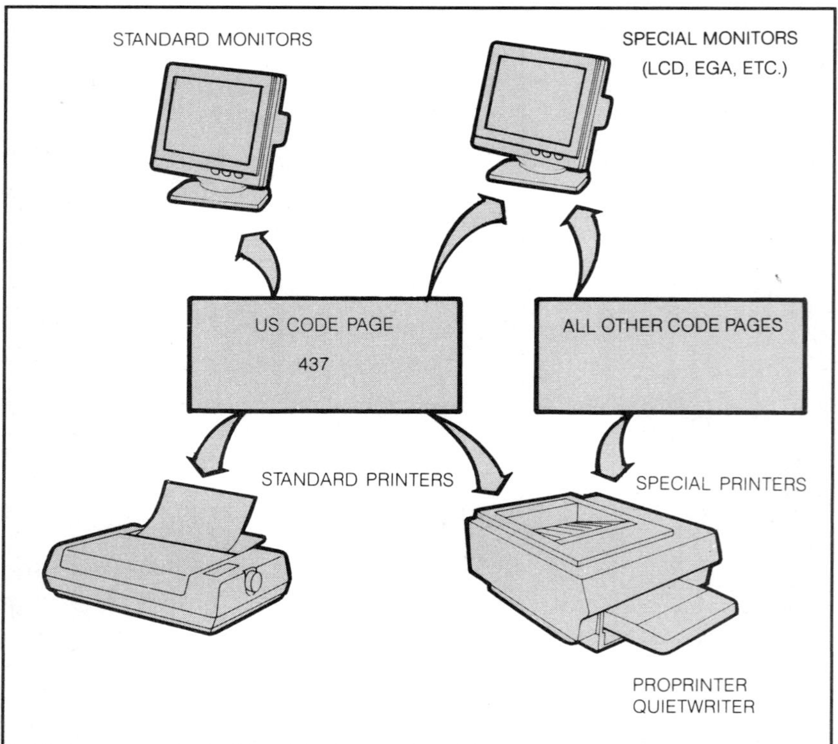

Figure 11.6: Sending output to standard and special devices

Some computers manufactured solely for foreign use have the foreign character set built in, as well as a keyboard with the appropriate key labels in place. These computers will not respond at all when you try to switch keyboard layouts with either the KEYB command or the Ctrl-Alt-function key combinations. No logic has been included to load in additional keyboard tables, since the necessary non-U.S. tables are already there.

translation tables in a file called KEYBOARD.SYS, which is loaded into the computer by using the KEYB command at the DOS prompt.

The output device drivers are loaded into memory from individual files. They are contained on the IBM startup disk in the files 4201.CPI, 5202.CPI, EGA.CPI, and LCD.CPI. CPI stands for code-page information; 4201 and 5202 refer to the IBM Proprinter and the IBM Quietwriter III Printer, respectively. EGA refers to both the standard Enhanced Graphics Adapter and the IBM Personal System/2 display types, while LCD will drive the IBM Convertible's LCD screen.

As you know, a DOS device driver has five different code pages to choose from. Each of these is referred to by a unique number, as shown in Table 11.5. Since code page 437 is the standard U.S. code page that is used with any monitor, 437 is the default when DOS boots up. This is the only code page that can be used with devices other than the two printers and two monitors supported by the drivers included with DOS 3.3 (see Figure 11.6).

Figure 11.7 ties all of the preceding sections together. It shows the entire process of moving information from beginning to end—from the keyboard interrupt to the final display or printed output.

Let's quickly run through a last example of the process. Assume you've loaded the Canadian French keyboard translation table into the computer (you'll learn how to do this in the next section). You've also loaded code page 863 and the 4201.CPI device driver, as you wish to print a character on the Proprinter. The character you want to print is the 3/4 symbol, which is not included in the normal ASCII

LANGUAGE	CODE PAGE
United States	437
Multilingual	850
Portuguese	860
Canadian French	863
Norwegian and Danish	865

Table 11.5: Code-page identification numbers

character set of U.S. computers or printers. The 3/4 symbol on the Canadian keyboard can be printed by using the key combination Alt-Shift- = .

When this key combination is pressed, a scan code is sent to the keyboard device driver, which routes the scan code to the keyboard

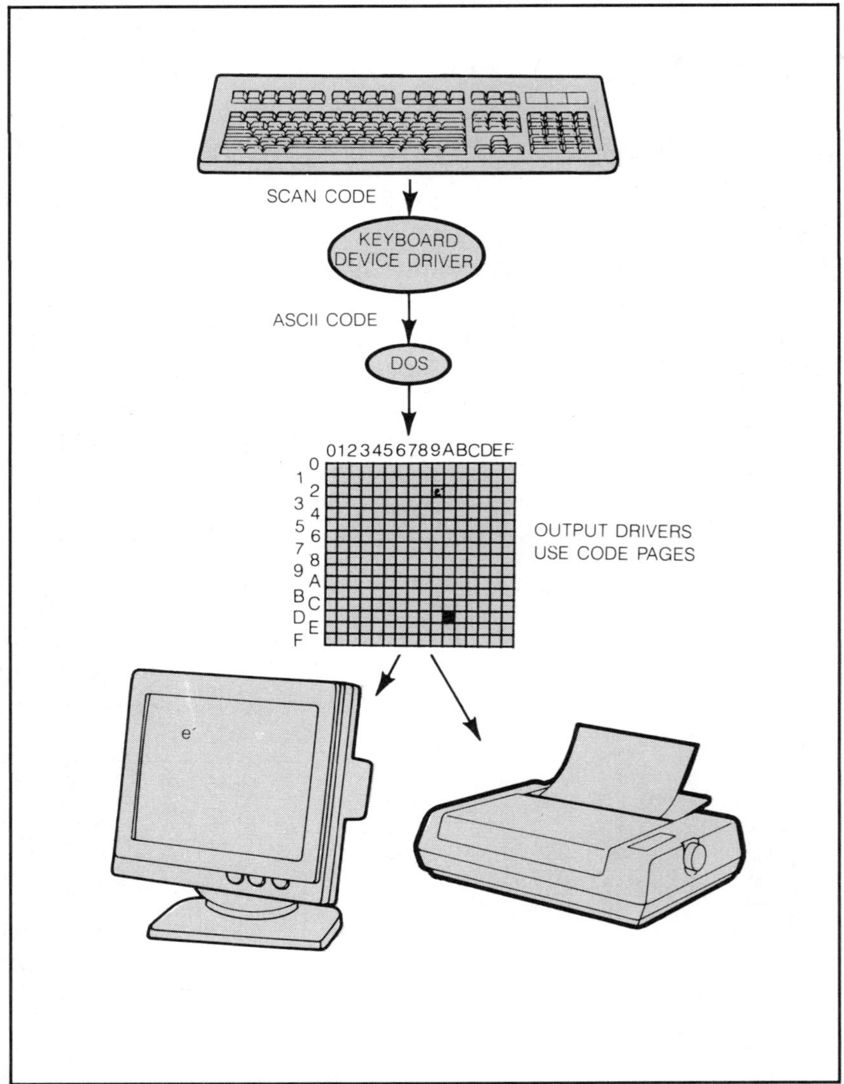

Figure 11.7: The overall code-page process

translation table. Here, the scan code is matched against the ASCII table, and an ASCII code (in this case, 173) is sent back to DOS. DOS sees that this character was destined for the printer and sends it on its way. The code is now processed by the Proprinter, which uses the installed code page. The Proprinter's driver now translates ASCII 173 to a set of hardware instructions that describe how to print a 3/4 symbol.

WORKING WITH CODE PAGES

Now that you understand how code pages are used, you must learn the required sequence of DOS 3.3 commands necessary to implement them. You first need to learn how to tell DOS that you will be using the national language-support scheme (NLS), which is just another name for the code-page mechanism. You also need to learn how to prepare, select, and switch between the various code pages. The following sections will teach you the mechanics of the process. Figure 11.8 provides an overview of the DOS command sequences necessary for a complete international setup, which you will explore in this chapter.

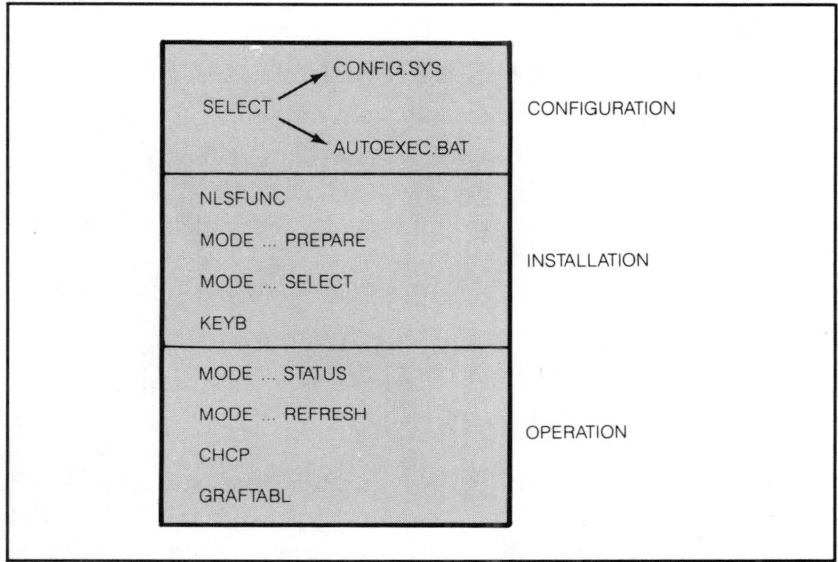

Figure 11.8: Command overview for international DOS operations

LOADING CODE-PAGE SUPPORT ROUTINES

NLSFUNC (short for national language-support functions) is a DOS 3.3 command that allows for the use of the new extended country information provided with DOS 3.3. This command will load in all of the required country-specific information. It must be run *before* you attempt to select any code page other than the default (437). As part of the format for the NLSFUNC command, you must tell DOS where you've placed the COUNTRY.SYS file. This file contains information that defines the country standards, such as the date and time format, the rules of capitalization, and special symbol usage for each of the 21 available country codes (see Table 11.2). U.S. standards will be assumed if you neglect to specify the location of the COUNTRY.SYS file.

Assuming you have created a DOS directory that contains COUNTRY.SYS, the command can be invoked as simply as

```
NLSFUNC \DOS\COUNTRY.SYS
```

The code-page support routines will be loaded into memory. No direct action or messages will be shown on the screen.

LOADING SPECIFIC CODE PAGES

After preparing DOS for national language-support operations, you can select specific code pages to use. The primary command for this purpose is a familiar one: MODE. In DOS 3.3 this command has several versions. They all have a similar format:

MODE *DeviceName* CODEPAGE *Clause*

DeviceName is any valid DOS output reserved name, such as CON or LPT2. *Clause* represents a parameter you can use with several different values:

- You can load the desired code pages with a PREPARE parameter; you specify that one to five code pages be available for output operations.

- Use the SELECT parameter to choose which of the code pages is to be the active one for a particular output device.
- Use the /STATUS parameter to display the status of all code pages and connected output devices supporting code-page operations.
- For advanced output devices that retain code-page information in memory located within the device itself (as opposed to main memory), use the REFRESH parameter to restore the information in case the device is turned off or loses power.

Let's discuss the processing managed by the MODE command in a bit more depth. You first use the PREPARE parameter to install the code-page information necessary for the output drivers to handle the special international characters. With the SELECT parameter you then select the code page to be activated on the specified device. This means you can have several code pages loaded into the device at once, but only one can be active at any one time. At any time, you can use the /STATUS parameter to display the active code page and all of the other code pages available. Finally, with REFRESH you can reinstall the currently active output driver into the specified device if it was erased due to power loss.

With the PREPARE parameter, you can load one or several code pages for a device with one MODE command. This requires that you specify the device reserved name, the list of allowable code pages (one or more), and the file containing the output driver. Code page 437 is the default code page; it is automatically loaded into the device. 437 is also the only code page that can access a nonspecified device (that is, one that IBM has not specifically written drivers for).

Think of it this way. A small buffer is set up for each device, and into this buffer can go from one to five code-page specifications, one of which is active at a time. For example, entering

```
MODE CON CODEPAGE PREPARE = ((850,437)
C:\DOS\EGA.CPI)
```

will load the code-page information file EGA.CPI, specify that code pages 850 and 437 be selected for possible activation, and attach these code-page values to the EGA display.

Suppose that later you decide that you want to replace 850 with 863, and that also you want to make code page 865 available. You would enter

```
MODE CON CODEPAGE PREPARE = ((863,,865)
C:\DOS\EGA.CPI)
```

The two commas hold the place of the second code page, thereby leaving 437 (the U.S. code page) as the second code page. If you had specified ((,850,437) instead, then the first code page would have been saved and the second and third written over and reset to 850 and 437.

In all versions of the MODE command, CODEPAGE can be contracted to CP. In addition, PREPARE can be abbreviated to PREP, SELECT to SEL, REFRESH to REF, and STATUS to STA. You can reduce your typing burden by using these abbreviations, as well as saving time and reducing the likelihood of errors. The full spelling is shown in this chapter for the sake of clarity only.

If you execute this command and the requested device is unavailable (not hooked up), you will get the message

```
Codepage operation not supported on this device
```

Assuming you really do have a device that supports code-page operations, check to see that it is connected properly to your system, that it is powered up, and that it is on-line.

The next parameter for the international version of the MODE command can only be used after you have properly prepared your code pages with PREPARE; the SELECT parameter will only work if the requested code-page device driver has been loaded. SELECT activates the specified code page on the specified device. For example, entering

If the device driver for your output device is resident in hardware, using PREPARE is unnecessary, since it will overwrite the hardware page. See your DOS user's manual for more detail on hardware code pages.

```
MODE CON CODEPAGE SELECT = 850
```

will make code page 850 the active code page for the console or the display device. Using this parameter in the previous example would make 850 active for an EGA display.

When you want to see information on the currently active code page, as well as a list of selectable code pages for a specific active device, you only need to enter

```
MODE CON CODEPAGE /STATUS
```

DOS will display information about the current code page assigned to the monitor and keyboard.

The last parameter, REFRESH, is very useful if for some reason you need to turn your printer off. The output device drivers stay resident inside the device they drive. The available code pages and their related information are available through DOS, which is resident in your computer. So, when a device driver is installed, a copy is made of the code-page information in the computer and loaded into the memory of the device. If the device is turned off, then its memory is lost, and hence its modified driver. However, the original copy is still in the computer's memory. Instead of having to load the code page again with PREPARE, REFRESH just makes another copy and sends it out to the device's memory.

For example, suppose you've entered the following sequence of commands:

```
MODE LPT1 CODEPAGE PREPARE=((850,437)
\DOS\4201.CPI)
MODE LPT1 CODEPAGE SELECT=850
```

This means you have installed code-page information for the IBM 4201 Proprinter and that you have two code pages to choose from, with 850 the currently active code page. Selecting a code page (with SELECT) causes the code-page driver to be copied into the hardware device (in this case, the printer connected to LPT1). Now, if you decide to turn the Proprinter off and then back on (perhaps to reset some switches), it would lose its local memory copy of the code-page information. To reload the code-page driver without spending the system's time to retrieve it from the disk, you would issue the command

```
MODE LPT1 CODEPAGE REFRESH
```

LOADING A KEYBOARD TRANSLATION TABLE

You have properly prepared your system to use national language support with the NLSFUNC command. You have also correctly installed the desired code-page information with MODE's PREPARE parameter, and you have selected a specific code page to use with MODE's SELECT parameter. The next step involves the KEYB command. This command is used to load in a new keyboard translation table for a specific country. In fact, it loads in a complete replacement for the keyboard driver resident in your computer's hardware (ROM BIOS). You can now select from the 21 different country codes you saw in Table 11.2.

If you were using alternate character sets in previous versions of DOS, then you need to use code page 850 in DOS 3.3, since the character sets and keyboard layouts of the previous versions are incompatible with this version (see Table 11.6).

Country	Keyboard Code	Existing Code Page	New Code Page
Australia	US	437	850
Belgium	BE	437	850
Canada—English	US	437	850
Canada—French	CF	863	850
Denmark	DK	865	850
Finland	SU	437	850
France	FR	437	850
Germany	GR	437	850
Italy	IT	437	850
Latin America	LA	437	850
Netherlands	NL	437	850
Norway	NO	865	850
Portugal	PO	860	850
Spain	SP	437	850
Sweden	SV	437	850
Switzerland—French	SF	437	850
Switzerland—German	SG	437	850
United Kingdom	UK	437	850
United States	US	437	850

Table 11.6: Old versus new code-page conversion table

The Multilingual code page (850) can support the primary character symbols used by all countries. If you switch between documents from different countries, it would be a good idea to load in code page 850 in addition to your native code page so that you can view these other documents.

The general format for the KEYB command is

KEYB *KeyCode, CodePage, FileSpec*

where *KeyCode* is one of the two-letter country codes in Table 11.2, *CodePage* is one of the five three-digit code-page numbers, and *FileSpec* is the full path name to the keyboard definition file KEYBOARD-.SYS. For example, entering the command

```
KEYB NL, 850, \DOS\KEYBOARD.SYS
```

will load the Netherlands keyboard translation table, based on code page 850, which is contained in the KEYBOARD.SYS file. Located in the DOS directory, the KEYBOARD.SYS file contains all of the keyboard translation tables for all possible countries.

Once you complete this initialization, the keys on the keyboard will no longer necessarily result in the letter, number, or character shown on the key. The assumption is that you will be using one of the scores of different keyboard layouts, each with its own key labels. In fact, if you're taking advantage of the keyboard reconfiguration capability but you are still using your original keyboard, it's a good idea to get new key labels, switch the key labels around, or simply to put new labels on the keys that have been changed.

There are often more accented characters than there are possible keys to assign. In this case, DOS understands special two-key sequences to represent the specially accented character. For instance, certain foreign letters require a circumflex over them. On the French keyboard, this symbol looks like the control, or "hat," symbol located over the 6 on the top row of a U.S. keyboard. In order to create this particular language-dependent effect, you must press the lowercase key just to the right of the letter p and *then* press the letter you want to put the circumflex over. In other words, you must employ a two-keystroke sequence to generate the two-part character symbol.

The set of these special keys that initiate a two-part character sequence are referred to as *dead keys* in DOS. If you make a mistake in typing the sequence, DOS will usually beep at you, show the erroneous result, and require you to erase the error and reenter the proper dead-key sequence. In this way, DOS provides yet another time-saving capability with the KEYB command, which saves you from having to touch up your text results with added accents and other special marks after the fact.

You can have up to two keyboard translation tables in memory at one time, but one of these must always be the standard U.S. table. To switch between the U.S. and another translation table, use these key combinations:

- Ctrl-Alt-F1 for the standard U.S. translation table
- Ctrl-Alt-F2 for a non-U.S. translation table

SWITCHING BETWEEN AVAILABLE CODE PAGES

Now that your system is prepared for code pages and you've selected one to be active, there may be times when you'd like to switch to a different code page. You'll need to do this when you are switching between documents written by personnel either in or for different contries. The CHCP command allows you to change the currently loaded code page. It is a very simple command to use. By issuing the command

```
CHCP 850
```

you can replace the currently active code page with code page 850. Any of the other four possible code-page numbers can be used if they have been properly prepared with the MODE command first.

If you only want to change the code page on a particular device, use the MODE command with SELECT. Use the CHCP command to change all prepared code-page devices at once.

The CHCP command does not have a parameter indicating which output device is being selected. That's because CHCP works on all prepared output devices, changing the active code page on all of them to the requested number.

DISPLAYING EXTENDED ASCII CODES ON A COLOR GRAPHICS ADAPTER

A CGA monitor shows less detail than EGA, PGA, and VGA monitors because it has fewer pixels. When your CGA monitor is in graphics mode, you must use the GRAFTABL command in order to display the nonstandard characters with ASCII codes above 128. Entering

```
GRAFTABL 860
```

will load the Portugese code page and display the following message:

```
Portugese Version of Graphic Character Set Table has just been
  Loaded.
```

This means that the characters—whether graphics symbols or national symbols—that occupy the ASCII codes above code 128 will be accessible, and the ones displayed will be those from the special Portuguese code page.

To dramatize the necessity of this command, Figure 11.9 shows the extended ASCII codes for the U.S. code page when a CGA

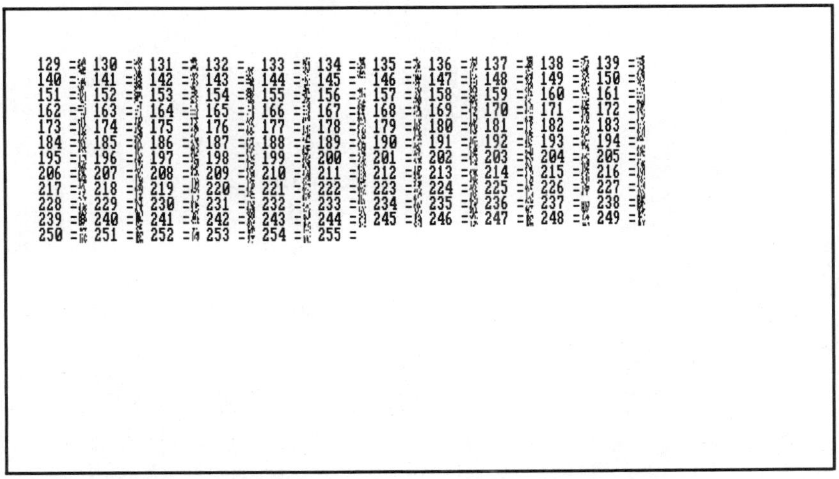

```
129 = 130 = 131 = 132 = 133 = 134 = 135 = 136 = 137 = 138 = 139 =
140 = 141 = 142 = 143 = 144 = 145 = 146 = 147 = 148 = 149 = 150 =
151 = 152 = 153 = 154 = 155 = 156 = 157 = 158 = 159 = 160 = 161 =
162 = 163 = 164 = 165 = 166 = 167 = 168 = 169 = 170 = 171 = 172 =
173 = 174 = 175 = 176 = 177 = 178 = 179 = 180 = 181 = 182 = 183 =
184 = 185 = 186 = 187 = 188 = 189 = 190 = 191 = 192 = 193 = 194 =
195 = 196 = 197 = 198 = 199 = 200 = 201 = 202 = 203 = 204 = 205 =
206 = 207 = 208 = 209 = 210 = 211 = 212 = 213 = 214 = 215 = 216 =
217 = 218 = 219 = 220 = 221 = 222 = 223 = 224 = 225 = 226 = 227 =
228 = 229 = 230 = 231 = 232 = 233 = 234 = 235 = 236 = 237 = 238 =
239 = 240 = 241 = 242 = 243 = 244 = 245 = 246 = 247 = 248 = 249 =
250 = 251 = 252 = 253 = 254 = 255 =
```

Figure 11.9: Extended ASCII codes before GRAFTABL is used

You should only consider using the GRAFTABL command if you run programs that set the video mode to graphics. Otherwise, you lose the memory occupied by the alternate character set and gain nothing in return.

monitor is in graphics mode. As you can see, the characters are indecipherable. After GRAFTABL 437 is executed, however, the codes are displayable, as shown in Figure 11.10.

If you use this command, make sure that the path is set properly for finding it. Also make sure that you run the GRAFTABL command *before* invoking the programs that use the CGA graphics mode. Naturally, if you will be facing this problem on a regular basis, you should add the GRAFTABL command to your AUTOEXEC.BAT file (you will learn how later in this chapter).

PREPARING AN INTERNATIONAL DOS SYSTEM DISK

DOS provides a special command, SELECT, which can save you a good deal of trouble if your principal goal is to have a system disk that supports code-page switching. With the following methods and commands, the delimiter format and keyboard information for each country can be installed permanently on a disk.

INSTALLING COUNTRY AND KEYBOARD INFORMATION

The SELECT command expects to read all the necessary DOS information from your startup and operating disks, now located on a diskette on drive A or B. It will manage the formatting of the destination disk and the copying of all necessary DOS files onto this other disk. (The destination disk must not be the same as the source disk.) You must specify the desired three-digit country code and the two-letter keyboard code, both from the list in Table 11.2.

The required format of the SELECT command is

SELECT *Source Destination xxx yy*

Source is either A or B; it must contain the KEYBOARD.SYS, COUNTRY.SYS, FORMAT.COM, and XCOPY.EXE files. *Destination* is the drive and path to which the DOS command files will be copied. (The root directory is the default, but if you use the SELECT command to set up a hard disk, you would be advised to arrange a

```
129 =ü 130 =é 131 =â 132 =ä 133 =à 134 =å 135 =ç 136 =ê 137 =ë 138 =è 139 =ï
140 =î 141 =ì 142 =Ä 143 =Å 144 =É 145 =æ 146 =Æ 147 =ô 148 =ö 149 =ò 150 =û
151 =ù 152 =ÿ 153 =Ö 154 =Ü 155 =¢ 156 =£ 157 =¥ 158 =₧ 159 =ƒ 160 =á 161 =í
162 =ó 163 =ú 164 =ñ 165 =Ñ 166 =ª 167 =º 168 =¿ 169 =⌐ 170 =¬ 171 =½ 172 =¼
173 =¡ 174 =« 175 =» 176 =░ 177 =▒ 178 =▓ 179 =│ 180 =┤ 181 =╡ 182 =╢ 183 =╖
184 =╕ 185 =╣ 186 =║ 187 =╗ 188 =╝ 189 =╜ 190 =╛ 191 =┐ 192 =└ 193 =┴ 194 =┬
195 =├ 196 =─ 197 =┼ 198 =╞ 199 =╟ 200 =╚ 201 =╔ 202 =╩ 203 =╦ 204 =╠ 205 =═
206 =╬ 207 =╧ 208 =╨ 209 =╤ 210 =╥ 211 =╙ 212 =╘ 213 =╒ 214 =╓ 215 =╫ 216 =╪
217 =┘ 218 =┌ 219 =█ 220 =▄ 221 =▌ 222 =▐ 223 =▀ 224 =α 225 =ß 226 =Γ 227 =π
228 =Σ 229 =σ 230 =µ 231 =τ 232 =Φ 233 =Θ 234 =Ω 235 =δ 236 =∞ 237 =φ 238 =ε
239 =∩ 240 =≡ 241 =± 242 =≥ 243 =≤ 244 =⌠ 245 =⌡ 246 =÷ 247 =≈ 248 =° 249 =∙
250 =· 251 =√ 252 =ⁿ 253 =² 254 =■ 255 =
```

Figure 11.10: Extended ASCII codes after GRAFTABL is used

specialized subdirectory to hold the appropriate files.) The *xxx* is the country code, and the *yy* is the keyboard code. Since the U.S. keyboard file is resident in the computer's memory, it does not need to be on the source disk.

If you are using a high-density drive as the destination drive for the SELECT command, you *must* use high-capacity diskettes. Also, since the SELECT command uses the FORMAT command, anything on the destination disk will be destroyed during the preparation of the disk. If you prepare a hard-disk drive in this way, you must be careful.

When you first execute SELECT, the following message appears on the screen:

```
SELECT is used to install DOS the first time. SELECT erases
everything on the specified target and then installs DOS.
Do you want to continue (Y/N)?
```

Entering Y will start the process, while N will abort it.

Here is an example of the SELECT command. Entering

```
SELECT B: C:\JUDD 001 US
```

will format and copy the DOS commands files to drive C, directory JUDD, executed from drive B, and install drive C with the U.S. rules for the date, time, and so on.

The SELECT command will also create two files on the destination disk. These are an initial AUTOEXEC.BAT file:

```
PATH \;\JUDD;
KEYB US 437 \JUDD\KEYBOARD.SYS
```

```
ECHO OFF
CLS
DATE
TIME
VER
```

and the CONFIG.SYS file:

```
COUNTRY = 001,437,\JUDD\COUNTRY.SYS
```

The next section provides more details about these two files. SELECT will also copy all of the contents of the source disk, including COMMAND.COM, into the specified directory. The six files that must be accessible on your source drive for this command to work are COMMAND.COM, FORMAT.COM, SELECT.COM, XCOPY.EXE, KEYBOARD.SYS, and, finally, COUNTRY.SYS.

MODIFYING THE REQUIRED SYSTEM FILES YOURSELF

The CONFIG.SYS and AUTOEXEC.BAT files can contain statements that will automate some of this setup for you if you don't want to rely on SELECT alone. You've already read about using CONFIG.SYS, and you'll read about AUTOEXEC.BAT in more detail in Chapter 15. You can make these adjustments with your own word processor, with DOS's EDLIN editor, or by using the COPY command. COPY can be used to add a line (say, *FileName*) to any ASCII file in the following way. You can type the command

COPY *FileName* + CON

When you are done entering lines to be added, press Ctrl-Z and Return. You will now be back at the DOS prompt.

UPDATING THE CONFIG.SYS FILE FOR INTERNATIONAL SUPPORT

The DEVICE configuration command in CONFIG.SYS can be used to load the various drivers needed for code-page switching.

Assuming you have typed the above command or are in an editor and are creating or modifying a CONFIG.SYS file, adding the following lines will install the various required drivers. In these cases, you need a different DEVICE line in your CONFIG.SYS for each different printer and display device.

The sample entry

DEVICE = *D:*\DISPLAY.SYS CON: = (*Type,Hwcp,x*)

in your CONFIG.SYS file loads the specialized display device drivers. *D* is the location of the DISPLAY.SYS file. *Type* is either LCD or EGA, depending on the display being used. *Hwcp* is the code-page number(s) supported directly by the hardware device, and *x* is how many code pages will be added. The value for *x* should be 1 if 437 is the current code page, and 2 if it isn't.

This entry loads the specialized device drivers supporting the Proprinter and Quietwriter:

DEVICE = *D:*\PRINTER.SYS LPT1: = (*Type,Hwcp,x*)

The parameters are the same as those just described, except that *Type* can be 4201 or 5202.

The IBM Proprinter Model 4201 reserves a hardware memory area in its own read-only memory (ROM) specifically for code-page information. The IBM Quietwriter III Printer Model 5202 uses hardware font cartridges to perform the same support purpose.

You can also have the country automatically set at the time your system boots up. The line to add to your CONFIG.SYS file is

COUNTRY = *xxx*

where *xxx* is the appropriate country code.

UPDATING YOUR AUTOEXEC.BAT FILE

Commands can be added to the AUTOEXEC.BAT file in the same way as they are for the CONFIG.SYS file. Including the KEYB command in the AUTOEXEC.BAT file lets the keyboard translation table and country codes be loaded in automatically. For example, adding the following line to your AUTOEXEC.BAT file:

```
KEYB FR 033
```

will automatically load the keyboard and country information for France.

You can also include versions of the NLSFUNC, MODE, and CHCP commands, which will work in conjunction with the CONFIG.SYS statements. As an example, the following lines included in your AUTOEXEC.BAT file would initialize national language-support operations, prepare code pages 863, 437, and 850, load the keyboard information file for France, and then select 850 as the active code page for both output devices:

```
NLSFUNC
MODE CON: CP PREPARE = ((863,437,850) \DOS\EGA.CPI)
MODE CON: CP PREPARE = ((863,437,850) \DOS\4201.CPI)
KEYB FR 033
CHCP 850
```

SUMMARY

Along with the PC family of computers, DOS has been a worldwide phenomenon. Recognizing this international influence, DOS provides certain features that allow you to customize your operating version. Although the specific commands and functions for national language support will be used primarily by only a small percentage of users, you may be one of that small group. This chapter is then critical to understanding the intertwined requirements of DOS setup.

- DOS supports many different languages and countries. DOS 3.3 supports five different groups of 256-character ASCII codes, called code pages.
- There are 11 different languages in 17 different countries, using 58 different keyboard layouts. DOS supports them all with a series of specialized commands.
- The code page is the fundamental table of information available to device drivers. Device drivers manage input from the

keyboard (KEYBOARD.SYS) and output to printers and monitors (DISPLAY.SYS).

- Special identification codes exist in DOS 3.3 for each country (21 different codes for 17 different countries) and for each keyboard used in those countries.
- Keyboard device drivers convert scan codes, which represent the key that was pressed, to ASCII codes. The precise ASCII code depends on which of five code pages is active.
- Output drivers for the IBM Quietwriter III Printer Model 5202 and the IBM Proprinter Model 4201 support printing of any of the specialized code-page symbols. Also available to support international output are the output drivers for the Enhanced Graphics Adapter, the IBM PC Convertible LCD display, and the IBM Personal System/2 displays.
- The DOS 3.3 NLSFUNC command loads national language-support functions. It is an essential first command for the installation of international operations.
- DOS 3.3 expands the roles of the MODE command to include new parameters, which allow you to prepare an output device for code-page use, select a specific code page for a particular display or printer, present the current code-page status of a device, and to restore the code page in the hardware of certain output devices.
- Code pages can be activated or changed for all connected and prepared output devices by specifying a CHCP command along with the number of the desired code page.
- The KEYB command is needed to specify which country and keyboard combination is to be activated for keyboard input, once your national language-support operations have been fully installed.
- Certain keys on some foreign keyboards understand two-key sequences to implement accents. The first key selects the accent mark, but displays nothing; it is called a dead key. The second key selects the character to be accented and displayed.
- A single keystroke can switch between U.S. and foreign code-page selections.

- You may not have a fancy new monitor, but you may want to display the extended ASCII characters (codes 128–255) on your CGA monitor when it is in graphics mode. You can do that by loading in an alternate character set with the GRAFTABL command.
- The SELECT command prepares a system disk that is properly configured for international operations. If you specify the desired code pages and the proper country code, DOS will create a system disk with all necessary files on it.
- SELECT also creates the useful CONFIG.SYS and AUTOEXEC.BAT files with the necessary initial lines for national language-support operations.
- You can adjust your own CONFIG.SYS file with the appropriate new DEVICE command for required keyboard and display output device drivers.
- You can update your own AUTOEXEC.BAT file to include the necessary NLSFUNC, MODE, KEYB, CHCP, and GRAFTABL commands for your system.

In the last four chapters, you've learned a good deal about customizing DOS. From controlling output and backups, to creating customized configurations and international layouts, you've done a good deal of work. The next chapter will present the last major subject in the "Revving It Up" section. It will focus on DOS's ability to redirect and filter all input and output information.

REDIRECTING THE ACTION

CHAPTER 12

A major benefit of DOS is its support commands, which affect whole files. Several additional features also enable you to manage your computer system more efficiently. These features offer you additional ways to control input and output in your system, as well as new ways to process your information. They are of great interest to programmers designing automated applications for DOS systems; they are also of practical value for anyone using DOS. In this chapter, you'll concentrate on three related features: redirection, filters, and pipes. These enable you to manage your computer information as it flows from one place to another in your system.

CONTROLLING THE FLOW OF INFORMATION BY REDIRECTION

Redirection refers to the ability of a program or a DOS command to choose an alternative device for input or output. As you know, most programs and commands have a default device. For example, when you enter the DIR command, the computer assumes that you want a directory to be displayed on the screen. This is because the default for DIR is the console (CON), which consists of the screen as the output device and the keyboard as the input device. Your normal ''interface'' with the microcomputer system is through the system console.

SENDING SCREEN OUTPUT TO THE PRINTER

You often need a hard-copy printout of the information that appears on your computer screen. As you learned in Chapter 7, the Shift-PrtSc key combination is limited to only one screenful of information at a time. However, it is often useful to send the complete output from a command such as DIR to another device, such as the printer. DOS has a simple way of redirecting the complete output, no matter how many screenfuls of data are involved.

Following a command with >PRN tells DOS to redirect the output to the printer. Think of the > sign as an arrow pointing to the destination. Entering the following command will redirect the standard DOS directory listing to the printer (PRN), instead of to the video screen:

```
DIR >PRN
```

The same principle of redirection applies to any DOS command that sends data to the screen. Entering

```
CHKDSK >PRN
```

will generate a status check of disk and memory and send it to the printer rather than to the video screen.

STORING SCREEN OUTPUT IN A DISK FILE

DOS can also direct the output to a text file. This means that the information displayed on the screen can be sent to a file on the disk. Screen displays are temporary; if a directory display is captured and stored in a file, however, its information can be used at a later time.

This redirection technique has many practical uses. If you're in a hurry and don't want to wait for printed output, you can quickly send the information to a disk file and then peruse it at your leisure. You can read it into your word-processing program and make modifications to it, or include it in reports. You can read it with a database management program and perform file management functions based on the information sent by DOS into the disk file.

An excellent use of redirection is to create a file that is a catalog of the contents of several diskettes. If you were working with a word processor or a database program, you could then get a master listing of all the files you have stored on all your working diskettes. If you were working with a hard disk, you could make a catalog of your backup disks.

The first step in creating your own diskette catalog is to decide where the master list will be placed. Let's assume you want to place the data in a file called CATALOG. The first cataloged directory will be that of the diskette in drive A. Entering

```
DIR A: > CATALOG
```

produces no visible result on the screen. You told DOS not to display the directory on the screen, but rather to store the information in a file called CATALOG. If you were watching, you would have seen the A drive light come on as the CATALOG file was being written.

To check the results of this command, you can ask DOS to type the contents of the CATALOG file:

```
TYPE CATALOG
```

The directory will be displayed just as if you had typed in the DIR command. However, this printout represents the directory when the original CATALOG file was created by DOS; it is like a snapshot of the original directory. It contains only the directory information that existed when the file was created.

Redirecting DOS output to a disk file can be misleading. Remember that the information contained in that file will not be current and will not be updated automatically to reflect any future changes to your system.

Try the following sequence now to reinforce your understanding of redirection. Redirect the output from the DIR and CHKDSK commands at the DOS prompt to a disk file. You can call this file CATALOG, or you can give it a name of your own. Then use the TYPE command to verify that the output was generated properly.

Later on, you can see that the contents of this file are unchanging. After doing some other work with the system, issue a DIR or CHKDSK command at the DOS prompt again. Then compare the results to the snapshot contained in your CATALOG file.

ADDING OUTPUT TO AN EXISTING FILE

Redirection also allows you to add the directory display of another drive to the CATALOG file. This requires a slightly different command. Look at the following two commands:

```
DIR A: > CATALOG
DIR A: >> CATALOG
```

They look quite similar. However, the first command has one > symbol and the second has two. What is the difference?

The first command simply replaces the old CATALOG file with a new one. The second command, on the other hand, causes the CATALOG file to contain the directory listings of *both* of the diskettes. The >> symbol indicates that the output from the DIR command should be *appended* to (added to) the existing CATALOG file. The directory listing of the new diskette placed in drive A will be appended to the directory listing of the diskette previously placed in drive A.

You can continue this process by placing other diskettes in drive A and repeating the >> command. CATALOG will grow as you store your diskette directories on it. If you are a hard-disk user, you can place your diskettes in A, and your CATALOG file will be updated on drive C.

To see the contents of this file, you can simply enter

```
TYPE CATALOG
```

The result will be a consolidated directory that spans the contents of a number of diskettes.

If you need a hard copy of the directories, you can redirect the data to your printer and use the TYPE command:

```
TYPE CATALOG > PRN
```

You can edit this command's output with your word processor, print the results on gummed labels, and attach them to your original diskettes. Some companies sell programs for $50 that do this simple task.

Try the redirection feature yourself right now. Create your own CATALOG file, listing all the file names on several diskettes. If you're interested only in the names themselves and not in the size or date and time information, use a DIR/W command to direct the output to your CATALOG file. Remember to use a single > sign to create the file and a double >> sign to append new directory output to it. Dual-diskette users should place the diskettes to be cataloged into drive B, creating the CATALOG file on drive A. Hard-disk users should place their diskettes into drive A, creating the CATALOG file on drive C.

RECEIVING INPUT FROM TEXT FILES

DOS can receive input from a text file. This means that instead of waiting at the console to enter data, make responses, or otherwise generate input for a DOS command or a program, you can type your responses in advance. DOS will then take each response from the input file as it is needed. Let's look at a simple example.

Input from a file is more unusual than output. In the normal course of computer use, most users will not take advantage of the feature described here. However, it can be useful.

You may have noticed that some DOS commands require the user to enter additional keystrokes after the program has begun. For example, the FORMAT command will always pause and ask you to press any key before actual formatting takes place. This safety precaution protects you from errors, giving you a moment to take a deep breath (and to check the disk in the drive) before actually committing yourself to the formatting process.

You could avoid that extra keystroke by creating an input file to be used with the FORMAT command. The input file would contain any keystrokes that you wanted typed in while the program was running. In this case, a simple press of the Return key will do. To create a file containing a Return character, you could use a word processor, or you could create the KEYS file from the DOS prompt using the COPY command you saw earlier. Enter

```
COPY CON: KEYS
```

and press Return. Then press Return again. Enter

```
N
```

and press Return. Then enter

```
^Z
```

and press Return. The KEYS file now contains the keystroke for the Return key. It also contains the No response (N) to the FORMAT command's request ''Do you want to format an additional diskette?''

To indicate that these responses are coming from a file and not from you at the keyboard, the < symbol is used:

```
FORMAT B:/S < KEYS
```

When you enter this command, the formatting does not pause—the Return keypress has been input from the KEYS file. When the single disk is completely formatted, the N tells FORMAT you're done, and the DOS prompt reappears. As you can see, this kind of feature can save you time and effort, and can be useful in many situations.

PROCESSING YOUR FILE INFORMATION WITH DOS FILTERS

Another powerful feature of DOS is its use of *filters* to process data directly. Just as a camera filter changes what you see through the lens, a DOS filter can process in unique ways any data that passes through it and can change what you see on the screen. There are three filters included in DOS: SORT, FIND, and MORE. They are stored on disk as the SORT.EXE, FIND.EXE, and MORE.COM files.

ARRANGING YOUR DATA WITH THE SORT FILTER

Let's look first at one of the most useful filters, the SORT filter. SORT rearranges lines of data. Take a look at the sample data files in Figures 12.1 and 12.2. These lists could have been prepared with a word processor, a database manager, a spreadsheet, or even with DOS itself. Lists like these usually grow in size, with the new entries added chronologically as your business acquires new clients or as you make new friends and acquaintances.

Every once in a while, you probably rewrite your own personal phone list. You usually want the list in last-name order, but you might want a special printout in nickname or first-name order. Even more often, businesses need to reprint their client list in some usable order. Perhaps the telephone receptionist needs an updated list in company-name order. The marketing department may need the

```
C>TYPE  BUSINESS.TXT
Cantonese Imports    134  Roberts    Joseph 212/656-2156
Brandenberg Gates    754  Bennett    Mary   415/612-5656
Sole Survivor,Inc.   237  Evans      Gail   415/222-3514
Presley Plastics     198  Presley    Robert 716/245-6119
Plymouth Granite Co  345  Williams   Peter  617/531-6145
Bucket Dance Wear    276  Lewis      Ann    415/635-2530
Intelli-Strategies   743  Griffiths  Robert 415/362-9537
Benicia Balloons     983  Franklin   Marie  212/524-4157
Standard Shelters    690  Rucker     Sally  415/532-1107
Panama Rain Corp.    576  Cook       Freda  408/534-9739

C>
```

Figure 12.1: A business contact list

```
C>TYPE PERSONAL.TXT
Klaar     Wim      213-968-2345   Ready
Torrance  Stan     415-567-4534   Stan
Quilling  Alan     415-526-4565   Al
Keepsake  Alice    415-249-3498   Jala
Bentley   Robert   415-654-4864   Speed
Hendley   Candice  415-212-3434   Candy

C>
```

Figure 12.2: A personal phone list

same list printed in telephone-number order. Then again, the accounts payable department may want the list in customer ID order. All of these are very easy to obtain with the SORT filter.

Using the redirection concept presented in the previous section, you can take each of these representative lists and rearrange the data to suit your needs. The easiest form of filtering is to enter the following command at the DOS prompt:

```
SORT < BUSINESS.TXT
```

The resulting screen will display the original lines of the file in company-name order (see Figure 12.3).

A similar arrangement of your personal phone list could be obtained by entering

```
SORT < PERSONAL.TXT
```

In this case, the arrangement is by last name (see Figure 12.4).

In both examples just given, the .TXT files were directed to be *input* to the SORT command—the < arrowhead points to SORT. Since there was no redirection specified for output, the sorted results appeared on the video screen. Each of these commands could also specify an output redirection that would place the sorted results in a disk file. You could then work with the sorted file as you liked, perhaps delaying the printing until a convenient time.

These lists are sorted by whatever data comes first on the line. Later in this chapter, you'll learn how to use SORT to arrange the data based on other information in each line.

The two sorted lists could be saved in the files CLIENTS.TXT and PHONES.TXT with the following commands:

```
SORT < BUSINESS.TXT > CLIENTS.TXT
SORT < PERSONAL.TXT > PHONES.TXT
```

```
C>SORT  <  BUSINESS.TXT
Benicia Balloons      983  Franklin  Marie   212/524-4157
Brandenberg Gates     754  Bennett   Mary    415/612-5656
Bucket Dance Wear     276  Lewis     Ann     415/635-2530
Cantonese Imports     134  Roberts   Joseph  212/656-2156
Intelli-Strategies    743  Griffiths Robert  415/362-9537
Panama Rain Corp.     576  Cook      Freda   408/534-9739
Plymouth Granite Co   345  Williams  Peter   617/531-6145
Presley Plastics      198  Presley   Robert  716/245-6119
Sole Survivor,Inc.    237  Evans     Gail    415/222-3514
Standard Shelters     690  Rucker    Sally   415/532-1107

C>
```

Figure 12.3: Sorting by company name

Figures 12.5 and 12.6 show the verification of these results with the TYPE command. Figure 12.7 shows how the SORT filter works.

PERFORMING TEXT SEARCHES WITH THE FIND FILTER

Let's look at another DOS filter, the FIND command. It permits you to scan any text file for a series of text characters and to locate any

```
C>SORT  <  PERSONAL.TXT
Bentley   Robert  415-654-4864   Speed
Hendley   Candice 415-212-3434   Candy
Keepsake  Alice   415-249-3498   Jala
Klaar     Wim     213-968-2345   Ready
Quilling  Alan    415-526-4565   Al
Torrance  Stan    415-567-4534   Stan

C>
```

Figure 12.4: Sorting by last name

```
C>SORT  <  BUSINESS.TXT  >  CLIENTS.TXT

C>TYPE CLIENTS.TXT
Benicia Balloons     983  Franklin  Marie  212/524-4157
Brandenberg Gates    754  Bennett   Mary   415/612-5656
Bucket Dance Wear    276  Lewis     Ann    415/635-2530
Cantonese Imports    134  Roberts   Joseph 212/656-2156
Intelli-Strategies   743  Griffiths Robert 415/362-9537
Panama Rain Corp.    576  Cook      Freda  408/534-9739
Plymouth Granite Co  345  Williams  Peter  617/531-6145
Presley Plastics     198  Presley   Robert 716/245-6119
Sole Survivor,Inc.   237  Evans     Gail   415/222-3514
Standard Shelters    690  Rucker    Sally  415/532-1107

C>
```

Figure 12.5: Sorted client list in text file

lines in the file that contain the specified characters. For instance, let's take the business contact list from Figure 12.1 and try to find all clients located in the area code 415:

FIND "415" BUSINESS.TXT

```
C>SORT  <  PERSONAL.TXT  >  PHONES.TXT

C>TYPE PHONES.TXT
Bentley    Robert   415-654-4864   Speed
Hendley    Candice  415-212-3434   Candy
Keepsake   Alice    415-249-3498   Jala
Klaar      Wim      213-968-2345   Ready
Quilling   Alan     415-526-4565   Al
Torrance   Stan     415-567-4534   Stan

C>_
```

Figure 12.6: Sorted phone list in text file

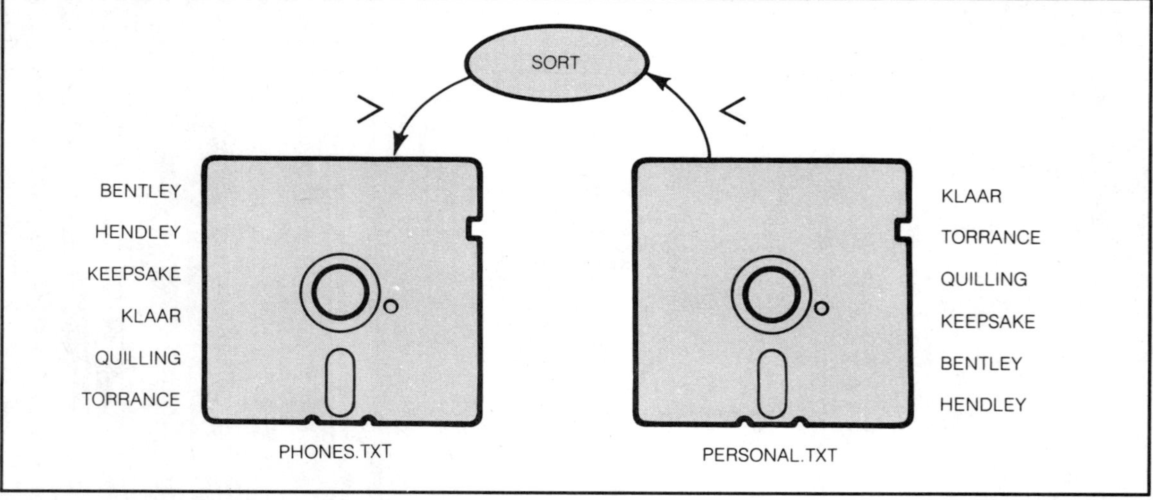

Figure 12.7: The SORT filter at work

The quotation marks around your character strings are delimiters. You must use them. They assist DOS in distinguishing a character string from the command line's other characters, which represent commands, file names, or parameters.

This command will locate all lines in the specified text file (the second argument) that contain the specified character string (the first argument). Figure 12.8 demonstrates the results. Note that the first line of the output identifies the input text file.

This is a typical database extraction request that has been handled by DOS *almost* satisfactorily. Notice that the Benicia Balloons company has been included in the results, even though its area code is not 415. You asked DOS to find every line in the file that included 415 anywhere in the line, and 415 is in the last four digits of that company's telephone number (524-4157). Therefore, the line was filtered into the resulting selection.

To solve this problem, you can specify "415/" as the character string. By including the slash you will be sure to extract only the telephone numbers that begin with the desired digits. Enter

Make sure your specified character string is unique enough to find only the data you're looking for. The fewer characters in your string, the greater the likelihood that DOS will find lines containing those characters.

```
FIND "415/" BUSINESS.TXT
```

Figure 12.9 shows the results. Your command has selected the correct lines from the file.

You can also name more than one file as input to the FIND filter. With the command shown in Figure 12.10, you could quickly see if any of your area code 212 business clients appeared on your personal phone list as well.

```
C>FIND  "415"  BUSINESS.TXT

---------- BUSINESS.TXT
Brandenberg Gates    754  Bennett    Mary    415/612-5656
Sole Survivor,Inc.   237  Evans      Gail    415/222-3514
Bucket Dance Wear    276  Lewis      Ann     415/635-253Ø
Intelli-Strategies   743  Griffiths Robert  415/362-9537
Benicia Balloons     983  Franklin   Marie   212/524-4157
Standard Shelters    69Ø  Rucker     Sally   415/522-11Ø7

C>■
```

Figure 12.8: Using the FIND filter to extract data

```
C>FIND  "415/"  BUSINESS.TXT

---------- BUSINESS.TXT
Brandenberg Gates    754  Bennett   Mary    415/612-5656
Sole Survivor,Inc.   237  Evans     Gail    415/222-3514
Bucket Dance Wear    276  Lewis     Ann     415/635-2530
Intelli-Strategies   743  Griffiths Robert  415/362-9537
Standard Shelters    690  Rucker    Sally   415/532-1107

C>_
```

Figure 12.9: Making sure your character string is sufficient

```
C>FIND  "212"  BUSINESS.TXT  PERSONAL.TXT

---------- BUSINESS.TXT
Cantonese Imports    134  Roberts   Joseph  212/656-2156
Benicia Balloons     983  Franklin  Marie   212/524-4157

---------- PERSONAL.TXT
Hendley   Candice 415-212-3434   Candy

C>_
```

Figure 12.10: Filtering multiple files

In these sample situations, business and personal lives have been kept apart. The FIND command could just as easily have been used as in Figure 12.11, with two different business mailing lists, in order to identify duplicate entries that should be removed from data lists. This is an example of how DOS can help you weed out extra entries.

The example in Figure 12.11 requires you to specify a FIND character string like "415/". Therefore, only duplicates for the 415

```
C>FIND  "617/"  BUSINESS.TXT  PROSPECT.TXT

---------- BUSINESS.TXT
Plymouth Granite Co 345  Williams  Peter  617/531-6145

---------- PROSPECT.TXT
Williams  Peter  Plymouth Granite Co 617/531-6145
Kingland  Benson Ranger Treadmills   617/222-4543
Brandeis  Judd   Scholar Support,Inc 617/298-4455

C>FIND  "415/"  BUSINESS.TXT  PROSPECT.TXT

---------- BUSINESS.TXT
Brandenberg Gates    754  Bennett   Mary   415/612-5656
Sole Survivor,Inc.   237  Evans     Gail   415/222-3514
Bucket Dance Wear    276  Lewis     Ann    415/635-2530
Intelli-Strategies   743  Griffiths Robert 415/362-9537
Standard Shelters    690  Rucker    Sally  415/532-1107

---------- PROSPECT.TXT
Simpson   Robert Wellington Services 415/446-2345

C>_
```

Figure 12.11: Finding duplicate entries in multiple lists

calling area will appear; you would have to respecify more area codes to be complete. However, other tools that you've learned about can do the job even better. First use the COPY command to join the two business files into one temporary file, which you can delete later; then use SORT to filter the resultant file.

Using TYPE with the sorted file would now show you all possible duplicates. You could proceed to find any subset of records of interest (for example, the 415 calling area) with FIND. In each case, you would not have to look back and forth between two lists. Duplicates would appear one right after the other, like the two entries for Plymouth Granite Company in Figure 12.12.

When you are joining two files to create a third, or when you are creating any temporary file, make sure your disk has enough space on it for the operation.

Although Figure 12.12 shows the duplicates for the 415 calling area on the screen, remember that the TEMP2.TXT file still contains the sorted collection of *all* records from both the BUSINESS.TXT and the PROSPECT.TXT files. This file could be erased now, or you could use it in further processing.

CONNECTING DOS OPERATIONS WITH PIPES

You've seen how the SORT and FIND filters can work with data files as input. Now you'll explore how filters can work in connection with other programs or DOS commands. When these connections are made, they are called *pipes*. Earlier in this chapter, you saw how you could change DOS's default input and output devices using redirection. Pipes allow you to combine the power of redirection with that of filters. You can simultaneously change (filter) your data while it is being moved (redirected) from one location to another.

Even with the redirection techniques you have learned so far in this chapter, if you want to do several things in a row, you might still have quite a bit of work to do. You might need to run one program, send its results to a disk file, and then run another program to process the resulting data. Then you might have to take the next program's input from that disk file to continue the processing chain, perhaps creating several intermediate files before getting the final result. Piping allows you to take the output of one command or program and make it the input of another command or program. You can do this several times in a row. An entire series of programs that generate intermediate output for one another can be automated by using the sophisticated combination of filters and pipes.

COMBINING PIPING AND SORTING

As you know, the SORT filter can be used to create a sorted directory listing. By adding pipes, you can use any column that appears in a directory listing as the criterion for a sorting order. This is very

```
C>COPY  BUSINESS.TXT + PROSPECT.TXT  TEMP1.TXT
BUSINESS.TXT
PROSPECT.TXT
        1 File(s) copied

C>SORT  < TEMP1.TXT  >  TEMP2.TXT

C>FIND  "617/"  TEMP2.TXT

---------- TEMP2.TXT
Brandeis  Judd   Scholar Support,Inc 617/298-4455
Kingland  Benson Ranger Treadmills   617/222-4543
Plymouth Granite Co 345  Williams  Peter  617/531-6145
Williams  Peter  Plymouth Granite Co 617/531-6145

C>_
```

Figure 12.12: Merging files before looking for duplicates

helpful, because a normal directory display does not arrange the files in any particular order. Using the SORT filter, you can produce your directory listings in order of file name, file extension, file size, date of creation, or even time of creation. As you'll see, you can take any text file and arrange it in any way you like as well.

Pipes are created by using the vertical bar symbol (¦). Entering the command

```
DIR ¦ SORT
```

sends the output of a DIR command to the SORT filter before it is sent to the screen. The filtered result is a sorted directory display. Figure 12.13 shows a standard directory listing before sorting. Figure 12.14 shows the SORT processing operation itself, and Figure 12.15 presents the sorted results.

This procedure required only a single piping sequence. Previously, you would have had to redirect the results of the DIR command into a disk file and then redirect the disk file so that it would be the input of the SORT filter. The pipe was created automatically by DOS to handle this job.

Note that the first three lines have also been sorted:

```
17 File(s)    205824 bytes free
Directory of A:\
Volume in drive A has no label
```

```
A>DIR

 Volume in drive A has no label
 Directory of  A:\

ANSI      SYS     1678   3-17-87  12:00p
RESTORE   COM    34643   3-17-87  12:00p
SORT      EXE     1977   3-17-87  12:00p
SUBST     EXE     9909   3-17-87  12:00p
XCOPY     EXE    11247   3-17-87  12:00p
DISPLAY   SYS    11290   3-17-87  12:00p
KEYBOARD  SYS    19766   3-17-87  12:00p
PRINTER   SYS    13590   3-17-87  12:00p
VDISK     SYS     3455   3-17-87  12:00p
DRIVER    SYS     1196   3-17-87  12:00p
FIND      EXE     6434   3-17-87  12:00p
FORMAT    COM    11616   3-18-87  12:00p
JOIN      EXE     8969   3-17-87  12:00p
MORE      COM      313   3-17-87  12:00p
REPLACE   EXE    11775   3-17-87  12:00p
       15 File(s)    206848 bytes free

A>_
```

Figure 12.13: Unsorted directory listing

The "17 File(s)" line is indented seven spaces beyond the "Directory" and "Volume" lines, which themselves are indented one space. The file names that follow are not indented.

The default drive must not be write-protected—DOS needs to create temporary files while it is performing its filtering job. In addition, the default drive must have sufficient available space to create the temporary files. Otherwise, the automatic piping process will be unable to continue.

Two extra files, 0A3B0550 and 0A3B0727, appear in the sorted listing. These files are temporary work files created during the sort-

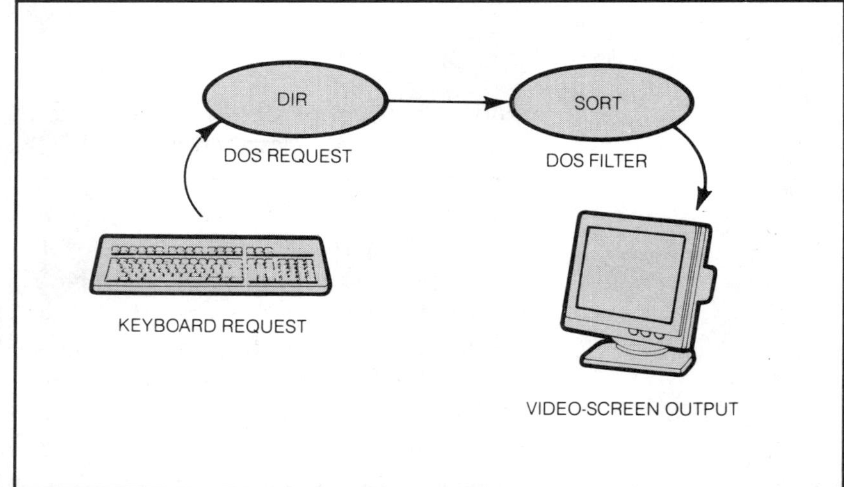

Figure 12.14: Information flow during filter operation

```
A>DIR | SORT

       17 File(s)    205824 bytes free
 Directory of  A:\
 Volume in drive A has no label
0A3B0550            0   7-26-87  10:59a
0A3B0727            0   7-26-87  10:59a
ANSI     SYS     1678   3-17-87  12:00p
DISPLAY  SYS    11290   3-17-87  12:00p
DRIVER   SYS     1196   3-17-87  12:00p
FIND     EXE     6434   3-17-87  12:00p
FORMAT   COM    11616   3-18-87  12:00p
JOIN     EXE     8969   3-17-87  12:00p
KEYBOARD SYS    19766   3-17-87  12:00p
MORE     COM      313   3-17-87  12:00p
PRINTER  SYS    13590   3-17-87  12:00p
REPLACE  EXE    11775   3-17-87  12:00p
RESTORE  COM    34643   3-17-87  12:00p
SORT     EXE     1977   3-17-87  12:00p
SUBST    EXE     9909   3-17-87  12:00p
VDISK    SYS     3455   3-17-87  12:00p
XCOPY    EXE    11247   3-17-87  12:00p

A>_
```

Figure 12.15: Sorted directory listing

ing operation by DOS on the default drive. They will be erased automatically after the piping operation is complete. Their obscure file names are based on the date and time of the actual SORT operation. They will always be different.

You can ignore these files completely if you wish. However, you may not want to have them appear in your sorted output—their inclusion may simply confuse others who read your output listing. To avoid this, you should set the default drive to a drive other than the one you want sorted. You can then use the PATH command to tell DOS where to find the SORT.EXE file. On a dual-diskette system, you might set the path to drive A; on a hard-disk system, you might set the path to the DOS directory on drive C.

Look at Figure 12.16 for further clarification. In this case, you first make drive C the default. The temporary files will be written on this new default drive. Then you ask for a directory listing of drive A. Finally, you ask DOS to direct the DIR command's output to the SORT command for filtering.

CUSTOMIZING YOUR DOS SORTS

Let's explore piping a little further, and in the process, look at some additional capabilities of DOS filters. The SORT filter allows

```
A>C:

C>DIR A: | SORT

       15 File(s)     206848 bytes free
 Directory of  A:\
 Volume in drive A has no label
ANSI     SYS      1678   3-17-87  12:00p
DISPLAY  SYS     11290   3-17-87  12:00p
DRIVER   SYS      1196   3-17-87  12:00p
FIND     EXE      6434   3-17-87  12:00p
FORMAT   COM     11616   3-18-87  12:00p
JOIN     EXE      8969   3-17-87  12:00p
KEYBOARD SYS     19766   3-17-87  12:00p
MORE     COM       313   3-17-87  12:00p
PRINTER  SYS     13590   3-17-87  12:00p
REPLACE  EXE     11775   3-17-87  12:00p
RESTORE  COM     34643   3-17-87  12:00p
SORT     EXE      1977   3-17-87  12:00p
SUBST    EXE      9909   3-17-87  12:00p
VDISK    SYS      3455   3-17-87  12:00p
XCOPY    EXE     11247   3-17-87  12:00p

C>_
```

Figure 12.16: Creating automatic piping files on the default drive

you several different ways to sort. For example, the /R switch tells the program to sort in reverse (descending) order. Entering

DIR A:¦SORT /R

produces a directory listing in reverse alphabetical order (see Figure 12.17).

SORT also allows you to specify the column on which you want the sorting to take place. Normally, SORT begins with the first character in the line. However, you can tell SORT to sort from another position in the data line, which allows you to sort your directory in a variety of ways. The following command will sort by file extension rather than by file name (see Figure 12.18):

DIR A:¦SORT / +9

The +9 in this command tells DOS to sort based on the ninth character space. Since DOS uses eight-character file names, the ninth character space is always blank (to separate the base name from the extension). Beginning the sort here sorts on the following three characters, the extension. Extending this idea to the sixteenth character space in a directory listing, you could just as easily sort the direc-

```
C>DIR A:  ¦ SORT /R
XCOPY     EXE    11247    3-17-87   12:00p
VDISK     SYS     3455    3-17-87   12:00p
SUBST     EXE     9909    3-17-87   12:00p
SORT      EXE     1977    3-17-87   12:00p
RESTORE   COM    34643    3-17-87   12:00p
REPLACE   EXE    11775    3-17-87   12:00p
PRINTER   SYS    13590    3-17-87   12:00p
MORE      COM      313    3-17-87   12:00p
KEYBOARD  SYS    19766    3-17-87   12:00p
JOIN      EXE     8969    3-17-87   12:00p
FORMAT    COM    11616    3-18-87   12:00p
FIND      EXE     6434    3-17-87   12:00p
DRIVER    SYS     1196    3-17-87   12:00p
DISPLAY   SYS    11290    3-17-87   12:00p
ANSI      SYS     1678    3-17-87   12:00p
 Volume in drive A has no label
 Directory of  A:\
       15 File(s)    206848 bytes free


C>_
```

Figure 12.17: Directory sorted in reverse alphabetical order

tory by file size (see Figure 12.19). Character space 16 gets you past the base name and extension, allowing sorting to begin with the file-size numbers.

DIR A:¦SORT / + 16

```
C>DIR A: | SORT /+9

MORE      COM      313   3-17-87  12:00p
FORMAT    COM    11616   3-18-87  12:00p
RESTORE   COM    34643   3-17-87  12:00p
SORT      EXE     1977   3-17-87  12:00p
FIND      EXE     6434   3-17-87  12:00p
JOIN      EXE     8969   3-17-87  12:00p
SUBST     EXE     9909   3-17-87  12:00p
XCOPY     EXE    11247   3-17-87  12:00p
REPLACE   EXE    11775   3-17-87  12:00p
DRIVER    SYS     1196   3-17-87  12:00p
ANSI      SYS     1678   3-17-87  12:00p
VDISK     SYS     3455   3-17-87  12:00p
DISPLAY   SYS    11290   3-17-87  12:00p
PRINTER   SYS    13590   3-17-87  12:00p
KEYBOARD  SYS    19766   3-17-87  12:00p
       15 File(s)    206848 bytes free
 Volume in drive A has no label
 Directory of  A:\

C>_
```

Figure 12.18: Sorting by file extension

```
C>DIR A: | SORT /+16

MORE      COM      313   3-17-87  12:00p
DRIVER    SYS     1196   3-17-87  12:00p
ANSI      SYS     1678   3-17-87  12:00p
SORT      EXE     1977   3-17-87  12:00p
VDISK     SYS     3455   3-17-87  12:00p
FIND      EXE     6434   3-17-87  12:00p
JOIN      EXE     8969   3-17-87  12:00p
SUBST     EXE     9909   3-17-87  12:00p
XCOPY     EXE    11247   3-17-87  12:00p
DISPLAY   SYS    11290   3-17-87  12:00p
FORMAT    COM    11616   3-18-87  12:00p
REPLACE   EXE    11775   3-17-87  12:00p
PRINTER   SYS    13590   3-17-87  12:00p
KEYBOARD  SYS    19766   3-17-87  12:00p
RESTORE   COM    34643   3-17-87  12:00p
 Directory of  A:\
 Volume in drive A has no label
       15 File(s)    206848 bytes free

C>_
```

Figure 12.19: Sorting by file size

COMBINING REDIRECTION WITH FILTERS AND PIPES

To make your job easier and quicker, a filter can also be combined with a redirection command. To print a sorted directory listing, you could enter

```
DIR A:¦SORT > PRN
```

As Figure 12.20 shows, the output of the DIR command is piped forward to become the input to the SORT command; the SORT command's output is then redirected from the screen to the printer.

As another example, you can create a text file containing a sorted directory listing by entering

```
DIR A:¦SORT > SORTDIR
```

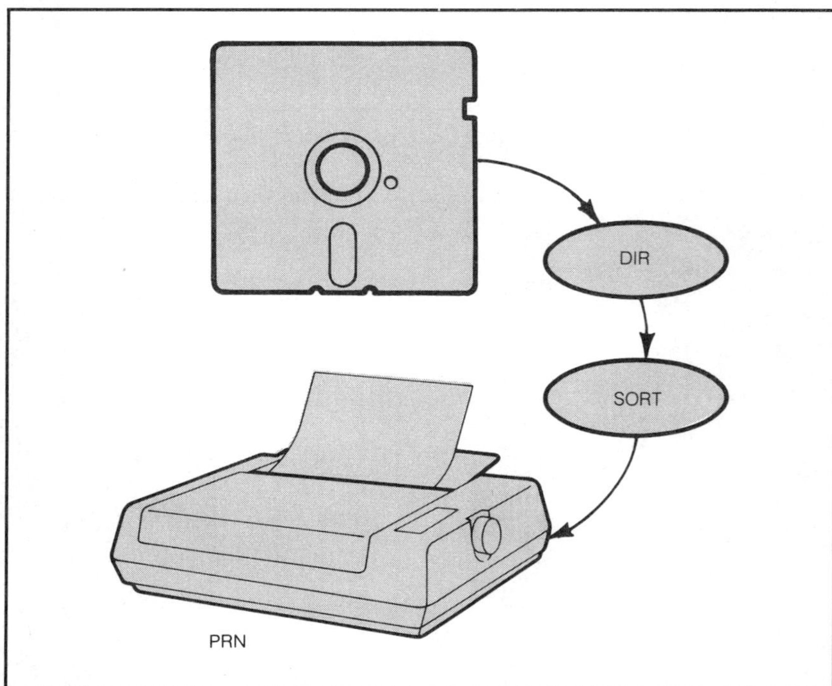

Figure 12.20: Combining pipes, filters, and redirection

As Figure 12.21 shows, this is similar to the previous example, except that the final sorted directory listing is not sent to the printer but is instead redirected to the SORTDIR disk file. To see the contents of the SORTDIR file, you could enter

```
TYPE SORTDIR
```

With pipes and filters, you can also make reference to files located elsewhere within the DOS directory structure. As an example, Figure 12.22 shows a file called CAD.KEY that is contained in the CAD\VWF directory. CAD.KEY lists the internal macros (mini-programs) of a computer-aided design (CAD) program. It contains three columns of information: the numeric key code, an ASCII indication of which key on the keyboard invokes the macro, and the name of the file containing the macro instructions.

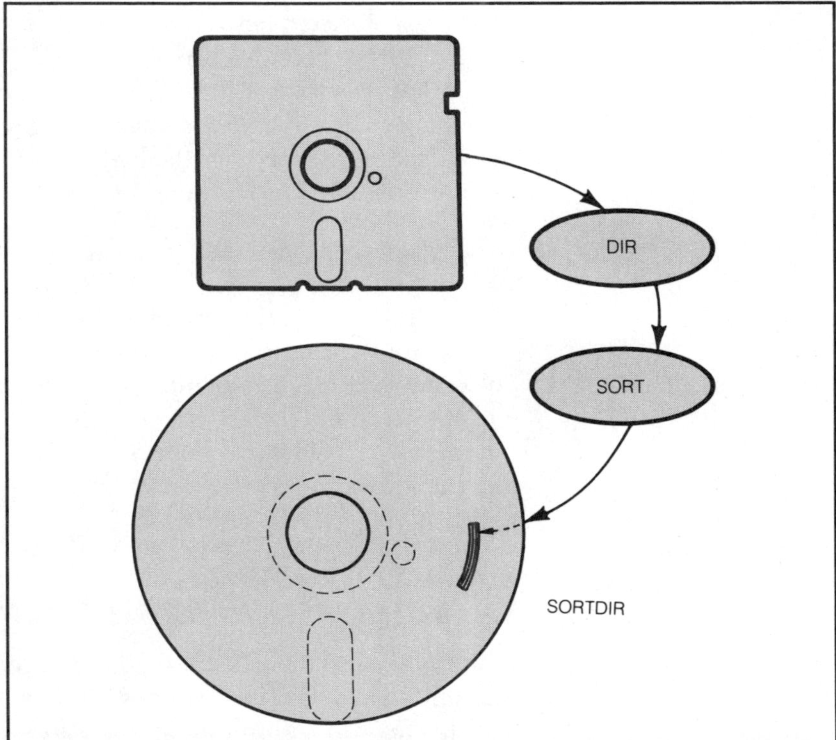

Figure 12.21: Creating a disk file with command combinations

```
C>TYPE \CAD\VWF\CAD.KEY
 316  F2 CLEARALL.MAC
  86   V VERTSNAP.MAC
 318  F4 EXAMPLE2.MAC
  79   O SNAPOFF.MAC
  71   G SNAPGRID.MAC
  66   B BACKUP.MAC
  76   L LINE.MAC
  49   1 ALAN1.MAC
  65   A ALAN2.MAC
  8Ø   P PLOTFIT.MAC
  51   3 ALAN3.MAC
  52   4 alan4.mac
 317  F3 EXAMPLE4.MAC

C>_
```

Figure 12.22: List of macro codes for a CAD program

The list of macro keys appears in the order in which the keys were created during previous use of the CAD program. Even with only a handful of possibilities, it is difficult to see which keys are taken and which are still available for macro assignment. A simple use of the SORT filter can rearrange the file lines within the same file, as shown in Figure 12.23. The command to use is

```
SORT < \CAD\VWF\CAD.KEY > \CAD\VWF\CAD.KEY
```

Figure 12.24 shows the results of this simple sorting.

Test your understanding now of filters, pipes, and redirection. Select any subdirectory of interest on your hard disk, or put any diskette of interest into a disk drive. Construct and enter the proper command to ask DOS to produce a directory listing, sort it by file size, and then print the sorted results on your printer.

SOPHISTICATED TEXT SEARCHES USING REDIRECTION

From the output of a command or program, FIND can select lines that contain a certain character or group of characters. You can combine this feature with a piping operation for a sophisticated search. For example, the following command lists only those files that

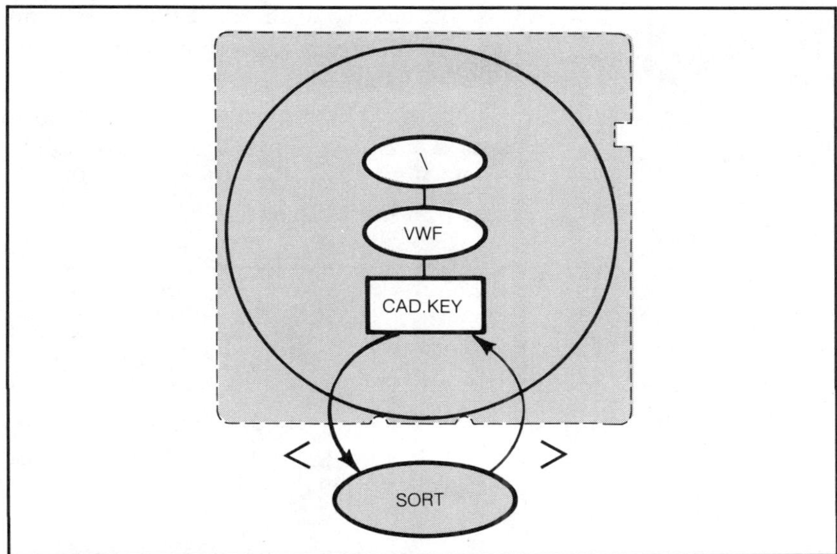

Figure 12.23: Sorting a file back into itself

```
C>SORT  <  \CAD\VWF\CAD.KEY  >  \CAD\VWF\CAD.KEY

C>TYPE  \CAD\VWF\CAD.KEY
  49    1  ALAN1.MAC
  51    3  ALAN3.MAC
  52    4  alan4.mac
  65    A  ALAN2.MAC
  66    B  BACKUP.MAC
  71    G  SNAPGRID.MAC
  76    L  LINE.MAC
  79    O  SNAPOFF.MAC
  8Ø    P  PLOTFIT.MAC
  86    V  VERTSNAP.MAC
 316   F2  CLEARALL.MAC
 317   F3  EXAMPLE4.MAC
 318   F4  EXAMPLE2.MAC

C>_
```

Figure 12.24: The sorted directory structure

> When you are doing character searches in DOS or any other processing language, the case (upper or lower) of the characters is critical. You must always specify the character string *exactly* as you expect to find it in the file.

contain the letters OR:

DIR A:¦FIND "OR"

This command would produce such files as MORE.COM and FORMAT.COM (see Figure 12.25), since they contain the letters

OR somewhere in their file names. Because FIND includes a line if the search criteria are found anywhere in that line, SYS.COM and ANSI.SYS are also found.

The FIND filter can be used in reverse as well. For example, if you wanted to *exclude* all files that have an .EXE extension, you could use the /V switch, as shown in Figure 12.26. All files are found except those that have the letters EXE in their complete name.

```
C>DIR A: | FIND "OR"
MORE      COM       313   3-17-87  12:00p
FORMAT    COM     11616   3-18-87  12:00p
RESTORE   COM     34643   3-17-87  12:00p
SORT      EXE      1977   3-17-87  12:00p

C>DIR A: | FIND "SYS"
DRIVER    SYS      1196   3-17-87  12:00p
ANSI      SYS      1678   3-17-87  12:00p
COUNTRY   SYS     11285   3-17-87  12:00p
DISPLAY   SYS     11290   3-17-87  12:00p
PRINTER   SYS     13590   3-17-87  12:00p
KEYBOARD  SYS     19766   3-17-87  12:00p
SYS       COM      4766   3-17-87  12:00p

C>_
```

Figure 12.25: Search capability with the FIND filter

```
C>DIR A: | FIND/V "EXE"

 Volume in drive A has no label
 Directory of  A:\

ANSI      SYS      1678   3-17-87  12:00p
RESTORE   COM     34643   3-17-87  12:00p
DISPLAY   SYS     11290   3-17-87  12:00p
KEYBOARD  SYS     19766   3-17-87  12:00p
PRINTER   SYS     13590   3-17-87  12:00p
VDISK     SYS      3455   3-17-87  12:00p
DRIVER    SYS      1196   3-17-87  12:00p
FORMAT    COM     11616   3-18-87  12:00p
MORE      COM       313   3-17-87  12:00p
       15 File(s)    206848 bytes free

C>_
```

Figure 12.26: Excluding files with the /V switch

The FIND filter can also assign line numbers to the output. You can request this by adding the /N switch to the command:

DIR A: ¦ FIND/N "EXE"

Figure 12.27 shows the results of this command. Lines 1 through 6 of the directory in drive A did not contain EXE, so they were discarded. The first line with an EXE in it was the seventh line input to the FIND filter; therefore, the /N switch put [7] in front of it. The next lines containing EXE were lines 8, 9, 15, 17, and 19.

As always, switches can be combined in a FIND command to do double duty. Figure 12.28 shows a file sorted by both numbering and exclusion, which was produced by using the /N and /V switches.

FIND can also be used to count the number of line matches by invoking the /C parameter. For example, you might like to know how many .EXE files are on a disk or in a directory. Let's assume for a moment that you have added a file called AUTOEXEC.BAT to a disk in drive A. The command

DIR A:¦FIND/C "EXE"

would produce an answer of 7, shown in Figure 12.29. This seems inaccurate, since only six files have the extension .EXE. However,

```
C>DIR A: ¦ FIND/N "EXE"
[7]SORT      EXE     1977   3-17-87  12:00p
[8]SUBST     EXE     9909   3-17-87  12:00p
[9]XCOPY     EXE    11247   3-17-87  12:00p
[15]FIND      EXE     6434   3-17-87  12:00p
[17]JOIN      EXE     8969   3-17-87  12:00p
[19]REPLACE   EXE    11775   3-17-87  12:00p

C>_
```

Figure 12.27: Numbering feature of the FIND filter with /N

```
C>DIR A: | FIND /N/V "EXE"
[1]
[2] Volume in drive A has no label
[3] Directory of  A:\
[4]
[5]ANSI      SYS      1678   3-17-87  12:00p
[6]RESTORE   COM     34643   3-17-87  12:00p
[10]DISPLAY  SYS     11290   3-17-87  12:00p
[11]KEYBOARD SYS     19766   3-17-87  12:00p
[12]PRINTER  SYS     13590   3-17-87  12:00p
[13]VDISK    SYS      3455   3-17-87  12:00p
[14]DRIVER   SYS      1196   3-17-87  12:00p
[16]FORMAT   COM     11616   3-18-87  12:00p
[18]MORE     COM       313   3-17-87  12:00p
[20]        15 File(s)    206848 bytes free

C>_
```

Figure 12.28: Combining FIND switches

```
C>DIR A: | FIND/C "EXE"
7

C>DIR A: | FIND "EXE"
AUTOEXEC BAT      152   7-05-87  11:32a
SORT     EXE     1977   3-17-87  12:00p
SUBST    EXE     9909   3-17-87  12:00p
XCOPY    EXE    11247   3-17-87  12:00p
FIND     EXE     6434   3-17-87  12:00p
JOIN     EXE     8969   3-17-87  12:00p
REPLACE  EXE    11775   3-17-87  12:00p

C>_
```

Figure 12.29: Counting occurrences with the /C switch

remember that FIND locates *all* occurrences of the specified string of characters—and AUTOEXEC.BAT contains these characters as well.

Once again, the solution is to specify a sufficiently unique character string. In this case, since the extension is always preceded by at least one space in the directory listing, the string " EXE" would correctly identify the six .EXE files, as shown in Figure 12.30.

```
C>DIR A: ¦ FIND/C " EXE"
6

C>DIR A: ¦ FIND " EXE"
SORT     EXE     1977   3-17-87   12:00p
SUBST    EXE     9909   3-17-87   12:00p
XCOPY    EXE    11247   3-17-87   12:00p
FIND     EXE     6434   3-17-87   12:00p
JOIN     EXE     8969   3-17-87   12:00p
REPLACE  EXE    11775   3-17-87   12:00p

C>_
```

Figure 12.30: Specifying a sufficiently unique character string

SAVING TIME BY COMBINING FILTERS

Once you are comfortable with DOS filters, you can save yourself both typing time and waiting time. You don't need to wait for the SORT filter to finish its work before you ask the FIND filter to begin. Since you can use the SORT and FIND filters together, you can tell DOS to execute both filters, one after the other. Enter

```
DIR A:¦SORT¦FIND "EXE"
```

to receive a sorted listing of the .EXE files (see Figure 12.31). AUTOEXEC.BAT is again included in the listing.

You have probably seen advertisements for sorting programs that promise to sort your files by any field within them. You can do all of that kind of sorting with simple DOS commands now. You've learned how to use switches on the SORT command to arrange your directory lines by categories other than the first category. You've also learned how to send the sorted results from one filter to another through piping.

For another example of sophisticated DOS manipulation, you could now take the original business contact list shown in Figure 12.1, sort it by telephone number, pipe the results into the FIND filter to extract the 415 entries, and finally pipe the results back into the SORT command to be rearranged alphabetically:

SORT / +43 < BUSINESS.TXT ¦ FIND "415/" ¦ SORT

Figure 12.32 demonstrates the results of this example. Notice that the first sort takes place using character space 43, the first space containing the phone number. If there were several contacts from the same

```
C>DIR A: ¦ SORT ¦ FIND "EXE"
AUTOEXEC BAT      152   7-05-87   11:32a
FIND     EXE     6434   3-17-87   12:00p
JOIN     EXE     8969   3-17-87   12:00p
REPLACE  EXE    11775   3-17-87   12:00p
SORT     EXE     1977   3-17-87   12:00p
SUBST    EXE     9909   3-17-87   12:00p
XCOPY    EXE    11247   3-17-87   12:00p

C>_
```

Figure 12.31: Combining SORT and FIND filters

```
C>SORT /+43  < BUSINESS.TXT ¦ FIND "415/" ¦ SORT
Brandenberg Gates    754  Bennett    Mary   415/612-5656
Bucket Dance Wear    276  Lewis      Ann    415/635-2530
Intelli-Strategies   743  Griffiths  Robert 415/362-9537
Sole Survivor,Inc.   237  Evans      Gail   415/222-3514
Standard Shelters    690  Rucker     Sally  415/532-1107

C>_
```

Figure 12.32: Sorting, extracting, and sorting again

company, their entries would appear in phone number order for each alphabetized company.

This is another example of how a well-written DOS command can save you the purchase of a functionally simple piece of additional software. In the next chapter, you'll see an example of how you can set up a batch file to provide yourself with this kind of capability.

CONTROLLING SCREEN OUTPUT

The last filter available in DOS is named MORE. It causes the screen display to pause, just as the /P switch does with the DIR command. Why not just use the /P with the SORT filter? Try it, and see what happens. If you enter

```
DIR A:/P¦SORT
```

you'll only get a blinking cursor if your directory required more than one screenful of information. This is because of the way the filter works. When data is filtered, it is stored in a temporary file; only then is the output filtered. Since the output is to be filtered, it's not sent to the screen. However, the now inappropriate pause required by the DIR A:/P command occurs anyway, so the computer is forced to pause when a screenful of information is sent *into* the pipe. This is not what you really want.

The proper way to handle pauses with filters is to use the MORE filter, like this:

```
DIR A:¦SORT¦MORE
```

The MORE filter works because it pauses the output of the SORT filter, rather than pausing the input from the DIR command. This sequence will only display one screenful at a time from the sorted directory listing, signaling you with the "More" message that more output remains to be viewed. Pressing Return will display the next screenful of information. The command

```
DIR¦MORE
```

will create a directory display like the one in Figure 12.33.

PIPES, FILTERS, AND REDIRECTION: AN EXAMPLE

Filters can help you overcome missing features in existing programs. One common problem is knowing how to sort a mailing list created by a word processor that does not contain a sorting feature. However, if you plan a bit, you can get the SORT filter to help you out.

Here is a typical mailing list, which uses commas to separate the name, address, and city fields (categories of information). WordStar uses a file arranged like this to produce MailMerge letters.

```
Smith,John, 12 Main St., Oakland
Goren,Nira, 10 Maple Dr., WC
Ornas,Diana, 1 Nut St., Pinole
```

Assume that this information is stored in a file called NAMES.TXT. The file could be created with the text mode of any word processor; in WordStar, you should use the nondocument mode to enter data for this special purpose. The data could also be entered using the COPY command, as you've seen earlier:

```
COPY CON: NAMES.TXT
Smith,John, 12 Main St., Oakland
```

```
 Volume in drive C is ROBBINS
 Directory of  C:\PROGRAMS\FW\SYBEX

.            <DIR>      3-16-87   4:34p
..           <DIR>      3-16-87   4:34p
FIG10-2  TXT      813   4-01-87   6:39p
DEMO     BAT       16   1-01-80  12:16a
FIG11-1B BAT       60   3-23-87  10:21p
FIG12-2A BAT       55   4-01-87   2:25a
FIG12-2B BAT       40   3-25-87  11:05a
FIG12-2C BAT       34   3-25-87  11:06a
FIG12-4  BAT       73   4-01-87   2:59a
HELP     BAT      412   3-24-87  11:41a
FIG11-1  CAP     4256   3-23-87   7:46p
FIG11-2  CAP     4256   3-23-87  11:39p
FIG11-3  CAP     4256   1-01-80  12:28a
FIG11-5  CAP     4256   3-24-87  11:42a
BOOKCRED FW2    13888   4-02-87   4:42p
FIG10-50 CAP     4256   4-13-87   4:22p
FIG10-1  TXT      569   3-30-87  10:53a
FIG10-8  TXT      335   3-30-87  10:53a
FIG10-51 CAP     4256   4-13-87   4:27p
FIG7-5   CAP     4256   1-01-80  12:11a
-- More --
```

Figure 12.33: The MORE filter

Goren,Nira, 10 Maple Dr., WC
Ornas,Diana, 1 Nut St., Pinole
^Z

To sort this file by last names, you would enter

TYPE NAMES.TXT ¦ SORT > LIST.TXT

This would create a new file, called LIST.TXT, that would contain the sorted list of names. To see the contents of LIST.TXT, you could enter

TYPE LIST.TXT

The list would appear as shown in Figure 12.34. Since it is already sorted, it could now be used more readily by your word-processing program or any other application program.

The FIND filter can also be used to select entries based on some common text. For example, you could select all the people in your mailing list that live in a certain city. Look at the following command:

TYPE LIST.TXT ¦ FIND "Pinole" > P.TXT

This selects only those lines in LIST.TXT that contain the characters "Pinole". (Remember, the string of characters to be matched

```
B>TYPE NAMES.TXT
Smith,John, 12 Main St., Oakland
Gable,Nina, 1Ø Maple Dr., WC
Omney,Diane, 1 Nut St., Pinole

B>TYPE NAMES.TXT ¦ SORT > LIST.TXT

B>TYPE LIST.TXT
Gable,Nina, 1Ø Maple Dr., WC
Omney,Diane, 1 Nut St., Pinole
Smith,John, 12 Main St., Oakland

B>_
```

Figure 12.34: Mailing list sorted by filters and redirection

must be entered in the same case in which the original text was entered.) The results of this selection are then redirected to P.TXT, the output disk file. P.TXT will contain only one of the mailing-list entries—the one containing "Pinole", as shown in Figure 12.35.

As in the earlier examples, this method is not a substitute for a real data management program. For example, if someone lived on Pinole street in Richmond, they too would appear on this DOS-generated "Pinole" list. However, features like FIND and SORT can be of great value, even to a new computer user. As you'll continue to learn in the next chapters on batch files, you can do many things with DOS alone that you otherwise would spend considerable money on.

SUMMARY

In this chapter, you've learned about powerful DOS features for specialized utility operations. You've seen that redirection allows you to specify alternative input and output devices for DOS commands. Pipes enable you to direct the flow of information with precision from one command to another. Filters permit you to process the data as it flows through your central processing unit under your direction. The

```
B>TYPE LIST.TXT | FIND "Pinole" > P.TXT

B>TYPE P.TXT
Omney,Diane, 1 Nut St., Pinole

B>_
```

Figure 12.35: File extraction with the FIND filter

chapter presented the following important points:

- Special symbols are used by DOS during redirection operations. The > sign indicates a new output device, and < indicates a new input source. If you use the >> sign, the output is appended to the specified file.
- Certain DOS commands can filter data. This data can be input at the keyboard, from an existing file, or even from another program or command.
- The FIND filter selects lines for output based on some selection characters. FIND offers three helpful switches: /N generates output lines that are numbered, /C counts the number of lines found, and /V excludes lines containing specified strings.
- The MORE filter performs the simple task of making the display pause when output fills the screen. This gives you the opportunity to read the complete display before continuing the processing.
- The SORT filter can easily arrange the lines of output from any command or data file. Optional switches add significant power to this command: /R produces a reverse-order listing, while / +*n* sorts the file by the *n*th character space instead of the first. This allows you to sort your data in meaningful orders.
- Pipes are preceded by the ¦ symbol. They transmit the output from one command to another, in effect making one command's output the next command's input.
- Pipes can be combined with both filters and redirection in sophisticated ways to produce powerful results.

The examples in this chapter should serve to spark your imagination—you can now create your own useful utility extensions. With the tools from this chapter alone, you can develop your own programs for file sorting, text searching, and diskette cataloging.

PART 4

LIFE IN THE FAST LANE

Part 4 deals primarily with advanced commands and features. Chapters 13, 14, and 15 teach you how to use batch files to execute groups of DOS commands automatically. Chapter 13 describes the basic features and limitations of batch files and gives you practice in building simple batch files. Chapter 14 extends your knowledge by teaching you the DOS batch-file subcommands and parameters, enabling you to build more complex batch files. Chapter 15 presents many batch files and techniques that you can use immediately on your computer. In Chapter 16, you will learn a number of advanced DOS commands. These include special commands for advanced file and directory manipulation, for managing the DOS command processor, and for modifying the DOS environment.

THE POWER OF DOS BATCH FILES

CHAPTER 13

IN THIS CHAPTER, YOU WILL BEGIN TO LEARN ABOUT batch files. you've already learned several DOS features that give you added power. Batch files can multiply the power of DOS dramatically, not just add to it. This chapter will show you what batch files are, and how they can be created and used. You will learn why they are so important to you and to your effectiveness as a DOS user.

Up to this point, you've learned quite a bit about individual DOS commands. You know that when you want to execute a DOS command, you just type in the command at the prompt. When the command is complete, DOS displays the prompt again; then you can enter another command. You've seen that when you work with DOS, you must enter these commands one at a time.

Batch files allow you to enter a *group* of DOS commands automatically. A batch file is a series of ordinary DOS commands that the computer can execute automatically as a group (a *batch*) instead of one at a time.

You create batch files to automate DOS activities that require more than one DOS command. As you will see, this simple idea has some unexpected benefits. DOS's ability to understand simple batch files allows you to create sophisticated DOS programs, which are more complex batch files containing a series of commands and also special elements called variables, conditional statements, and subroutines.

BUILDING A BATCH FILE

Batch files can be as simple or complex as you want them to be. Let's take a simple task first. Assume you're working on a hard disk and would like to find out what .COM and .EXE files are available to you in the version of DOS installed on your disk. You would first need to change the active directory to the directory that contains the DOS files. Then you might clear the screen (with CLS) before you entered the appropriate DIR commands. You might successively enter each of the following DOS commands to obtain the desired output:

```
CD \DOS
CLS
DIR/W *.COM
DIR/W *.EXE
```

The result of this sequence would be the screen shown in Figure 13.1.

To complete the task, you had to issue four commands. If this were a task that you did often, you could automate the task with a batch file containing the commands. To do so, however, you'd need to know the rules for building batch files.

RULES FOR BATCH FILES

In order for DOS to properly recognize and process a file as a batch file, there are several rules you must follow. These rules apply to

- File type,
- Naming conventions,
- Limitations of the batch-file mechanism, and
- Running and stopping batch files.

BATCH FILES MUST BE STANDARD ASCII TEXT FILES

Standard text files contain normal ASCII characters, and each line ends with a carriage return (CR) and a line feed (LF). This definition

```
C>DIR/W *.COM

 Volume in drive C is ROBBINS
 Directory of  C:\DOS

ASSIGN   COM    BACKUP   COM    BASIC    COM    BASICA   COM    CHKDSK   COM
COMMAND  COM    COMP     COM    DISKCOMP COM    DISKCOPY COM    EDLIN    COM
FDISK    COM    FORMAT   COM    GRAFTABL COM    GRAPHICS COM    KEYBFR   COM
KEYBGR   COM    KEYBIT   COM    KEYBSP   COM    KEYBUK   COM    LABEL    COM
MODE     COM    MORE     COM    PRINT    COM    RECOVER  COM    RESTORE  COM
SELECT   COM    SYS      COM    TREE     COM    DEBUG    COM
       29 File(s)    2383872 bytes free

C>DIR/W *.EXE

 Volume in drive C is ROBBINS
 Directory of  C:\DOS

ATTRIB   EXE    FIND     EXE    JOIN     EXE    REPLACE  EXE    SHARE    EXE
SORT     EXE    SUBST    EXE    XCOPY    EXE    EXE2BIN  EXE    LINK     EXE
       10 File(s)    2383872 bytes free

C>_
```

Figure 13.1: DOS program-file listings

may not mean much to novice computer users; it is more important to know how to produce such files.

You can create a batch file using the DOS COPY CON command (see Chapter 12), the EDLIN line editor, or a word-processing program that can create an ASCII standard file or convert its files to ASCII standard. You can use the following word-processing programs to produce ASCII files directly:

- WordPerfect, using TEXT IN/OUT
- WordStar in nondocument mode
- WordStar 2000, using the UNFORM format
- Microsoft Word, saving the file as UNFORMATTED
- DisplayWrite III, using BLOCK ASCII SAVE
- Framework II, using DISK EXPORT ASCII

You can use the following programs to convert files to DOS standard text files after they have been saved as word-processing files:

- MultiMate, running the CONVERT program
- Samna, using the DO TRANSLATE ASCII command
- Symphony, using the PRINT FILE command

The best way to create and manipulate your batch files is to use one of these word processors, because a word processor offers the greatest range of commands for manipulating text. The next best way is with EDLIN; while it is less flexible than a word processor, EDLIN does have the advantage of being available with DOS. The "least-best" way is to use COPY CON, because it only allows text entry; it does not permit any manipulation of already entered text.

Because you may not have a word processor, this book assumes you are using EDLIN to create your batch files. If you need to refresh your memory on EDLIN, refer to Chapter 6.

BATCH FILES MUST FOLLOW CERTAIN NAMING CONVENTIONS You've probably noticed by now that there are certain classes of files on your system: .COM and .EXE program files, .BAS BASIC language files, .WK1 spreadsheet files, .DBF database files, and probably many others. DOS must be able to distinguish a batch file from these other types of files on your system.

You can give a batch file almost any name you like, as long as you use the .BAT extension. Of course, the name must adhere to standard DOS file-naming rules, with no more than eight letters or numbers in the base name. SIMPLE.BAT and START.BAT are examples of acceptable batch-file names.

Batch-file names should be unique. Never give a batch file the same name as either a DOS command or a program name (that is, the name of an .EXE or .COM file).

You should never create a batch file that has the same name as a DOS command (for example, DIR.BAT or FORMAT.BAT). If you do, DOS will become confused as to whether you wanted to execute the command with that name or the batch file with that name. DOS always assumes you want to execute a DOS command first; only if it can't find a DOS command (or any .EXE or .COM files) will it look to see if there is a batch file with the name that you typed in. DOS expects you to enter the command or batch-file name without typing the extension. Thus, you could create a file named DIR.BAT, but you could never use it—DOS would always assume when you entered DIR that you wanted the Directory command, not the DIR.BAT file.

BATCH FILES HAVE CERTAIN LIMITATIONS Only commands that work at the DOS prompt can be included in a batch file. You'll soon see that there are some additional controlling commands (called subcommands) that can be used in a batch file; you can also use variable input parameters, which will be covered in detail later in this chapter. However, the main commands that do something for you are always going to look just as they would if they were typed at the DOS prompt.

Users of diskette systems should be aware that exchanging a diskette containing an executing batch file for another diskette will force DOS to stop after it completes the current instruction and prompt you to reinsert the original diskette. Only then can the next instruction in the batch file be executed properly.

RUNNING AND STOPPING BATCH FILES Executing all the instructions within a batch file is as simple as typing the name of the .BAT file containing those instructions. As with commands and programs, however, if you don't precede the batch-file name with a drive identifier and a directory name, the assumption will be the current drive and current directory.

You can stop batch-file execution at any time by pressing the Break key combination (Ctrl-ScrollLock). DOS will ask you if you want to terminate the batch job. Usually, you answer Y for Yes, since that's why you pressed the Break combination in the first place. However, if you have a change of heart and answer N, the current step in the batch file will be ignored and the rest of the commands will be executed.

CREATING YOUR FIRST BATCH FILE

Take a moment now to create your first batch file. Create your own version of SIMPLE.BAT, including all the statements seen in Figure 13.2. Use the EDLIN program unless you are familiar with an available word processor and plan to use it for all your batch-file work.

When you enter

```
EDLIN SIMPLE.BAT
```

```
CD \DOS
CLS
DIR/W *.COM
DIR/W *.EXE
```

Figure 13.2: The SIMPLE.BAT file

DOS will create a file called SIMPLE.BAT. Remember that when you use EDLIN, you are entering text into a file. This means that nothing appears to happen when you type in a command. Only after the SIMPLE.BAT file has been written can you tell DOS to read, process, and execute the instructions contained in it.

Write the file now using EDLIN's simple I (Insert) command. Leave insertion mode by pressing Ctrl-C, and then enter E (to end the edit). The DOS prompt returns, and you are ready to execute the batch file by typing in its name *without* the .BAT extension:

```
SIMPLE
```

The results of typing in this one-word command are the same as those produced when all four commands were typed in separately. DOS executes each of the commands automatically, one after the other, without further assistance from you.

Like programs or disk-resident DOS commands, batch files can be located on any disk and in any directory, and they can be referenced by simply specifying the full path name to them. For example, if SIMPLE were located in a directory called UTILITY\MISC on drive C, you could execute it by entering

```
C:\UTILITY\MISC\SIMPLE
```

Remember, if you wish to prevent the batch instructions from continuing to execute, you only need to press the Break key combination.

EDITING A BATCH FILE

You will notice that the batch file you just wrote displays the command lines contained within it as each one executes. This echoing of the commands to the screen is controlled by the ECHO command. The default status of ECHO is ON, which means that DOS commands executed from a batch file are displayed as they are executed. However, output results are sometimes more attractive or readable if the commands are *not* displayed. Let's add a line to the batch file that will set ECHO to OFF.

Notice the extra DOS prompt on your screen after a batch file completes. This second prompt appears because EDLIN has inserted a carriage return before the end-of-file marker in SIMPLE.BAT. Don't be concerned; it won't cause any harm.

Bring up EDLIN again, specifying the full name of the file you want to edit, SIMPLE.BAT. Use the I command to enter

```
ECHO OFF
```

as the new line 1. To list the resulting file, enter the L command and press Return. EDLIN will display the five lines of your batch file:

```
*L
1: ECHO OFF
2: CD\DOS
3: CLS
4: DIR/W *.COM
5:*DIR/W *.EXE
```

You can then save the file and return to DOS with the End command.

Now you can try the modified batch file. As before, just enter

```
SIMPLE
```

That's all it takes to execute all the individual DOS commands contained within the SIMPLE.BAT file. Note that since ECHO is OFF, only the results of the commands, not the commands themselves, will be displayed (see Figure 13.3).

```
 Volume in drive C is ROBBINS
 Directory of  C:\DOS

ASSIGN   COM     BACKUP   COM     BASIC    COM     BASICA   COM     CHKDSK   COM
COMMAND  COM     COMP     COM     DISKCOMP COM     DISKCOPY COM     EDLIN    COM
FDISK    COM     FORMAT   COM     GRAFTABL COM     GRAPHICS COM     KEYBFR   COM
KEYBGR   COM     KEYBIT   COM     KEYBSP   COM     KEYBUK   COM     LABEL    COM
MODE     COM     MORE     COM     PRINT    COM     RECOVER  COM     RESTORE  COM
SELECT   COM     SYS      COM     TREE     COM     DEBUG    COM
       29 File(s)    2342912 bytes free

 Volume in drive C is ROBBINS
 Directory of  C:\DOS

ATTRIB   EXE     FIND     EXE     JOIN     EXE     REPLACE  EXE     SHARE    EXE
SORT     EXE     SUBST    EXE     XCOPY    EXE     EXE2BIN  EXE     LINK     EXE
       10 File(s)    2342912 bytes free

C>
C>_
```

Figure 13.3: Results of running SIMPLE.BAT

VARIABLES IN BATCH FILES

Until now, you've only seen batch files that have been designed for a specific use: for example, a batch file that quickly and easily lists all the .COM and .EXE files in the DOS directory. In such cases, the batch file works with constant values (*.COM or *.EXE). If batch files could accept variables, as more sophisticated programming languages do, they could be much more flexible.

You can create DOS batch files that will do just that. Variables in any language allow you to construct programs that differ in a well-defined way each time the program is run. In other words, the program stays the same, but the value used by the program to complete its tasks varies. You can consider the DOS batch-file feature to be a simple programming language.

Let's take a moment to look at the terminology involved. As you have seen throughout this book, many DOS commands accept a variety of parameters. These parameters are just additional pieces of information needed by DOS to clarify the task specified in the command. For example, the command COPY REPORT.DOC FEBRUARY.DOC contains the COPY command, and the REPORT and FEBRUARY documents are its respective source and destination parameters. Next month, however, you might want to run the COPY command again, with the REPORT.DOC file as the source and the MARCH.DOC file as the destination. Thus, the second parameter can be considered a variable parameter, since it needs to be changed each month.

Batch files can accept variables as easily as they can accept DOS commands. Variables always begin with a percentage sign (%) and are followed by a number from 0 to 9. Thus, DOS allows variables named %0, %1, %2, and so on.

To see how this system works, create a simple batch file called DEMO.BAT, consisting of the following two lines:

```
CLS
DIR *.%1
```

This batch file will clear the screen and then display a directory of all file names that have similar extensions (.COM, .BAT, .EXE, .WP, and so on).

Note that instead of entering .EXE or some other extension, you used the variable %1. This means that the batch file is not ''locked in'' to DIR *.EXE, DIR *.COM, or anything else. Instead, %1 can stand for anything you want.

Here's how the % symbol works. When you type in any DOS command, DOS assigns variable names to each section of that command. Look at the following command:

```
DEMO EXE
```

If this command were entered at the prompt, DOS would internally assign %0 to the first phrase (DEMO), %1 to the second phrase (EXE), and if there were other parameter entries on the line, % values up to %9. This allows you to refer to the phrases within your batch file. Since the DEMO batch file makes reference to %1, DEMO will actually use whatever phrase follows DEMO (in this case EXE) to complete the DIR command. Thus, the command

```
DIR *.%1
```

will be treated as if you had originally typed

```
DIR *.EXE
```

and the batch file will display all files with an .EXE extension, as shown in Figure 13.4.

Running the batch file again with a different value for the first parameter generates a different result.

```
DEMO COM
```

causes only the .COM files to be listed. You can refer to parameter %1 any number of times inside the batch file, even though DEMO-.BAT referred to it only once.

This technique is called *deferred execution,* since the decision as to what parameter will be used is deferred until the time of batch-file execution. In this example, a Directory command will be executed, but the decision as to what specific directory listing will be produced is deferred until the batch file has actually been called and the %1

```
A>DIR *.EXE

 Volume in drive A has no label
 Directory of  A:\

ATTRIB   EXE     8247  12-30-85  12:00p
IMSHOW   EXE    20090   6-20-85  10:09a
FIND     EXE     6416  12-30-85  12:00p
JOIN     EXE     8955  12-30-85  12:00p
REPLACE  EXE    11650  12-30-85  12:00p
SHARE    EXE     8580  12-30-85  12:00p
SORT     EXE     1911  12-30-85  12:00p
SUBST    EXE     9911  12-30-85  12:00p
XCOPY    EXE    11200  12-30-85  12:00p
        9 File(s)      6144 bytes free

A>
A>_
```

Figure 13.4: Running DEMO.BAT with one variable parameter (EXE)

parameter has been specified as the first parameter after the batch-file name.

Let's take another example of a batch file using variable parameters. This time, you'll use a second variable to create MOVE.BAT, a batch file whose purpose will be to move files from one drive or directory to another. As you know, you must do two things to move a file:

1. Copy the file to the new drive or directory.
2. Erase the file from the old drive or directory.

Your task is to create a batch file that will issue all the necessary commands, so that you only need to supply the file names to be moved and the identifier of the new drive.

The batch file MOVE.BAT requires two variables, %1 and %2. The first one will be a file name or a wild card to use for selecting a file or files. The second variable will be the letter specifying the destination drive. For example, you might want to move all the .EXE files from the current directory to drive B. To do that, you could enter the following four lines at the DOS prompt:

```
CLS
COPY *.EXE B:
ERASE *.EXE
DIR/W B:
```

Then again, you might want to move all the .PRG files from your DBASE\TEST subdirectory on drive C to the ACTIVE directory on drive C:

```
CLS
COPY C:\DBASE\TEST\*.PRG C:\ACTIVE
ERASE C:\DBASE\TEST\*.PRG
DIR/W C:\ACTIVE
```

There will probably be many occasions when you need to perform this operation between drives, between directories, or both, so this is a perfect opportunity to use variables. Write a batch file called MOVE.BAT, which contains these lines:

```
CLS
COPY %1 %2
ERASE %1
DIR/W %2
```

This batch file issues the proper commands for you if you merely indicate the desired file source and destination. For example,

```
MOVE *.EXE B:
```

will move all the .EXE files from the current directory to drive B.

```
MOVE C:\DBASE\TEST\*.PRG C:\ACTIVE
```

will move all the .PRG files from the DBASE\TEST subdirectory on drive C to the ACTIVE directory on drive C. The results are shown in Figure 13.5.

The MOVE.BAT batch file includes a dangerous command, ERASE. Since there is no automatic protection built into this batch program, a mistake can have serious consequences. If the COPY command in the MOVE batch file fails, the succeeding ERASE command will not allow you to effectively run the MOVE command again, since the original files will have been deleted. This can be a problem when your destination disk fills up or if you have a bad sector. Chapter 9 emphasized the importance of backup copies for your important files; writing and running a batch file such as MOVE.BAT reaffirms the need for such backup procedures.

The same batch file can be used to move the files the other way. Simply reverse the parameters. Entering

```
MOVE B:*.EXE C:
```

will move all the .EXE files from drive B to drive C. (Substitute A for C in this command if you are using a dual-diskette system.)

Variable parameters are a mainstay of batch-file creation. You should stop here for a while and try out these new tools. Create a batch file called PARA.BAT that uses three variables: %1, %2, and %3. Have this program make a new directory (MD) using the first variable as the complete path name and directory name. Have it use

```
C>COPY \DBASE\TEST\*.PRG \ACTIVE
C:\DBASE\TEST\DB3BOOK.PRG
C:\DBASE\TEST\START.PRG
C:\DBASE\TEST\INVOICE.PRG
C:\DBASE\TEST\CERTIF.PRG
C:\DBASE\TEST\RECOMM1.PRG
C:\DBASE\TEST\RECOMM2.PRG
C:\DBASE\TEST\PAYROLL.PRG
C:\DBASE\TEST\PAYROLL2.PRG
C:\DBASE\TEST\EXPERT.PRG
C:\DBASE\TEST\EXPERT1.PRG
C:\DBASE\TEST\EXPERT2.PRG
C:\DBASE\TEST\EXPERT3.PRG
C:\DBASE\TEST\EXPERT4.PRG
C:\DBASE\TEST\MESSAGE.PRG
C:\DBASE\TEST\LEDGER.PRG
C:\DBASE\TEST\INVOICE2.PRG
C:\DBASE\TEST\BOOKS2.PRG
C:\DBASE\TEST\DISKPREP.PRG
        18 File(s) copied

C>ERASE \DBASE\TEST\*.PRG

C>DIR/W \ACTIVE
-- More --
```

```
 Volume in drive C is ROBBINS
 Directory of  C:\ACTIVE

.                .                DB3BOOK  PRG    START    PRG    INVOICE  PRG
CERTIF   PRG    RECOMM1  PRG    RECOMM2  PRG    PAYROLL  PRG    PAYROLL2 PRG
EXPERT   PRG    EXPERT1  PRG    EXPERT2  PRG    EXPERT3  PRG    EXPERT4  PRG
MESSAGE  PRG    LEDGER   PRG    INVOICE2 PRG    BOOKS2   PRG    DISKPREP PRG
       20 File(s)   1413120 bytes free

C>
```

Figure 13.5: Running the MOVE.BAT file

the second variable as a wild-card file name. Then have it copy all file names meeting the wild-card specification in the current directory to the directory specified in %1. The batch file should do a DIR/W on this new directory after the transfer, and should end with a CHKDSK on the disk drive specified in the third variable, %3. For example, if you wanted the following lines to be executed in your batch file:

```
MD \TRIAL
CD \TRIAL
```

```
COPY EX*.COM \TRIAL
DIR/W \TRIAL
CHKDSK B:
```

you should be able to invoke your batch file as follows:

```
PARA \TRIAL EX*.COM B:
```

SUMMARY

In this chapter, you took your first look at the DOS batch-file mechanism. It extends the power of your operating system by allowing you to build your own new set of commands. The new set of commands can be used just like any existing DOS command, except that it is your customized batch file that executes when requested, and not a prewritten command provided by DOS.

You learned the following key points about batch files:

- Batch files can be as simple as one line or as complex as many hundreds of lines.
- Batch files can contain a series of sequentially executed commands or programs, or even other batch files.
- Batch files can be invoked as easily as any DOS command—by simply typing the name of the batch file. This allows you to create your own set of specialized add-on DOS commands.
- You can terminate the execution of your batch program by pressing the Break key combination.
- Variable parameters make your batch files very flexible in terms of when and how you can use them. These variables are referred to as %0, %1, %2, %3, and so on through %9.

The next chapter will take your batch-file construction skills one giant step further. You'll learn about the set of specialized subcommands designed to work only within the batch-programming mechanism. These unique commands can be incorporated into any batch file, making DOS comparable to a high-level computer language.

SUBCOMMANDS IN BATCH FILES

CHAPTER 14

The SHIFT subcommand provides the virtually unnecessary capability of running a batch file that needs more than the allowable variable parameters (%0 to %9). Most DOS books make you struggle through the concept of shifting parameters, using trumped-up examples. However, no realistic batch file needs more than a few input parameters; this chapter won't waste your time on such an impractical subcommand.

BATCH FILES HAVE THEIR OWN SET OF SPECIALIZED support commands, known as *subcommands*. You don't need them to create simple batch files, but you greatly expand your possibilities when you learn them. You'll learn about all of these extra built-in tools in this chapter. Depending on what type of batch program you write, you may need to use one or several subcommands.

Some subcommands will be commonplace in your batch files; for example, you will frequently use ECHO or REM to insert messages both in the batch file itself and on the video screen. You'll use others only occasionally; for example, you'll use PAUSE only for batch files that must allow users sufficient time to read information on the screen. Still others will be used in specific situations only. In this category, you'll see the FOR subcommand, which allows the repetition of operations, the IF subcommand, which provides decision making, and the GOTO subcommand, which manages the flow of control.

In the preceding chapter, you looked at some simple examples of batch files, in which each command was executed successively. DOS also allows you to execute these commands nonsequentially, according to your own specified order. Changing the order of command execution is known as modifying the flow of control, or simply branching.

This chapter deals with elements that make the DOS batch-file feature into a simple but practical high-level programming language. A final section in the chapter discusses the distinction between creating a standard batch-file chain (which allows you to transfer control of execution from one file to another) and emulating true programming subroutines.

INCORPORATING MESSAGES INTO BATCH FILES

In the last chapter, you briefly used the ECHO subcommand to suppress the display of the commands themselves while a batch file was processing. ECHO has some other uses. If ECHO is followed by text instead of by ON or OFF, it will print the text. Thus, ECHO can be used to display information on the screen during the execution of a batch file.

To see how this works, create a new batch file, called HELP1.BAT, containing several ECHO subcommands, each of which contains helpful information for a user (see Figure 14.1). This batch file will explain how the previously created MOVE.BAT file can be used. (The figure contains a few sample lines of text to demonstrate the method of using the ECHO subcommand; the dots at the bottom indicate where you can add additional lines of text.) Running this batch file by typing in

```
HELP1
```

at the DOS prompt results in Figure 14.2.

Notice that the first two commands set ECHO to OFF and clear the screen, so the remaining "echoed" messages appear without your seeing the actual ECHO subcommand for each line. Regardless of whether ECHO is on or off, the textual information on the ECHO line is always displayed. ECHO OFF only suppresses the display of any succeeding DOS commands in the batch file.

One of the command lines that is usually suppressed—and purposely so—is a REM statement. You will see many REM statements in batch-file listings. Here is an example:

```
REM This is a simple internal commenting line.
REM So is this... for the TYPICAL.BAT file
```

A REM (Remark) statement is used for internal documentation in a batch file. It usually contains notes to the programmer or to the future user of the batch program. Anything from the file name to information about algorithms and techniques will be welcomed by someone trying to understand the inner workings of a batch program. Nearly all of the remaining batch files in this book will have at

```
ECHO OFF
CLS
ECHO  The batch file MOVE.BAT is designed to
ECHO  transfer a file(s) from one drive or
ECHO  directory to any other drive/directory.
ECHO  ========================================
ECHO  MOVE first copies, then deletes the
ECHO  originals.  The general form is:
ECHO        MOVE  source  destination
.
.
.
```

Figure 14.1: The HELP1.BAT file

```
The batch file MOVE.BAT is designed to
transfer a file(s) from one drive or
directory to any other drive/directory.
---------------------------------------
MOVE first copies, then deletes the
originals.  The general form is:
     MOVE  source  destination

C>_
```

Figure 14.2: Results of executing the HELP1.BAT file

least one REM statement containing at least the name of the batch file itself.

If ECHO is set to OFF, then the REM statements will not be shown on the video screen during program execution. The more complex or obscure your batch-file logic, the more you need to have several REM lines built into it.

INTERRUPTING BATCH FILES DURING EXECUTION

There are two kinds of interruptions in life: permanent and temporary. DOS provides batch-file equivalents to these types of interruptions with the PAUSE subcommand and the Break key combination.

When a PAUSE subcommand is used in a batch file, the execution of the commands in the file stops temporarily, and DOS displays the message "Strike a key when ready...." When you press the Return key or the spacebar (or virtually anything else), the next command in the batch file will execute.

In a batch file like HELP1.BAT, which displays text, it's a good idea to add PAUSE as a final command so that the screen information can be read. Information that is displayed to a user is usually only one part of a more complex batch file; pausing the execution allows the user to read the messages before continuing the program.

The PAUSE subcommand is not necessary to the functioning of the program, but it has a practical function. Filling the screen with a lot of instructions is a sure way to lose a user's attention. Instead, you can display a little information, pause the display, clear the screen, and display a little more information. This will keep the user alert.

HELP2.BAT, an expanded version of the batch file that you saw in the last section, represents a two-screen help system (see Figure 14.3). This is implemented by inserting the two commands PAUSE and CLS into the middle of the batch file. PAUSE temporarily interrupts the execution of the batch file, prompting you to press any key when you are ready to go on. CLS simply erases the messages you've already read, so that you can concentrate on the new messages displayed. When you run the HELP2.BAT program, the results will be like those shown in Figure 14.4.

When a PAUSE subcommand is issued, almost any key will cause the batch-file processing to resume. One exception to this rule is

```
REM The HELP2.BAT File
ECHO  OFF
CLS
ECHO The batch file MOVE.BAT is designed to
ECHO transfer a file(s) from one drive or
ECHO directory to any other drive/directory.
ECHO .
ECHO MOVE first copies, then deletes the
ECHO originals.  The general form is:
ECHO      MOVE  source  destination
ECHO .
ECHO ***********************************************************
ECHO Press Ctrl-BREAK key to terminate these messages, or
PAUSE
CLS
ECHO .
ECHO ***********************************************************
ECHO Make sure you have a backup copy of all important files.
ECHO This batch file does an unconditional ERASE of
ECHO all the files requested to be moved.  It does this
ECHO even if the COPY command fails, and the files never
ECHO make it to the destination drive or directory (%%2)
```

Figure 14.3: The HELP2.BAT file

pressing Ctrl-ScrollLock, the Break key combination. If you press this, the batch file will be interrupted. DOS first displays a ^C on the screen and then asks if you wish to terminate the batch job. Figures 14.5 and 14.6 demonstrate the screen results of your answer. In Figure 14.5, your Y answer causes the batch file to cease immediately and returns control to the DOS prompt. This is a permanent interruption.

Notice in Figure 14.6 that the ^C occurred in the middle of the third ECHO statement's output. Because you answered N, the currently

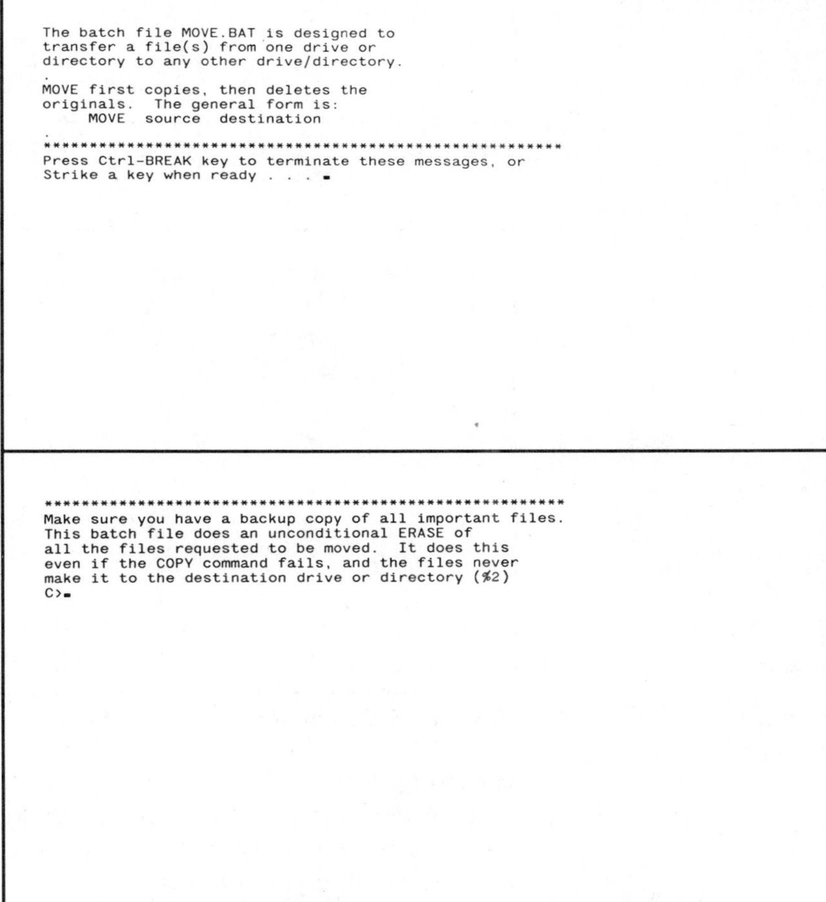

Figure 14.4: A two-screen help system created with PAUSE and CLS

```
 The batch file MOVE.BAT is designed to
 transfer a file(s) from one drive or
 directory to any other drive/directory.
 --------------------------------------
^C

Terminate batch job (Y/N)? Y
C>_
```

Figure 14.5: Permanent batch-file interruption with the Break key combination

```
 The batch file MOVE.BAT is designed to
 transfer a file(s) from one drive or
 d^C

Terminate batch job (Y/N)? N --------------------------------------
 MOVE first copies, then deletes the
 originals.  The general form is:
      MOVE  source  destination

C>_
```

Figure 14.6: Continuing a batch file after interrupting its execution

executing statement does not complete, and the batch file continues with the next line. In short, DOS's message gets in the way of normal batch-file output, which is another reason to avoid asking a batch file to continue after you interrupt it.

The Break key combination will also work with DOS commands that have built-in pauses, such as FORMAT and DISKCOPY.

When these commands display such messages as "strike ENTER when ready," the Break combination will cancel the command. You may also want to use Break to stop the execution of a batch file that is not working as you desire.

DECISION MAKING IN BATCH FILES

DOS can test the value of certain variables and parameters during the execution of a batch file. Performing this test is known as *decision making,* or *logical testing.* A logical test allows branching within a program, which means that different actions will be performed based on the results of the test.

A branching statement (also called a *conditional* statement) might look like this:

```
IF Something = Something Else   Do This   Otherwise Do That
```

A more formal way of stating this is

```
IF A = B Then Perform Action C   Otherwise Perform Action D
```

A = B is called a *logical expression.* As in any language, it can stand for such things as Wage = 500 or Lastname = Robbins. If A = B is a true statement, then C will happen. On the other hand, if A = B is false, then action D will take place. This branching ability allows you to create batch files that evaluate circumstances and perform different actions according to the conditions found.

AN EXAMPLE BRANCHING PROGRAM

To get an idea of the usefulness of branching, let's create a batch file that takes advantage of it and also uses what you've learned already in this chapter. This program's purpose will be to help you to search a disk for a certain file and report if it is there or not.

After you've worked with your computer for a while, you probably will accumulate many diskettes with many files. Once in a while, you'll need to locate one file among those diskettes. Which diskette is usually the big question. You can easily miss the file name on a complete disk directory listing, even if you printed the listing out and kept it with the disk.

A new batch file, LOCATE.BAT, is just the ticket. Type in the LOCATE.BAT file as shown in Figure 14.7. (The line numbers are for your convenience only—don't enter them!) Once you've typed in this batch file, you can simply enter

LOCATE *FileName*

to learn if the file is on the diskette.

The batch program presented here for diskettes can also be used to locate a file in a hard-disk directory.

Figure 14.8 depicts the step-by-step flow of execution for the branching that occurs in the LOCATE.BAT file you've just entered. The first two commands, ECHO OFF and CLS, are familiar to you by now. The next subcommand is new: the IF subcommand. It is used to test a condition that the computer can evaluate as true or false.

The IF subcommand can be used in three ways:

1. IF EXIST or IF NOT EXIST. This form of IF is used to test if a file exists.
2. IF A == B or IF NOT A == B. This form tests the equality of A and B, where A and B represent character strings. Note that DOS uses == as the symbol for equality. The character strings can be literals or variables. A *literal* (also known as a constant) is any unchanging character string, such as JUDD or END. A variable is one of the changing parameters %0 through %9, which you learned about in Chapter 13. For example, the command

   IF %1 == END

   tests to see if the first variable parameter in the batch-file

DOS usually doesn't care whether information is entered in upper- or lowercase letters. However, when you are testing for the equality of groups of characters, as you do with the IF and the FIND subcommands, case does matter. If you enter the lowercase letters *end* as the first parameter in IF %1 == END, DOS will evaluate the IF as false. If you enter the uppercase letters *END,* the logical expression will be true.

```
ECHO OFF
CLS
IF NOT EXIST %1 GOTO NOFIND
ECHO The file %1 has been located!
GOTO END
:NOFIND
ECHO The file %1 cannot be found.  Look elsewhere.
:END
ECHO ON
```

Figure 14.7: The LOCATE.BAT file

command, %1 (a variable), is equal to the letters END (a literal). This is the most common use of the IF subcommand.

3. IF ERRORLEVEL #. This form tests to see if the preceding command has been executed correctly and failed. DOS or any individual application program can set a return code equal to a number from 0 to 255. Usually, a value of 0 means that the preceding command completed successfully; a number greater than 0 indicates a failure, the value indicating the different reasons for that failure. Only DOS commands like BACKUP, FORMAT, and RESTORE will affect this return-code value. (You can, of course, write your own programs to set the return code, but that requires a course in

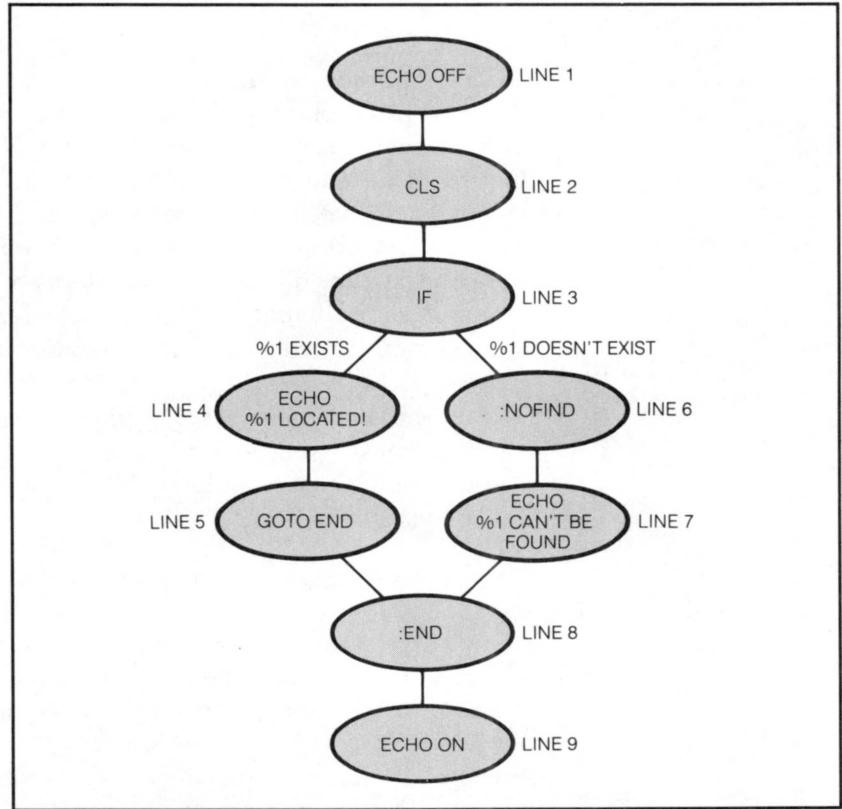

Figure 14.8: Flow of control in the LOCATE.BAT file

programming and goes beyond the scope of this book.) Note that ERRORLEVEL # means a return code of # *or greater.*

If any of these three DOS commands fail, the error level can be compared to a particular number, #, and different action can be taken depending on the severity of the error. The higher the return code, the more severe the error. The IF statement can control which succeeding section of the batch file receives control, depending on the value of this error level.

In this batch file you are using the IF NOT EXIST form of the IF subcommand to test whether a certain file exists. Line 3 is

```
IF NOT EXIST %1 GOTO NOFIND
```

What does GOTO NOFIND mean? The GOTO subcommand tells DOS to continue executing the batch file at a new place. NOFIND is a special placeholder, or label, that you enter into the batch file to indicate that desired location. Where is NOFIND? Look again at Figure 14.7. You will see :NOFIND on line 6. If the file name entered in the batch-file command line as %1 cannot be found on the disk (in other words, does not exist), then batch-file processing jumps from line 3 to line 6. The label line does nothing except facilitate this jumping, so the actual next line executed is on line 7. This branching technique is referred to in programming languages as the *flow of control.*

If, however, the file does exist, then the next command to execute will be the next available one in the batch file, the one on line 4. This is just an ECHO subcommand, which states that the sought-after file has been located:

```
ECHO The file %1 has been located!
```

The displayed message will contain the actual file name specified, typed in by you as %1, the first parameter on the command line.

The next line, line 5, is called an *unconditional transfer of control.* It is necessary in this batch-file language to enable the processing sequence to skip over the :NOFIND section of the program. The label :END is again just a placeholder to mark where processing can continue. If the desired file has been located (line 4), then the flow of execution should skip over the :NOFIND section, and the next line of code to be executed would be line 9.

Line 8 is called a *nonexecutable instruction,* because it does not represent any steps that the processor takes. It is simply a label for that place in the program. It can be compared to the address on your house, which is just a label that helps friends and the postal service find their way to you.

Let's go back now to the LOCATE command. To see how it works, try it with a file on a diskette or in a directory. Assuming your DOS operating disk is in drive A,

```
LOCATE A:chkdsk.com
```

will produce the message "The file A:chkdsk.com has been located!" The command

```
LOCATE A:topview.exe
```

will probably not find a file by that name. It will produce the message "The file A:topview.exe cannot be found. Look elsewhere." If you wanted to search a large directory on your hard disk for the VTREE.COM file, you could enter

```
LOCATE C:\utility\vtree.com
```

You might receive the message "The file C:\utility\vtree.com has been located!".

It's easy to see that the task performed by this batch file can be done in other—perhaps simpler—ways. However, you've used an IF subcommand, a GOTO subcommand, the label mechanism, and variable parameters. That's the main point of this batch file, not the actual job being performed. You can use these tools to make your own batch files, which will do meaningful work for you on your own system.

USING LOOPING AND REPETITION IN BATCH FILES

The FOR subcommand is similar to commands in other programming languages that facilitate repetition. Often, one or more commands in a program need to be repeated, sometimes a fixed number of times and sometimes a variable number of times. In either situation, the FOR subcommand enables you to meet this need.

The general form of the FOR subcommand is

```
FOR %%Letter IN (Possibilities) DO Command
```

Letter can be any single alphabetic letter. It is similar to the variable parameters you saw in Chapter 13 (%0, %1, %2, and so on). In this situation, however, double percent-sign variables are used. The %% tells DOS that you are referring to a batch-file variable in the looping FOR statement.

The *Command* in the FOR statement that will be executed repeatedly can change slightly during each repetition. This works similarly to the variable parameter method, which required you to write the batch file originally using %1 or %2 to refer to possible first or second input parameters. This method deferred execution so that when the batch file actually executed, it used the actual values typed in after the batch-file name, instead of using the placeholder % expressions.

In a FOR subcommand, execution is similarly deferred until the command executes. At that time, the *Possibilities* are evaluated, and the *Command* is executed for each possibility. When written into a batch file, this command can represent a more concise form of coding. For example, suppose you have a program called QRTLY.EXE that generates a quarterly business report. This program requires only that you specify the desired quarter for the current fiscal year. Entering the following at the DOS prompt would produce a report for quarter 3:

```
QRTLY 3
```

At the end of the fiscal year, you might want to generate current copies of the quarterly reports for each quarter. You would enter

```
QRTLY 1
QRTLY 2
QRTLY 3
QRTLY 4
```

and press Return after each line. All four of these successive requests could be replaced in a batch file called REPORTS.BAT with one automatic FOR subcommand, as shown in Figure 14.9.

FOR is a batch-file subcommand. This means it can only be executed from within a batch file.

Using this looping mechanism would not require you to wait for each quarterly report to finish before you requested the next to begin:

```
FOR %%Y IN (1 2 3 4) DO QRTLY %%Y
```

Your first reaction might be that this is an awfully complicated-looking expression just to save typing in four simple QRTLY report requests. Again, it just demonstrates the technique. If you had a monthly report program called MONTHLY.EXE, you could just as easily request the printing of twelve monthly reports with

```
FOR %%Y IN (1 2 3 4 5 6 7 8 9 10 11 12) DO MONTHLY %%Y
```

The modified REPORTS file would look like REPORTS2.BAT, shown in Figure 14.10.

As you've seen in the general form of the FOR subcommand, there can be only one *Command* parameter executed after the DO portion of the command. It can be a program name, as you've just seen demonstrated, or it can be another DOS command, like DIR or CHKDSK. The following FOR subcommand exemplifies this:

```
FOR %%A IN (%1 %2 %3 %4) DO DIR %%A
```

This command would perform a DIR command for each variable

```
ECHO OFF
REM The REPORTS.BAT File
REM Produce the Four Quarterly Reports
FOR %%A IN (1 2 3 4) DO QRTLY %%A
ECHO ON
```

Figure 14.9: The REPORTS.BAT file

```
ECHO OFF
REM The REPORTS2.BAT File
REM Produce the Twelve Monthly Reports
FOR %%A IN (1 2 3 4 5 6 7 8 9 10 11 12) DO MONTHLY %%A
ECHO ON
```

Figure 14.10: The REPORTS2.BAT file

parameter (presumably, four different file names). If this FOR subcommand were in a batch file called HUNT.BAT, as shown in Figure 14.11, you might invoke HUNT in the following manner to determine if any of the four specified files were located in the current directory:

```
HUNT HEART.EXE, LUNGS.EXE, LIVER.COM, BRAIN.EXE
```

The result might look something like Figure 14.12. Even though you've suppressed the display of the DOS commands themselves with ECHO OFF, the remaining output still appears cluttered.

Using a batch subcommand as the object of DO can produce a more concise and attractive result. An IF subcommand can be used to replace the DIR command:

```
FOR %%A IN (%1 %2 %3 %4) DO IF EXIST %%A ECHO %%A
   FOUND
```

The results, shown in Figure 14.13, speak for themselves. The desired information about whether the files exist is not obscured by any additional DOS directory information. In this FOR subcommand, the actual command executed by DO is IF EXIST %%A ECHO %%A FOUND.

Note, however, that the ECHO OFF command itself is still displayed. This is because the echoing feature is on until ECHO OFF shuts it off. DOS 3.3 users can surmount this limitation by preceding the command with the @ symbol.

```
@ECHO OFF
```

will turn the echoing feature off for all succeeding commands, and the @ symbol will suppress the display of this command as well.

Try out all of the sample batch files in this section to affirm your understanding of the subcommands. In some cases, you will have to

```
ECHO OFF
REM The HUNT.BAT File
FOR %%A IN (%1 %2 %3 %4) DO DIR %%A
ECHO OFF
```

Figure 14.11: The HUNT.BAT file

```
C>HUNT HEART.EXE LUNGS.EXE LIVER.COM BRAIN.EXE

C>ECHO OFF

C>
C>_
```

```
 Volume in drive C is ROBBINS
 Directory of  C:\PROGRAMS\FW\CHAP11

HEART    EXE   186787   2-26-84  11:45a
        1 File(s)   1335296 bytes free

 Volume in drive C is ROBBINS
 Directory of  C:\PROGRAMS\FW\CHAP11

File not found

 Volume in drive C is ROBBINS
 Directory of  C:\PROGRAMS\FW\CHAP11

LIVER    COM   236398   1-13-86   9:55a
        1 File(s)   1335296 bytes free

 Volume in drive C is ROBBINS
 Directory of  C:\PROGRAMS\FW\CHAP11

File not found

C>
C>_
```

Figure 14.12: Executing HUNT.BAT to repeat a DOS command

change the directory references to references that will work on your system. Either in addition to or in place of the examples in this section, create a new batch file—for example, GYRO.BAT—that will provide extra information to a user about your chosen topics. The batch file could be invoked as follows:

GYRO HEART

This would determine if a text file called HEART.HLP existed. If it did, the screen would clear and the contents of the HEART.HLP file

```
C>TYPE HUNT2.BAT
ECHO OFF
REM The HUNT2.BAT File
FOR %%A IN (%1 %2 %3 %4) DO IF EXIST %%A ECHO %%A FOUND
ECHO OFF

C>HUNT2 HEART.EXE LUNGS.EXE LIVER.COM BRAIN.EXE

C>ECHO OFF
HEART.EXE FOUND
LIVER.COM FOUND

C>_
```

Figure 14.13: Subcommands within subcommands

would be displayed. If it did not, the message "No help is available on subject HEART" would be displayed. Create your own sample .HLP text files to test your batch file.

USING BATCH CHAINS AND BATCH SUBROUTINES

Since a batch file can execute any command that otherwise could be entered directly at the DOS prompt, a batch file can invoke another batch file. By simply entering the name of the second batch file, you can pass control from the first to the second file. Execution continues with the instructions in the second batch file and does not return to the first (calling) batch file. This is known as *chaining*. It is different from the calling procedure familiar to programmers.

Look at the listings of the three batch files in Figures 14.14, 14.15, and 14.16. These three files together demonstrate both the capabilities and the limitations of chaining. Carefully read the steps of each of the three batch files, while looking at the output results in Figure 14.17.

The first batch file executes three simulated instructions and then invokes the second batch file as its last instruction. These simulated instructions take the place of any other successive batch-file

```
ECHO OFF
REM The FIRST.BAT File
ECHO Simulated Instruction 1 in First.bat
ECHO Simulated Instruction 2 in First.bat
ECHO Simulated Instruction 3 in First.bat
SECOND
```

Figure 14.14: The FIRST.BAT file

```
ECHO OFF
REM The SECOND.BAT File
ECHO Simulated Instruction 1 in Second.bat
ECHO Simulated Instruction 2 in Second.bat
ECHO Simulated Instruction 3 in Second.bat
THIRD
ECHO Last Instruction in Second.bat
```

Figure 14.15: The SECOND.BAT file

```
ECHO OFF
REM The THIRD.BAT File
ECHO Simulated Instruction 1 in Third.bat
ECHO Simulated Instruction 2 in Third.bat
ECHO Simulated Instruction 3 in Third.bat
```

Figure 14.16: The THIRD.BAT file

```
C>FIRST

C>ECHO OFF
Simulated Instruction 1 in First.bat
Simulated Instruction 2 in First.bat
Simulated Instruction 3 in First.bat
Simulated Instruction 1 in Second.bat
Simulated Instruction 2 in Second.bat
Simulated Instruction 3 in Second.bat
Simulated Instruction 1 in Third.bat
Simulated Instruction 2 in Third.bat
Simulated Instruction 3 in Third.bat

C>_
```

Figure 14.17: Batch-file chaining

commands that you might write. (You should focus on chaining here, rather than on other command lines; the simulated instructions are displayed merely to give you a representative context for the chaining technique.)

After FIRST is done, it passes control to SECOND by invoking as its last instruction the name of the file (SECOND) to which control will be passed. Then batch file SECOND executes another three simulated instructions before passing control to batch file THIRD. THIRD executes its own three simulated instructions before the chain process is complete. However, the line "Last instruction in Second.bat" is never executed, because the third batch file was invoked *in the middle* of the second batch file!

Proper chaining of batch files requires the new batch-file name to be the last instruction of the preceding batch file in the chain.

True subroutines provide you with the ability to write modular batch files that perform well-defined task sequences, and to temporarily leave one batch file to execute a sequence *without losing your place* in the first batch file. If you need to run a batch file while in the middle of another batch file, you can do this in two ways. If you are using DOS 3.3, you can use the CALL subcommand. If you are using an earlier version of DOS, you must invoke the COMMAND.COM program itself. The forms required are

CALL *BatchFileName*

for DOS 3.3 users, and

COMMAND/C *BatchFileName*

for all earlier versions. Since under most circumstances DOS batch files can only chain, the COMMAND/C version brings into memory a completely separate copy of DOS for the express purpose of running the named batch file.

With either the CALL or COMMAND/C method, when the batch file has executed all its commands, control will be returned to the very next line in the running batch file—the one *following* the CALL or COMMAND/C instruction—and execution will continue from there.

Look again at the THIRD.BAT file shown in Figure 14.16, and then look at FOURTH.BAT, shown in Figure 14.18. You can use these two files and the secondary command processor technique to invoke and run the instructions within the THIRD.BAT file, as shown in Figure 14.19. The results are different from the results of chaining.

Running FOURTH by this method will result in the same first three simulated instructions as with chaining. When those three have executed, control will be transferred to the THIRD batch file, at which point its three simulated instructions will execute. However, unlike the previous chaining example, control returns to FOURTH, which can execute its last instruction. If there were another instruction in FOURTH, or another hundred instructions, they would then all execute. In this way, sophisticated, structured application environments and systems can be built up by using only DOS commands and the batch-file mechanism.

```
@ECHO OFF
REM The FOURTH.BAT File
ECHO Simulated Instruction 1 in Fourth.bat
ECHO Simulated Instruction 2 in Fourth.bat
ECHO Simulated Instruction 3 in Fourth.bat
CALL THIRD
ECHO Last Instruction in Fourth.bat
```

Figure 14.18: The FOURTH.BAT file

```
C>FOURTH
Simulated Instruction 1 in Fourth.bat
Simulated Instruction 2 in Fourth.bat
Simulated Instruction 3 in Fourth.bat
Simulated Instruction 1 in Third.bat
Simulated Instruction 2 in Third.bat
Simulated Instruction 3 in Third.bat
Last Instruction in Fourth.bat
C>
```

Figure 14.19: DOS supports true subroutines

SUMMARY

In this chapter, you extended your understanding of batch files. You learned about a variety of specialized commands that only work from within batch files. These subcommands provide DOS with the kind of features normally reserved for a high-level computer language:

- Messages can be included for internal documentation with the REM subcommand. You can also include messages to be displayed during the execution of the batch program with the ECHO subcommand.
- All batch-file command lines are displayed on the console as they execute. You can suppress any particular one by preceding it with the @ character in column 1 of the command line (DOS 3.3 only), or you can suppress all succeeding command lines with the ECHO OFF command.
- Batch files can contain the standard logic seen in most programming languages. Branching is managed by the GOTO subcommand in conjunction with simple labels.
- Decision making is provided with the IF subcommand. DOS allows decisions on whether a file exists or not (EXIST), decisions on whether character strings equal each other or not (==), and decisions about the severity of command errors (ERRORLEVEL #).
- The FOR subcommand controls the sophisticated features of looping and command repetition.
- You can interrupt your own batch program temporarily with the PAUSE subcommand or permanently with the Break key combination.
- You can implement true programming subroutines by using the CALL subcommand (DOS 3.3 only) or by invoking a secondary command processor with COMMAND/C (for earlier versions of DOS).

Now that you possess these fundamental batch-file construction skills, the next chapter will make a more advanced user out of you. You will learn many tricks and techniques that will lead you to develop fancy implementations and systems of your own.

SOPHISTICATED BATCH-FILE EXAMPLES

CHAPTER 15

YOU'VE SEEN IN CHAPTER 13 THAT THE PRIMARY ROLE of batch files is to allow you to conveniently group together a collection of DOS commands, other programs, and other batch files. You've also seen how this entire collection of commands can be run by entering the batch-file name with any special parameters at the DOS prompt.

As you've learned in the last two chapters, there are two situations in which you should write batch files:

1. When you have a time-consuming sequence of unattended operations to be performed.
2. When you need to run a complex sequence of commands frequently, and you would like to ensure that they are performed consistently.

If a batch file you write works, *it's right*. It may not be the fastest, most efficient, or most elegant file, but it's still right.

In this chapter, you will see a wide range of batch files. These examples provide you with usable programs: you can type them in yourself, or you can send for the diskette with the files already on it (see the coupon at the end of this book). These examples will also give you ideas for creating similar programs for your own computer system.

AUTOMATING SYSTEM JOBS

DOS does not supply a default AUTOEXEC.BAT file. However, many application programs do supply one on their system disks. When loading a new application program, be sure that the program's AUTOEXEC.BAT file does not overwrite an existing AUTOEXEC-.BAT file that you carefully created.

When you turn on your computer and load DOS, DOS scans the root directory of the disk for a batch file called AUTOEXEC.BAT. If it finds that file, it executes the commands within it automatically.

AUTOEXEC.BAT is a valuable tool. In both diskette and hard-disk systems, it can be used to execute any number of DOS commands or other programs. For example, you can set the time and date if you have a battery-powered clock in your computer, or you can configure your PROMPT and MODE commands for specific serial-port and video-screen requirements. There is no limit to the variations you can make in your AUTOEXEC.BAT file.

Let's take a look at some of these AUTOEXEC.BAT variations. You'll look first at how to load and run a specific program automatically when you power up your computer. Then you'll see how to set up a customized PROMPT command. Finally, you'll explore some possibilities for more complex system setup.

AUTOMATING THE SYSTEM STARTUP

The AUTOEXEC-.BAT file must be stored in the root directory of the disk. It will be ignored if it is stored in any other directory.

It's easy to add an automatic startup feature to your system disk. As soon as DOS is loaded, the computer will run a particular program. Let's assume you want to run the BASICA program each time you start your system. Since BASICA is totally self-contained, all you need to do is use the COPY command to place a copy of BASICA-.COM on your new system disk.

Assuming your new system disk is on drive B for dual-diskette systems and on drive C for hard-disk systems, you would use the command

```
COPY BASICA.COM B:
```

for a dual-diskette system, or the command

```
COPY BASICA.COM C:
```

for a hard-disk system.

A simple task your AUTOEXEC.BAT file can do is to enter the name of a particular application program you want to execute. The principle shown here will apply to any program that you want to start up automatically when your system boots. For this example, you'd like to invoke BASICA.COM automatically on startup. Use whatever text-editing method you like to create an AUTOEXEC.BAT file containing the one line that invokes the BASICA program:

```
BASICA
```

If you'd like to try out this method with another program such as a word processor—say, WP.COM—make sure you copy WP.COM to the new system disk. In this case, your AUTOEXEC.BAT file will contain one line:

```
WP
```

Since many application programs include overlay files, you must be sure to copy those files to your new system disk. For instance, suppose your word processor requires a file called WP.OVL. You would need to have that file on the system disk containing your new AUTOEXEC.BAT file.

To see if your new setup will work as planned, restart the computer from your system disk. You can do this in two ways. First, you can turn off the computer, wait a few seconds, and then turn the computer on again. When the disk spins, DOS should be loaded and the program should run automatically.

As an alternative, you can use the keyboard rebooting procedure produced by the Ctrl-Alt-Del key combination. This will also restart the computer. However, it will not perform the same internal hardware and memory checks that occur with an actual startup.

Don't get casual about the Ctrl-Alt-Del rebooting method. If you are in the middle of running a program like a word processor, a database manager, or a spreadsheet, rebooting may destroy your current working file.

Using the Ctrl-Alt-Del key combination is also simple. If you have a hard-disk system, remember to remove any disk that is currently in drive A, since the computer defaults to that drive automatically. Hold down the Ctrl and the Alt keys, and press the Del key at the same time. Then release all of the keys. The system will load, and your AUTOEXEC.BAT will be executed. This is called a *warm boot,* since the computer has already been turned on. A *cold boot* occurs when you first turn on the computer's power; the same sequence takes place then, with the addition of several internal hardware tests.

Either of these rebooting procedures can be followed with most programs, and any main program can be run automatically at system startup. However, keep in mind that some copy-protected programs have their own instructions for automatic startup.

CHANGING THE DEFAULT SYSTEM PROMPT

Changing your default system prompt is often so useful that you might want to have it set automatically when you turn on the computer. You can use the AUTOEXEC.BAT file to accomplish this. Not only individual software programs, but also DOS commands themselves can be executed automatically during startup.

Create an AUTOEXEC.BAT file in the root directory that contains the single line

```
PROMPT $p$g
```

Even though this AUTOEXEC.BAT file contains only one command, there is no limit to the number of automatic commands you can have in this file. To see how this particular command is activated, reboot your system.

OTHER POSSIBILITIES WITH AUTOEXEC.BAT

There is no limit to the number of command lines you can have in any batch file. However, you should not write batch files with too many commands in them. They become harder to read, understand, modify, and debug as they get larger.

The possibilities are limitless when it comes to adding useful instructions to your AUTOEXEC.BAT file. Just about everything else you'll read about in this chapter could be included in it. For that matter, just about anything you've already learned, from setting the prompt uniquely to initializing function keys, could be included in your startup AUTOEXEC.BAT file.

For example, suppose that you want to simply press the function key F9 or F10 to generate a wide directory listing or a clean screen. As you learned in Chapter 10, the following two commands will provide that setup:

```
PROMPT $e[0;67;"DIR/W";13p
PROMPT $e[0;68;"CLS";13p
```

Include these in your AUTOEXEC.BAT file, and voila—your wish has become DOS's command. Use the more sophisticated versions of the PROMPT command presented in Chapter 10 if you'd like an even more useful prompt than this.

Use your own judgement and creativity in including commands in your AUTOEXEC.BAT file. The rest of this chapter contains a host of tips, tricks, and techniques that can be used with batch files. You'll want to include some of these in your AUTOEXEC.BAT file. The next section provides a good example of using batch files in AUTOEXEC.BAT.

CREATING YOUR OWN MENU SYSTEM

It's always helpful to set up a mechanism that makes it easy for you and others to run programs. Hard-disk menu systems are designed to provide that very capability. Of course, you can always buy one. However, an inexpensive way to set up a menu system is to use DOS's batch-file feature. A series of batch files stored on your hard disk can enable anyone to access the programs you have installed. You'll now see one possible design for such a series of batch files.

Remember that nearly everyone designs and programs differently, and that all of the batch files you see here are demonstrations. Feel free to add embellishments or to design the instruction sequences differently.

The first step in creating your own menu system is to create a file that will contain a listing of the programs available on your system. Let's put this display menu into a text file called MENU.SCR, as shown in Figure 15.1.

This file of text can be displayed each time your system boots up. All you must do is write an AUTOEXEC.BAT file containing these two simple commands:

```
CLS
TYPE MENU.SCR
```

```
          MENU OF AVAILABLE HARD DISK PROGRAMS

TO SELECT ONE, TYPE ITS NUMBER AND PRESS <RETURN>


1  -  INVENTORY MANAGEMENT SYSTEM

2  -  BUDGET ANALYSIS SYSTEM

3  -  WORD PROCESSING

4  -  SYSTEM UTILITIES


ENTER YOUR CHOICE NOW, PLEASE:
```

Figure 15.1: Menu management file

To make this menu work, you must create other DOS batch files for each option listed on the menu. For example, to run your inventory management system, you need to create a batch file called 1.BAT. Because the file's base name is the number 1, and all batch files have the extension .BAT, typing 1 and pressing Return will execute the commands in that file.

A typical batch file for a menu system would contain a set of actions like the following:

1. Changing the directory to the correct one (for example, C:\DBMS\INVNTORY).
2. Running the program. For example, to run a dBASE III PLUS customized inventory program called INVENT.PRG, the batch file would execute the command DBASE INVENT.
3. Returning to the root directory after the program has completed.
4. Displaying the menu again, so that the user can make another choice.

Of course, many other things could be done in a file like 1.BAT; for example, it could set a specialized path and then reset it at the end of the program. The rest of this chapter will focus on the many different things you can do in any batch file.

Figure 15.2 shows the contents of example .BAT files that perform three minimum steps. The three sets of commands shown in this figure perform the actions required for choices 1, 2, and 3 on the menu in Figure 15.1. The 1.BAT file brings up a database management program, the 2.BAT file brings up a spreadsheet program, and the 3.BAT file brings up a word-processing program. The contents of each of these batch files are almost exactly the same, except that the directory and program have been changed in each.

The fourth choice on your sample menu, SYSTEM UTILITIES, is interesting because it suggests the possiblity of a flexible multilevel menu system. You could create a batch file called 4.BAT that would contain a new screen display, listing several utility choices. The utility operations could be safely nestled inside other batch files, and another entire set of menu choices could be automated.

```
CD \DBMS\INVNTORY
DBASE  INVENT
CD \
TYPE MENU.SCR

-----------------

CD \LOTUS
LOTUS
CD \
TYPE MENU.SCR

-----------------

CD \WP
WP
CD \
TYPE MENU.SCR
```

Figure 15.2: The 1.BAT, 2.BAT, and 3.BAT files

At this point, you should write your own 4.BAT batch file and any necessary subordinate batch files to complete the menu example. Although you can use your imagination, start off with the following simple tasks:

1. Clear the screen, and display a file of new choices with TYPE. Call this file UTIL.SCR, and give the user these options:

    A. Display the current date and time
    B. Format a new diskette in drive A

    Remember that 1.BAT, 2.BAT, and so on are already used for your main menu, so your utility files will have to be named differently. For example, you might want the two options just presented to be contained in batch files named A.BAT and B.BAT. Or you could display the menu choices as 1 and 2, and then name the files U1.BAT and U2.BAT. (The latter method is preferable, since it presents a consistent appearance to any user; all choices are numbered 1, 2, 3, and so on.) In fact, you could even create new batch files called 1.BAT, 2.BAT, and so on, but you would have to place them in a separate directory and run them from there.

2. When done, display the main menu again (MENU.SCR).

Remember to add REM statements for documentation to all batch files that aren't transparently simple. Use them for your successor, for another programmer who uses your batch file, and for yourself—after all, *you* could be the one who, two months later, tries to figure out why a certain statement was included.

3. The final step is to create a new AUTOEXEC.BAT file that will start up your menu system automatically when the computer is turned on. Although you may come back throughout this chapter to change the file, start off with an AUTOEXEC.-BAT file that looks like the one in Figure 15.3. This file contains commands that change the prompt, open a path, clear the screen, and display the menu.

You are now ready to test the menu system you've created. Before you do, let's review the several files that make up your menu system:

- MENU.SCR. This file contains the menu display. It has no DOS function. Its only purpose is to tell the user what options are available on the hard disk.
- AUTOEXEC.BAT. This file executes when the computer is turned on or booted. It opens the path needed for hard-disk operation and displays the menu for the user to read.
- 1.BAT, 2.BAT, 3.BAT, 4.BAT. These files execute the choices listed on the menu. You should create one batch file for each choice.
- If you completed the exercise, you also wrote UTIL.SCR and several other batch files.

To test the entire menu system, reboot your computer. When the computer starts up, it should display your menu. You should test each option on the main menu, as well as each option you programmed into the submenu. Be careful to use a new disk or scratch disk when testing the FORMAT choice on your Utility menu.

IMPROVING PERFORMANCE WITH BATCH FILES

There are many ways to improve performance with batch files. Some of these are ridiculously easy—what's hard is thinking of them at all. In this section, you'll learn a host of simple possibilities for batch files. Since the lines of code are few, you can implement these approaches quickly if you choose.

```
ECHO OFF
PROMPT $P$G
PATH \;\DBMS;\WP;\LOTUS;\DOS
CLS
TYPE MENU.SCR
```

Figure 15.3: AUTOEXEC.BAT file for hard-disk menu management

SIMPLIFYING CONSISTENT SEQUENCES

Most of us are not great typists. Even for those who can speed along, there is great value to be gained in reducing the number of keys to be pressed. In the music world, there is much debate on the value of pressing one button and getting the sound of an entire rhythm section. No such debate rages in the PC world; anything that gets the same result with fewer keypresses receives a broad welcome.

ABBREVIATIONS Any DOS command can be abbreviated to the ultimate in simplicity with a one-line batch file. For example, the CHKDSK command can be shortened to the letter C simply by creating a batch file called C.BAT, and including in it the one instruction

```
CHKDSK
```

When you type C at the DOS prompt, the batch file C.BAT will be given control, and its one instruction will be executed as if you had typed it at the DOS prompt.

This technique can also be used for commands that normally take parameters, such as the RENAME or the XCOPY command. You could just as easily create a batch file called R.BAT that only contains the one executable instruction

```
RENAME %1 %2
```

When you wanted to use this command, you could type R instead of typing RENAME along with the variables. For instance, if you wanted to rename OLD.TXT to NEW.TXT, you could now type

```
R OLD.TXT NEW.TXT
```

DOS would quickly discover that R is a batch file, and the job would be handled through the batch-file invocation of the RENAME command, using the parameters represented as %1 and %2.

This simplification technique can be extended to commands with multiple lines. If you frequently do a CHKDSK on your A and C drives, your version of C.BAT could contain the following lines:

```
CHKDSK A:
CHKDSK C:
```

In this case, you won't even have to type C twice and press Return twice. On the other hand, the C.BAT file will be less flexible for other purposes, since it will always issue the CHKDSK command for two disk drives, A and C.

SHORTHAND NOTATION FOR COMMANDS Certain commands that perform fixed chores can also be simplified with batch files. For instance, you learned in Chapter 8 how to use the MODE command to manage various aspects of different devices. If your system has both a color and a monochrome monitor, you could use a batch file to invoke the proper version of the MODE command. To switch output to the monochrome monitor, you could enter

```
MODE MONO
```

in a file called MONO.BAT. To switch output to the color monitor using 80 columns with color enabled, you could enter

```
MODE CO80
```

in a file called COLOR.BAT. Then, whenever you needed to switch, you would only have to enter the simple batch name, MONO or COLOR, to obtain the desired result. With this method a user doesn't have to remember (or even know) the actual DOS command or command/parameter sequence that produces a particular result.

Another good use of this technique is turning on the compressed printing mode for your Epson- or IBM-compatible printer, which you learned about in Chapter 7 as well. You could create a batch file called COMPRESS.BAT that contains one line:

```
MODE LPT1: 132
```

You could create another batch file called NORMAL.BAT that would also contain only one line:

```
MODE LPT1: 80
```

Anyone could now type COMPRESS at the DOS prompt to send a wide spreadsheet or database information to the printer. When they were done, they could enter the command NORMAL to return the printer to its normal configuration.

Another benefit of this method appears when you acquire new printers at a later date. Only the inside portion of the batch file has to be changed once, and only by one knowledgeable person. Everyone else using the system still only has to remember to type COMPRESS or NORMAL.

REPEATED AUTOMATIC INVOCATION

Any time you need to execute the same command repeatedly, the following technique can come in handy. Perhaps you need to find a text string in a series of files located in different directories; or perhaps you just need to obtain a directory listing of several diskettes successively. This method relies on the fact that %0, as a batch-file variable, represents the actual name of the batch file itself.

Take a look at the CONTENTS.BAT file shown in Figure 15.4. In this batch file, the PAUSE command prompts you to enter a new diskette into drive A and then waits for you to do so (see Figure 15.5).

Remember that the line numbers in this batch file and in the other files listed in this chapter are there for reference only. If you type in these batch programs for yourself, leave out the line numbers.

If you press the Return key at this point, you will receive a directory listing of the diskette you placed in drive A, as shown in the top portion of the figure. However, this is also the point in the batch program at which you can terminate the otherwise unending sequence by pressing Ctrl-C. If you do not, the batch file will retype its own

```
REM  CONTENTS.BAT

PAUSE Load diskette into drive A:
DIR  A: /P
%0
```

Figure 15.4: The CONTENTS.BAT file

```
COLORBAR BAS      1427  12-30-85  12:00p
COMM     BAS      4254  12-30-85  12:00p
DEBUG    COM     15799  12-30-85  12:00p
DONKEY   BAS      3572  12-30-85  12:00p
EXE2BIN  EXE      3063  12-30-85  12:00p
LINK     EXE     39076  12-30-85  12:00p
MORTGAGE BAS      6178  12-30-85  12:00p
MUSIC    BAS      8575  12-30-85  12:00p
MUSICA   BAS     13431  12-30-85  12:00p
PIECHART BAS      2180  12-30-85  12:00p
SAMPLES  BAS      2363  12-30-85  12:00p
SPACE    BAS      1851  12-30-85  12:00p
VDISK    LST    136315  12-30-85  12:00p
       18 File(s)     107520 bytes free

C>contents

C>REM  CONTENTS.BAT

C>
C>PAUSE Load diskette into drive A:
Strike a key when ready . . . ^C

Terminate batch job (Y/N)? y
C>
```

Figure 15.5: Running the CONTENTS.BAT file

name and the word "contents," and the batch file will begin to execute again; you will be prompted to enter another diskette.

The key to this repetitive behavior is in line 5 of the listing. The %0 is only a variable parameter that substitutes for the original batch-file name typed at the DOS prompt.

PROGRAM SETUP AND RESTORATION

This section offers different approaches for initiating your own programs. You've already seen a typical small application method in Figure 15.2. In that example, a main program was run (perhaps with initial parameters) after the proper directory was entered. Now let's look at two other times you'll want to consider using batch files.

INVOKING THE SAME SEQUENCE OF PROGRAMS You sometimes perform a recurring series of steps in the computing world. For instance, you may run your word processor (WP.EXE) to create a new document and then, as a matter of course, run your grammar and style checker (STYLE.COM). You may also run a specialized spelling checker (SPELL.EXE) before you rerun your word processor to implement any suggested changes. The sequence, then, is as follows:

1. Word processor runs.
2. Style checker runs.
3. Spelling checker runs.
4. Word processor runs again.

If these programs do not allow parameter passing, you could write a batch file called WRITE.BAT, which would consist of the following lines:

```
WP
STYLE
SPELL
WP
```

On the other hand, many programs now allow you to specify a parameter to indicate the name of a file to be selected. If a program allows such a specification, then a batch file can be even more useful. Suppose you are working on a proposal called PROPOSAL.DOC. Your WRITE.BAT file could do more work if it contained these lines:

```
WP PROPOSAL.DOC
STYLE PROPOSAL.DOC
SPELL PROPOSAL.DOC
WP PROPOSAL.DOC
```

Simply typing WRITE at the DOS prompt would bring you successively through all four program invocations, each one bringing in the specified PROPOSAL file.

Here's another example. You may be working on the Great American Novel, and each chapter you write undergoes the same painstaking care and attention as the rest of your word-processed documents. You can take the simplifying process one step further by using the variable parameter technique. Look at the following batch file:

```
WP CHAPTER%1
STYLE CHAPTER%1
SPELL CHAPTER%1
WP CHAPTER%1
```

If you've named your files CHAPTER1, CHAPTER2, and so on, you can then invoke your four-program sequence by typing at the DOS prompt the chapter number as the parameter:

```
WRITE 5
```

Keep in mind that if your novel has more than nine chapters, you'll have to name them differently so that you don't exceed DOS's maximum limit of eight characters in a file name.

SETUP AND RESTORATION FOR TWO-DRIVE OPERATIONS Some programs assume that the data they use is available on the default disk drive and directory. Since DOS allows you to run a program that isn't in the current drive and directory, you can first switch to the drive or directory containing your data and then run the program. After the program is done, you can change back to your original drive or directory. This is usually the root for hard-disk systems, and drive A for dual-diskette systems. The technique for returning to the root was shown in Figure 14.2. On a dual-diskette system, you can perform a similar sequence of steps.

Figure 15.6 shows a typical configuration, in which programs reside on drive A and data files on drive B. Suppose you want to run a main program called ESTATE.EXE, which is on your program

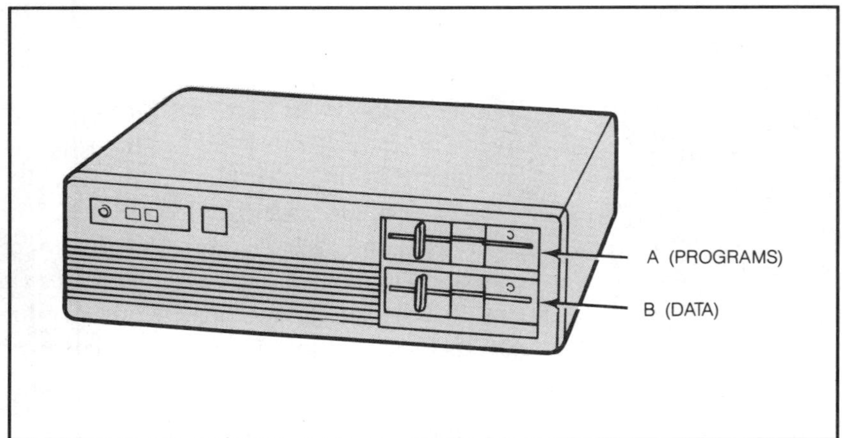

Figure 15.6: Typical configuration for a two-drive operation

disk and which uses several real estate data files on the data disk in drive B. The following batch file (SWITCH.BAT) will change the default drive to B for the duration of the execution of ESTATE.EXE, and then reset the default drive back to A. DOS will look on B for any files referenced by the ESTATE program.

```
REM SWITCH.BAT
B:
A:ESTATE
A:
```

CHAINING FOR DISKETTE-SWITCHING APPLICATIONS

As you know, any batch file can contain references to other batch files. Now you'll learn how those referenced batch files can also be on different drives. You can use this technique to develop sophisticated multidiskette applications. For example, you could have a batch file called FIRST.BAT on drive A, which has a number of instructions in it, ending with an invocation of a SECOND.BAT file, located on drive B. A segment of the FIRST.BAT file might look like Figure 15.7.

The SECOND.BAT file, which could control the backing up of your files onto a clean diskette, could be located on your data disk. SECOND.BAT might look like Figure 15.8. When control transfers to SECOND.BAT, its first instruction pauses the computer, prompting you to remove the main program diskette from A and replace it with a backup diskette. After performing the XCOPY backup sequence, the batch file pauses again so you can reinsert your original system diskette in drive A.

The last statement in SECOND.BAT is your opportunity to continue the execution chain. This ''last line'' can be the name of

```
Instruction 1
Instruction 2
.
.
.
Last instruction
B:
SECOND
```

Figure 15.7: Segment from FIRST.BAT file

```
PAUSE Place your data backup diskette into drive A:
XCOPY  *.*  A:
PAUSE Replace your original system diskette in drive A:
**** last line ****
```

Figure 15.8: Sample SECOND.BAT file

another batch file to execute, on either A or B. You can even include a variable such as %1 in this last line, transferring it from the original FIRST.BAT file to a THIRD.BAT program. The %1 could also be a command that would be executed as the last instruction of the SECOND.BAT file. In short, the last line in the SECOND.BAT file could contain A:FIRST, which would rerun the original starting program; %1, which would run a command passed from FIRST-.BAT to SECOND.BAT; or the name and location of any other batch file to continue the chain. If your last line uses %1, then of course the FIRST.BAT file should be modified to include a parameter in the final line.

INITIALIZING YOUR RAM DISK

A batch file is an obvious place for the series of commands necessary to set up your RAM disk. If you use the VDISK or RAM-DRIVE options of your CONFIG.SYS file, your RAM disk will already be created. However, some memory boards (like AST boards) come with a program that can initialize a RAM disk whenever you choose. If this is the case on your system, you should invoke the program with a batch file.

Say you have created a RAM disk called D. The following RAMINIT.BAT file could copy programs and files to it—for instance, commonly used batch files like HELP.BAT and frequently used DOS programs like CHKDSK.COM, SORT.EXE, and the command processor COMMAND.COM.

```
COPY HELP.BAT D:
COPY CHKDSK.COM D:
COPY SORT.EXE D:
COPY COMMAND.COM D:
```

You could also set the COMSPEC environment here to tell DOS

where to find the command processor. (COMSPEC is a special DOS variable, designed to specify where a copy of COMMAND.COM can be found. You will learn more about this variable in Chapter 16.)

Finally, you could reset the path to check the RAM disk for referenced files that are not in the default directory:

> If you use this RAM disk method for improving your system's performance, remember to put the RAM disk on your path *before* any other references to directories that may contain the original copies of the files. Then the fast-access RAM copy of the referenced file is located first, before the slower disk-resident version of the same file.

```
SET COMSPEC = D:\COMMAND.COM
PATH D:\;C:\LOTUS;C:\WP;C:\UTILITY;C:\DOS
```

In Chapter 10, you learned about a wide range of uses for a RAM disk. Placing all of those things in this RAMINIT.BAT file is a good technique, even if you eventually include a reference to RAMINIT-.BAT in your AUTOEXEC.BAT file for automatic initialization of your RAM drive.

INITIALIZING YOUR COLOR MONITOR

You learned in Chapter 10 how to use the PROMPT command to set up the foreground and background colors on a color monitor. Having to look up or remember the codes can be tedious. This is a perfect opportunity for a batch file. RGB.BAT will expect two parameters, each specifying what colors the monitor should use for the foreground and background. The calling sequence will be

RGB *Foreground Background*

Entering the following sequence at the DOS prompt will cause all future output to appear in blue letters on a white background:

```
RGB BLUE WHITE
```

The batch file itself can be seen in Figure 15.9.

Several interesting points are demonstrated in this file:

- There are two major sections in the logical flow. The first section (lines 3–28) controls the setting of the background colors, according to the second color parameter specified after the

```
REM  RGB.BAT

ECHO OFF
IF ARG==ARG%2 GOTO FOREGROUND
GOTO BK%2
:BKBLACK
PROMPT $e[40m
GOTO FOREGROUND
:BKWHITE
PROMPT $e[47m
GOTO FOREGROUND
:BKRED
PROMPT $e[41m
GOTO FOREGROUND
:BKGREEN
PROMPT $e[42m
GOTO FOREGROUND
:BKBLUE
PROMPT $e[44m
GOTO FOREGROUND
:BKMAGENTA
PROMPT $e[45m
GOTO FOREGROUND
:BKCYAN
PROMPT $e[46m
GOTO FOREGROUND
:BKBROWN
PROMPT $e[43m

:FOREGROUND
ECHO ON
ECHO OFF
CLS
IF ARG==ARG%1 GOTO DONE
GOTO %1
:BLACK
PROMPT $p$g$e[30m
GOTO DONE
:WHITE
PROMPT $p$g$e[37m
GOTO DONE
:RED
PROMPT $p$g$e[31m
GOTO DONE
:GREEN
PROMPT $p$g$e[32m
GOTO DONE
:BLUE
PROMPT $p$g$e[34m
GOTO DONE
:MAGENTA
PROMPT $p$g$e[35m
GOTO DONE
:CYAN
PROMPT $p$g$e[36m
GOTO DONE
:BROWN
PROMPT $p$g$e[33m
:DONE
ECHO ON
CLS
```

Figure 15.9: RGB.BAT sets foreground and background colors

batch-file name RGB. The second section (lines 30–58) controls the foreground color settings, based on the value of the first parameter on the batch file line.

- This batch file is not case-sensitive, as other batch programs that relied on the IF subcommand would be. In other words, each of the following commands would produce the same result:

```
RGB    BLUE WHITE
rgb    blue white
```

- You can use the IF ARG = = ARG%1 technique to test for the absence of a variable parameter. This IF test will only be true if the variable is missing.

- ECHO ON and OFF, followed by a screen clearing, is necessary between the setting of the foreground and background colors. The foreground prompt must take effect while ECHO is off and before the background color is set.

The overall flow of this program can be seen in Figure 16.10.

SOPHISTICATED BATCH FILES

This section deals with some specific batch files used by experienced DOS users. People's perceptions of advanced subjects differ dramatically; what one person views as sophisticated, another views as old hat. The batch-file techniques presented here are beneficial. If they're new to you, that's all the better. If they're old hat, perhaps

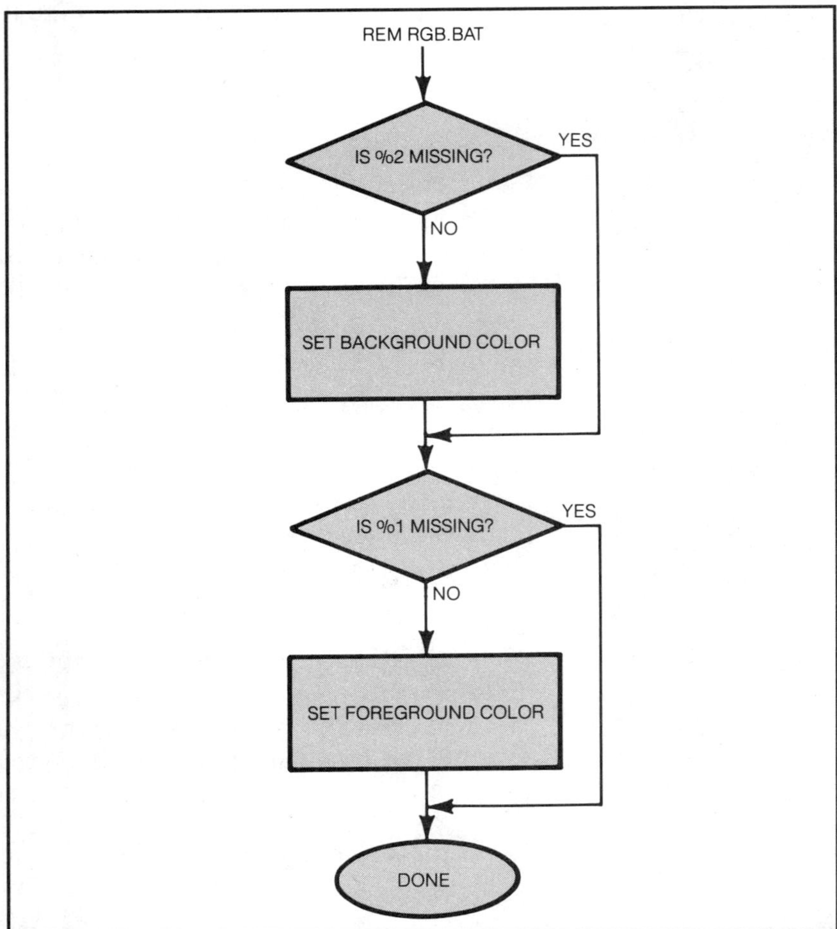

Figure 15.10: Logical flow in the RGB.BAT file

you'll learn some new approaches by the manner in which these batch programs are implemented.

CUSTOMIZED SYSTEM HELP SCREENS

Some systems are used by many people at different times. A desirable feature for such a system is customizable help screens. You can use the batch-file mechanism in DOS to easily set up this capability. All it takes is the INFO.BAT file, shown in Figure 15.11.

```
1   REM  INFO.BAT
2
3   ECHO OFF
4   IF EXIST %1.HLP  GOTO OK
5   ECHO Sorry.  No help available for %1
6   GOTO END
7
8   :OK
9   TYPE %1.HLP
10  PAUSE
11
12  :END
```

Figure 15.11: Customizable help screens with INFO.BAT

Once you've installed this batch file in your path, you can use it from any directory. All you need to do is write a text file with an .HLP extension. This file should contain the text information you'd like displayed for anyone requesting help. The user, in turn, will only need to run the INFO.BAT file, specifying the first parameter as the topic for which help is desired.

For example, if there is a subject named GOBBLEDY for which you wish to provide users with helpful on-line information, you should place the information in a text file called GOBBLEDY.HLP. Then the user need only enter

INFO GOBBLEDY

to display the predefined textual information (see Figure 15.12). If help is not available on your system (that is, an .HLP file does not exist for the subject), then a simple message to that effect is given (see Figure 15.13).

In this example of a help file, no CLS instruction is executed. It was omitted so that Figures 15.12 and 15.13 could show the entire resulting sequences. If you were to write a similar INFO system for yourself, you might want to consider inserting CLS instructions before lines 5 and 9, the output lines in the INFO.BAT batch file.

The program in Figure 15.11 can be understood quickly by looking at the logic-flow diagram in Figure 15.14. The heart of the batch program begins at line 4, after the initial REM and ECHO OFF statements. If an .HLP file exists for the subject (entered as %1), then the batch file continues executing at line 8. This is really only the label :OK, which is needed by the GOTO statement in line 4. The help information is presented to the user by the TYPE statement in line 9. The PAUSE statement ensures that the user will have time to read the information before anything else appears on the screen or before the screen is cleared.

If no help file exists, the IF statement in line 4 causes line 5 to be executed next. The ECHO statement displays a "Sorry ..." message

```
C>INFO GOBBLEDY

C>REM  INFO.BAT

C>
C>ECHO OFF
GOBBLEDYGOOK is a specially coined phrase which means wordy and
generally unintelligible jargon.  It is symptomatic of many
computer textbooks.  No one believes that the phrase could
possibly apply to their writings or utterances.

Strike a key when ready . . . ▪
```

Figure 15.12: INFO.BAT makes on-line help available

```
C>INFO ARRAYS

C>REM  INFO.BAT

C>
C>ECHO OFF
Sorry.  No help available for ARRAYS

C>▪
```

Figure 15.13: Screen display when help is not available

to the user, and the batch program ends immediately. This is handled by the GOTO statement in line 6, which ensures that none of the instructions between lines 7 and 11 execute.

APPOINTMENT REMINDER SYSTEM

Some computer systems offer the luxury of automatic appointment reminders. In addition, some utility packages like SideKick

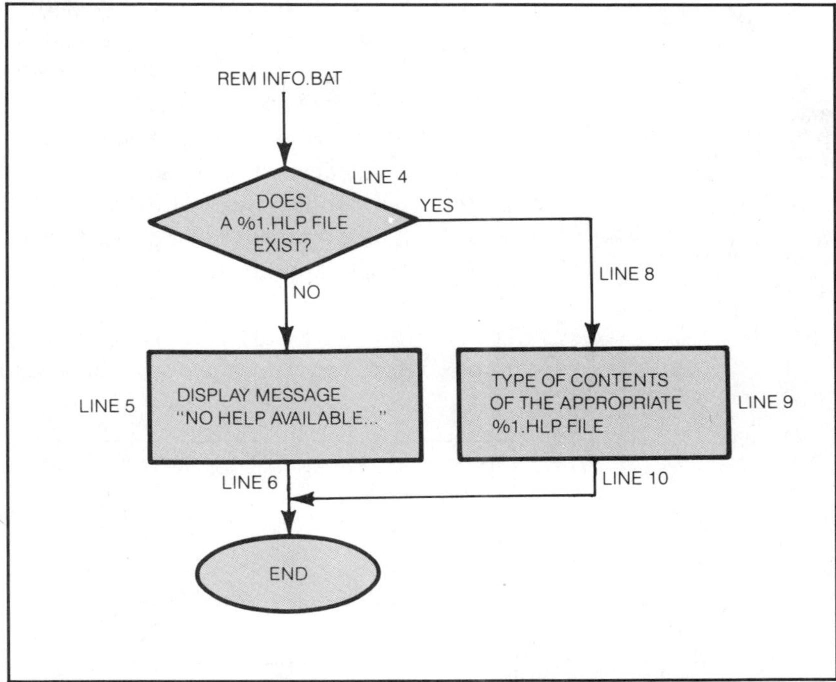

Figure 15.14: Logic flow for INFO.BAT

permit the entry and retrieval of date-oriented information (however, this is not automatic). The following example can take away the problem of forgetting to check your message or appointment log.

Unless you're very self-disciplined, the easiest way to implement this method begins by including a couple of reminders in your AUTOEXEC.BAT file. For instance, these three lines should jog your memory:

```
ECHO Remember to enter the following command to
ECHO get your messages for today (or any day).
ECHO TODAY mm-dd-yy
```

When you want to see the message or appointment file for, say, January 1, 1988, you only need to enter

```
TODAY 01-01-88
```

The results of this sequence can be seen in Figure 15.15.

The naming convention for date files must be adhered to precisely. If you use dashes, slashes, or even leading zeros to create the text files, then you must also use them when you call up the TODAY.BAT file.

The actual batch file that manages this simple operation is shown in Figure 15.16. As you can see, it is only a variation on the help method of the preceding section. The date files are text files, differing only in name and content from the .HLP files.

The way in which these text files are used (via the TYPE command) also reflects a similar batch-file approach. With the INFO method, all the files were similarly named with an .HLP extension, and their base names reflected the actual topic for which help was desired. In this appointment reminder system, the actual file name is understood (via %1) to be the date itself, a simple enough naming convention. The batch file types out the text file by that precise name. Here, you cannot assume that the batch-file code has the intel-

```
C>TODAY Ø1-Ø1-88

C>REM  TODAY.BAT

C>
C>ECHO OFF
Happy new year!
You probably shouldn't be at work today at all.
However, since you are, don't forget to start writing 1988
         on all your checks, memos, etc.
Also, don't forget the paperwork for the new tech writer
      beginning work tomorrow.

C>TODAY 1/1/88

C>REM  TODAY.BAT

C>
C>ECHO OFF
No messages for 1/1/88

C>_
```

Figure 15.15: Running the TODAY.BAT file

```
REM  TODAY.BAT

ECHO OFF
IF NOT EXIST %1 GOTO ERROR

TYPE %1
GOTO END

:ERROR
ECHO No messages for %1

:END
```

Figure 15.16: The TODAY.BAT file

ligence of the DOS DATE command; in other words, 01-01-88 could not be replaced by 1/1/88 or any other variation.

The logic flow for this batch file can be found in Figure 15.17. You can see that it is only slightly different from the logic flow in the INFO.BAT file.

Remember to erase your older date files when you no longer need them. Date files tend to proliferate quickly if they are not erased after use.

One of many additions to this batch file could be the simple addition of the line

```
DATE %1
```

just before line 6 (the TYPE instruction). In systems that do not have a battery-backed clock/calendar, you usually have to run the DATE command when you bring up the system. Since you must enter the date once for your appointment-making system, you can let the batch-parameter mechanism do the work of setting the date as well. Programmers are always looking for ways to reduce user intervention time, system program time, or both. Minor improvements like this will add up dramatically over time.

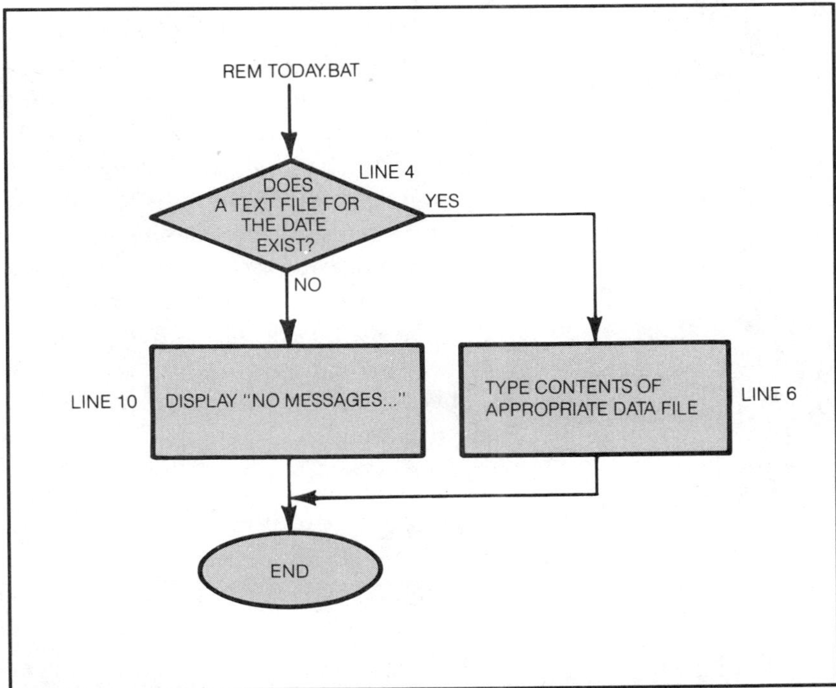

Figure 15.17: Logic flow for TODAY.BAT

BROADCASTING SYSTEM MESSAGES

Yet another variation on the theme of this section can be seen in the ANNOUNCE.BAT file of Figure 15.18. This batch program uses an area in memory called the *DOS environment,* which contains a set of variables and the values assigned to them. The DOS environment always includes the COMSPEC variable and the values you assign to PATH and PROMPT variables, as well as other arbitrarily named variables used by some programs or by the batch files described here.

A little-known technique of referencing DOS environment variables from within batch files allows you to broadcast messages to your system's users. This technique is useful for systems that have a number of different users, with perhaps one primary user. The goal is to have a simple command like

```
ANNOUNCE
```

display any and all current system messages for a user (see Figure 15.19).

In this figure, the first line is the key to the technique. You initialize a DOS environment variable (MESSAGE) equal to the name of this week's message file. In this case, the primary system operator only has to make the assignment of WEEK34.TXT to MESSAGE once, usually at the beginning of the day. For the rest of the time that the system is up, simply typing ANNOUNCE at the DOS prompt will display the current message file. Only the system operator needs to know the name of the actual message file, and from week to week, everyone's procedure for displaying system messages remains the same. Even the naming conventions can change, and the system operator is the only one who needs to know it.

This batch program can be modified slightly to allow for recurring messages that don't change from week to week. For instance, you could insert another line before line 5, like

```
TYPE ALWAYS.TXT
```

Then the ALWAYS.TXT file could contain any constant that you wished to display always, regardless of the week. This could contain such things as the operator's name and phone number, the service bureau's phone number, the security guard's extension, and so forth.

```
REM ANNOUNCE.BAT

ECHO OFF
ECHO Current System Messages:
TYPE %message%
```

Figure 15.18: The ANNOUNCE.BAT file

```
C>SET MESSAGE=WEEK34.TXT

C>TYPE WEEK34.TXT
Messages for Week 34 of FY88:
     Ted Bishop is on vacation.  Susanne Powers will be filling in.
     Next Saturday is the company picnic.  Mary has the tickets.
     Don't forget.  Backup, backup, backup.
     Time cards due on Thursday this week!

C>ANNOUNCE

C>REM ANNOUNCE.BAT

C>
C>ECHO OFF
Current System Messages:
Messages for Week 34 of FY88:
     Ted Bishop is on vacation.  Susanne Powers will be filling in.
     Next Saturday is the company picnic.  Mary has the tickets.
     Don't forget.  Backup, backup, backup.
     Time cards due on Thursday this week!

C>_
```

Figure 15.19: ANNOUNCE.BAT displays all current system messages

USING BATCH-FILE SUBROUTINES FOR STATUS TRACKING

Programmers use a variety of techniques for debugging their code. One of those techniques places additional printing statements at critical points in the source code. These are like snapshots. When the execution flow reaches these points, various parameters and variable values are printed out. The current program status can then be assessed and the problem discovered.

Programmers using this technique quickly learned the value of sending these debugging snapshots to a disk file instead. In this way, their program is not slowed down, and normal screen output is not compromised by debugging output.

You can borrow a page from the programmer's book for your own batch-file programming. Your batch files may at times become complicated, especially if you use the multifile technique of chaining. In writing any batch file, consider writing your own SNAPSHOT.BAT file. In a simple implementation, it could consist solely of the following two commands:

```
DIR >> AUDIT.TXT
CHKDSK >> AUDIT.TXT
```

Whenever SNAPSHOP.BAT was invoked, the current directory and disk status would be noted, and the >> redirection symbol would ensure that the AUDIT.TXT file would receive this information. You could later peruse the contents of this "tracking file" at your leisure.

The CALL subcommand in DOS 3.3 (or the COMMAND/C feature of earlier DOS versions) is also critical to effective use of the snapshot method. You may want to note the current disk directory and memory status at various points during the execution of one of your batch files.

The ANYOLD1.BAT file shown in Figure 15.20 is representative of any batch file you might write; the vertical dots just stand for your own instructions. Some example DOS commands, like COPY, DIR, and ERASE, have been included. The snapshot is taken by inserting a line that runs the SNAPSHOT.BAT file immediately.

In the figure, lines 8 and 18 use the CALL subcommand. If you're using a version of DOS earlier than 3.3, you could just replace the CALL subcommand with the following:

```
COMMAND/C SNAPSHOT
```

This invokes a secondary copy of the command processor, which then runs the SNAPSHOT batch file before continuing with other statements in the batch program you are testing.

When you are creating your batch file, you can insert as many of these secondary command processor lines as you need to assess the actual actions of your batch program. All of the snapshot results will be placed in the AUDIT.TXT file. You can erase this file any time you'd like to clear it out, since the >> redirection parameter will recreate the AUDIT.TXT file if it does not exist. After your batch file is complete and working just the way you want it to, you can remove all of the snapshot lines.

Note the use of the PAUSE command in ANYOLD1.BAT. Since the next command is ERASE, you're giving the user of your batch program a last chance to cancel out the continuation of the batch file. This is made especially useful by the preceding display of the A and C directories in the ANYOLD1 program.

Several creative variations on this method are available to you. Look at the modified SNAPSHOT.BAT file in Figure 15.21. In this version, two additional lines have been added before the DIR and CHKDSK lines. In fact, the DIR and CHKDSK commands are now being executed for both of the disks affected by commands in ANYOLD1.BAT. Line 4 is an add-on utility program that displays the system date and time. It is one of the Norton Utilities and it presents this information in an attractive and readable format.

You could, of course, use DOS's DATE and TIME commands instead of an additional utility, redirecting their output to the AUDIT.TXT file. However, doing this would require you to press the Return key twice. This is because DOS will place its normal request for any date and time changes in the AUDIT.TXT file

```
REM ANYOLD1.BAT
          .
          .
          .
COPY A:*.DBF  C:\DATABASE
CALL SNAPSHOT
          .
          .
          .
DIR C:\DATABASE
DIR A:
PAUSE Everything look OK? BREAK, if not.
ERASE A:\*.WK1
CALL SNAPSHOT
```

Figure 15.20: The ANYOLD1.BAT file

```
1  REM  SNAPSHOT.BAT
2
3  ECHO Snapshot at point %1  >> AUDIT.TXT
4  TM          >> AUDIT.TXT
5  DIR/W  A:   >> AUDIT.TXT
6  CHKDSK A:   >> AUDIT.TXT
7  DIR/W  C:   >> AUDIT.TXT
8  CHKDSK C:   >> AUDIT.TXT
```

Figure 15.21: The SNAPSHOT.BAT file

instead of on your video monitor. You won't see the requests, but DOS will wait for your response anyway.

Naturally, you can modify the snapshot examples presented here to include any other utility program lines or DOS commands that will provide you with useful information.

Line 3 represents another useful variation. The AUDIT.TXT file will expand to include many entries, depending on the complexity of your batch file and how often you invoke the COMMAND/C instruction. Each entry can be tagged so that it indicates where the snapshot was taken.

Figure 15.22 shows the beginning of the AUDIT.TXT file. The first AUDIT entry sequence is labeled anyold1-A. When the secondary processor begins each time, it runs the SNAPSHOT program, passing the first parameter (%1) along. Line 3 accounts for the value of this parameter (anyold1-A) appearing in the output file AUDIT.TXT. You need only type a different string of characters each time you make a COMMAND/C entry in a batch file you want to trace through.

TIPS, TRICKS, AND TECHNIQUES

Earlier in this chapter, you used several batch files that will be useful in your system either directly or with slight modification. They represent stand-alone batch files that can provide you and others with useful additional tools, like the customized help screens or the color monitor initialization. This section will present a number of techniques that you can apply to your batch files. The methods can either be used as you see them, or they can be incorporated into the more sophisticated batch programs you may write.

USING RAM DISKS EFFECTIVELY

You learned in Chapter 10 how to initialize a RAM disk. You only needed to include one of the following two lines in your CONFIG.SYS file:

```
DEVICE = VDISK.SYS 256
```

for PC-DOS, or

```
DEVICE = RAMDRIVE.SYS 256
```

for MS-DOS. You've then created a 256K RAM disk (of course, the

```
Snapshot at point anyold1-A
                                         5:56 pm, Wednesday, June 17, 1987

 Volume in drive A is INVENTORY
 Directory of  A:\

INVENT   EXE     INVENT2  EXE     STORES   DBF     STORES   NDX     PRICES   DBF
ANALYSIS WK1
        5 File(s)     43008 bytes free
Volume INVENTORY created Nov 23, 1987 3:37p

   362496 bytes total disk space
        0 bytes in 1 hidden files
   319488 bytes in 5 user files
    43008 bytes available on disk

   524288 bytes total memory
   132304 bytes free

 Volume in drive C is ROBBINS
 Directory of  C:\PROGRAMS\FW\CHAP13

.                ..              1        BAT     2        BAT     3        BAT
QUANCHAH FW2     CHAP12A  FW2    CHAP12B  FW2     FIG12-4  TXT     FIG12-5  TXT
-- More --
```

```
FIG12-6  TXT     FIG12-1  TXT    FIG12-2A TXT     FIG12-2B TXT     FIG12-2C TXT
FIG12-3  TXT     FIG12-10 TXT    FIRST    BAT     GOBBLEDY HLP     C        BAT
R        BAT     MONO     BAT    RGB      BAT     COMPRESS BAT     NORMAL   BAT
COLOR    BAT     01-01-88        CONTENTS BAT     FIG12-8  CAP     ANYOLD1  BAK
FIG12-7  TXT     FIG12-14 CAP    TODAY    BAT     HELP     BAT     FIG12-13 CAP
FIG12-12 TXT     FIG12-17 TXT    FIG12-16 CAP     ANNOUNCE BAT     WEEK34   TXT
ANYOLD1  BAT     FIG12-19 TXT    FIG12-20 CAP     AUDIT    TXT     FIG12-21 TXT
ANYOLD1  TXT     SNAPSHOT BAT    FIG12-22 TXT     FIG12-21 BAK     SNAPSHOT BAK
FIG12-22 BAK
       51 File(s)   1292288 bytes free
Volume ROBBINS      created Mar 22, 1987 4:43p

 21204992 bytes total disk space
   108544 bytes in 4 hidden files
   149504 bytes in 62 directories
 19654656 bytes in 1442 user files
  1292288 bytes available on disk

   524288 bytes total memory
   132304 bytes free


C>
```

Figure 15.22: Contents of AUDIT.TXT after running ANYOLD1.BAT

disk's size can vary according to what you intend to use it for), and you can proceed to transfer the proper files to it.

These examples assume that you have previously transferred the correct main programs, help files, overlays, and so on, to your RAM disk.

If you want your RAM disk to run a word processor, you could use the lines

```
REM RAMWP.BAT

CD\PROGRAMS\WORDPROC
D:
WP
```

```
C:
CD\
```

to create a file called RAMWP.BAT.

Storing the RAMWP.BAT file in your root directory, and assuming your root is on your path, you could switch to rapid RAM-based word processing easily and quickly by simply typing

```
RAMWP
```

If you use this RAM drive technique for running more than one major program (for example, both a word processor and a DBMS), you must have enough space reserved for both. If you do not, you may need to write a separate batch program to copy the required programs onto the RAM drive. Of course, you can use the IF and EXIST subcommands to check the RAM drive itself. They will do the work for you, determining what files are needed and whether any existing files need to be erased to make room for the new ones.

You can use the same technique for your database management program, or for any other program that is slow because of normal disk-access speed. A variation of the RAMWP.BAT file for a database management system might contain these lines:

```
REM RAMDBMS.BAT

CD\PROGRAMS\DATABASE
D:
DBMS
C:
CD\
```

This batch file also makes the C hard-disk directory the obvious one for containing your document or data files. D, the RAM disk, is made the current drive so that the WP or DBMS program that executes is the one found on the RAM disk. Any references to C alone, with no directory path, will access the files in the current default directory on the C drive (in this case, either PROGRAMS\WORDPROC or PROGRAMS\DATABASE).

CONTROLLING USER ACCESS

Entire books have been written on the subject of password protection. Even more advanced tomes discuss the subject of *resource allocation,* which involves usage as well as access. Resource allocation means controlling access to both the contents of data files and the running of program files. Let's look at a simple but subtle form of password protection that you can implement with DOS alone.

The DOS environment affords you a special password feature. You can initialize a PASSWORD variable at the DOS prompt or in another batch file. For instance, you can enter

SET PASSWORD = EELS

Then the code segment shown in Figure 15.23 must be contained in a batch file to restrict access to only those people who know the password. If PASSWORD was set correctly to EELS before a batch file containing this code was run, then PROGRAM will run. Otherwise, the invalid password message will be echoed, and the batch file will terminate. In short, only those users who know that the password is EELS and set it correctly will be able to run the particular program. The program could be contained in any .EXE or .COM file, and of course, the batch file could properly reset the directory if necessary in the :RUN section.

This password code uses IF statements to check for entry of the password in uppercase and in lowercase. You never know what case a user's keyboard might be in when he or she tries to run your batch file or menu system.

The password feature can easily be extended by using several DOS environment variables, each containing different passwords. Your batch programs can check for the proper values. For instance, you can have three passwords controlling access to the inventory, personnel, and accounting programs. Doing this might require several blocks of code like the code just seen, and three passwords, PASS1, PASS2, and PASS3, controlling access to INVENTRY.EXE, PRSONNEL.EXE, and ACCOUNTS.EXE.

You might have a menu system that passes control to three batch files (see Figure 15.24) instead of directly to the three main programs. Only users who properly knew and set the appropriate DOS environment variable would be allowed access to the program they chose

```
IF %PASSWORD%==EELS GOTO RUN
IF %PASSWORD%==eels GOTO RUN

ECHO Sorry. That's an invalid password.
GOTO END

:RUN
PROGRAM
:END
```

Figure 15.23: Code segment for password protection

```
IF %PASS1%==STORE GOTO RUN
IF %PASS1%==store GOTO RUN

ECHO Sorry.  That's an invalid password.
GOTO END

:RUN
INVENTRY


:END
------------------------------------------------

IF %PASS1%==JOSHUA GOTO RUN
IF %PASS1%==joshua GOTO RUN

ECHO Sorry.  That's an invalid password.
GOTO END

:RUN
PRSONNEL

:END
------------------------------------------------

IF %PASS1%==1812 GOTO RUN

ECHO Sorry.  That's an invalid password.
GOTO END

:RUN
ACCOUNTS

:END
```

Figure 15.24: Three batch files for a multiple password system

from the menu. Notice in the figure that the third password contains digits only, so IF tests for upper- and lowercase do not have to be performed.

SUMMARY

You've come a long way in this book. Not only have you learned a wide variety of commands and DOS features, but you've learned how to knit those features into seamless and sophisticated automatic batch files. This chapter presented the following examples:

- The AUTOEXEC.BAT file offers you a host of useful applications. Besides automating the system startup, you can change the default system prompt and automate anything you wish at power-up time. This ranges from automatically running any DOS command to automatically running add-on utility software packages.

- Batch files can be used to create simple but functional menu systems to drive the most sophisticated application setup.
- Batch files can simplify consistent instruction sequences. Through the use of abbreviations and shorthand notation, you can reduce your typing burden while simultaneously speeding up your system processing.
- The variable parameters allowed in batch files can provide a valuable tool for repeating critical application tasks automatically.
- A batch file quickly and automatically invokes any application program that is nested in its own subdirectory structure. The current directory and DOS path can be set up before program execution and restored afterwards.
- Operations involving multiple disks and diskettes, as well as sophisticated modular batch systems, can easily be developed with batch-file chaining.
- You can make batch files that will prepare and initialize your RAM disk automatically. This increases system efficiency and improves response time.
- Color monitors can be controlled easily through judicious batch-file development. You saw how a single batch file can make short work of setting the foreground and background colors on color screens.
- With batch files, you can create customized system help features, as well as an appointment reminder system. You can also broadcast messages to system users. These features can be very useful on systems that involve many people sharing the computer at different times.
- The CALL subcommand (DOS 3.3 only) or a secondary command processor can be woven into sophisticated applications. You saw how to do this for capturing system status snapshots, which can help you debug and analyze your system.

- You also learned a couple of new tricks for dealing with RAM disks. Batch programs can load main word-processing, spreadsheet, or database programs onto a RAM disk, and then execute the RAM-resident version of the main program using data files from your hard disk.
- The DOS environment can be used with batch files to manage a password control system.

Congratulations! There is nothing more you need to know in terms of DOS itself to consider yourself an advanced DOS user. However, keep reading. Chapter 16 offers you a chance to learn about advanced DOS commands.

ADVANCED DOS COMMANDS

CHAPTER 16

YOU HAVE NOW LEARNED ALL THE COMMANDS NECessary for using your DOS system effectively. In this chapter, you'll extend your knowledge to include a special advanced set of commands. None of the standard uses of DOS require these commands, but they can help you immeasurably in dealing with special situations. With their help, you can tailor your system to your specific needs and increase the overall efficiency of your applications.

The commands presented in this chapter will allow you to expand the range of ways in which you manage and manipulate files. Others will enable you to use and traverse your directory and disk structures more easily and more quickly. A final group of commands will help you get more mileage from the main DOS controlling program, COMMAND.COM.

ADVANCED FILE MANIPULATION

A file attribute is something that describes that file. Height is an attribute of a person; disk storage space is an attribute of a file. Another attribute of a file, indicated by the archive bit, is whether it has been changed since the last time it was backed up with the BACKUP command. Yet another attribute, indicated by the read/write bit, is whether you are allowed to make or delete permanent changes. Several advanced DOS commands have been designed to work specifically with files and attributes such as these.

CHANGING A FILE'S ATTRIBUTES

Most files can be read from and written to; they are said to be *read/write* and to have an attribute of −R. Some files are restricted, only permitting data to be read from them. These files are called *read-only* and have an attribute of +R.

ATTRIB, a DOS disk-resident command, is used to change the read/write and archive file attributes. This command can be very useful; since you can change a file's read/write attribute bit to read-only, you can block the deletion of the file, which could prevent accidental erasure or changes to a file or group of files.

Influencing the archive bit allows you to control which files will be backed up. If you are using many temporary files, for example, you can reset their archive bits to 0 (off). Those files will then be ignored by the BACKUP /M and XCOPY /M commands. No backup or copy will take place; as a result, the backup and copy operations for the rest of your files will be faster, and less disk space will be required.

One version of the ATTRIB command affects the attributes of one or more files. A second, simpler version displays the current attributes of one or more files. The format of the command is

ATTRIB *Switches FileNames*

The *Switches* parameter controls the on/off status of the two file attributes. If *Switches* is not specified, the current attribute values of the specified files are displayed. *FileNames* is any standard file name. Wild cards are allowed, as well as drive and path-name prefixes.

Figure 16.1 shows the ATTRIB command applied to the root directory on drive C of a sample system. It indicates that three files have the A bit (archive attribute) set (files COMMAND.COM, AUTOEXEC.BAT, AND QD2.LOG), while only one file has the R bit (read/write attribute) set to read-only (COMMAND.COM). The CONFIG.SYS file has no attributes set, which means that it does not need to be backed up, and it can be read from and written to with no restrictions.

If switches are included, both the archive and read/write attributes can be modified simultaneously with one ATTRIB command. The first switch, which affects the read-write bit, is specified either as +R for read-only or −R for read/write. If the read-only status is set (+R), then the file may not be deleted or modified in any way.

The second switch affects the archive bit. It is specified either as +A, which sets the archive bit, or −A, which resets the archive bit. The archive bit is normally set whenever a file is rewritten to disk (after it has been changed). When a BACKUP command is issued, it

If read-only status is set, it may not always be obvious why later operations become difficult. Trying to use EDLIN on a read-only file, for example, produces the understandable message "File is READ-ONLY," but trying to erase such a file produces "Access denied," a less than obvious message. Worse still, you may be in another application program like dBASE III PLUS, which only produces the cryptic message "File cannot be accessed!"

checks the archive bit. If the archive bit is set, BACKUP will back up the file; otherwise, it won't. After BACKUP has scanned a file and either backed it up or not, the archive bit will be reset to 0. Using the −A switch forces the archive bit to be reset, so that a file will be skipped over during a backup. This allows you some measure of control over whether your files will be backed up.

Table 16.1 shows the different states of a file's attributes when different combinations of these two switches are used. Remember that 1 in a binary system indicates that the attribute bit is on, and 0 indicates that it is off.

```
C>DIR

 Volume in drive C is ROBBINS
 Directory of  C:\

COMMAND  COM     25307   3-17-87  12:00p
CONFIG   SYS       160   8-10-87   6:03p
WP            <DIR>      8-10-87   9:44p
FW            <DIR>      8-10-87   9:45p
AUTOEXEC BAT       276   8-10-87   6:08p
QD2      LOG      3206   8-11-87   4:46p
DBASE         <DIR>      1-01-80  12:06a
DOS           <DIR>      1-01-80  12:10a
UTILITY       <DIR>      1-01-80  12:14a
        9 File(s)   3715072 bytes free

C>ATTRIB *.*
  A    R  C:\COMMAND.COM
          C:\CONFIG.SYS
  A       C:\AUTOEXEC.BAT
  A       C:\QD2.LOG

C>
```

Figure 16.1: Attribute status of sample root files

COMMAND	READ/ WRITE BIT	ARCHIVE BIT
ATTRIB +R +A SAMPLE.TXT	1	1
ATTRIB +R −A SAMPLE.TXT	1	0
ATTRIB −R +A SAMPLE.TXT	0	1
ATTRIB −R −A SAMPLE.TXT	0	0

Table 16.1: Attribute combinations with the ATTRIB command

As Figure 16.1 showed, you can determine the current status of a file by using the ATTRIB command without switches. Using the switches, however, lets you control those attribute values yourself. If the command

```
ATTRIB +R -A SAMPLE.TXT
```

were used to set the read/write attribute to read-only (on), and the archive attribute off, then the command

```
ATTRIB SAMPLE.TXT
```

would produce the following result:

```
R   A:\SAMPLE.TXT
```

This shows that the read/write bit for the SAMPLE.TXT file is set to read-only, and that the archive bit is not set—no A indicator appeared.

UPDATING SETS OF FILES

If you work with a specific application program (for example, a word processor or a spreadsheet), you might want a backup disk to contain only copies of the most recently modified files. REPLACE allows you to make selective backups of files without using the BACKUP command. It can replace (update) the files on the backup disk that were recently changed or newly created on your working disk. It can also ignore any of your older and unchanged files.

The format of this command is

REPLACE *Source Destination Switches*

As always, the command may be prefixed by an optional drive and path name indicating where the REPLACE command file is located. *Source* represents the changed or newly created files that are to be written to the destination disk. *Destination* is optional; it specifies the destination drive and path to receive the copies of the specified files. If no destination path is given, the default is the current directory.

The *Switches* parameter represents one or more switches: /A, /P, /R, /S, or /W. Because the REPLACE command is defined primar-

The REPLACE command is simply an advanced, selective version of the COPY command. It is most commonly used when you change versions of DOS and need to update various system files. REPLACE can also be used to update an entire DOS directory on your hard disk when you upgrade your version of DOS. It also comes in handy when regularly backing up a small set of files at the end of a workday, either adding new files or updating modified files on your designated backup diskette.

ily by these switches, some of them cannot be used together. Let's use the two directories in Figure 16.2, SOURCE and DEST, to demonstrate the behavior of the REPLACE command with its switches.

The /A switch allows you to add files to the destination directory. DOS will only copy source files that are not in the destination directory. The /P (Prompt) switch instructs DOS to pause and ask you if it is all right to copy each file that meets the criteria of *any other* switch that is used.

Let's use the /A and /P switches together. If you issue the command

```
C> REPLACE \SOURCE\*.* \DEST /A /P
```

for the files shown in Figure 16.2, the results on your screen will be

```
Add C:\DEST\FILE2.TXT? (Y/N) Y
Adding C:\DEST\FILE2.TXT

1 file(s) added
```

The one file in the source directory (FILE2.TXT) that did not already exist by name in the destination directory was selected for replacement. As Figure 16.3 shows, FILE2.TXT was added to the DEST directory; FILE1.TXT and FILE3.TXT were left as they were.

```
C>DIR

 Volume in drive C is ROBBINS
 Directory of  C:\SOURCE

.            <DIR>       3-05-88   3:00p
..           <DIR>       3-05-88   3:00p
FILE3          12176    11-16-88  10:30a
FILE1           1056     8-18-88   4:23p
FILE2           3616     9-26-88   6:42a
        5 File(s)    2535424 bytes free

C>DIR \DEST

 Volume in drive C is ROBBINS
 Directory of  C:\DEST

.            <DIR>       3-05-88   3:00p
..           <DIR>       3-05-88   3:00p
FILE3          12784     8-15-88   7:06a
FILE1           1040     1-08-88   4:57p
        4 File(s)    2535424 bytes free

C>_
```

Figure 16.2: Example directories

```
C>DIR \DEST

 Volume in drive C is ROBBINS
 Directory of  C:\DEST

.            <DIR>      3-Ø5-88   3:ØØp
..           <DIR>      3-Ø5-88   3:ØØp
FILE3          12784    8-15-88   7:Ø6a
FILE1           1Ø4Ø    1-Ø8-88   4:57p
FILE2           3616    9-26-88   6:42a
        5 File(s)    2525184 bytes free

C>_
```

Figure 16.3: Adding files with the REPLACE command

The /R switch overrides the read/write attributes of read-only files on the destination directory. It allows you to replace those read-only files without generating an error message, so you will not be denied the implicit file update performed by REPLACE. This switch should be used with caution, since you or someone else may have set the read/write attribute bit to read-only for a good reason.

Be careful to enter the source and destination directories in the correct order in your command. Performing a REPLACE backwards could copy your old data over your new versions.

The /S switch will only replace or update old files, not add new ones. Therefore, it cannot be used with the /A switch. Be careful when you use the /S switch with a wild-card character—it will replace *all* files matching the source specification, including those in any subdirectories of the destination directory.

Figure 16.4 shows how the /S switch works. This example uses the original DEST directory from Figure 16.2, which only contained FILE1.TXT and FILE3.TXT. The command shown in the figure tells the computer to use files in the SOURCE directory to replace any files they match in the DEST directory. Since only FILE1.TXT and FILE3.TXT are common to both directories, only they are replaced in the DEST directory.

The /W switch allows you time to insert a new source diskette before the replacement process begins. DOS pauses to give you time to place a new source diskette into a drive. For example, you can execute a REPLACE command from a DOS diskette in drive A, replace that disk

```
C>REPLACE  \SOURCE\*.*  \DEST  /S
Replacing C:\DEST\FILE3 file.
Replacing C:\DEST\FILE1 file.
2 files were replaced.

C>DIR \DEST

 Volume in drive C is ROBBINS
 Directory of  C:\DEST

.            <DIR>       3-Ø5-88   3:ØØp
..           <DIR>       3-Ø5-88   3:ØØp
FILE3           12176   11-16-88  1Ø:3Øa
FILE1            1Ø56    8-18-88   4:23p
        4 File(s)   2525184 bytes free

C>_
```

Figure 16.4: Updating matching files with REPLACE

with the correct source disk, and then proceed to replace files on B with files from the newly inserted source diskette in A.

RESCUING LOST FILES

RECOVER is DOS's "Humpty Dumpty" command—it puts a file or a complete disk back together again. There may be times in your future when something will happen to a file or to a part of the disk containing your file. A file may become unreadable, and access to that file may be denied. (This usually stems from the deterioration of the magnetic disk surface, rather than from the simple attribute modification discussed in the last section.)

File loss may also be due to corruption of the file allocation table (FAT). Even RECOVER is not likely to help you much in this instance.

The RECOVER command can read a file part by part (actually, disk cluster by disk cluster), skipping over the parts that have gone bad. This command rewrites the file without the bad data and allows you to access what's left. The format to recover specific files is

RECOVER ***FileNames***

and the format to recover an entire disk is

RECOVER ***DriveName***

Like all DOS commands, RECOVER can be prefixed with a drive and path name to indicate where the disk-resident DOS command file may be found. In the first format, the file names to be recovered can also be prefixed by their directory locations.

RECOVER is not designed to work properly on a network disk. Disengage a disk completely from any network before you try to recover files with this command.

Recovering all files on a disk is necessary when the directory or file allocation table of the disk has been damaged. After you use the second version of this command, the directory will be made up of files of the form FILE*nnnn*.REC, where *nnnn* is a number. All of the recovered files will be numbered sequentially in the order in which they were recovered. This is not necessarily the order in which they appeared in the directory before the damage was done.

Only try to recover an entire drive when your disk's directory has been damaged completely. RECOVER does not distinguish between normally accessible and inaccessible files, so all files in the directory will be renamed in this format.

When you try to recover all files on a disk, you are limited to the maximum number of files that can fit into the root directory of the disk. If your disk has a subdirectory structure that contains more than this maximum, you'll have to invoke RECOVER several times, clearing out the recovered files from the root in between invocations. When you have finished recovering your text files, you will probably need to go through each one and edit the end of the recovered files, since the recovery process is likely to capture meaningless data at the end of the last disk cluster occupied by your original file.

IMPROVING DISK AND DIRECTORY REFERENCING

The following commands influence the way that DOS looks at its disk drives and disk directory structures. These commands can be very useful when you are running older programs that make fixed assumptions about drives, when your programs do not contain a changeable path specification, or when a path name simply gets too long. These commands will also make your DOS application references easier and faster.

TREATING DISKS AS DIRECTORIES

JOIN is used to make DOS treat a whole disk drive as if it were a subdirectory on another drive. This extraordinary command allows individual DOS commands to treat files on multiple disk drives as if they were part of one sophisticated directory on a single drive.

The JOIN command can be very helpful when it is used with a directory management program like XTREE. Each time XTREE switches disks, it totals all of the files to determine the amount of space already used and the amount of space still available. This takes quite some time and can be a burden to power users. Switching a new disk with JOIN allows you to switch the current directory rather than current drive, and is a significantly faster operation.

There are three versions of the JOIN command. As usual, all of them allow you to precede the command itself with a drive and path name specifying where DOS can find the JOIN.EXE file. Entering JOIN with no parameters at the command prompt will display all the current directory and disk names that have been joined. Entering JOIN with two parameters specifies what directory and drive are to be joined. Entering JOIN with only one parameter (a drive identifier) and the /D switch *disjoins* the drive from a directory to which it had been joined.

Executing the following JOIN command will connect the two drives internally:

```
JOIN D: C:\ACCOUNT
```

This can be read as "Join the entire drive *D* to the C:\ACCOUNT directory." Any disk drive identifier may be substituted for D, and any empty directory of files may be substituted for C:\ACCOUNT. To see how this works, look at Figure 16.5, which shows two disk directory structures. Figure 16.6 shows the new directory structure after this JOIN command was executed. Drive D appears to be a subdirectory on drive C.

When you invoke JOIN with no parameters, DOS will display the results of any joining. The computer will show the joined drives and the directories they have been attached to. For example, entering

```
JOIN
```

The JOIN command applies only to root directories and the first level of subdirectories beyond root directories. You'll receive an "invalid parameter" message if you try to join to a directory any further into your hierarchical structure.

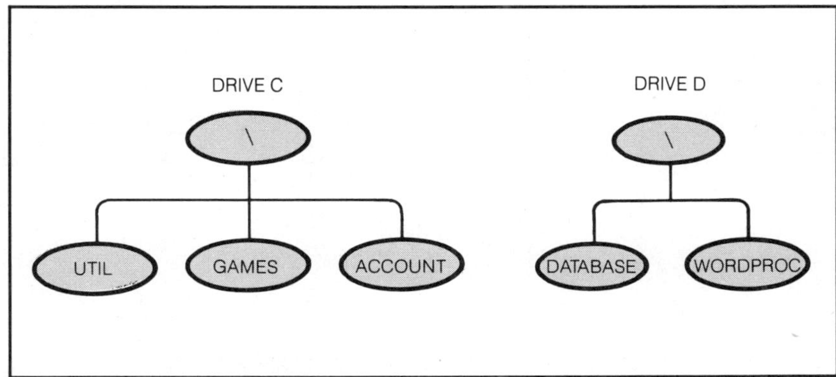

Figure 16.5: Sample disk directory structures

produces

```
D: => C:\ACCOUNT
```

This tells you that the root directory of drive D can only be accessed now through the ACCOUNT directory on drive C. In effect, C:\ACCOUNT is the new root directory of drive D, and all of drive D's subdirectories are now subdirectories of C:\ACCOUNT.

When you use the primary form of the JOIN command, in which you specify a drive and a directory to be joined, DOS will simply respond with a new prompt if everything went well. You won't receive any notice that the join was made—and in this case, no news is good news. For example, if ACCOUNT is an empty directory, the command

```
JOIN D: C:\ACCOUNT
```

will produce no obvious result.

You must use a completely empty directory when you join another disk drive to it.

If the proposed root directory (C:\ACCOUNT) had not been empty of files, you would have received the error message "Directory not empty," and the JOIN command would have failed. Although a proposed root directory *may* have subdirectories and the JOIN command can still be made, any subdirectories in existence will be sup-

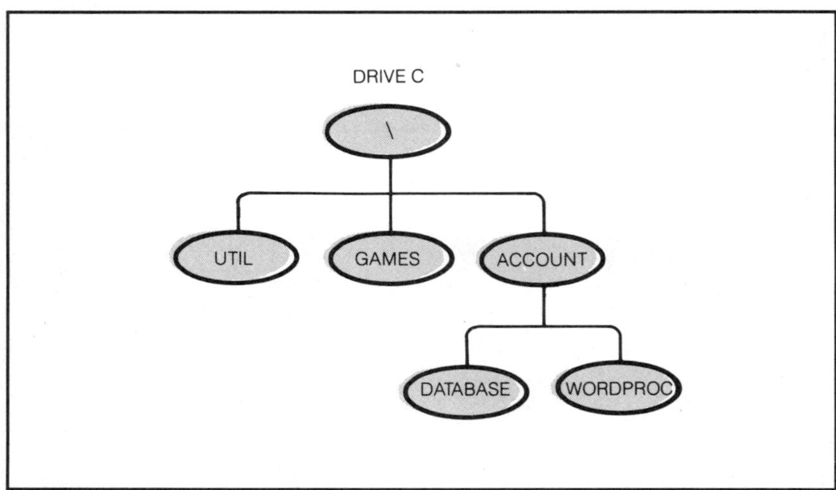

Figure 16.6: Results of joining a disk drive to a directory

pressed temporarily until the drive and directory are disjoined. You won't be able to access any information in that part of your directory structure.

Continuing with this example, if a DIR command is executed on drive C after the join has been made, the remaining amount of disk storage shown will be that of drive C, not of drive D. If anything is saved in the ACCOUNT subdirectory (actually, drive D), then disk storage will be used on drive D, not on C. Thus, it is possible to save in ACCOUNT (drive D) a file that is larger than the apparent amount of disk storage space left. In addition, access to drive D will be denied, so any command using drive D explicitly (such as DIR D:) will generate the error message "Invalid drive specification."

The last version of the JOIN command cancels the effects of a previous JOIN command. You must specify the JOIN command you wish to disengage (there may have been many). The following command would disengage the join just executed in our example:

```
JOIN D: /D
```

If the destination drive (that is, the proposed root directory of the JOIN command in question) is omitted, with the intention of undoing all joinings, the error message "Incorrect number of parameters" will appear. Similarly, disjoining a drive that has not been joined will generate the error message "Invalid parameter."

Now let's work through an actual session with the JOIN command. The following sequence will show what happens if you are using drives A and B on a dual-diskette system. The drives contain the directories shown in Figure 16.7. The first JOIN command in Figure 16.8 appends the root directory of B to the directory A:\ACCOUNT, as a DIR command shows. A:\ACCOUNT has become drive B's root directory.

The two commands in Figure 16.9 change the active directory and then create a file in that directory; this file is actually being created in drive B. To see that the file is actually on drive B, you need to disjoin the directories and take a look at the files on drive B (see Figure 16.10).

TREATING DIRECTORIES AS DISKS

The SUBST (Substitute) command is the opposite of the JOIN command: it will create a new disk drive out of any existing directory.

```
A:\> DIR A:

 Volume in drive A has no label
 Directory of  A:\

UTIL         <DIR>        6-04-87   2:12p
GAMES        <DIR>        6-04-87   2:12p
ACCOUNT      <DIR>        6-04-87   2:12p
JOIN     EXE      8955  12-30-85  12:00p
SUBST    EXE      9911  12-30-85  12:00p
       5 File(s)     339968 bytes free

A:\> DIR B:

 Volume in drive B has no label
 Directory of  B:\

WORDPROC     <DIR>        6-04-87   2:12p
DATABASE     <DIR>        6-04-87   2:12p
        2 File(s)     359424 bytes free

A:\> _
```

Figure 16.7: Directory listings of drives A and B

```
A:\> JOIN B: A:\ACCOUNT
A:\> DIR A:\ACCOUNT

 Volume in drive A has no label
 Directory of  A:\ACCOUNT

WORDPROC     <DIR>        6-04-87   2:12p
DATABASE     <DIR>        6-04-87   2:12p
        2 File(s)     339968 bytes free
A:\> _
```

Figure 16.8: Joining drive B to the ACCOUNT directory on A

To visualize this, look at Figure 16.6 first and Figure 16.5 next. Starting with one directory structure, you can take a directory (ACCOUNT) and all of its subdirectories and make that directory the root directory of a new drive.

A frequent use for this command is running older software packages that cannot reference files in a hierarchical directory structure. By fooling these packages into thinking they are only addressing files

```
A:\> CD \ACCOUNT
A:\ACCOUNT> COPY CON: TEST.TXT
This is a test file.  This will be saved in the
\ACCOUNT directory which is actually the root directory
of drive B.  Therefore, the available storage space
shown with the DIR command will be that remaining on
drive A.  When this file is saved, it will actually use
space on drive B, so the available storage space shown
on the screen (for A:) will not change.  However, it
will be decreasing the available disk space on drive B.
^Z
        1 File(s) copied

A:\ACCOUNT> DIR

 Volume in drive A has no label
 Directory of  A:\ACCOUNT

WORDPROC     <DIR>       6-04-87   2:12p
DATABASE     <DIR>       6-04-87   2:12p
TEST     TXT        380  6-04-87   2:58p
        3 File(s)    339968 bytes free

A:\ACCOUNT>
```

Figure 16.9: Directory files as files on another drive

```
A:\ACCOUNT> CD \
A:\> JOIN B: /D
A:\> DIR B:

 Volume in drive B has no label
 Directory of  B:\

WORDPROC     <DIR>       6-04-87   2:12p
DATABASE     <DIR>       6-04-87   2:12p
TEST     TXT        380  6-04-87   2:58p
        3 File(s)    358400 bytes free

A:\>
```

Figure 16.10: Disjoining a drive and directory

The SUBST command also reduces your typing burden. You can redefine any directory, no matter how deep in your hierarchical structure, as a single-letter drive identifier. All future command references will be shorter, faster, and less liable to contain typing errors.

on a disk drive, you can still make use of the DOS directory structure for file storage.

The SUBST command comes in handy in another common situation. If you have a hard disk with a directory structure containing many levels of subdirectories, this command allows you to avoid typing long path names. For the same reason, it is useful when you have a program that requests a file name and path but only allows a certain amount of characters to be entered. WordPerfect is an example of this type of program.

Like the JOIN command, SUBST has three versions. The first actually performs a substitution, the second displays all current substitutions, and the third cancels a previous substitution.

Since a substituted drive is really only a portion of another drive, don't mistake it for a RAM drive. SUBST offers convenience, not increased performance.

Let's look at an example. Specify a directory structure, as shown in Figure 16.11. Then suppose you need to run an older general ledger program that needs the files in ACCOUNT\GL, but the older program does not support paths. You would issue the following command:

```
SUBST F: C:\ACCOUNT\GL
```

This command makes DOS assume there is a disk drive F, and that the contents of this drive are the contents of the ACCOUNT\GL subdirectory on drive C. Drive F now includes all of the directory's subdirectories (in this example, however, there are no subdirectories).

You can refer to the directory just as you would a normal disk drive. If you typed

```
DIR F:
```

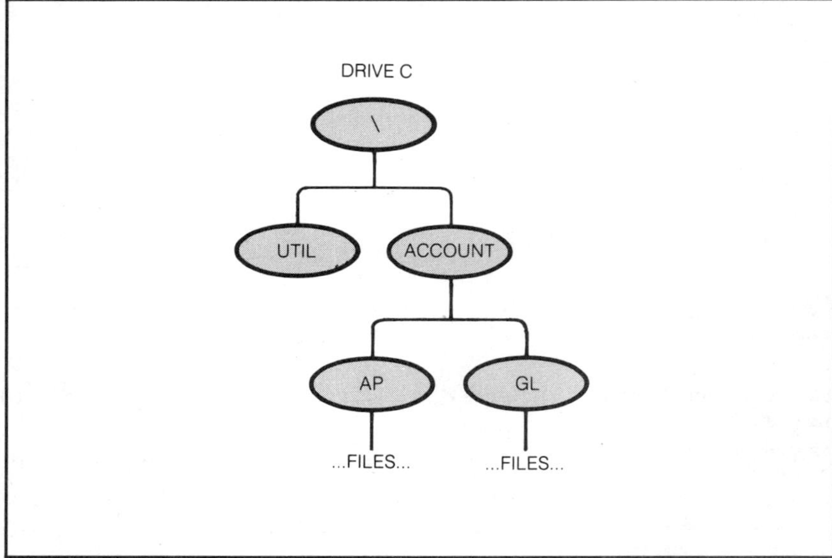

Figure 16.11: Sample directory structure

DOS would return the same result as if you had typed

```
DIR C:\ACCOUNT\GL
```

Unlike the JOIN command, the SUBST command allows you to access the specified subdirectory directly after the SUBST command has been issued. If you save a file on F (or in the subdirectory), it will also be saved in the subdirectory (or on F), because both access the same part of the disk (see Figure 16.12). In effect, this command opens up another "window" into a directory, and you can access that directory's contents through the window simply by using a drive specifier.

By default, DOS only supports drives lettered A through E. In order to create and access drives lettered beyond E, you must include in your CONFIG.SYS file the command LASTDRIVE = *n*, where *n* is the last letter allowed for a drive. For example, LASTDRIVE = E is the default condition, whereas LASTDRIVE = Z allows drives labeled A through Z.

The second version of SUBST causes all currently active substitutions to be displayed. DOS will show you the created drive identifier and the drive and directory to which it is linked. For example,

```
C:\> SUBST
F: => C:\ACCOUNT\GL
```

shows you that drive F is being used as a substitute for

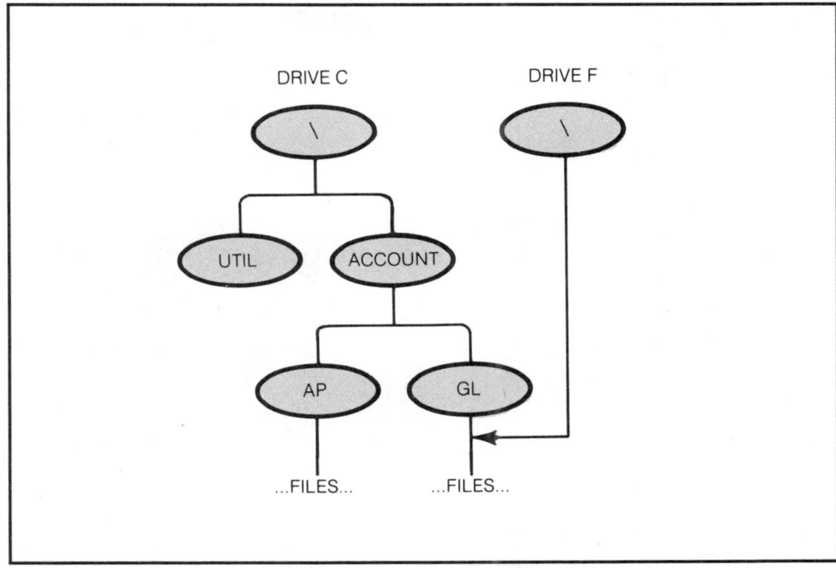

Figure 16.12: Directory references with SUBST and a fictitious disk-drive identifier

ACCOUNT\GL on drive C. As a result, the ACCOUNT\GL directory can be accessed normally (on drive C) or through its substitute (on the fictitious drive F).

The final version of SUBST is used to undo a substitution. To undo the SUBST command shown in the previous example, you would type

```
SUBST F: /D
```

The /D switch disjoins, or disassociates, the directory from the fictitious drive F.

Let's take a look at an example of using all three versions of this command. The first step is to examine the root directory on drive A to verify that no drive F exists (see Figure 16.13). Next, issue the SUBST command to create drive F, as shown in Figure 16.14. Then activate the "windowing" feature of this command by creating a file on drive F and verifying that it actually resides in the linked subdirectory (see Figure 16.15).

Finally, you can undo the SUBST command to restore the system to its original state by issuing this command:

```
A:\> SUBST F: /D
```

```
A>DIR

 Volume in drive A is DEMO
 Directory of  A:\

UTIL         <DIR>        3-05-88   2:40p
ACCOUNT      <DIR>        3-05-88   2:40p
        2 File(s)    358400 bytes free

A>DIR ACCOUNT

 Volume in drive A is DEMO
 Directory of  A:\ACCOUNT

.            <DIR>        3-05-88   2:40p
..           <DIR>        3-05-88   2:40p
GL           <DIR>        3-05-88   3:35p
AP           <DIR>        3-05-88   3:35p
        4 File(s)    358400 bytes free

A>_
```

Figure 16.13: Root directory of drive A

Trying to use the DIR command on drive F will now result in the following:

```
A:\> DIR F:
Invalid drive specification
```

```
A>SUBST F: \ACCOUNT\GL

A>DIR F:

 Volume in drive F is DEMO
 Directory of  F:\

.            <DIR>       3-Ø5-88   3:35p
..           <DIR>       3-Ø5-88   3:35p
        2 File(s)    35328Ø bytes free

A>_
```

Figure 16.14: A directory treated as a disk drive

```
A>COPY CON: F:TEST.TXT
This file should appear in both F: and \ACCOUNT\GL^Z
        1 File(s) copied

A>DIR F:

 Volume in drive F is DEMO
 Directory of  F:\

.            <DIR>       3-Ø5-88   3:35p
..           <DIR>       3-Ø5-88   3:35p
TEST     TXT        5Ø   3-Ø5-88   4:31p
        3 File(s)    347136 bytes free

A>DIR \ACCOUNT\GL

 Volume in drive A is DEMO
 Directory of  A:\ACCOUNT\GL

.            <DIR>       3-Ø5-88   3:35p
..           <DIR>       3-Ø5-88   3:35p
TEST     TXT        5Ø   3-Ø5-88   4:31p
        3 File(s)    347136 bytes free

A>_
```

Figure 16.15: Substituted and original drive

REROUTING DISK INPUT AND OUTPUT

Some older programs have hard-coded drive references, which means they are internally frozen, with no way for you to make use of a hard disk. The ASSIGN command can help you solve this problem. It causes any requests for one drive to be carried out on another drive. ASSIGN is very useful with older software packages designed to work only with drives A and B. You can have your files in a directory on your hard disk, and the older program will be tricked into believing it is accessing the files on a single drive without any hierarchical structures.

This command has two versions. The first will make or break assignations, while the second cancels all assignations currently in effect. The first version is the most frequently used:

> You should not use ASSIGN with BACKUP, RESTORE, LABEL, JOIN, SUBST, or PRINT. These commands act on the contents of drives and directories; serious problems can result if your intended destination drive has previously been reassigned to another drive. As a matter of protection, DOS ignores reassignments when you invoke the even more dangerous FORMAT, DISKCOPY, and DISKCOMP commands.

ASSIGN *DriveX* = *BigDrive*

In this version, DOS will cause all future references to files and directories on *DriveX* to be treated as if they had been made to *BigDrive*. As always with DOS transient commands, you can prefix the command name with a drive identifier and a path name.

A simple example of this command is assigning to drive C any references to the files on drive A.

```
ASSIGN A = C
```

can be read as "Let the current working directory on drive C handle everything requested of drive A." When the command DIR A: is executed, a directory of drive C will appear. To undo ASSIGN commands, use ASSIGN by itself without any drive assignments:

```
ASSIGN
```

SPEEDING UP DISK ACCESS

When you have a directory structure that contains many levels of subdirectories, DOS can take a very long time to search for a file or directory. To combat this problem, Microsoft developed the new DOS 3.3 FASTOPEN command, which maintains a list of the most recently accessed directory and file locations. This means that if you repeatedly reference a directory or file, DOS will be able to locate it more quickly on the disk. The FASTOPEN memory buffer will contain the disk location of that directory or file; DOS can then access it without having to check the disk directory structure itself.

The general format of this command is

```
FASTOPEN Drive: = Size
```

Drive is the drive you want FASTOPEN to work for. You must repeat the *Drive:* and =*Size* parts of the command for each drive you want FASTOPEN to affect. *Size,* an optional parameter, represents the number of directory or file entries that FASTOPEN will remember.

Make sure that the FASTOPEN command file is available on the current directory or path. As with all DOS 3.3 commands, you can precede the command name with the full path name leading to it.

FASTOPEN may not be used on a drive defined by the JOIN, SUBST, or ASSIGN command. In addition, it should not be used on network drives.

The most common use of the FASTOPEN command is simply to specify the disk drive whose performance you want to improve. For example, entering

```
FASTOPEN C:
```

will enable DOS to remember the last 34 directories and files accessed (the default), and thus be able to go right to them on the disk.

FASTOPEN can only be used once per boot session and reserves 35 bytes per entry. A buffer size of 100 (FASTOPEN C: = 100) would therefore consume about 3500 bytes of memory. It is recommended that *Size* be at least as great as the highest number of levels in the directory structure, so that any file in the directory can be quickly found. In fact, unless you are only working with one file, *Size* should be larger. The default is reasonable, unless you have special usage requirements and perform some actual timing tests.

INFLUENCING THE COMMAND PROCESSOR AND ITS ENVIRONMENT

The command processor on your system disk, COMMAND-.COM, is the program that interprets all of the commands you type in from the keyboard. It has been primarily responsible for interpreting all the commands you've learned so far. It takes your command

and first scans its own internal command list to see if it can handle your request without going to the disk. If the command is a resident command, then the way in which that command will work is defined somewhere in COMMAND.COM. If it is a transient command, COMMAND.COM will check the directory to see if the command file is present. If it is not, and your command is not in a batch file, you will get an error message. However, if it does find the command file, control will be transferred to that file.

Let's look at some examples. TYPE is a resident command used to display the contents of ASCII files. When COMMAND.COM is ready to accept a command, it displays the DOS prompt. Say you type in the command TYPE OUTLINE.TXT. COMMAND-.COM first determines that TYPE is a resident command. It then looks internally for the instructions that tell it what to do when the TYPE command is used. Following these instructions, it gets the file name you typed in and displays the file.

Transient commands are not really commands at all—each transient command request actually runs a program contained in a separate file. These files are called .COM or .EXE files. For example, a file named ASSIGN.COM contains the program that performs an ASSIGN command. Say you issue the command ASSIGN A = B. COMMAND.COM first checks that it is not a resident command. After first checking the current working directory, it will then find the file called ASSIGN.COM somewhere along the specified path and transfer control of the system to that file. When ASSIGN is done assigning, control passes back to COMMAND.COM. Of course, this assumes you've set the path properly (PATH \DOS).

When COMMAND.COM is doing all of this, it must not only access those parts of itself that contain definitions and instructions, but it also must access the DOS environment. This contains user-defined definitions, such as the current path and the last available drive (LASTDRIVE in CONFIG.SYS). The SET command gives you direct control over the contents of the DOS environment.

RENAMING COMMANDS

The SET command is used to change character strings and definitions within the DOS environment. Both you and DOS can set aside named areas of this environment for character strings. You can use them for anything you like—for example, individual path names for future commands, file names for later DOS operations, or variable values used by several batch files.

The SET command with no parameters

```
SET
```

can display the current DOS environment settings. A modified format can erase any existing entry:

SET *Name* =

will erase the DOS environment variable *Name*. To create a completely new DOS environment string or to change one that already exists, use the format

SET *Name* = *String*

where *Name* is either a variable name defined by you, or one of the system's predefined names like PROMPT, PATH, LASTDRIVE, or COMSPEC.

You are limited by default to 127 bytes of total available DOS environment space, although this default may be increased by using the /E switch of the SHELL command (see Chapter 18).

Let's take a look at a sample sequence that demonstrates this command. First, you can display the existing DOS environment, which includes all externally defined system defaults and user definitions. For example, issuing the SET command at the DOS prompt:

```
A:\> SET
```

will display the following:

```
COMSPEC = A:\COMMAND.COM
PATH = \
PROMPT = $p$g
LASTDRIVE = Z
FILES = \wordproc\wordperf\files
```

The first four of these environment names are predefined and have special meaning to the system. You've seen all of these except for COMSPEC, which is only modified infrequently, when you've relocated your command processor to some drive or directory other than the root of the boot disk. COMSPEC is usually used when you place

COMMAND.COM on a RAM disk to speed up applications that invoke the command processor frequently.

The next version of the SET command will remove an entire string definition from the DOS environment. With the DOS environment defined as just shown, executing the command

```
SET PATH =
```

will clear the value of the PATH variable. If you then execute the SET command, you will see that the PATH variable has been removed:

```
A:\> SET
COMSPEC = A:\COMMAND.COM
PROMPT = $p$g
LASTDRIVE = Z
FILES = \wordproc\wordperf\files
```

The entire path definition has been removed. Asking for the current path at the DOS prompt now will result in a "No Path" message.

The last version of SET will define or modify a DOS environment string. Say you want to replace the path. You can do it in one of two ways: by using the PATH command (see Chapter 5), or by using the SET command. Using the command

```
SET path = \utility
```

would change or create the path definition, as shown here:

```
A:\> set
COMSPEC = A:\COMMAND.COM
PATH = \utility
PROMPT = $p$g
LASTDRIVE = Z
FILES = \wordproc\wordperf\files
```

Notice that the variable name "path" was changed to "PATH," but "utility" stayed in the same case. This is because the case of the DOS environment's character string may have meaning to you and affect how you intend to use it.

Definitions contained in the DOS environment can only be used (that is, actually referred to) by programs or batch files. For example, typing CD FILES at the DOS prompt will not work. You can, however, create a batch file that accesses the DOS environment string FILES:

```
A:\> COPY CON: TEST.BAT

dir %FILES%
^Z
```

As you learned in Chapter 15, a leading percent sign indicates a batch variable, while leading and trailing percent signs together indicate a DOS environment string.

The command dir %FILES% would cause the command processor to look up FILES in the DOS environment and, when found, substitute its definition (in this case, \wordperf\wordproc\files) for %FILES%. Remember, this is *not* available directly from the DOS prompt.

As you can see, the DOS environment can be used by programs and batch files and is a convenient way to pass information to these programs. For example, suppose a program needs a certain file name or path, but for some reason the program does not ask the user directly for this information. (Security reasons often account for this situation.) The path information can be put into the DOS environment, which then can be made inaccessible to the user but readily obtainable from the program.

CREATING A SECOND COMMAND PROCESSOR

There will be times when it may be useful to create or invoke a second command processor. COMMAND.COM, the first command processor, is invoked when the computer is turned on. It is the part of DOS that takes in, translates, and executes your standard commands. However, invoking a second command processor with COMMAND can give you the ability to execute DOS commands from inside a program (written in BASIC, Pascal, and so on) and then return to that program. This command also allows you to load and customize a command processor that has special functions and abilities or altered command definitions. The COMMAND command has several switches: one to specify the memory residency status of the new command processor, one to name a file to be run upon invocation, and one to change the size of the DOS environment.

The general format of this command is

COMMAND *Location Switches*

Location is the optional drive and path where the command processor to be invoked is located. This parameter gives you the ability to prepare and then use a nonstandard or restricted version of a command processor. The *Switches* parameter represents any or all of the optional switches /P, /C *String*, and /E:*xxxxx*.

The new command processor must be named COMMAND.COM as well. Once the new processor is invoked, however, the directory containing the new processor will not become the new root directory. Everything will run as it did before you reassigned the processor, but the processing rules of the new processor will be in effect.

The optional switches define the new processor's environment. The /P (Permanent) switch causes the new command processor to become the primary processor. DOS will assume as initial values all the existing DOS environment variables defined by the prior command processor. You may change any of them, but you will not be able to exit to the previous DOS environment. Without /P, the new DOS environment exists only temporarily, and you can exit from it only by using DOS's EXIT command. This comes in handy if you are using a modified command processor for security reasons.

The /C *String* parameter tells the new processor to execute the command in *String* when it is invoked. If this is left out, the new command processor will be invoked and prompt you for commands. For example, the normal processor that is run every time you start the computer, COMMAND.COM, has a built-in *String* value of AUTOEXEC.BAT, which causes the AUTOEXEC.BAT file to be run when the system starts.

The /E:*xxxxx* parameter can define a new DOS environment size, so that extensive use of the SET command will be permitted. This is only necessary when you begin doing fancy things with your batch files (as you saw in the previous chapter) or your application programs.

For example, suppose you have a command processor in the UTILITY directory, in which the ERASE command has not been defined. You would like 500 bytes of DOS environment, and you would like this processor to supplant the COMMAND.COM processor permanently. The following command will do all of this:

```
COMMAND \UTILITY /P /E:500
```

COMMAND is the command name, and UTILITY is the directory containing the new command processor. The /P switch makes the newly active command processor (the secondary command processor) the permanent primary processor, and /E:500 tells the computer to allow half a kilobyte of DOS environmental memory.

Invoking a secondary processor without the /P parameter will cause the DOS environment to appear as in Figure 16.16. You may terminate the secondary processor invoked without /P by using the DOS EXIT command. This will deactivate the secondary DOS environment and reactivate the main processor. On exiting from the secondary processor, the computer will reenter the DOS environment of the first processor. Therefore, any changes made to any of the DOS environment variables of the secondary command processor will be lost when you exit to the primary DOS environment.

While any changes you make to the DOS environment while you are running the secondary processor will be lost when you exit to the primary processor, anything else you have done—such as changing drives and deleting files—will be permanent.

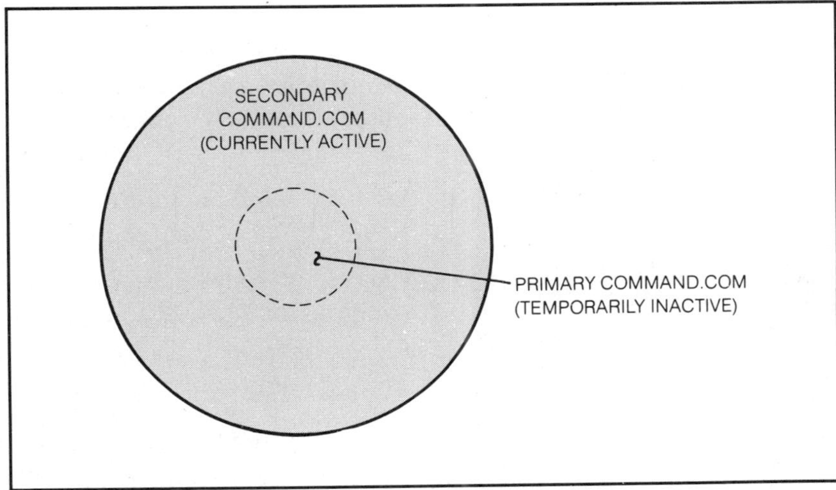

Figure 16.16: Invoking a secondary command processor

This can come in handy in a number of instances. If necessary, you could even use this command to increase the available DOS environment. Simply reinvoking the original command processor with

```
COMMAND \ /P /E:5000
```

would activate the same processor, but expand the DOS environment to 5000 bytes and make the new processor the primary processor.

You should not invoke a secondary command processor lightly, since each new invocation of COMMAND.COM requires a finite additional amount of physical memory to be allocated. Permanent attachment of a secondary processor is better used as a technique for customization or security, rather than for simply expanding the DOS environment.

SUMMARY

You have now mastered some of the most advanced features of DOS. The sophisticated capabilities you've seen in this chapter often lie buried under unreadable documentation. In this chapter, however, you've seen how these advanced features can be used to your advantage.

- The ATTRIB command gives you complete control over the file attributes that govern whether and when the file can be erased, modified, or backed up.
- Files, and even entire disks, that have become physically damaged stand an improved chance of being recovered with the RECOVER command.
- You can upgrade backups and software easily and quickly by using the REPLACE command.
- Entire disk drives can be seen as only a single directory branch of another disk structure by using the JOIN command.
- The SUBST command allows you to treat an entire directory branch as a separate and unique (but fictitious) disk drive. This is useful with older programs that don't allow directory

path references. The ASSIGN command is also useful for hard-coded programs; it lets you reroute disk references.

- Speedier disk access can be obtained by DOS 3.3 users with the FASTOPEN command, which enables DOS to remember the disk locations of recently used files and directories.
- You can create sophisticated application environments with the SET command, which controls the creation and modification of DOS environment string variables.
- You can exercise control over the command processor itself by invoking a secondary processor with the COMMAND command. This allows unique security and customization possibilities.

APPENDICES

APPENDIX A DOS PROMPT, BATCH-FILE, AND CONFIGURATION COMMANDS

This appendix provides capsule summaries of all DOS 3.3 commands. The majority of these commands are described in more detail in previous chapters of this book (see the index for specific pages); however, the summaries presented here can be used for quick reference to each of the individual commands.

Some commands not covered previously in this book are only needed occasionally, but are presented here for completeness. All batch-file subcommands and all configuration (CONFIG.SYS) commands are reviewed in this chapter as well.

Each capsule summary begins with a general description of the command, followed by its format or formats and the definitions of its switches and parameters. Brackets indicate optional switches and parameters. Vertical bars indicate "either/or" choices. The command's type, and any restrictions on the command's use, close each command capsule.

APPEND

The APPEND command causes the computer to search through a predetermined set of directories. It will not, however, search for files ending in .COM, .BAT, or .EXE, but for files with extensions other than these. The APPEND command allows DOS to open files that will be read from or written to. The PATH command must therefore still be used to find executable files.

Format

[*D*:*Path*]APPEND[*D1*:*Path1*][;*D2*:*Path2*...][/X][/E][;]

D:*Path* is the drive and path where the command file is located if it is not in the current directory.

D1:Path1 is the first drive and directory searched after the default drive and directory.

D2:Path2... is the second drive and directory searched after the default drive and directory, and so on.

/X causes APPEND to process the searching methods SEARCH FIRST, FIND FIRST, and EXEC (for programmers only).

/E stores the paths in the DOS environment (which means they can be changed through SET, but that they will be lost when a secondary processor exits).

The ; symbol alone nullifies the APPEND command by erasing the path list.

Unless specified, files will be saved by APPEND in the default directory instead of in the directory they were called from, if that directory was not the default directory.

Type

Transient upon first execution, resident after first execution.

Restrictions

There are 128 bytes of space in which to specify the paths. Do not use this command in conjunction with the different APPEND command used in the IBM PC Network program 1.00 or in the IBM PC LAN program 1.10.

ASSIGN

The ASSIGN command causes any requests for one drive to be carried out on another drive. With parameters, assignments are made. Without parameters, ASSIGN cancels all current assignments.

Format

[*D:Path*]ASSIGN [*SourceD* = *DestD*] [...]

D:Path is the drive and path where the command file is located if it is not in the current directory.

SourceD is the drive to be rerouted.

DestD is the drive that will handle *SourceD*'s requests.

... are additional assignments.

Type

Transient.

Restrictions

Do not use ASSIGN with BACKUP, RESTORE, LABEL, JOIN, SUBST, or PRINT. ASSIGN is ignored by FORMAT, DISKCOPY, and DISKCOMP.

ATTRIB

The ATTRIB command is the command used to change the read/write and archive file attributes. When used with parameters, ATTRIB changes the attributes of a file. When used without the parameters, ATTRIB displays the attributes.

Format

[*D*:*Path*]ATTRIB [+R¦--R][+A¦--A][*FileSpec*][/S]

D:*Path* is the drive and path where the command file is located if it is not in the current directory.

+R makes *FileSpec* read-only.

--R makes *FileSpec* read/write operations possible.

+A sets the archive bit of *FileSpec*.

--A resets the archive bit of *FileSpec*.

FileSpec is an optional drive and path, plus the file name and extension, of the file that is the object of the command. Wild cards are allowed.

/S causes all files in the directory and its subdirectories to be modified.

Type

Transient.

BACKUP

This command performs a backup of your hard disk. Since many errors may occur on such a large volume of data, backing up is a must. BACKUP saves all of your current data, file by file, directory by directory, to diskettes.

Format

[*D:Path*]BACKUP *SourceD*:[*FileSpec*] *DestD*:
[/S][/M][/A][/D:*mm-dd-yy*] [/T:*hh:mm:ss*][/F][/L[:*LogFileSpec*]]

D:Path is the drive and path where the command file is located if it is not in the current directory.

SourceD is the drive specification of the source drive to be backed up; this can be a diskette or a hard disk.

FileSpec is an optional drive and path, plus the file name and extension, of the file that is the object of the command. Wild cards are allowed.

DestD is where the backups will be stored (a diskette or a hard disk).

/S backs up files of the current specified directory.

/M backs up modified files.

Unless the /A parameter is used, BACKUP will erase all the files on *DestD*. The target disk will be formatted according to the capacity of the drive. Mismatches in capacity and formatting are not allowed.

/A appends the backup files to the files already on *DestD* instead of writing over them.

/D:*mm-dd-yy* works like /M, but the "modified since" date is specified by *mm-dd-yy,* not the last backup date.

/T:*hh:mm:ss* backs up files on or after the indicated time when /D is used.

/F causes BACKUP to format the destination disk if it has not already been formatted.

/L creates a log file.

LogFileSpec is an optional name for the log file (the default name is BACKUP.LOG).

Type

Transient.

Restrictions

You cannot back up files that you are sharing but do not currently have access to. Do not use BACKUP with JOIN, SUBST, APPEND, or ASSIGN. FORMAT must be available for use in the same directory as BACKUP, since it may be needed to format the target disk.

BREAK

This command makes programs easier to interrupt. Turning BREAK on makes DOS check more often for the Ctrl-Break key combination. For example, if you are compiling a long program and the compiler encounters an error and gets stuck in a loop, you will want to halt execution. Having BREAK set to ON will allow you to do this.

Format

```
BREAK [ON ¦ OFF]
```

ON enables Ctrl-Break.

OFF disables the Ctrl-Break function (this is the default).

Type

Resident.

BUFFERS

This command causes a certain number of file-transfer buffers to be set aside in memory. While most programs only require a few buffers, remember that every disk access requires one. It is recommended that you set BUFFERS equal to the appropriate number, as shown in Table A.1. Note that a value of 3 buffers for system RAM of less than or equal to 128K is used only for high-capacity drives.

BUFFERS VALUE	SYSTEM RAM (K)
2 or 3	<=128
5	129–256
10	257–512
15	513 and up

Table A.1: BUFFER settings per system RAM

Format
BUFFERS = *x*

> *x* is the number of buffers to be set up. If this command is not specified, DOS 3.3 will determine the number of buffers automatically, based on the current system memory.

Type
Configuration.

CALL

CALL allows a true subroutine capability in DOS 3.3. When you are executing a batch file, it may sometimes be necessary to run a second batch file and then return to the first batch file at the place where the second file was called. In other words, you may want to run a second batch file without having to completely restart the first one. This can be done with the CALL command.

Format
CALL *FileSpec*

> *FileSpec* is the optional drive and path name, plus the file name, of the second batch file to be executed.

Type
Batch, resident.

Restrictions

CALL should not be used to pipe or redirect output. Recursive calls are allowed, but you are responsible for ensuring that the logic eventually ends.

CHCP

This command allows you to change the currently loaded code page for all eligible installed devices. The NLSFUNC command must be loaded prior to using CHCP. Although this command is internal, it may need to access the COUNTRY.SYS file. Should this be the case, and should the COUNTRY.SYS file not be on the default drive, DOS will display the message "File not found."

Format

CHCP [*xxx*]

xxx is the code-page number.

Type

Resident.

Restrictions

The corresponding device drivers for the specified code page must be available. NLSFUNC must have been executed previous to this command.

CHDIR (CD)

When moving through the directory structure, you must change the directory you are in. CHDIR (or simply CD) is an easy way to do that. Executing CHDIR .. will put you in the immediate parent directory of the directory you are in. (The two-dot symbol denotes this particular parent directory.)

Format

C[H]D[IR] [*D:Path*]

D:*Path* is the optional drive and path specifying which directory you wish to make the default directory.

Type
Resident.

CHKDSK

A problem in the system area can prevent you from using your disk. The correctional facilities of CHKDSK will help you solve such a problem by resolving errors in the disk's file allocation table.

Format
[*D:Path*]CHKDSK [*FileSpec*][/F][/V]

D:Path is the drive and path where the command file is located if it is not in the current directory.

FileSpec is an optional drive and path, plus the file name and extension, of the file that is the object of the command. Wild cards are allowed.

/F allows corrections on the disk.

/V lists all files and their paths.

Type
Transient.

Restrictions
CHKDSK will not work on drives created by JOIN or SUBST, or on networked drives.

CLS

Sometimes the screen becomes cluttered, or you have a batch file that does many different things, and you no longer need to see everything put on the screen. To clear the screen, you can use the CLS command. After the screen erasure, the cursor is placed at the top left of the screen.

Format
CLS

Type
Resident.

COMMAND

The COMMAND.COM command processor, invoked when the computer is turned on, is the part of DOS that takes in, translates, and executes commands. Invoking a second command processor can give you the ability to execute DOS commands from inside a program and then return to that program. The COMMAND command also allows you to load a custom command processor that has special functions and abilities or altered command definitions.

Format
COMMAND [*D*:*Path*][/P][/C *String*][/E:*xxxxx*]

D:*Path* is the drive and path where the command file is located if it is not in the current directory.

/P makes the new processor the primary processor.

/C *String* executes the command represented by *String*.

/E:*xxxxx* sets the DOS environment size to *xxxxx* bytes.

Type
Resident.

COMP

This command compares the contents of two or more files to see if they are the same.

Format
[*D*:*Path*]COMP [*FileSpec1*] [*FileSpec2*]

D:*Path* is the drive and path where the command file is located if it is not in the current directory.

FileSpec1 is the optional drive and path, plus the file names and extensions, of the first set of files to be compared. Wild cards are allowed.

FileSpec2 is the optional drive and path, plus the file names and extensions, of the second set of files to be compared. Wild cards are allowed.

Type
Transient.

COPY

Copies of read-only files created with COPY will *not* be read-only.

The COPY command has three distinct uses. You can use it to duplicate files, to access devices, or to concatenate files.

Duplicating files with COPY, using the first format of this command, allows you versatility in moving files around the disk system. Whole directories can be copied and thus moved to another location or to another disk. Without COPY, you would never be able to transfer newly purchased programs from diskettes to your hard disk, or copy files to a diskette for another system.

The second format of COPY is especially useful for printing multiple files at once, which cannot be done with the TYPE command. It is also the only way for you to directly send information to a device from DOS.

The third format of the COPY command allows files to be concatenated; that is, ASCII-type files can be added to the end of one another to form one big file.

Format
COPY [/A][/B]*SourceFile* [[/A][/B][*DestFile*][/A][/B][/V]]
COPY [/A][/B]*Source* [/A][/B][*Dest*][/A][/B][/V]
COPY [/A][/B]*SourceFile1* + *SourceFile2*[/A][/B] + ...
[*ConcatFile*][/A][/B][/V]

These switches will affect the file immediately preceding the place where the switch is used, as well as all files following it, until the next time the switch is used.

The /A switch is used with *SourceFile, Source,* or *SourceFile1, SourceFile2* to read data up to but not including the first Ctrl-Z (end-of-file) character; the file is treated as an ASCII file. This is the default when concatenating (format 3).

The /A switch is used with with *DestFile, Dest,* or *ConcatFile* to write a Ctrl-Z at the end of the file.

The /B switch—(the default for duplicating files (format 1))—is used with *SourceFile, Source,* or *SourceFile1, SourceFile2* to copy the entire file up to the last Ctrl-Z.

The /B switch is used with *DestFile, Dest,* or *ConcatFile* to make sure that no Ctrl-Z will be written at the end of the file.

/V causes DOS to check that all of the specified files were copied successfully.

SourceFile is the drive, path, file name, and extension of the file to be copied.

Not specifying a destination file in the third format of the COPY command will result in all source files being appended to the end of the first source file.

DestFile is the drive, path, file name, and extension of the file to which *SourceFile* will be copied.

Source and *Dest* can be either device or file specifications, although DOS only allows ASCII files to be read from a device.

SourceFile1 and *SourceFile2* are a list of files to be added together (*SourceFile2* to the end of *SourceFile1,* etc.).

ConcatFile is the file composed of the concatenation of the source files.

Type

Resident.

COUNTRY

Since the format of such things as the date and time may change from country to country, your computer must be able to recognize and adapt to these different formats. The COUNTRY command has provisions for up to 21 country codes, and it will also call up a specified code page.

Format

COUNTRY = *xxx*,[*yyy*] [,*FileSpec*]

xxx is the three-digit international code of each country.

yyy is the specified code page.

FileSpec is the location and name of the file containing the country information; the default is \COUNTRY.SYS.

Type

Configuration.

CTTY

If you have a special system configuration or another workstation connected through one of the auxiliary serial ports (AUX, COM1, COM2, COM3, or COM4), CTTY can change the current input and output device (which is usually the keyboard and screen) to something else. You could, for example, specify a teletype as a console.

Specifying a non-input device such as LPT1 in a CTTY command will hang the system. The computer will try to input data from this port, which cannot be done.

Format

CTTY *Device*

Device is a valid device name.

Type

Resident.

Restrictions

The keyboard and monitor will be reset as the main console when you use BASIC and other programs that do not use DOS function calls.

DATE

This command changes the date. Use it either to update or to simply find out what day of the week a certain date is. DATE also resets a permanent clock's date, should one be installed.

If the *mm-dd-yy* specification is left off, you will be prompted for it. The order of *mm-dd-yy* is dependent on the country you have selected.

Format

DATE [*mm-dd-yy* ¦ *dd-mm-yy* ¦ *yy-mm-dd*]

mm is the month (01 to 12).

dd is the day (01 to 31).

yy is the year, either 80 to 99, or 1980 to 1999.

Type

Resident.

DEBUG

Although DEBUG is not discussed in the DOS 3.3 user's manual, it *is* included on the DOS 3.3 master disk.

DEBUG fixes and changes assembly-language programs. It provides a way to run and test any program in a controlled environment: you can change any part of the program and immediately execute the program without having to reassemble it. You can also run machine-language (object) files directly. Programmers often use this DOS tool to make quick program changes, to test variations, and to rapidly isolate errors in assembly-language code.

Format

[*D*:*Path*]DEBUG [*FileSpec*] [*Param1*] [*Param2*]

> *D*:*Path* is the drive and path where the command file is located if it is not in the current directory.
>
> *FileSpec* is an optional drive and path, plus the file name and extension, of the file that is the object of the command.
>
> *Param1* and *Param2* are any optional parameters that are needed by *FileSpec*.

Type

Transient.

DEL

When issuing the command DEL *.*, which deletes all files in the current directory, DOS will issue the warning "Are you sure (Y/N)?" to verify that you really wish to take such a drastic action. Issuing the DEL command with a subdirectory as the *FileSpec* parameter deletes all of the files in that subdirectory, but not the subdirectory itself.

This command removes a file from the directory. The file is still physically present on the disk and can be retrieved by using certain non-DOS disk utilities (such as the Norton Utilities), but it is not accessible using the directory structure.

Format

DEL *FileSpec*

> *FileSpec* is an optional drive and path, plus the file name and extension, of each file to be deleted. Wild cards are allowed.

Type

Resident.

Restrictions

You cannot use DEL to delete read-only files or any subdirectory still containing files.

DEVICE

This command loads a device driver. A driver can be anything from a keyboard enhancement routine to a RAM disk specification. DEVICE can be used many times in the CONFIG.SYS file, limited only by how the drivers use the system's memory.

Format

DEVICE = *FileSpec*[*Switches*]

FileSpec is the optional drive and path, plus the file name and extension, of the specified driver file.

Switches are the switches corresponding to the specific driver files.

Type

Configuration.

DIR

The DIR command offers several ways to see what files you have. Without this command, it would be extremely difficult, if not impossible, to operate a computer system of any size.

Format

DIR [*FileSpec*][/P][/W]

All DIR parameters represented by *FileSpec* are completely independent from one another. They can be used in any combination, either alone or together, to narrow down the directory listing.

FileSpec is an optional drive and path, plus the file name and extension, of the file that is the object of the command.

/P causes the computer to prompt you to continue listing the directory entries if the listing is longer than one screen.

/W causes the listing to be displayed in wide format (without the size, date, and time, and in a horizontal listing).

Type
Resident.

Restrictions
Hidden files will not be shown when you use the DIR command.

DISKCOMP

Unlike the COMP command, which compares two sets of files, the DISKCOMP command compares two diskettes (not hard disks). It is usually used to verify a COPY or BACKUP operation.

Format
[*D*:*Path*]DISKCOMP [*D1*:[*D2*:]][/1][/8]

> *D*:*Path* is the drive and path where the command file is located if it is not in the current directory.
>
> *D1* and *D2* are the two drives to be compared.
>
> /1 forces the computer to compare the diskettes as if they were single-sided (no matter what they really are).
>
> /8 forces the computer to read and compare only the first eight sectors on each track, even if they are 9- or 15-sector diskettes.

Type
Transient.

Restrictions
DISKCOMP will not work on a hard disk or with the JOIN, ASSIGN, or SUBST commands.

DISKCOPY

This command gives you a quick way to copy a diskette with a lot of data on it that would otherwise take forever to copy with the COPY command. DISKCOPY copies the raw data of the diskette, so if the diskette is a system diskette, the new copy will also be a system diskette. If the source diskette is not a system diskette, then the copy will not be a system diskette either, even if the destination diskette originally was a system diskette. The second diskette will be an *exact* copy of the first. This command also formats a nonformatted destination diskette during the copying process.

Format
[*D*:*Path*]DISKCOPY [*SourceD*:*DestD*:][/1]

D:*Path* is the drive and path where the command file is located if it is not in the current directory.

SourceD is the source drive to be copied.

DestD is the destination drive to be copied onto.

/1 forces the computer to copy only the first side of the source diskette to the first side of the destination diskette, as if they were both single-sided, even if they are double-sided.

Type
Transient.

Restrictions
You cannot use this command with a hard disk; also, it does not recognize an assigned or substituted drive, and should not be used with JOIN. DISKCOPY cannot reliably read a double-sided disk formatted in a high-capacity drive, and it will not work with network drives.

ECHO

ECHO can be used to send a line of text to the printer or a file; for example, ECHO Hello >LPT1 will cause "Hello" to be printed. To print a character that has some other function, enclose it in double quotation marks.

When you set up a batch file, there are times when you don't want the executing commands to be displayed on the screen. ECHO suppresses the screen's presentation of batch-file command execution.

Format
ECHO [ON ¦ OFF ¦ *String*]

ON turns on the display of commands (the default).

OFF turns off echoing.

String is a message that is to be displayed regardless of whether ECHO is ON or OFF.

Type
Batch, resident (acceptable on a DOS command line).

EDLIN

EDLIN is the DOS line editor. Unlike many word processors, it is not a full-screen editor. EDLIN has no formatting commands, and you must change data a line at a time. It is good for modifying short ASCII files and for creating and modifying simple batch files.

Format
[*D*:*Path*]EDLIN *FileSpec*[/B]

D:*Path* is the drive and path where the command file is located if it is not in the current directory.

FileSpec is an optional drive and path, plus the file name and extension, of the file that is the object of the command.

/B causes EDLIN to load a file containing embedded Ctrl-Z codes.

Type
Transient.

ERASE

When you enter the command ERASE *.*, which will erase all files in the current directory, DOS will issue the warning "Are you sure (Y/N)?" to ensure that you wish to take such drastic action. Issuing the command ERASE *FileSpec,* where *FileSpec* is the name of a subdirectory, deletes all files in the subdirectory but not the subdirectory itself.

The ERASE command removes a file from the directory. The file is still physically present on the disk and can be gotten back by using a disk utility, but it is not accessible using the directory structure.

Format
ERASE *FileSpec*

FileSpec is the optional drive, optional path, file name, and extension of each file to be erased. Wild cards are allowed.

Type
Resident.

Restrictions

You cannot use ERASE to delete read-only files or to remove a subdirectory.

EXE2BIN

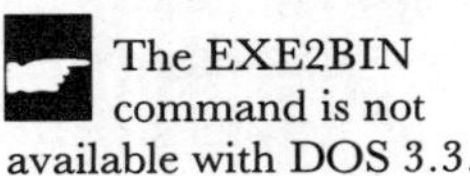
The EXE2BIN command is not available with DOS 3.3.

This advanced command formally converts executable files to command files. A file with an .EXE extension is used as the source file, and a file with a .COM or .BIN extension is created.

Format

[*D:Path*]EXE2BIN *SourceFile* [*DestFile*]

> *D:Path* is the drive and path where the command file is located if it is not in the current directory.
>
> *SourceFile* is the drive, path, file name, and extension of the file to be converted; .EXE is the default for the extension.
>
> *DestFile* is the drive, path, file name, and extension for the converted file; .BIN is the default for the extension. If this parameter is not included on the command line, the resultant file will have the same drive, path, and file name as the source file, but its extension will be .BIN.

Type

Transient.

Restrictions

SourceFile must be a programmer's object file created with the LINK program. The code and data of the file must be less than 64K.

FASTOPEN

DOS can take a long time to search for a file or directory, especially if it is located in subdirectories. The FASTOPEN command maintains a list of the most recently accessed directory and file locations on the disk. This means that when you repeatedly access a directory or file, all DOS has to do is check in memory where that directory or file is located and then access it, without having to check through the disk's directory tree. This process can save a good deal of time.

Format

[*D*:*Path*]FASTOPEN *D1*:[= *Size*]

D:*Path* is the drive and path where the command file is located if it is not in the current directory.

D1 is the drive to which FASTOPEN will be attached (the command can be issued for each drive separately).

Size is the number of directory or file entries that FASTOPEN will remember.

Type

Transient.

Restrictions

FASTOPEN will not work with JOIN, SUBST, or ASSIGN, or with network drives.

FCBS

On older-style DOS versions—specifically, version 1—files were accessed via file control blocks (FCBs). These are approximately 40-byte sections in memory that tell DOS the file's name and other attributes. The FCBS command allows you to access these.

Format

FCBS = *MaxNum*,*PermNum*

MaxNum is the number of FCBs that may be opened concurrently (the default is 4).

PermNum is the minimum number of FCBs that will remain open when DOS tries to close files automatically (the default is 0).

Restrictions

If *PermNum* is less than *MaxNum,* DOS can close an FCB without alerting the program that is using the FCB. This can cause major problems.

FDISK

Hard disks can be set up to have more than one type of operating system on them. For example, you can have DOS 3.3 managing one part of a disk and UNIX managing another. Each of these sections is called a *partition.* You can have from one to four partitions on a disk (see Appendix C).

Partitions must be set up before the disk is logically formatted. If your disk is already being used and you wish to make a partition, you will have to back up all of your data, run FDISK on the system diskette, and then reformat your disk.

All data on your hard disk will be destroyed when you create partitions with FDISK.

Two types of partitions can be set up for DOS: a primary partition and an extended partition. DOS only needs the primary partition, which can be as large as 32Mb. If you have more hard-disk space available than that on one hard disk, you will need to create an extended partition, which you assign the next logical drive letter. You can also subdivide the extended partition into more logical drives, up to the letter Z. Partitioning is done because DOS is limited to 32Mb per drive.

Format

[*D:Path*]FDISK

> *D:Path* is the drive and path where the command file is located if it is not in the current directory.

Type

Transient.

Restrictions

FDISK can only be used on hard-disk systems. A disk must be reformatted logically after being partitioned. FDISK will not work if another process is accessing the disk.

FILES

Just as the number of buffers to be used by DOS can be specified, so may the number of files open at any one time. The FILES command specifies the size of the file control area in which file control blocks are created.

When you are using the FILES command, keep in mind that the size of DOS increases by 48 bytes for each file beyond the eight default files.

Format

FILES = *x*

x is a number between 8 and 255 (8 is the default) specifying the number of files that can remain open at one time.

Type

Configuration.

FIND

FIND allows you to search through a file to locate any particular string of text characters.

Format

[*D*:*Path*]FIND [/V][/C][/N]*"String"* [*FileSpec*...]

D:*Path* is the drive and path where the command file is located if it is not in the current directory.

/V causes FIND to display each line not containing *String*.

/C counts the number of lines containing *String* and shows the total.

/N shows the relative line number of each line containing *String*.

String is the string of characters to be searched for.

FileSpec is the drive, path, file name, and extension of each file to be searched. Multiple files should be separated by a space.

Type

Transient.

Restrictions

Wild cards not allowed with this command. FIND will end its search at the first Ctrl-Z encountered in a file.

FOR

FOR sets up a repeating loop in a batch file. This is useful for repeating an operation with a different parameter a specified number of times.

Format

FOR %%*Var* IN (*ComSet*) DO *Command*

Var is a variable name.

ComSet is the set of values to be used successively by *Command.*

Command is the command to be executed using %%*Var* as a varying parameter (which uses the values given in *ComSet*).

Type

Batch, resident.

Restrictions

The variable name used in a FOR command cannot be a DOS reserved word.

FORMAT

When you want to use a new disk with your system, it must be formatted. Certain markings must be placed on the disk to help the computer know where it is when it accesses the disk. The disk is not actually erased but is reset to a state in which nothing is on it.

The FORMAT command destroys the contents of a disk, so be careful. Write-protecting any disks in other drives during a format may help prevent errors.

The FORMAT command can create both a data disk, in which all storage space is available for use, and a system diskette, which is bootable and contains DOS's two hidden system files and the COMMAND.COM file. FORMAT will also check the disk for any areas that have gone bad and mark them accordingly, so that no data will be saved in those areas.

Format

[*D*:*Path*]FORMAT *D1*:[/S][/1][/8][/V][/B][/4][/N:*xx*][/T:*yy*]

D:*Path* is the drive and path where the command file is located if it is not in the current directory.

D1: is the drive to be formatted.

/S causes a system disk to be made.

/1 formats only one side of the disk.

/8 formats the disk with 8 sectors instead of 9.

/V prompts for a volume label when formatting is complete.

/B formats the disk with 8 sectors and leaves room for the hidden system files, but does *not* transfer the system to the diskette. This allows for the use of the SYS command with any DOS version.

/4 causes a high-capacity drive to create a 360K, double-sided diskette.

/N:*xx* specifies that the disk be formatted with *xx* sectors per track.

/T:*yy* specifies that the disk be formatted with *yy* tracks.

Type

Transient.

Restrictions

FORMAT ignores assignments made with ASSIGN. /V cannot be used to format a diskette for DOS 1.1.

GOTO

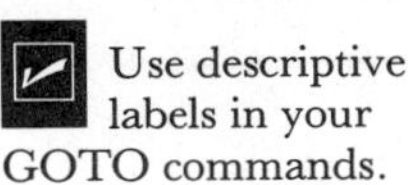
Use descriptive labels in your GOTO commands.

During a batch file's execution, it may become necessary to skip over some commands and execute others in a file. Or it may be necessary to jump back to another point in a file, perhaps for some logical looping. GOTO allows you to transfer execution.

Format
GOTO [:]*Label*

Label is the line identifier used by the batch file to indicate the line to which GOTO will transfer control.

Type
Batch, resident.

GRAFTABL

It is nice to be able to display the full ASCII range of characters on the screen so that you can see exactly what you are dealing with. If you have a Color Graphics Adapter, this command will enable you to display the ASCII characters that have codes from 128 to 255.

Format
[*D*:*Path*]GRAFTABL [437¦860¦863¦865¦/STATUS]

D:*Path* is the drive and path where the command file is located if it is not in the current directory.

437 loads the U.S. code page.

860 loads the Portuguese code page.

863 loads the Canadian code page.

865 loads the Norwegian and Danish code page.

/STATUS shows the number of the code page currently in use.

Type
Transient.

GRAPHICS

This command allows you to transfer graphics screens to your printer using the Shift-PrtSc key combination. The printing time will depend on what graphics mode you are in.

Format

[*D:Path*]GRAPHICS [*PrinterType*] [/R][/B][/LCD]

D:Path is the drive and path where the command file is located if it is not in the current directory.

PrinterType is an optional printer-type specification. It can be COLOR1, COLOR4, COLOR8, COMPACT, GRAPHICS, or THERMAL.

/R prints a reverse-video image.

/B prints the background color when *PrinterType* is COLOR4 or COLOR8.

/LCD prints the image produced on a liquid crystal display.

Type

Transient.

IF

Conditional statements play an important role in any type of programming. A conditional statement simply says "Do one thing if a certain condition is true; otherwise, do another thing." This allows branching, or decision making, in your programs.

In most high-level programming languages, conditionals are defined with the IF command. IF A=B THEN GOTO :START is executed as "If A equals B, then transfer control to the line labeled :START; otherwise, just go on to the next instruction."

Format

IF [NOT] *Condition Command*

NOT inverts the truth of the condition. If NOT is included, a true condition would be regarded as false, and a false condition as true.

Condition is the criterion for the execution of *Command*. *Condition* can be in one of the following formats:

ERRORLEVEL *Code* is used to determine if the return code of the last program or command that was executed equals *Code* or is higher.

String1 = =*String2* specifies that *String1* must equal *String2* for the condition to be true.

EXIST *FileSpec* causes the condition to be true if the file defined by *FileSpec* resides in the specified directory.

Command is the action (usually a command) that is executed when *Condition* is true or not false.

Type

Batch, resident (acceptable on a DOS command line).

Restrictions

DOS is case-sensitive for *String* values.

JOIN

JOIN makes DOS treat a whole disk drive as if it were a subdirectory of another drive. The JOIN command has three main formats. The first displays all directory and disk names that have been joined; the second actually performs the joining; and the third disjoins a directory and disk.

Formats

[*D:Path*]JOIN
[*D:Path*]JOIN *Drive2 Drive1*
[*D:Path*]JOIN *Drive2* /D

D:Path is the drive and path where the command file is located if it is not in the current directory.

Drive2 is the drive to which a directory will be attached or released.

Drive1 is the drive and path of the directory to be joined.

/D causes any previous joining of *Drive2* to be unjoined.

Type

Transient.

Restrictions

Use JOIN only on multidrive systems. JOIN cannot be used to join a SUBST-created drive.

KEYB

This command is used to load a new keyboard translation table for a specific country. There are 21 country codes to choose from.

Format

[*D*:*Path*]KEYB [*xx*[,[*yyy*],[*FileSpec*]]]

D:*Path* is the drive and path where the command file is located if it is not in the current directory.

xx is a keyboard code representing a country.

yyy is the code page to be used.

FileSpec is the drive, path, file name, and extension of the keyboard definition file (the default is \KEYBOARD.SYS).

Type

Transient.

LABEL

LABEL allows you to give a disk a volume label electronically. You will then see your disk's name each time you call up a directory.

Format

[*D*:*Path*]LABEL [*D1*:][*String*]

D:*Path* is the drive and path where the command file is located if it is not in the current directory.

D1: is the drive containing the disk whose label is to be changed or displayed.

String, when specified, will become the label of the disk in *Drive2*.

Type

Transient.

LASTDRIVE

If you have more than five drives hooked up to your system, or if you are using the SUBST command often and need to declare a drive name beyond E, you need this command. LASTDRIVE configures the system so that you can access drives up to the specified drive, which may even be Z.

Format
LASTDRIVE = *D*

D is the last accessible drive; the default is E.

Type
Configuration.

Restrictions
If you specify a letter range that is not sufficient for the number of drives currently hooked up to the system, LASTDRIVE will not be accepted. For example, if you specify G as the final drive, and have eight drives hooked up to your system, LASTDRIVE will not work—you've only assigned seven letters to cover your eight drives.

MKDIR (MD)

The MKDIR command (or MD for short) creates a new directory, either in the current working directory or at the specified path location in an existing tree. This new directory will be empty of files initially, but it is usable immediately.

Format
M[K]D[IR] [*D*:*Path*]

D:*Path* is the optional drive and path specifying which directory you wish to create.

Type
Resident.

MODE

The MODE command controls and redirects output. There are ten formats for this useful command. The first selects various print modes on parallel printers, the second redirects output, and the third changes the parameters of the serial port. The fourth format changes the display type, and the fifth sets the video mode and, simultaneously, adjusts the horizontal alignment of the monitor.

The MODE command can also work with code pages. The sixth and seventh formats install code-page device drivers in the specified device. The eighth format selects the code page to be activated for the specified device. (You can have several code pages loaded into the device at once, but only one can be active at any one time.) The ninth format displays the active code page and then displays all of the code pages that can be activated for the specified device.

The tenth format reinstalls the currently active device driver in the specified device if it was erased. This comes in handy if for some reason you need to turn your printer off. Instead of using the first or second format to reload the driver, which in fact is already in computer memory anyway, you can use the tenth format to make another copy and place it into the device's memory.

Formats

[*D*:*Path*]MODE LPT*x*: [*CPL*][,[*LPI*][,P]]
[*D*:*Path*]MODE LPT*x*: = COM*y*
[*D*:*Path*]MODE COM*y*[:]*Baud*[,[*Parity*][,[*Bits*][,P]]
[*D*:*Path*]MODE *Type*
[*D*:*Path*]MODE [*Type*], *Shift* [,T]
[*D*:*Path*]MODE *Device* CODEPAGE PREPARE = ((*CP*)*FileSpec*)
[*D*:*Path*]MODE *Device* CODEPAGE PREPARE = ((*CPList*)*FileSpec*)
[*D*:*Path*]MODE *Device* CODEPAGE SELECT = *CP*
[*D*:*Path*]MODE *Device* CODEPAGE[/STATUS]
[*D*:*Path*]MODE *Device* CODEPAGE REFRESH

D:*Path* is the drive and path where the command file is located if it is not in the current directory.

x is a printer number.

CPL is the number of characters per line.

LPI is the number of lines per inch.

P causes the computer to continuously retry accessing the port during time-out errors.

y is a serial-port number.

Baud is a baud rate for the COM port (110, 150, 300, 600, 1200, 2400, 4800, 9600, or 19200).

Parity is a parity value for the COM port; it can be even, odd, or none (the default is even).

Bits is a combination of two parameters specifying the number of stop and data bits used.

Type is the display type being used. It is specified as 40, 80, BW40, BW80, CO40, CO80, or MONO.

Shift is the direction for a screen shift, either L or R.

T puts a test pattern on the screen for checking the screen alignment when shifting.

Device is a valid device name (CON, LPT1, and so on).

CP is a code-page number (437, 850, 860, 863, or 865).

CPList is a list of code-page numbers.

FileSpec is the file containing the code-page data. Its value is 4201.CPI for the IBM Proprinter; 5202.CPI for the IBM Quietwriter III Printer; EGA.CPI for EGA displays; or LCD.CPI for LCD displays.

/STATUS displays the active code page and the other available code pages for *Device*.

Type

Transient.

MORE

This command is similar to the DIR/P command, which pauses the directory listing after each screenful of data and asks you to press a key to continue. MORE is a filter—that is, data is sent to it, and MORE processes the data and sends it out in a new format. In this case, the filter simply prints the data a screenful at a time and prints "-- MORE --" at the bottom of the screen until you press a key.

Format

[*D*:*Path*]MORE

D:*Path* is the drive and path where the command file is located if it is not in the current directory.

Type

Transient.

NLSFUNC

NLSFUNC supports national-language features and code-page switching. It uses the new extended country information provided with DOS 3.3 to load the part of the keyboard translation table containing the country-specific information.

Format

[*D*:*Path*]NLSFUNC [*FileSpec*]

D:*Path* is the drive and path where the command file is located if it is not in the current directory.

FileSpec specifies the location and name of the country-specific code file (the default is \COUNTRY.SYS).

Type

Transient.

PATH

You often need to access a program in a directory other than the one you are in. The PATH command gives DOS a list of drives and directories to search through, in the order given, until it finds the requested program file. Beware of the order given, however: if there are two different files with the same name in different directories along the path, then the first one encountered will be used.

Format
PATH [*D1*:*Path1*][;*D2*:*Path2*...]

[*D1*:*Path1*] is the first drive and directory searched.

[*D2*:*Path2*...] is the second drive and directory searched, and so on.

Type
Resident.

Restrictions
PATH will not work for data files, overlay files, or other non-executable files (see APPEND).

PAUSE

This command temporarily halts the execution of a batch file. A message will be printed on the screen telling you to strike a key when you are ready to continue.

Format
PAUSE [*String*]

String prints a specified string (a message) on the screen before "Strike any key when ready."

Type
Batch, resident (acceptable on a DOS command line).

PRINT

The PRINT command invokes, modifies, and adds files to an internal software-based queue. Queues offer you a way to set up the computer to output multiple files in order automatically.

Format
[*D*:*Path*]PRINT [*Params*][/C][/T][/P][*FileSpec*,...]

D:*Path* is the drive and path where the command file is located if it is not in the current directory.

Params contains optional switches and parameters that redefine queue characteristics. They are as follows:

> /D:*Device* specifies the output device.
>
> /B:*BuffSize* specifies the output buffer's size in bytes.
>
> /U:*BusyTicks* specifies how long the queue will wait each cycle if the printer is too busy to print new data.
>
> /M:*MaxTicks* specifies how much time the queue has to send data to the printer.
>
> /S:*TimeSlice* specifies the number of time slices.
>
> /Q:*QueueSize* specifies the maximum number of entries in the queue.

/C cancels previous and following entries on the command line.

/T terminates the queue; everything is canceled and stopped.

/P adds previous and following entries on the command line to the queue.

FileSpec, ... is an optional list of the paths, names, and extensions of files to be queued for printing.

Type

Transient.

Restrictions

You cannot use a printer without the PRINT command while a queue is printing. PRINT cannot be used on a network. The disk where the files are located cannot be removed from the drive until the queue has completed printing.

PROMPT

This command changes the system prompt to whatever you like—it can display the time, the date, or a simple message. This is useful for finding out which directory you are in before you modify or delete any files.

Format

PROMPT [*String*]

String is a string of characters that can contain special-purpose entries. Possible values are shown in Table A.2.

CHARACTERS	DESCRIPTION
$$	$ sign
$t	Time
$d	Date
$p	Current directory
$v	DOS version number
$n	Default drive identifier
$g	> symbol
$l	< symbol
$b	¦ symbol
$q	= symbol
$h	Erasing backspace
$e	Escape character
$ _	Carriage return and line feed

Table A.2: Special-purpose PROMPT codes (meta strings)

Type

Resident.

RECOVER

Sometimes a part of a disk goes bad—that is, the computer cannot read it, and access to the files in that area may be denied. The RECOVER command reads the file part by part, skipping over the bad data, and rewrites the file without the bad data, allowing the user access to what's left. RECOVER can be used to recover specific files or an entire disk.

Format
[*D*:*Path*]RECOVER [*D1*][*FileSpec*]

D:*Path* is the drive and path where the command file is located if it is not in the current directory.

D1 is the drive identifier for the disk to be recovered.

FileSpec is an optional drive and path, plus the file name and extension, of the file that is the object of the command. Wild cards are allowed.

Type
Transient.

Restrictions
RECOVER should not be used on a network disk.

REM

It is often helpful to place comments in your file code, so that if you come back to those files later, you can quickly and easily understand what they contain and how they work. In batch files, this is done with the REM command. The contents of a REM command line are not executed or displayed if ECHO is OFF, but they will be readable if you look at the file itself.

Format
REM *String*

String represents nonexecutable comments.

Type
Batch, resident (acceptable on a DOS command line).

Restrictions
Comments may be up to 123 characters long per REM statement. Enclose characters that have special meanings to DOS (such as ¦) in double quotation marks ("¦").

RENAME

The RENAME command (which can be shortened to REN) performs the very useful function of renaming a file.

Format

REN[AME] *OldFile NewFile*

OldFile is the optional drive and path, plus the file name and extension, of the file that will be renamed. Wild cards are allowed.

NewFile is a new file name and extension for *OldFile*. Wild cards are allowed. The *NewFile* parameter does not require or accept a prefixed drive and path.

Type

Resident.

Restrictions

You cannot use RENAME to give a subdirectory a new name.

REPLACE

The REPLACE command is an advanced, selective version of the COPY command. It is useful for changing versions of DOS when files need to be updated. It is also useful for selective backups of files without the BACKUP command. For example, if you work with a single-disk word processor, then a backup disk might only contain copies of the text files you've worked on. REPLACE would only replace the files on the backup disk that were changed on the original, or it would only make copies of newly created files—not older, unchanged files.

Format

[*D*:*Path*]REPLACE *SourceFile* [*Dest*][/A][/P][/R][/S][/W]

D:*Path* is the drive and path where the command file is located if it is not in the current directory.

SourceFile is the optional drive and path, plus the file name and an optional extension, of each file that will be a replacing file.

Dest is the optional drive and path of the files to be replaced.

/A adds files to those already present.

/P prompts you before replacing a file.

/R replaces both normal and read-only files on *Dest*.

/S replaces all files in the directory structure that have matching file names.

/W waits for you to insert a diskette.

Type
Transient.

RESTORE

This command is the reverse of BACKUP: it restores files to the disk and directory from which they were backed up.

Format
[*D:Path*]RESTORE *SourceD FileSpec*[/S][/P][/B:*mm-dd-yy*]
[/A:*mm-dd-yy*][/M][/N][/L:*hh-mm-ss*][/E:*hh-mm-ss*]

D:Path is the drive and path where the command file is located if it is not in the current directory.

SourceD is the drive containing the backed-up files to be restored.

FileSpec is the optional drive and path, plus the file names and extensions, of the files on *SourceD* to be restored. Wild cards are allowed.

RESTORE will overwrite files with the same name if they are in the specified directory. Use the /P switch (or the REPLACE command) to avoid rewriting a file.

/S restores files in subdirectories of the files specified in *FileSpec*.

/P prompts you before a file is restored if that file was modified since it was last backed up.

/B:*mm-dd-yy* causes all backed-up files that were last modified on or before *mm-dd-yy* to be restored.

/A:*mm-dd-yy* causes all backed-up files that were last modified on or after *mm-dd-yy* to be restored.

mm-dd-yy represents a date in months, days, and years.

/M compares the backed-up files and the files on the destination disk; it then restores the files that have been changed or erased since the last backup.

/N restores files that no longer exist on the destination disk.

/L:*hh-mm-ss* restores all files changed since the time specified by *hh-mm-ss*.

/E:*hh-mm-ss* restores all files changed prior to the time specified by *hh-mm-ss*.

hh-mm-ss represents time in hours, minutes, and seconds.

Type

Transient.

Restrictions

Only files created with BACKUP will be restored. Do not use RESTORE if SUBST, JOIN, or ASSIGN was invoked in a BACKUP operation.

RMDIR (RD)

You may find it necessary to delete or remove a directory. You must first delete all files or subdirectories in the directory, and then use the RMDIR command.

Format

R[M]D[IR] [*D*:*Path*]

D:*Path* is the drive and path of the directory to be removed.

Type

Resident.

SELECT

SELECT is an advanced version of the FORMAT command. It allows you to specify a new keyboard layout and country-specific date and time formats.

Format

[*D*:*Path*]SELECT [[A: ¦ B:]*DestD*:[*DestPath*]] *xxx yy*

D:*Path* is an optional drive and path where the command file is located.

A: or B: is the source drive that contains the command files and country information (A: is the default).

DestD:*DestPath* is the drive and optional path of the disk to be formatted. The root directory is the default for an unspecified *DestPath*.

xxx specifies the country code.

yy specifies the keyboard code.

Type

Transient.

Restrictions

SELECT uses FORMAT, so anything on the destination disk will be destroyed after this command is used. SELECT may be used on a hard disk, so be careful.

Drives A and B are the only source drives, and the destination drive must not be the same as the source drive. The U.S. keyboard file is resident in the computer's memory, so it does not need to be on the source disk. CONFIG.SYS and AUTOEXEC.BAT files are created on *DestD*. High-capacity diskettes must be used in high-capacity drives.

SET

The SET command changes strings and definitions within the DOS environment of your computer. This area of memory set aside for special definitions and defaults can be used by the system and also can be changed by the user. With SET you can display the current DOS environment, erase the current definition of *Name,* create a new DOS environment string, or change one that already exists.

Format
SET [*Name* = [*Param*]]

Name is a user-specified string used in place of *Param.* It can also contain the DOS environment strings PROMPT, PATH, LASTDRIVE, or COMSPEC.

Param is what *Name* will represent, or it is the new setting for one of the DOS environment strings.

Type
Resident.

Restrictions
There are only 127 bytes of total available DOS environment by default. You can, however, change this with the SHELL command's /E switch.

SHARE

This command loads routines that enable file sharing and allows you to "lock" a disk or all or part of a file so that it cannot be used by another process on the same computer. SHARE does not prevent the use of a file by another computer when you are using networks; that kind of protection should be provided with your network software.

Format
[*D:Path*]SHARE [/F:*FileMem*][/L:*Locks*]

D:Path is the drive and path where the command file is located if it is not in the current directory.

/F:*FileMem* sets aside the memory to be used for keeping track of file sharing (the default is 2048 bytes).

/L:*Locks* specifies the number of locks that can be in effect at once (the default is 20).

Restrictions

You may only load the SHARE command once. Subsequent attempts at loading will yield an error message. You must reboot to remove SHARE.

SHELL

If you are a system programmer or if you have your own command processor, this command is for you. When DOS loads, SHELL can specify and load your command processor instead of COMMAND.COM. You can also use SHELL with the /E switch to load in the standard COMMAND.COM file, but with an expanded DOS environment.

Format

SHELL = *ComFileSpec* [/E:*xxxxx*][/P]

ComFileSpec is the drive, path, and file name of the new command processor.

/E:*xxxxx* defines, in bytes, the size of the DOS environment.

/P keeps the specified command processor resident and causes AUTOEXEC.BAT to be executed after the processor has been loaded.

Type

Configuration.

SHIFT

Batch files often need information from the user—a drive identifier, a file name, a yes-or-no answer, and so on. These temporary values can be put into the variables %0 through %9 and be made available to the batch file when it is run. For those applications that require more than ten variables, Microsoft has developed the SHIFT command. This command simply shifts all of the variables down one number. For example, executing SHIFT would cause the new %1 to equal the old %2, the new %2 to equal the old %3, and so on. %9 could reference a formerly inaccessible eleventh parameter value.

Format
SHIFT

Type
Batch, resident (acceptable on a DOS command line).

SORT

SORT is another filter command. Data is sent in, and depending on the parameters, sorted and displayed, or routed to another file. Directories may be displayed in a sorted format, but the files will not be physically sorted on the disk.

Format
[*D:Path*]SORT [/R][/ + *Col*]

D:Path is the drive and path where the command file is located if it is not in the current directory.

/R sorts in reverse-alphabetical order.

/ + *Col* starts the sorting with column *Col* (the default is column 1).

Type
Transient.

STACKS

This command is intended for very advanced users. It allows you to change the stack resources that are normally defined for you. Stack frames are used for interrupt processing.

Format
STACKS = *n*,*s*

n specifies the number of stack frames.

s specifies the number of bytes in each frame.

Type
Configuration.

SUBST

The SUBST command is the opposite of the JOIN command. It creates a new disk drive corresponding to a directory. Starting with one directory structure, you can take a directory and all of its subdirectories and make that branch of the tree into the root directory of a new, fictitious drive. This new drive accesses all of its data from a physically existing drive, and thus cannot be considered a RAM disk.

Like the JOIN command, SUBST has three distinct formats for its use. The first displays all of the current substitutions, the second actually performs a substitution, and the third cancels out a substitution.

Formats
[*D*:*Path*]SUBST
[*D*:*Path*]SUBST *NewD Path2*
[*D*:*Path*]SUBST *NewD* /D

D:*Path* is the drive and path where the command file is located if it is not in the current directory.

NewD is the drive to be created or abolished.

Path2 is the drive and directory specification to be made into drive *NewD*.

/D abolishes an existing *NewD* substitution.

Type
Transient.

Restriction
The last available drive is drive E unless the LASTDRIVE command is used.

SYS

If you have made a data diskette and wish to make it into a system diskette, or if you wish to transfer a new version of DOS to an older-version DOS diskette, this command may be the answer. When FORMAT /S is used to format a disk, SYS is invoked automatically to transfer the system files. The SYS command does not transfer COMMAND.COM, but does transfer the two hidden BIOS and DOS files.

Format

[*D*:*Path*]SYS *DestD*:

D:*Path* is the drive and path where the command file is located if it is not in the current directory.

DestD is the drive the system files will be transferred to.

Type

Transient.

Restrictions

There must not be any files on the data diskette, since the two system files must be the first two files on the disk. SYS will not work on a network drive.

TIME

This command is used to set the system time. It may also be used to reset an internal clock. Setting the time comes in very handy when errors occur—you can tell exactly when a file was last written to or changed. It also provides a trail by which a programmer can trace the file-saving flow of a program. It is advisable to set the time and date every time you boot the system.

Format

TIME [*hh*:*mm*[:*ss*[.*xx*]]]

hh is the current hour, in 24-hour format. To translate from 12-hour to 24-hour if the time is between 1:00 P.M. and 12:00 A.M., add 12 to the hour (for example, 7:45 P.M. = 19:45).

mm is the current number of minutes.

ss is the current number of seconds.

xx is the current number of hundredths of seconds.

Type
Resident.

TREE

TREE displays a listing of all of your directories and subdirectories and the files in them. This is especially useful for identifying long directory specifications that should be cut down.

Format
[*D*:*Path*]TREE [*D2*:][/F]

D:*Path* is the drive and path where the command file is located if it is not in the current directory.

D2 is the drive identifier of another drive you want TREE to affect.

/F displays all paths and names of files in the directories.

Type
Transient.

TYPE

Using TYPE on a non-ASCII file could have no effect, or it could display meaningless symbols on your screen. It could also lock up your system entirely. If this happens, you'll need to reboot.

TYPE displays the contents of an ASCII file. ASCII files contain no control codes that would affect the screen display; they appear as straight listings of data.

Format
TYPE *FileSpec*

FileSpec is the optional drive and path, plus the file name and extension, of the file to be displayed.

Type
Resident.

VER

The VER command displays the current version of DOS in which you are working.

Format
VER

Type
Resident.

VERIFY

This command turns the global verify feature of DOS on or off. When it is on, everything written to a file will be checked buffer by buffer, to ensure the accuracy of the transmission. This is a useful feature, but your system will run more slowly. Use VERIFY ON when you must be completely sure of the validity of the file data being transferred—for example, during BACKUP operations.

Format
VERIFY [ON ¦ OFF]

ON turns the feature on.

OFF turns VERIFY off. This is the default.

Type
Resident.

Restrictions
VERIFY will not work with network disks.

VOL

The VOL command shows you the volume label of the disk contained in a specified drive.

Format

VOL [*D*:]

D is a specified drive, if different from the default drive.

Type

Resident.

XCOPY

XCOPY is a modified version of the COPY command. It does the same thing, only better. Instead of reading and writing files one at a time, XCOPY reads files into a buffer that is equal in size to available memory, and then writes out the contents of the buffer (this is usually several files). XCOPY can be used for a single file or for several different groups of files. You can combine its switches as well.

Format

[*D*:*Path*]XCOPY [*FileSpec1*][*FileSpec2*][/A][/D:*mm-dd-yy*]
[/E][/M][/P][/S][/V][/W]

D:*Path* is the drive and path where the command file is located if it is not in the current directory.

FileSpec1 is the necessary drive, path, and file-name specifications for the files to be copied. Wild cards are allowed.

FileSpec2 is the necessary drive, path, and file-name specifications for the files to be written to. Wild cards are allowed.

/A copies only files with a set archive bit.

/D:*mm-dd-yy* copies only files created or modified on or after the specified date; the format depends on the COUNTRY specification.

/E creates corresponding subdirectories on *FileSpec2* before copying is done (even if *FileSpec1* contains no files to transfer).

/M copies files with a set archive bit and resets the archive bit on the source file.

/P prompts you before each file is copied.

/S also copies files from all subdirectories within the specified directory. Corresponding subdirectories will be created on *FileSpec2* for all *FileSpec1* directories that contain files.

/V turns VERIFY on during execution of this command only.

/W causes XCOPY to prompt you to insert different disks before it executes.

Type

Transient.

Restrictions

XCOPY will not copy to or from devices. It also will not copy hidden files from the source and will not overwrite read-only files on the destination.

APPENDIX B GLOSSARY

This appendix defines all of the important DOS-related terms used in this book. Although these terms are defined in the text when they are first introduced, the glossary presented here offers concise definitions that will refresh your memory when you read a chapter later in the book, or when you simply can't remember the meaning of a particular term.

active partition The section of a hard disk containing the operating system to be used when the hardware powers up.

ANSI driver A device driver, contained in the ANSI.SYS file, that loads additional support for advanced console features.

application program A program that performs or replaces a manual function, such as balancing a checkbook or managing inventory.

archive bit A bit in a file specification used to indicate whether the file in question needs to be backed up.

ASCII American Standard Code for Information Interchange; the coding scheme whereby every character the computer can access is assigned an integer code between 0 and 255.

assembly language A symbolic form of computer language used to program computers at a fundamental level.

asynchronous communications *See* serial communications.

AUTOEXEC.BAT A batch file executed automatically whenever the computer is booted up.

background task A second program running on your computer; usually, a printing operation that shares the CPU with your main foreground task.

base name The portion of a file name to the left of the period separator; it can be up to eight characters long.

BASIC Beginner's All-purpose Symbolic Instruction Code. A computer language similar to the English language.

batch file An ASCII file containing a sequence of DOS commands that, when invoked, will assume control of the computer, executing the commands as if they were entered successively by a computer user.

baud rate The speed of data transmission, usually in bits per second.

binary A numbering system that uses powers of the number 2 to generate all other numbers.

bit One-eighth of a byte. A bit is a binary digit, either 0 or 1.

bit mapping The way a graphics screen is represented in the computer. Usually signifies point-to-point graphics.

booting up *See* bootstrapping.

boot record The section on a disk that contains the minimum information DOS needs to start the system.

bootstrapping When the computer initially is turned on or is rebooted from the keyboard with Ctrl-Alt-Del, it "pulls itself up by its bootstraps." *See also* warm booting, cold booting.

branching The transfer of control or execution to another statement in a batch file. *See also* decision making.

break key The control-key combination that interrupts an executing program or command; activated by pressing the ScrollLock key while holding down the Ctrl key.

buffer An area in memory set aside to speed up the transfer of data, allowing blocks of data to be transferred at once.

byte The main unit of memory in a computer. A byte is an eight-bit binary-digit number. One character usually takes up one byte.

cache A portion of memory reserved for the contents of recently referenced disk sectors. Facilitates faster reaccess of the same sectors.

case sensitivity Distinguishing between capital letters and lowercase letters.

chaining Passing the control of execution from one batch file to another. This represents an unconditional transfer of control.

character set A complete group of 256 characters that can be used by programs or system devices. Consists of letters, numbers, control codes, and special graphics or international symbols. *See also* code page.

cluster A group of contiguous sectors on a disk. This is the smallest unit of disk storage that DOS can manipulate.

COBOL A programming language usually used for business applications.

code page A character set that redefines the country and keyboard information for non-U.S. keyboards and systems.

cold booting When the computer's power is first turned on and DOS first boots up. *See* bootstrapping.

COMMAND.COM The command processor that comes with DOS.

command line The line on which a command is entered. This line contains the command and all of its associated parameters and switches. It may run to more than one screen line, but it is still one command line.

command processor The program that translates and acts on commands.

compressed print Printing that allows more than 80 characters on a line of output (usually 132 characters, but on newer printers up to 255 characters per line).

computer-aided design (CAD) program A sophisticated software package containing advanced graphics and drawing features. Used by engineers, architects, and designers for drawing and design applications.

concatenation The placing of two text files together in a series.

conditional statement A statement in a batch file that controls the next step to be executed in the batch file, based on the value of a logical test.

CONFIG.SYS An ASCII text file containing system configuration commands.

configuration An initial set of system values, such as the number of buffers DOS will use, the number of simultaneously open files it will allow, and the specific devices that will be supported.

console The combination of your system's monitor and keyboard.

contiguity The physical adjacency on a disk of the disk sectors used by a file.

control codes ASCII codes that do not display a character but perform a function, such as ringing a bell or deleting a character.

copy protection Special mechanisms contained in diskettes to inhibit the copying of them by conventional commands.

CPU Central Processing Unit. The main chip that executes all individual computer instructions.

Ctrl-Z The end-of-file marker.

cursor The blinking line or highlighting box that indicates where the next keystroke will be displayed or what the next control code entered will affect.

cutting and pasting Selecting text from one part of a document or visual display and moving it to another location.

cylinder Two tracks that are in the same place on different sides of a double-sided disk. May be extended to include multiple platters. For example, Side 0 Track 30, Side 1 Track 30, Side 2 Track 30, and Side 3 Track 30 form a cylinder.

daisy-wheel printer A printer that uses circular templates for producing letter-quality characters.

data area The tracks on a disk that contain user data.

database A collection of data organized into various categories. A phone book is one form of database.

database management system A software program designed to allow the creation of specially organized files, as well as data entry, manipulation, removal, and reporting for those files.

data bits The bits that represent data when the computer is communicating.

data disk A disk that has been formatted without the /S switch. The disk can contain only data; no room has been reserved for system files.

data stream The transmission of data between two components or computers.

dead key A reserved key combination on international keyboards, which outputs nothing itself but allows the next keystroke to produce an accent mark above or below the keystroke's usual character.

debugging The process of discovering what is wrong with a program, where the problem is located, and what the solution is.

decimal A numbering system based on ten digits.

decision making A point in a batch file at which execution can continue on at least two different paths, depending on the results of a program test. Also known as logical testing or branching.

default The standard value of a variable or system parameter.

deferred execution In a program or batch file, when execution is delayed until a value for some parameter is finally entered or computed.

delimiter A special character, such as a comma or space, used to separate values or data entries.

destination The targeted location for data, files, or other information generated or moved by a DOS command.

device Any internal or external piece of peripheral hardware.

device driver Also known as an interrupt handler. A special program that must be loaded to use a device. Adds extra capability to DOS.

device name Logical name that DOS uses to refer to a device.

digital A representation based on a collection of individual digits, such as 0's and 1's in the binary number system.

digitizer A device with a movable arm that can take an image and break it up into small parts, which the computer translates into bits.

directory A grouping of files on a disk. These files are displayed together and may include access to other directories (subdirectories).

directory tree The treelike structure created when a root directory has several subdirectories, each of the subdirectories has subdirectories, and so on.

disk drive A hardware device that accesses the data stored on a disk.

diskette A flexible, oxide-coated disk used to store data. Also called a floppy diskette.

disk optimizer A program that rearranges the location of files stored on a disk in order to make the data in those files quickly retrievable.

DOS Disk Operating System. A disk manager and the program that allows computer/user interaction.

DOS environment A part of memory set aside to hold the defaults needed in the current environment, such as COMSPEC, PATH, LASTDRIVE, and so on.

DOS prompt Usually C> or A>. The visual indication that DOS is waiting for a command or prompting you for input.

dot-matrix printer A printer that represents characters by means of tiny dots.

double-density diskette A diskette on which magnetic storage material is arranged twice as densely as usual, allowing the storage of twice the usual amount of data. Generally refers to a 360K, 5¼'' diskette.

drive identifier A single letter assigned to represent a drive, such as drive A or drive B. Usually requires a colon after it, such as A:.

DRIVER.SYS A file containing a device driver for an extra external disk drive. Used in the CONFIG.SYS file.

dual tasking Causing two tasks or programming events to occur simultaneously.

echoing Displaying on your video monitor the keystrokes you type in.

EDLIN The DOS line editor.

end-of-file marker A Ctrl-Z code that marks the logical end of a file.

environment The context within which DOS interfaces with you and with your commands.

error level A code, set by programs as they conclude processing, that tells DOS whether an error occurred, and if so, the severity of that error.

expansion cards Add-on circuit boards through which hardware can increase the power of the system, such as adding extra memory or a modem.

expansion slots Connectors inside the computer in which expansion cards are placed so that they tie in directly to the system.

extended ASCII codes ASCII codes between 128 and 255, which usually differ from computer to computer.

extended DOS partition A hard-disk partition used to exceed the 32Mb, single-disk barrier; it can be divided into logical disk drives.

extended memory Additional physical memory beyond the DOS 1Mb addressing limit.

extension The one to three characters after the period following the base name in a file specification.

external buffer A device, connected to the computer and another device, that acts as a buffer.

Family Application Programming Interface (FAPI) The suggested subset of OS/2 system service calls that enable a developed .EXE program to run under either DOS or OS/2.

file A collection of bytes, representing a program or data, organized into records and stored as a named group on a disk.

file allocation table (FAT) A table of sectors stored on a disk, which tells DOS whether a given sector is good, bad, continued, or the end of a chain of records.

file name The name of a file on the disk. Usually refers to the base name, but can include the extension as well.

file version A term that refers to which developmental copy of a software program is being used or referenced.

filter A program that accepts data as input, processes it in some manner, and then outputs the data in a different form.

fixed disk IBM's name for a hard disk.

floppy diskette *See* diskette.

flow of control The order of execution of batch-file commands; how the control flows from one command to another, even when the next command to be executed is not located sequentially in the file.

foreground task The main program running on your computer, as opposed to the less visible background task (usually a printing job).

formatting The placement of timing marks on a disk to arrange the tracks and sectors for subsequent reading and writing.

fragmentation A condition in which many different files have been stored in noncontiguous sectors on a disk.

function keys Special-purpose keys on a keyboard, which can be assigned unique tasks by DOS or by application programs.

gigabyte (Gb) 1024 megabytes.

global characters *See* wild cards.

graphics mode The mode in which all screen pixels on a monitor are addressable and can be used to generate detailed images. Contrasts with text mode, which usually allows only 24 lines of 80 characters.

hard disk A rigid platter that stores data faster and at a higher density than a floppy diskette. Sealed in an airtight compartment to avoid contaminants that could damage or destroy the disk.

hardware The physical components of a computer system.

hardware interrupt A signal from a device to the computer, indicating that an event has taken place.

head A disk-drive mechanism that reads data from and writes data to the disk.

head crash Occurs when the head hits the disk platter on a hard disk, physically damaging the disk and the data on it.

help file A file of textual information containing helpful explanations of commands, modes, and other on-screen tutorial information.

hexadecimal A numbering system in base 16. A single eight-bit byte can be fully represented as two hexadecimal digits.

hidden files Files whose names do not appear in a directory listing. Usually refers to DOS's internal system files, but can also refer to certain files used in copy-protection schemes.

high-capacity diskette A 1.2Mb, 5¼'' floppy diskette.

high-resolution mode The mode on a video monitor in which all available pixels are used to provide the most detailed screen image possible. On a color monitor, this mode reduces the possible range of colors that can be output.

horizontal landscape When output to a printer is not done in the usual format, but rather with the wider part of the paper laid out horizontally, as in a landscape picture.

hot key A key combination used to signal that a memory-resident program should begin operation.

housekeeping Making sure the directory stays intact and well organized, and that unnecessary files are deleted.

hub The center hole of a diskette.

IF A conditional statement in a batch file.

ink-jet printer A printer that forms characters by spraying ink in a dot pattern. *See* dot-matrix printer.

interface The boundary between two things, such as the computer and a peripheral.

interrupt A signal sent to the computer from a hardware device, indicating a request for service or support from the system.

keyboard translation table An internal table, contained in the keyboard driver, that converts hardware signals from the keyboard into the correct ASCII codes.

key combination When two or more keys are pressed simultaneously, as in Ctrl-ScrollLock or Ctrl-Alt-Del.

key redefinition Assigning a nonstandard value to a key.

kilobyte (K) 1024 bytes.

laser printer A printer that produces images (pictures or text) by shining a laser on a photostatic drum, which picks up toner and then transfers the image to paper.

LCD Liquid Crystal Display. A method of producing an image using electrically sensitive crystals suspended in a liquid medium.

letter-quality printer A printer that forms characters that are comparable to those of a typewriter.

line editor A program that can make textual changes to an ASCII file, but can only make changes to one line of the file at a time.

line feed When the cursor on a screen moves to the next line, or when the print head on a printer moves down the paper to the next line.

literal Something that is accepted exactly as it was submitted.

lockup Occurs when the computer will not accept any input and may have stopped processing. Requires that the computer be warm or cold booted to resume operating.

log file A separate file, created with the BACKUP command, that keeps track of the names of all files written to the backup diskette(s).

logging on Signing onto a remote system, such as a mainframe or telecommunications service.

logical Something that is defined based on a decision, not by physical properties.

logical drives Disk drives, created in an extended DOS partition, that do not physically exist, but DOS thinks they do. A means for DOS to access a physical disk that has more than 32Mb available.

logical testing *See* decision making.

machine language The most fundamental way to program a computer, using instructions made up entirely of strings of 0's and 1's.

macro A set of commands, often memory-resident. When executed, they appear to the program executing them as if they were being entered by you.

medium-resolution mode The mode on a Color Graphics Adapter in which only 320 × 200 pixels of resolution are allowed.

megabyte (Mb) 1024 kilobytes.

memory The circuitry in a computer that stores information. *See also* RAM and ROM.

memory-resident Located in physical memory, as opposed to being stored in a disk file.

menu A set of choices displayed in tabular format.

meta symbols Special single-character codes used by the PROMPT command to represent complex actions or sequences to be included in the DOS prompt.

microfloppy diskette The 3½'' diskette format used in the new Personal System/2 and many other computers.

modem A device that transmits digital data in tones over a phone line.

monitor The device used to display images; a display screen.

monochrome Using two colors only—the background and foreground.

mouse A device that moves the screen cursor by means of a hand-held apparatus moved along a surface such as a desk. The computer can tell how far and in which direction the mouse is being moved.

multitasking When two or more computing applications are executing simultaneously.

national language-support operations The DOS 3.3 feature that supports displays and printers, using a new range of code and character groupings.

network Several computers, connected together, that can share common data files and peripheral devices.

nibble Four bits, or half a byte.

octal A numbering system in base 8.

OS/2 Operating system/2. The latest advanced operating system from Microsoft and IBM, which manages computer/user interaction, enhanced memory features and multitasking.

operating system *See* DOS.

overlay files Files containing additional command and control information for sophisticated and complex programs. An overlay file is usually too large to fit into memory along with the main .EXE or .COM file.

overwriting Typing new data over what is already there.

parallel communications Data transmission in which several bits can be transferred or processed at one time.

parameter An extra bit of information, specified with a command, that determines how the command executes.

parity The bit, added to the end of a stream of data bits, that makes the total of the data bits and the parity bits odd or even.

partition The section of a hard disk that contains an operating system. There can be at most four partitions on one hard disk.

Pascal A programming language used mainly in computer science.

password A sequence of characters that allows entry into a restricted system or program.

path The list of disks and directories that DOS will search through to find a command file ending in .COM, .BAT, or .EXE.

peripheral Any physical device connected to the computer.

piping Redirecting the input or output of one program or command to another program or command.

pixel The smallest unit of display on a video monitor—in short, a dot—which can be illuminated to create text or graphics images.

platter The rigid disk used in a hard-disk drive.

plotter A device that draws data on paper with a mechanical arm.

port A doorway through which the computer can access external devices.

Presentation Manager The windowing interface of OS/2's Version 1.1, which displays executing programs within separate screen windows on the same display monitor.

primary DOS partition Up to the first 32Mb of a hard disk. Contains the boot record and other DOS information files.

printer A device that outputs data onto paper using pins (dot matrix), a daisy wheel, ink jets, laser imaging, and so on.

process *See* task.

protected mode The principal operating environment of OS/2 that supports multitasking, process protection, and advanced memory management.

public domain Something not copyrighted or patented. Public domain software can be used and copied without infringing on anyone's rights.

queue A series of files waiting in line to be printed.

RAM Random Access Memory. The part of the computer's memory to which you have access; stores programs and data while the computer is on.

RAM disk An area of RAM that acts as if it were a disk drive. All data in this area of memory is lost when the computer is turned off or warm booted. Also known as a virtual disk.

range A contiguous series of values (minimum to maximum, first to last, and so on).

read-after-write verification An extra level of validity checking, invoked with the VERIFY command or the /V switch. Rereads data after writing it to disk, comparing the written data to the original information.

read-only status Indicates that a file cannot be updated but can be read.

read/write bit The bit in a file specification that indicates whether a file can accept changes or deletions, or can only be accessed for reading.

real mode The single tasking unprotected operating environment that runs old DOS programs under OS/2.

redirection Causing output from one program or device to be routed to another program or device.

REM statement A line in a BASIC program containing remarks or comments for program explanation or clarification.

reserved names Specific words, in a programming language or operating system, which should not be used in any other application context.

resident commands Commands located in random-access memory.

resource allocation Making system facilities available to individual users or programs.

reverse video Black letters on a white background.

ROM Read-Only Memory. The section of memory that you can only read from. This contains the basic computer operating system and system routines.

root directory The first directory on any disk.

scan code The hardware code representing a key pressed on a keyboard. Converted by a keyboard driver into an ASCII code for use by DOS and application programs.

scrolling What the screen does when you're at the bottom of it and press Return—all of the lines roll up.

secondary command processor A second copy of COMMAND.COM, invoked either to run a batch file or to provide a new context for subsequent DOS commands.

sector A division of a disk track; usually, 512 bytes.

serial communications Data transmission in which data is transferred and processed one bit at a time. Also known as asynchronous communications.

Session Manager The OS/2 program that presents a menu of choices enabling you to switch your video display between your DOS program and any of the active OS/2 protected mode programs.

shareware Public domain software. *See also* public domain.

snapshot program A program used in debugging to store the status of system or application program variables.

software The programs and instruction sets that operate the computer.

software interrupt A signal from a software program that calls up a routine that is resident in the computer's basic programming. Also, a software signal to the computer that the software program has finished, has a problem, and so on.

source The location containing the original data, files, or other information to be used in a DOS command.

spooling Simultaneous Peripheral Operations On-Line. Using a high-speed disk to store input to or output from low-speed peripheral devices while the CPU does other tasks.

spreadsheet program An electronic version of an accountant's spreadsheet; when one value changes, all other values based on that value are updated instantly.

start bit The bit sent at the beginning of a data stream to indicate that data bits follow.

stop bit The bit sent after the data bits, indicating that no more data bits follow.

string A series of characters.

subcommands Several special commands used only within batch files.

subdirectory A directory contained within another directory or subdirectory. Technically, all directories other than the root directory are subdirectories.

switch A parameter included in DOS commands, usually preceded by the slash (/) symbol, which clarifies or modifies the action of the command.

synchronization The coordination of a sending and receiving device, so that both simultaneously send and receive data at the same rate.

system disk A disk containing the necessary DOS system files for system booting.

task An OS/2 program and the set of system resources that it uses.

text mode The mode in which standard characters can be displayed on a monitor.

thread A logical sequence of code in an OS/2 program. This is the fundamental entity that is assigned CPU time in the OS/2 multitasking environment.

time slice The smallest unit of time managed and assigned by the operating system to programs and other processing activities.

toggle A switch or command that reverses a value from off to on, or from on to off.

track A circular stream of data on the disk. Similar to a track on a record, only not spiraling.

transient command A command whose procedures are read from the disk into memory, executed from memory, and then erased from memory when finished.

utility A supplemental routine or program designed to carry out a specific operation, usually to modify the system environment or perform housekeeping tasks.

variable parameter A named element, following a command, that acts as a placeholder; when you issue the command, you replace the variable parameter with the actual value you want to use.

verbose listing A listing of all files and subdirectories contained on the disk and path specified in the command. Activated by the CHKDSK command with the /V switch.

vertical portrait The conventional 8¼-by-11-inch output for printed information, with the long side of the paper positioned vertically.

virtual disk *See* RAM disk.

volume label A name, consisting of up to 11 characters, that can be assigned to any disk during a FORMAT operation or after formatting with the LABEL command.

warm booting Resetting the computer using the Ctrl-Alt-Del key combination. *See* bootstrapping.

wide directory listing An alternate output format that lists four columns of file names.

wild cards Characters used to represent any other characters. In DOS, * and ? are the only wild-card symbols.

word processor A computerized typewriter. Allows the correction and reformatting of documents before they are printed.

write-protection Giving a disk read-only status by covering the write-protect notch.

APPENDIX C ASCII CODES

This appendix presents information on how ASCII codes are created, used, and manipulated in DOS. It discusses the different numbering systems used to create these codes, as well as how codes are grouped to form identifiable character sets. Using this information, you can both manage your DOS system more readily and manipulate file data for yourself.

CHARACTER SETS

Just as you use an alphabet and a decimal numbering system, the computer uses its own character and numbering system. DOS maintains, in memory, all of the characters of the English alphabet, including numbers and symbols, as well as some foreign symbols (such as accented vowels). This group of symbols is called a character set. By changing the symbols in this set, you can obtain completely new character sets. This is especially useful for people living in other countries, who have less daily need of U.S. standard characters and who would rather work with their own characters.

ASCII CODES

A character is any letter, number, punctuation symbol, or graphics symbol. In other words, it is anything that can be displayed on a video screen or printed on a printer.

Each character in a character set has a number assigned to it, which is how the computer refers to the various characters in the set. For example, code 65 refers to a capital A, and code 97 refers to a lowercase a. These codes are called ASCII codes (pronounced "*ask-ee* codes"); ASCII stands for American Standard Code for Information Interchange.

Codes 0 through 31 are used as control codes. Displaying one of these codes will cause something to happen instead of causing a symbol to be displayed. For example, displaying code 7 will result in the computer's bell or beeper being sounded. Displaying code 13 will result in a carriage return.

Codes 32 through 127 are ASCII character codes for numbers, letters, and all punctuation marks and symbols. Codes 128 through 255, known as extended ASCII codes, vary from computer to computer. They usually comprise foreign characters, Greek and mathematical symbols, and graphics characters. (Graphics characters consist of small lines and curves that can be used to create geometric patterns.)

DOS 3.3 has several available ASCII tables, called code pages. The most common is the standard U.S. code page (see Table C.1); the next most common is the Multilingual code page (see Table C.2).

MAPPING ONE CHARACTER SET ONTO ANOTHER

Any device that displays characters has a device driver that literally drives, or controls, the device. When the computer tells a printer to print the letter A, DOS sends the code 65 to the printer driver, which converts the 65 into a series of control codes that will print the A.

For the sake of consistency, computers, printers, and displays all have the same character sets and coding system for ASCII codes 32 through 127. This ensures that when you press a key, the desired character will be displayed, and the same character will be printed by your printer.

The process of matching ASCII codes against characters in a character set is called *mapping*. The following section describes how you map a set of numbers onto a set of characters so that they correspond exactly to each other.

HEX DIGITS 1st / 2nd	0-	1-	2-	3-	4-	5-	6-	7-	8-	9-	A-	B-	C-	D-	E-	F-
0-		►		0	@	P	`	p	Ç	É	á	░	└	╨	α	≡
1-	☺	◄	!	1	A	Q	a	q	ü	æ	í	▒	┴	╤	β	±
2-	☻	↕	"	2	B	R	b	r	é	Æ	ó	▓	┬	╥	Γ	≥
3-	♥	‼	#	3	C	S	c	s	â	ô	ú	│	├	╙	π	≤
4-	♦	¶	$	4	D	T	d	t	ä	ö	ñ	┤	─	╘	Σ	⌠
5-	♣	§	%	5	E	U	e	u	à	ò	Ñ	╡	┼	╒	σ	⌡
6-	♠	▬	&	6	F	V	f	v	å	û	ª	╢	╞	╓	µ	÷
7-	•	↨	'	7	G	W	g	w	ç	ù	º	╖	╟	╫	τ	≈
8-	◘	↑	(	8	H	X	h	x	ê	ÿ	¿	╕	╚	╪	Φ	°
9-	○	↓	)	9	I	Y	i	y	ë	Ö	⌐	╣	╔	┘	Θ	∙
A-	◙	→	*	:	J	Z	j	z	è	Ü	¬	║	╩	┌	Ω	·
B-	♂	←	+	;	K	[	k	{	ï	¢	½	╗	╦	█	δ	√
C-	♀	∟	,	<	L	\	l	|	î	£	¼	╝	╠	▄	∞	^{n}
D-	♪	↔	-	=	M	]	m	}	ì	¥	¡	╜	═	▌	ϕ	^{2}
E-	♫	▲	.	>	N	^	n	~	Ä	Pt	«	╛	╬	▐	ε	■
F-	☼	▼	/	?	O	_	o	⌂	Å	ƒ	»	┐	╧	▀	∩	

Table C.1: U.S. ASCII table (code page 437 in DOS 3.3)

HEX DIGITS 1st / 2nd	0-	1-	2-	3-	4-	5-	6-	7-	8-	9-	A-	B-	C-	D-	E-	F-
0-		►		0	@	P	`	p	Ç	É	á	░	└	ð	Ó	-
1-	☺	◄	!	1	A	Q	a	q	ü	æ	í	▒	┴	Đ	β	±
2-	☻	↕	"	2	B	R	b	r	é	Æ	ó	▓	┬	Ê	Ô	=
3-	♥	‼	#	3	C	S	c	s	â	ô	ú	│	├	Ë	Ò	¾
4-	♦	¶	$	4	D	T	d	t	ä	ö	ñ	┤	─	È	õ	¶
5-	♣	§	%	5	E	U	e	u	à	ò	Ñ	Á	┼	ı	Õ	§
6-	♠	▬	&	6	F	V	f	v	å	û	ª	Â	ã	Í	µ	÷
7-	•	↨	'	7	G	W	g	w	ç	ù	º	À	Ã	Î	þ	¸
8-	◘	↑	(	8	H	X	h	x	ê	ÿ	¿	©	╚	Ï	Þ	°
9-	○	↓	)	9	I	Y	i	y	ë	Ö	®	╣	╔	┘	Ú	¨
A-	◙	→	*	:	J	Z	j	z	è	Ü	¬	║	╩	┌	Û	·
B-	♂	←	+	;	K	[	k	{	ï	ø	½	╗	╦	█	Ù	^{1}
C-	♀	∟	,	<	L	\	l	|	î	£	¼	╝	╠	▄	ý	^{3}
D-	♪	↔	-	=	M	]	m	}	ì	Ø	¡	¢	═	¦	Ý	^{2}
E-	♫	▲	.	>	N	^	n	~	Ä	×	«	¥	╬	Ì	¯	■
F-	☼	▼	/	?	O	_	o	⌂	Å	ƒ	»	┐	¤	▀	´	

Table C.2: Multilingual ASCII table (code page 850 in DOS 3.3)

NUMBERING SYSTEMS

Computers use a variety of numbering systems to operate. The most basic numbering system is the binary system, in which there are only two digits, 0 and 1. The digital circuitry used in computers operates by using small voltages that turn magnetic bits on or off. Therefore, 0 and 1 are used to represent the two states of off and on, respectively.

Counting in binary is not difficult, but it does require some adjustment from your standard decimal-numbering scheme. The progression of numbers and their matching decimal conversions are shown in Table C.3.

Chapter 8 contains a detailed explanation of the binary numbering system. The general rule for converting numbers from binary to decimal is to multiply the number in every binary number column by 2 raised to the column-number power. You count column numbers from the right, starting with 0. For the binary number 1101, for example, you would obtain

$$(1 \times 2^0) + (0 \times 2^1) + (1 \times 2^2) + (1 \times 2^3)$$

BINARY	DECIMAL
0	0
1	1
10	2
11	3
100	4
101	5
110	6
111	7
1000	8
1001	9
1010	10

Table C.3: Binary-to-decimal conversion

where any number to the 0 power (2^0 in this case) is defined as equal to 1. This is called *counting in base 2.*

The *decimal* system counts in base 10. Using the same method of converting binary numbers, you can see that breaking down the decimal number 2014 into its component parts works like this:

$$(4 \times 10^0) + (1 \times 10^1) + (0 \times 10^2) + (2 \times 10^3)$$
$$= 4 + 10 + 000 + 2000$$
$$= 2014$$

Another numbering system is called *octal,* or base 8. This system has only eight digits, 0–7. The octal number 701 is converted to base 10 (decimal) by the following computation:

$$(1 \times 8^0) + (0 \times 8^1) + (7 \times 8^2)$$
$$= 1 + 0 + 448$$
$$= 449$$

The last major numbering system in computers is called *hexadecimal,* which counts in base 16. This system has 16 digits in it: 0–9 and A–F, which form the counting sequence 0123456789ABCDEF. To count in this system, you use the same method you use for other numbering systems. The hexadecimal number BA7 translates to decimal as

Hexadecimal notation is convenient for byte values because a hexadecimal digit is equivalent to 4 ($2^4 = 16$) binary digits (called a *nibble*) and there are 8 bits ($2^8 = 256$-character set) in a byte. A byte can therefore be represented by two hexadecimal digits.

$$(7 \times 16^0) + (A \times 16^1) + (B \times 16^2)$$

which is equal to

$$7 + (10 \times 16^1) + (11 \times 16^2)$$

which is also equal to

$$7 + 160 + 2816$$
$$= 2983$$

Table C.4 demonstrates how to count in hexadecimal.

HEXADECIMAL	DECIMAL
0	0
.	.
.	.
9	9
A	10
B	11
.	.
.	.
F	15
10	16
.	.
.	.
1A	26

Table C.4: Hexadecimal-to-decimal conversion

APPENDIX D PARTITIONING YOUR HARD DISK

Hard disks are usually so large that they can contain more than one type of operating system. For example, you can have DOS 3.3 manage one part of a disk and UNIX manage another. Each of these sections is called a *partition.* You can have from one to four partitions on a disk.

Partitions are used to make the hard disk, especially a very large one, a more economical investment. They allow you to effectively have up to four completely different computer systems resident in one set of hardware. However, since they do not share a common software environment, they cannot share data directly.

Two types of partitions can be set up for DOS: a *primary DOS partition* and an *extended DOS partition.* The primary DOS partition is the partition that contains DOS and is the first partition on the disk. This is the only partition that must be on the disk if your disk is no larger than 32Mb. The extended DOS partition is a separate partition that cannot be used for booting, but can be divided into separate logical drives.

If you have more than 32Mb available on one hard disk, you will need to create an extended DOS partition, which is assigned the next logical drive letter. For example, if you had a 60Mb hard-disk drive, and wanted access to all of it, you would create a 32Mb primary partition and a 28Mb extended partition. The primary partition could be accessed as drive C, while the extended partition would be called drive D. You could also subdivide the extended partition into more logical drives (up to the letter Z).

You must create partitions before using a hard-disk drive. You will probably take the easiest route by simply making the entire disk into one primary partition. The FDISK program presented here, however, is necessary in several more advanced situations. For example, you may plan on using multiple operating systems from the same disk. FDISK will let you set up unique partitions for each system. (Each of these would be a primary partition, but only one could be designated the active partition, the one that will gain control at boot up.) Then again, you may be using one of the large hard disks (40–70Mb) that are increasingly common. Since DOS can only access a logical drive of 32Mb or less, you'll need to partition a larger physical drive into multiple logical drives. Only in this way can you store and retrieve information on the larger hard disk.

If your disk is already being used and you wish to make a new partition, you will have to first back up all of your data and then run FDISK from a system diskette. Finally, you'll need to reformat your disk before restoring your files to it.

CONFIGURING A DOS PARTITION

In this section, you will see exactly how to use the FDISK command. This procedure is very important, and it can have serious consequences if done incorrectly. However, it can also make your system more efficient, when done properly. FDISK is only usable on hard-disk systems.

Invoking the FDISK command is as simple as typing

```
FDISK
```

and pressing Return. (Remember to have your path set properly to include the directory containing the FDISK command file.) After this command creates the appropriate partition(s), you must then logically format the disk.

All data on your disk will be destroyed when you create partitions with FDISK.

When you first execute FDISK, the screen will clear and the FDISK Options screen will appear. This contains the menu used to get around in FDISK (see Figure D.1).

As you can see, there are four choices. If you have a system with more than one hard-disk drive, the number in the "Current Fixed Disk Drive: 1" line would be changed to the number of drives in your system. Also, a fifth option, "Select Next Fixed Disk Drive," would be displayed on the screen. You can only work on one hard-disk drive at a time, but you can switch from the drive you are working on to another drive. For now, let's assume you have one hard-disk drive and that the screen in Figure D.1 is what you see.

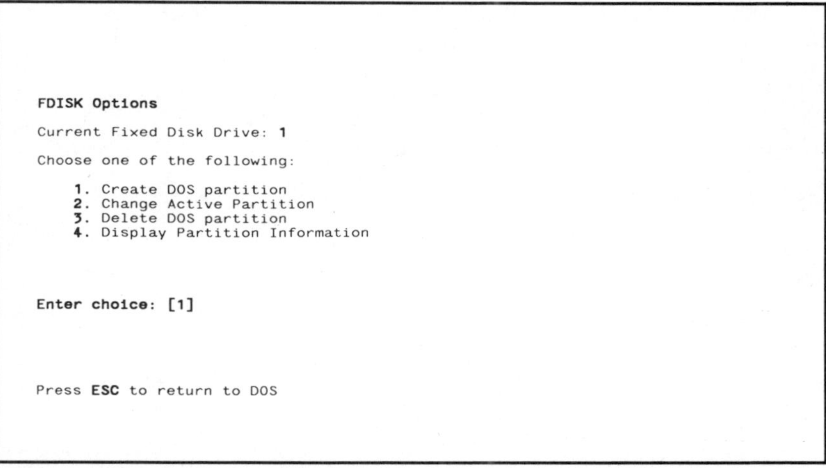

```
FDISK Options

Current Fixed Disk Drive: 1

Choose one of the following:

    1. Create DOS partition
    2. Change Active Partition
    3. Delete DOS partition
    4. Display Partition Information


Enter choice: [1]


Press ESC to return to DOS
```

Figure D.1: The FDISK Options menu

CREATING A PARTITION

If you plan to use your hard disk to support another operating system, do not partition the whole disk. Leave some room so that another system can be loaded onto the disk.

The first option on the FDISK Options menu is to create a DOS partition. Since you are using DOS, and not another operating system like UNIX, you can only create DOS partitions. Should you wish to put another operating system onto the disk, that system would have its own version of FDISK and could then create its own partitions next to DOS's.

Choosing the first option to create a DOS partition results in Figure D.2. If you select option 2 at this point, intending to create an extended DOS partition *before* creating a primary partition, DOS will display a message indicating that you cannot do so, and will suggest that you press Esc to return to the main FDISK Options menu. Assuming you are starting from scratch, you would select choice 1 to create the primary DOS partition. You will then see the screen shown in Figure D.3.

If you want to use the whole disk for DOS, then you answer Y on this screen. Doing so makes DOS use the whole disk. The computer will allocate the entire disk, and then come back with the message

```
System will now restart

Insert DOS diskette in drive A:
Press any key when ready . . .
```

```
Create DOS Partition

Current Fixed Disk Drive: 1


    1. Create Primary DOS partition
    2. Create Extended DOS partition




Enter choice: [1]




Press ESC to return to FDISK Options
```

Figure D.2: The Create DOS Partition menu

```
Create Primary DOS Partition

Current Fixed Disk Drive: 1

Do you wish to use the maximum size
for a DOS partition and make the DOS
partition active (Y/N).........? [n]






Press ESC to return to FDISK Options
```

Figure D.3: Creating the primary DOS partition

Since you just created the partition, there is still nothing on the hard disk. The system must be rebooted from the disk drive. You can now format the entire hard disk just as you would a floppy diskette.

If you answer N, as shown in Figure D.3, you have the opportunity to create a smaller partition, as shown in Figure D.4. As you can see, there are 305 *cylinders* available on the total disk. A hard disk consists of several platters, similar to a diskette; each platter consists of a

```
Create Primary DOS Partition

Current Fixed Disk Drive: 1




Total disk space is  3Ø5 cylinders.
Maximum space available for partition
is  3Ø5 cylinders.

Enter partition size...........: [ 2ØØ]


No partitions defined

Press ESC to return to FDISK Options
```

Figure D.4: Defining the primary DOS partition's size

series of concentric tracks made up of sectors. Each platter lies above another and is read by a different disk head. Viewed vertically, a series of tracks (with the same track number, but on different platters) located one above the other constitute a cylinder. The brackets in the screen shown in Figure D.4 indicate the place where you may enter a number for cylinders that is less than the default maximum (305 on this disk).

Notice that the second-to-last line on the screen tells you that no partitions have been defined yet. If you are using your disk for DOS alone, you should accept the default maximum cylinder value. All disk space will then be available for DOS and your DOS files. If you plan on splitting up your disk between DOS and another operating system, however, you'll have to decide for yourself what percentage of total disk space is needed for the other operating system. In this example, you intend to create an extended DOS partition, so 200 was entered for the number of cylinders in the primary DOS partition.

Entering 200 results in the screen shown in Figure D.5. This screen tells you that the first partition on drive C is a primary DOS partition (PRI DOS) that starts at cylinder 0 and ends at cylinder 199, constituting a total of 200 cylinders. Pressing Esc at this point returns you to the FDISK Options menu. If you again try to create a primary partition, DOS will show the following message on your

```
Create Primary DOS Partition

Current Fixed Disk Drive: 1

Partition Status   Type   Start  End  Size
 C: 1             PRI DOS    Ø   199   2ØØ





Primary DOS partition created

Press ESC to return to FDISK Options
```

Figure D.5: Primary DOS partition screen

There can only be one primary DOS partition. When DOS boots up, the system files from this partition are loaded into memory for your operations.

screen:

> Primary DOS partition already exists.
> Press ESC to return to FDISK Options

In this example, you have only used 200 cylinders out of a possible 305, so you can make an extended DOS partition. To do so, you select choice 1 on the FDISK Options menu (see Figure D.1) and then select choice 2 on the Create DOS Partition menu (see Figure D.2).

The resulting screen, shown in Figure D.6, allows you to create an extended DOS partition. This screen tells you the current partition information—that is, that there are 305 total cylinders available for use—and also tells you that 105 cylinders remain unused. The 105 value is used as the default entry at this stage. You only need to type in a number over the 105 to override the default. In Figure D.6, 55 was entered for the desired extended DOS partition, leaving 50 cylinders unused on the disk for another operating system.

The screen will now clear, redisplay the partition information (including that on the new extended DOS partition), and print the message

> Extended DOS Partition created
> Press ESC to return to FDISK Options

```
Create Extended DOS Partition

Current Fixed Disk Drive: 1

Partition Status   Type  Start  End Size
 C: 1             PRI DOS    0  199  200


Total disk space is  305 cylinders.
Maximum space available for partition
is  105 cylinders.

Enter partition size...........: [  55]



Press ESC to return to FDISK Options
```

Figure D.6: Creating an extended DOS partition

near the bottom of the screen. Pressing Esc will result in the next step of the process (see Figure D.7).

Since you have just created an extended DOS partition, DOS wants to know if you want to create logical drives within this new partition. It tells you the total available cylinders in the partition and asks you to enter a size for the logical drive. In this example, you enter 45. The resulting screen will contain the logical drive information (drive name, starting cylinder, ending cylinder, and total cylinders used).

Suppose you wanted to create another logical drive, E, using the remaining ten cylinders. You could again choose option 1 on the FDISK Options menu. You would go again to the Create DOS Partition menu, but there would be one new choice displayed:

> 3. Create logical DOS drive(s) in
> the Extended DOS partition

This would bring you back to the screen for defining logical drives, where you could then enter the information for drive E. Going through this same sequence again in order to use the remaining ten cylinders will result in Figure D.8. Notice that the cylinder numbers are within the bounds of the extended DOS partition. You are told that DOS created two logical drives, D and E, with sizes of 45 and 10 cylinders. Furthermore, you're reminded that no more space remains for any other logical drives. Press Esc, and you will once again be back at the FDISK Options menu.

If you try to create another extended partition, you will get a partition information screen and the message

Extended DOS partition already exists.
Press ESC to return to FDISK Options

```
Create Logical DOS Drive(s)




No logical drives defined


Total partition size is   55 cylinders.

Maximum space available for logical
drive is   55 cylinders.

Enter logical drive size........: [  45]


Press ESC to return to FDISK Options
```

Figure D.7: Defining logical drives

```
Create Logical DOS Drive(s)

Drv Start End  Size
 D:  200   244   45
 E:  245   254   10






All available space in the Extended DOS
partition is assigned to logical drives.

Logical DOS drive created, drive letters
changed or added
Press ESC to return to FDISK Options _
```

Figure D.8: Logical drive summary screen

CHANGING THE ACTIVE PARTITION

The *active* partition is the partition that is used to boot the system. It is the default partition. Choosing option 2 on the main FDISK Options menu leads you to a menu like that shown in Figure D.9, in which the partition information is displayed along with the total number of cylinders available on the disk. FDISK now wants to know the number of the partition that you wish to make active.

If you enter the number 2, as shown in the figure, DOS will inform you that only the primary DOS partition (1) may be made active. Type the number 1 so that the primary DOS partition will have control when the system comes up. Pressing Return will result in the adjusted partition information display seen in Figure D.10.

Notice the letter A on the first line of this display. An A under "Status" tells you that partition 1 is the active partition. Pressing Esc takes you back to the FDISK Options menu.

DISPLAYING PARTITION INFORMATION

Option 4 on the FDISK Options menu is used to display information about the partitions. This is useful because no extra functions will be executed at the same time; you can simply look at the information. Choosing option 4 yields the screen shown in Figure D.11.

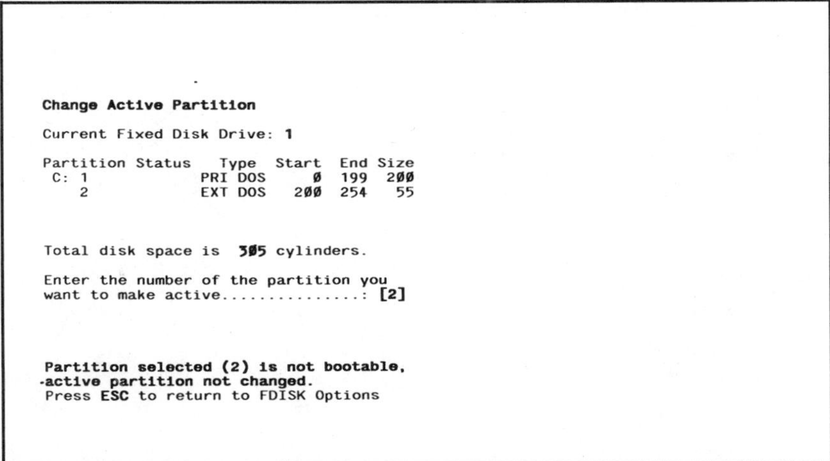

Figure D.9: The Change Active Partition menu

The information at the top of the screen is familiar by now. But what if you want to see information about the logical drives that have been defined? Look at the bottom half of the screen, where you are asked you if you want to see this information. Replying with Y results in a display of information about these logical drives (see Figure D.12). Pressing Esc at this point will return you to the FDISK Options menu.

```
Change Active Partition

Current Fixed Disk Drive: 1

Partition Status   Type  Start  End Size
 C: 1         A   PRI DOS     0  199  200
    2             EXT DOS   200  254   55


Total disk space is  305 cylinders.




Partition 1 made active

Press ESC to return to FDISK Options
```

Figure D.10: Display of the active partition

```
Display Partition Information

Current Fixed Disk Drive: 1

Partition Status   Type  Start  End Size
 C: 1         A   PRI DOS     0  199  200
    2             EXT DOS   200  254   55


Total disk space is  305 cylinders.


The Extended DOS partition contains
logical DOS drives. Do you want to
display logical drive information?  [Y]


Press ESC to return to FDISK Options
```

Figure D.11: Displaying partition information

DELETING DOS PARTITIONS

As with most things, what DOS giveth, DOS can taketh away—with a little prodding from you. Selecting choice 3 on the FDISK Options menu produces the Delete DOS Partition menu, shown in Figure D.13.

```
Display Logical DOS Drive Information

Drv Start End  Size
 D:  200   244   45
 E:  245   254   10




Press ESC to return to FDISK Options
```

Figure D.12: Logical drive information

```
Delete DOS Partition

Current Fixed Disk Drive: 1

Choose one of the following:

     1.  Delete Primary DOS partition
     2.  Delete Extended DOS partition
     3.  Delete logical DOS drive(s) in
         the Extended DOS Partition


Enter choice: [ ]


Press ESC to return to FDISK Options
```

Figure D.13: The Delete DOS Partition menu

Using this menu, you can delete any of the information you've already set up. You may want to expand or contract other partitions, or you may no longer want to use a partition in the manner you originally designed. In any case, you can only make changes in a certain order. You cannot delete the primary DOS partition without first deleting the extended DOS partition. If you try, DOS will give you this message:

```
Cannot delete Primary DOS partition on
drive 1 when Extended partition exists

Press ESC to return to FDISK Options
```

In addition, you cannot delete an extended DOS partition without first "undefining" (deleting) the logical drives in that partition. Trying to delete the extended DOS partition before deleting the drives in it will simply display the current partition information with the patient message

```
Cannot delete Extended DOS partition
while logical drives exist.
Press ESC to return to FDISK options
```

Choice 3 in the Delete DOS Partition menu is probably the first selection you will need to make; you work your way backwards through the order in which you created things. (Actually, you will find that this is a fairly natural process.) Selecting choice 3 produces the screen shown in Figure D.14, which contains the logical drive information and the size of the extended DOS partition the drives are in. You are also warned that any data contained in the logical disk drive to be deleted will also be deleted.

If you still want to delete the drive, simply enter the drive identifier. You will then be asked to confirm this step. In Figure D.14, you have selected drive E to delete first, and confirmed the choice by typing Y. If you had entered N, you would have been returned to the FDISK Options menu.

Once FDISK deletes the logical drive, it updates the display at the top of the screen and asks for another drive to delete. If you wanted to regain all the space used by this partition, you would then enter drive D, confirm your entry, and end up with the screen shown in

Figure D.15. Pressing Esc twice at this point will bring you back up through the menu screens to the main FDISK Options menu.

Now that the logical drives are gone, you can delete the extended DOS partition itself if you chose to do so. Choosing option 2 on the Delete DOS Partition menu results in the familiar form of an FDISK screen (see Figure D.16). Again, you are shown the partition infor-

```
Delete Logical DOS Drive

Drv Start End  Size
 D:  200   244   45
 E:  245   254   10




Total partition size is   55 cylinders.

Warning! Data in the logical DOS drive
will be lost. What drive do you wish
to delete.........................? [e]

Are you sure......................? [y]

Press ESC to return to FDISK Options
```

Figure D.14: Deleting a logical drive

```
Delete Logical DOS Drive

Drv Start End  Size
 D: drive deleted
 E: drive deleted




Total partition size is   55 cylinders.
All logical drives deleted in the
Extended DOS partition



Press ESC to return to FDISK Options.
```

Figure D.15: Summary of logical drive deletions

```
Delete Extended DOS Partition

Current Fixed Disk Drive: 1

Partition Status   Type  Start  End Size
 C: 1        A   PRI DOS     Ø  199  2ØØ
    2            EXT DOS   2ØØ  254   55




Warning! Data in the Extended DOS
partition will be lost. Do you wish
to continue......................? [y]


Press ESC to return to FDISK Options
```

Figure D.16: Deleting the extended DOS partition

mation display (as in Figure D.11), warned that data will be lost, and asked if you really want to delete the extended DOS partition. If you reply Y, the screen will be updated to show only the primary DOS partition and the message

Extended DOS partition deleted

Press ESC to return to FDISK Options

Press Esc to return once again to the FDISK Options menu.

CHAPTER 1 EXERCISES

1. Identify the physical portions of your computer system. Use any available purchasing documents, or simply look at your hardware. Determine the following information:

   In your system unit, how much conventional memory is installed? How much expanded memory is installed? How much extended memory is installed?

   What type of disk drives do you have? Do you have a hard disk? If so, what is its size in megabytes? Do you have floppy disk drives? How many 3½″ drives do you have? How many 5¼″ drives do you have?

   What type of video monitor do you have? Monochrome? CGA? EGA? VGA? 8514?

   What type of printer do you have? Dot matrix? Laser? Color? Letter quality?

   Do you have any of the following additional devices installed on your computer? Mouse, modem, plotter, battery backup (size in watts), backup device (tape or disk), special purpose devices?

2. Look in the rear of your computer's system unit. Identify the connectors, plugs, and cables there. Trace the connections from the computer's system unit to each connected device. Determine the following:

   Number of serial ports? Is a modem connected? Is a plotter connected? What else is connected to a serial port?

   Number of parallel ports (connected typically to printers)?

   Is a keyboard cable connected? Is a video monitor cable connected? Is a backup device connected? (either tape or disk). Is a scanner cable connected? Are any special purpose devices connected?

3. Perform a warm boot on your system. Don't perform this exercise if anything important is happening on your computer.

4. What is the storage size of the following disk types?

   Double-sided, double-density (5¼″)

   Double-sided, high-density (5¼″)

   Double-sided, double-density (3½″)

   Double-sided, high-density (3½″)

CHAPTER 2 EXERCISES

1. Study your keyboard to discover which of the possible standard designs it uses. Compare your keyboard to the ones shown in Figures 2.3–2.5 to determine if it is one of the standard types.
2. Determine from which drive your system boots DOS—that is, from a hard or floppy disk.
3. When your system boots, you may be asked to verify (or correct) the date and time. You can perform these procedures even if these requests don't appear automatically. Do this now by changing the system date to 11 P.M. yesterday.
4. Change the default disk drive. If your system prompt begins as A>, change the default drive to B and back again. If the first prompt you see is C>, make A the default drive.
5. To practice correcting mistakes, place any floppy disk into drive A and, without pressing Return, type the following command:

   ```
   DOR A:
   ```

   Use the Backspace key to return to and correct the mistyped O. After correctly reentering the command, press Return to have DOS display a list of the file contents of the disk in drive A.
6. Practice cancelling a command completely. Type a slightly longer command without pressing the Return key:

   ```
   DIR A:*.EXE
   ```

   Cancel this command with the Esc key. You are now ready to reenter this or any other command, even though no new prompt appears.
7. Suppose that you want to see what is on several different diskettes. Place the first diskette in drive A and type

   ```
   DIR A:
   ```

   Use F3 to repeat the command for the remaining disks.

8. Place a diskette in drive A and enter

   ```
   DOR A:*.EXE
   ```

   After receiving DOS's error message, use the F1 and F3 keys to fix just the incorrect position of the command and enter the correction.

9. At this point, you probably have different pieces of information in various portions of your screen. Clear your screen.

10. To prepare a new (scratch) diskette for data use, you must format it. Do this now. (If you have a dual-floppy system, you'll be formatting the disk in drive B. If you have a hard disk, you'll be formating the disk in drive A).

11. Prepare a system disk—one capable of booting the DOS system later from drive A. (Again, if you have a dual-floppy system, format the disk in B. If you have a hard disk, format the disk in A.)

12. Use the DISKCOPY command to make a backup copy of a floppy disk. If you have a write-protect tab, place it over the notch along the edge of the orginal diskette.

13. Use the CHKDSK command to determine information about your hard disk, if you have one. Pay particular attention if CHKDSK indicates bad sectors on your disks. Although it's OK to have bad sectors, you should watch whether the number of bad sectors increases. This is often a sign that the disk in question may be deteriorating.

CHAPTER 3 EXERCISES

1. Use the DIR command to explore the contents of the disks on your system. Take a directory of one floppy disk and the root directory of your hard disk if you have one.
2. Determine if someone has configured your system to use other disk drive letters. (If you receive the response "Invalid drive specification," there are no other drives available on your system.)
3. Take a directory of a floppy disk or your hard disk, but this time list the files in wide format.
4. Take a directory again, but this time make it so the listing pauses at the end of each screenful.
5. Try limiting the number of files displayed by using the * and ? wild-card symbols. Display all executable command files on your diskette (those files whose ending extensions are either .COM or .EXE).
6. Use the * wild card to display all file names that begin with a specific letter. For example, display all files that begin with A or S.
7. Use the DIR command to see a complete list of file names stored on a diskette. Choose one of these file names, and make a second copy of that file on the same disk. Change the name on the second copy to the conventional .BAK extension.
8. You can also make a backup copy on a completely separate disk. Do this now, using the file from the previous exercise. If your original file is on drive C, copy it to drive A. If your original file is on a diskette in the default A drive, copy it to drive B.
9. Now make a copy of every file that shares a common extension (.BAK, .DOC, and so on). Use the * character and issue only one command COPY *.EXT and so on).
10. If you have two floppy drives, try the following. Copy all files from one disk to another using the * character and issuing only one command (hint: *.*).

    If you have a hard drive and only one floppy drive, make a backup of a floppy disk by copying all files from the floppy to your hard disk. Then copy those files to another floppy.

11. Create a simple text file by copying text from your keyboard directly onto the disk. Use the COPY CON: command and remember to enter Ctrl-Z when you are finished entering text. Use the DIR command to see the file you've just made.
12. If your version of DOS is 3.2 or higher, you can use the XCOPY command. This is a more efficient command for copying multiple files from one disk location to another. Repeat exercises 9, 10, and 11 using this command.
13. Use the DIR command to find a file name that seems to contain only text (for example, look for a file whose extension is .TXT, .DOC, or .BAT). Display its contents on the screen. Do this with the file you created in Exercise 12.
14. Try renaming a file with the RENAME command. Use the DIR command to verify the change in file name.
15. First, copy the SAMPLE.TXT file to a SAMPLE.BAK file. Then, use the ERASE command to delete the backup version. Use the DIR command, both before and after the ERASE command, to verify that this file has been created and then deleted.

CHAPTER 4 EXERCISES

1. Use the CHKDSK command to determine the size and volume label of your hard disk.
2. If your hard disk has no volume label, use the LABEL command to give it one now.
3. Place the label SAMPLES on a scratch floppy disk using the FORMAT command. (Be sure not to use a disk containing any needed data.)
4. Create a sample directory structure on the newly formatted SAMPLES diskette. First, change the default directory to drive A. Then, create a \UTIL directory located in the root. Take a piece of blank paper and begin to draw your own directory tree. The first branch from the root will be \UTIL.
5. Type the DIR command now. You should see one entry for \UTIL—the <DIR> indicator by the name tells you that it is a directory entry and not a data or program file. Change to that new directory now.
6. Identify three file names—either on your hard disk or on your B drive if you have a dual-floppy system—that you will shortly copy onto your SAMPLES diskette. You should use their real names in the next exercises; I'll call them FILENAME.1, FILENAME.2, and FILENAME.3.
7. Switch the default drive to C (or B in a dual-diskette system). Now, copy FILENAME.1 into the \UTIL directory of drive A. You don't need to precede FILENAME.1 with a drive identifier because it is located on the default drive (C).
8. Switch the default drive back to A. Now, copy FILENAME.2 into the \UTIL directory (now the current directory again). You must precede FILENAME.2 with the drive identifier C:, since the default drive is now A. DOS assumes that your target drive for the COPY command is the current default drive (A) if you don't specify it on the command line.
9. Now change the current directory on drive A back to the root. Copy your third sample file from a different drive (C or B) into the \UTIL directory on the current drive. The source drive identifier is required, because it is not the current default (A). Also, the target destination must contain the directory path name because it is not the current directory on drive A. You are currently located in the root directory.

10. Create a subdirectory of the \UTIL directory called \SPECIAL. Use the DIR command to confirm that you've done this correctly.
11. Use the /V switch on the CHKDSK command to explore the current structure and contents of your SAMPLES diskette.
12. Use the COPY command to move a file from the \UTIL directory into the \SPECIAL directory. Use the DIR command to verify that the COPY command succeeded.
13. If the COPY command in Exercise 11 worked, erase the original copy of the file that you copied. This COPY and ERASE combination is the equivalent of a MOVE command, although DOS 3.3 does not have such a direct command.
14. To obtain a summary of the directory and subdirectory structure on your disk, use the TREE command—like CHKDSK, one of DOS's disk-resident commands. Run the TREE command and specify your SAMPLES diskette (either in drive A or B) as the target of the operation. Try printing a copy of this tree by adding DOS's special redirection request (>PRN).
15. Set up a PATH for your hard disk to save yourself typing. Include the root directory and the \DOS directory in your path. Then verify that this new PATH has been set.
16. Test this new PATH by running any of the hard-disk commands used in earlier exercises.
17. Suppose that you no longer need the files in the \SPECIAL directory. In fact, since there is only one file located there, you can erase it to leave an empty directory. Then, prune the \SPECIAL directory from the hierarchical tree structure by using the Remove Directory command. Run a TREE command now to verify that the \SPECIAL directory is no longer in the \UTIL directory or anywhere else in the SAMPLES disk hierarchy.

CHAPTER 5 EXERCISES

1. Make a bootable floppy disk using the FORMAT command.
2. Create a directory on the hard disk for storing the DOS support files, if one doesn't exist. Verify your new directory structure with the DIR command.
3. Place each DOS diskette in drive A and type the following command:

    ```
    COPY A:*.* \DOS
    ```

    Some DOS support files reside on each of the original DOS diskettes. When you're done, a copy of all disk-resident DOS programs will be in your \DOS directory.
4. To learn how the PATH command interacts with the concept of a current directory, first switch to drive A and ask for a DIR listing of the \DOS directory. Since \DOS is on drive C, you'll receive an error message. Try this command again from drive A, but this time specify the drive that contains the \DOS directory. Now, change back to drive C. Since the current drive is C, you can successfully ask for a directory listing of the \DOS directory. Lastly, make \DOS the current directory and then enter the DIR command. Without any other specifications, DIR will display the file names in the current directory on the current drive.
5. The default DOS prompt only supplies the drive identifier for the current drive. You can use the PROMPT command to change the prompt to a more useful display. Change the prompt so that it displays the current drive and directory followed by a greater than (>) character.
6. The remaining examples in this chapter concentrate on loading application programs onto your hard disk and running those programs from their subdirectory locations. You may have a word processor, a spreadsheet, a database management system, or some other useful application program. Tailor the following instructions accordingly.

    First, create a subdirectory on your hard disk to house the application files. Choose an appropriate name. Next, copy the application files from the original floppy diskettes into this new directory.
7. To run your application program, you can always change to the directory that contains the program itself. Then, you can just type the name of the program.

8. You can create multiple subdirectories for data files, either by some logical grouping of the data used (for example, Accounting, Budgeting, Projecting, and so on) or by actual user name (for instance, Samuelson, Robbins, Carlson, and so forth). In the former case, you would enter several MD commands (choose appropriate names for your application program's subject areas). To store data by user name, choose user names for your actual personnel. Do this now using names of your classmates.
9. Add the directory containing the application program to your path. Switch to one of the subdirectories in which you intend to store data files for your application program. Then, run the application.
10. As a final exercise, use the TREE and CHKDSK commands to map your new hard-disk directory structure. These commands work because they are disk-resident DOS commands, and are found in the \DOS directory because of your PATH command.

    If your printer is turned on and connected, you can use redirection to print copies of these structure maps. Do so now.

CHAPTER 6 EXERCISES

1. Create the new file TEST.DTA with the EDLIN program. EDLIN will respond with a "New file" message and its asterisk prompt (*).

2. Switch EDLIN into insert mode by typing the I command and pressing Return. You can now type several lines of text, ending each by pressing the Return key. For example, type

   ```
   This is an interesting but limited text processor.
   It's not full screen, but you can edit any lines.
   EDLIN depends on line numbers, which are automatically assigned.
   You must refer to text lines by these numbers.
   ```

   EDLIN numbers each line before you type it. When you've entered all the text you wish, press Ctrl-C to exit the text insertion mode and return to the EDLIN prompt.

3. Change the second line of this text file by typing the number 2 and pressing Return. Now press F2 and then the comma symbol (,). This keeps the first portion of the line, up to the comma. Press the period key, followed by the spacebar. Now type the letters

   ```
   Nev
   ```

   You are overtyping the word "but" at this point. Now, press the Ins key, finish typing

   ```
   ertheless
   ```

   and press the F3 key to add the remainder of the original line without retyping any of it. Press Return, and the result should be:

   ```
   2:*It's not full screen. Nevertheless, you can edit any lines.
   ```

4. Move (cut and paste) line three to just after line one by typing

   ```
   3,3,2M
   ```

5. Review the current arrangement of your text lines by typing the L, or List, command. The result should be

```
This is an interesting but limited text processor.
EDLIN depends on line numbers, which are automatically assigned.
It's not full screen. Nevertheless, you can edit any lines.
You must refer to text lines by these numbers.
```

6. Locate any lines in your file that contain the word "line." Type the command:

```
1,4 ? Sline
```

Line two appears, and EDLIN asks if this is the line you want:

```
O.K.?
```

If this is the desired line, simply press Return. EDLIN will return to its normal prompt and you can proceed with the next EDLIN command. In this example, however, type N for No. EDLIN then displays line three, which also includes the string of characters "line." Type N again two more times. When EDLIN runs out of lines, or it can't find your text string in the remaining lines, it displays the message "Not found."

7. Suppose that you decide to replace all occurrences of the word "Nevertheless" with "However." Type this command:

```
1,4?RNevertheless^ZHowever
```

The ? means that you want EDLIN to show you the changed lines and ask for confirmation about making the changes permanent. You create the ^Z that appears after the original text and before the new substituted text by pressing the Ctrl-Z key combination.

Use the L command to verify what your text file looks like now:

```
This is an interesting but limited text processor.
EDLIN depends on line numbers, which are automatically assigned.
It's not full screen. However, you can edit any lines.
You must refer to text lines by these numbers.
```

8. Use the D command to delete the fourth line of this file. Use the L command to verify that only three lines remain.
9. Save your file and end the editing session by typing the E, or End, command.
10. You are now back at the DOS prompt. Use the DIR command to verify that your TEST.DTA file has been successfully saved.
11. Return to editing mode once again, as you might with a normal text file. Use the I command to add a line of text to the end of the file. You can now type a fourth line, press Return, and press Ctrl-C to switch back to the EDLIN prompt. For example:

    ```
    4:*EDLIN always saves the previous version on disk
    5:*^C
    ```

    Now, type the E command once again to return to DOS, saving this newer version of your text file.
12. Once you are back at the DOS prompt, again use the DIR command to look for TEST.DTA. This time, EDLIN has saved the newer, larger version of your file under the expected name TEST.DTA. However, EDLIN has also saved the preceding version of the file under the name TEST.BAK. Remember that you can always revert to a previous version by erasing the latest copy of your file and renaming the .BAK version of the same file name.

CHAPTER 7 EXERCISES

1. Turn on your printer, make sure it is online, and check that all computer cable connections are correct. Type

    DIR/W

   to place some text information on the screen. Now, print a copy of your screen.

   Note: Perform Exercises 2, 3, and 4 only if you have an IBM Graphics, or compatible, printer.

2. If you have any application program that can create graphic images on the screen, bring it up now. Use that program's commands to generate a graphic image on your screen; then use Shift-PrtSc to attempt to print that graphic image. You'll discover that normal graphics don't print at all.

3. Load the DOS program that will enable PrtSc to print graphics.

4. Using the same command, reverse the black and white aspects of the screen image in the preceding exercise.

5. Try printing any text file (for example, TEST.DTA from the preceding chapter's exercises) with the COPY command.

6. If you have several files with similar names, try using the COPY command with wild cards to print them all at once. Notice that this command does not automatically start each new file on a separate page in your printed output. Note also that you can do nothing else with your computer until the printing has completed.

7. Use the PRINT command to initiate background printing. Use the same file names you selected in the last exercise. Notice that each text file is printed beginning on a separate page. Also, note that the DOS prompt returns immediately after you are told that printing is being initiated. You can continue working on other programs in the foreground while your specified files are printed in the background.

8. Reenter the PRINT command, this time specifying several different files located in different directories and even on different drives. Construct your own background printing request and note how much time it takes to print the files. This is precisely how much time you have saved by using this DOS

command. You can continue to do useful work while you wait for the printing to complete.

9. Resubmit the command in the preceding exercise. This time, however, cancel all spooling operations with the appropriate switch If you've thrown the correct switch, you'll see a message on your screen that the print queue is now empty, and you'll receive a message on your printed output that all files were cancelled by the operator.

CHAPTER 8 EXERCISES

1. Become comfortable with decimal to binary conversion by converting these decimal numbers to their binary equivalents. Also practice converting hexadecimal to and from decimal. Use the ASCII code tables in Appendix B to verify the following equivalences:

DECIMAL	BINARY	HEXADECIMAL	ASCII
33	00100001	21	!
123	01111011	7B	{

2. Using the ASCII code tables in Appendix B, determine the sequence of hexadecimal or decimal numbers necessary to transmit the following sequence of characters: FACSIMILE.

   Note: Assuming that your printer is an IBM graphics or compatible, or one of the Epson MX series, use the MODE command in the remaining exercises to control some of your system device characteristics.

3. First, use the COPY or PRINT command to print an initial copy of the TEST.DTA file (or any other text file), which you created in the last chapter's exercises. Then, use the MODE command to adjust the size of the characters printed (that is, by adjusting the number of columns in the printout).

4. The DOS default is to print six lines per inch. Using MODE, change DOS's lines per inch to eight. Print the TEST.DTA file to see the result.

5. Using one command, change the lines per inch to eight and change the characters per inch to 132 (the maximum allowable).

6. If you have a serial printer attached to output port COM1, use MODE to connect it to the LPT1 output port name. Now copy the TEST.DTA file to the LPT1 port name.

7. Switch the mode of your video display from 80 characters per line to 40. Now try typing a DIR command at your DOS prompt. Switch the number of characters back to 80 per line.

8. If you have two monitors on your system (typically a monochrome and a color monitor), switch between them with the MODE command.

CHAPTER 9 EXERCISES

1. Obtain two formatted scratch diskettes to use in this series of exercises. Select a directory to back up from your hard disk, and back it up using the DOS BACKUP command. (If your \WP directory contains many files, you may be directed to place your second formatted diskette into drive A at some point.)

2. Note the file sizes for the BACKUP.001 and CONTROL.001 files. (If your backup procedure required two diskettes, use the second diskette as the target for this DIR command.) You'll compare these file size numbers later as you make further BACKUP requests.

3. See what happens when you try to delete the BACKUP.001 file created by the BACKUP program.

4. If you have a directory containing many files grouped by file extension, back up just one set of these files according to a specific file extension. (For example, back up just those files in the \WP directory that have .WPB extensions, or whatever extension your word processor uses to store its document files.)

5. Choose another directory containing files you want to include with the backup set created in Exercise 1. Back up these new files *making sure that you add them to this previous backup set.* When you are done, compare the size of the BACKUP and CONTROL files with the sizes noted in Exercise 2.

6. Choose a directory on your hard disk that contains subdirectories, and back up the entire directory tree. (You can reuse current backup diskettes by simply reissuing the BACKUP command.)

7. Pick one file extension (.TXT, .BAT, .COM, and so on) and back up *all* files on your hard disk that have it.

8. Repeat Exercise 7, but this time create a log file that contains the names of all backed up files. Use the TYPE command to view the contents of the BACKUP.LOG file produced and stored in the root of drive C.

9. Use the CHKDSK command to determine how many bytes of storage might be required to back up all files on your hard disk. Use the "bytes available on disk" number to determine roughly how many diskettes you'll need to store your files. Subtract "bytes available" from "total disk space" to estimate how many bytes are used and therefore (roughly) how many bytes you'll need on the

backup diskettes. Second, divide this number by the number of bytes on each diskette you're using for backup. Third, round off this number to the next higher integer. This is how many diskettes you'll need.

10. Suppose that you wish to maintain a current backup set of files from your hard disk. You may have 20 or 30 megabytes of storage on this hard disk. Making a complete backup from scratch each time could take an hour.

    Using the /M switch is a much better idea. This switch guarantees that only the most recently modified (or created) files are sent to the diskettes in the backup drive. Combining this switch with the /A switch ensures that you spend the minimum time to write out new or changed files, and that the one backup set contains the most complete and current set of files from your hard disk.

    Spend a few minutes creating some new files or modifying some old ones. Then type the following command to ensure that these new or updated files (not yet backed up) are now added to your backup set of diskettes:

    ```
    BACKUP C:\ A: /S /A /M
    ```

    Store this set of diskettes now. It is a valuable backup of your entire hard disk!

CHAPTER 10 EXERCISES

1. Change directories to the root of your boot drive and review your current CONFIG.SYS file.
2. Use EDLIN (or your word processor) to make all adjustments to your CONFIG.SYS file in this set of chapter exercises. Place the line FILES=20 in your CONFIG.SYS.
3. Look in your CONFIG.SYS file for a line that sets the number of buffers. If the line BUFFERS=10 does not appear, add it or make the necessary changes.
4. Create a 256K RAM disk on your system if you have the memory available. If you have an extended memory board in your system, you may create a 1024K RAM disk.
5. Review your new RAM disk with the CHKDSK command. (When the RAM disk is created, VDISK uses the next available drive letter on your system.)
6. A simple way of assessing the improved speed of a RAM disk is to fill it with files and then run the DIR command. First, take any diskette and copy all of its files onto your RAM disk. Now, type these two commands:

   ```
   DIR A:
   DIR D:
   ```

   This contrasts a RAM disk's speed with that of a diskette. To compare RAM disk speed with a hard disk further, copy the same files onto a new directory of your hard disk. Now run the DIR command for all three file sites:

   ```
   DIR A:
   DIR C:\SAMPLES
   DIR D:
   ```

7. If your CONFIG.SYS file does not have a DEVICE line for the ANSI.SYS file, add this command line to your CONFIG.SYS file:

   ```
   DEVICE = C:\DOS\ANSI.SYS
   ```

   Reboot your system to make ANSI.SYS customizing capabilities available to you.

8. Practice adjusting your DOS system prompt now. If your prompt is currently just the drive identifier, change it to the current drive/directory followed by the greater than symbol (>).

9. If you have a color monitor, change your screen's output to reverse video (black becomes white, and vice versa). Type a DIR command to see the dramatic difference in screen appearance.

10. Use Table 10.1 to construct a new PROMPT command to make all subsequent characters underlined, bold, or blinking. Type a DIR command. After verifying the result, restore your screen to normal attributes. Type

    ```
    CLS
    ```

    to clear any existing earlier display information from your screen.

11. Use the PROMPT command to make your display blinking and reverse video. Use Table 10.1 to combine other codes for your monitor.

12. Add some text of your own choosing to a new DOS prompt.

13. Include the date and time in a new prompt, shown in reverse video.

14. Use Table 10.2 to experiment with other combinations of new DOS prompts. Create multiline prompts, as well as combining color and attribute possibilities from Table 10.1. For example, if you have a color monitor, try creating a prompt that consists of current directory and system time in blue letters over white background.

15. Redefine a function key with the PROMPT command. Make it possible to run the CHKDSK command by simply pressing F10. Use Table 10.3 to experiment with changing the default results from pressing other function keys.

CHAPTER 11 EXERCISES

1. You can store invisible control symbols in text files almost as easily as you can store visible letters or numbers.

   For example, type this command:

   ```
   COPY CON: BEEP.COD
   ```

   Hold the Alt key down with one hand, and then press the three digits 007 on the numeric keypad at the right side of your keyboard. You've just entered the control code for a beep into this file. Now terminate the file by pressing ^Z and the Return key.

   To sound a beep on your computer, you just need to copy this file to the CON device. Try this now:

   ```
   COPY BEEP.COD CON:
   ```

2. Temporarily change the COUNTRY command entry in your CONFIG.SYS file to the Netherlands (or include such a command, if it is not there currently). This changes the date and time formats. Type the DATE and TIME commands to see how DOS automatically adjusts the format appearance.
3. Load the national language support functions for your system. Specify where the COUNTRY.SYS file is located.
4. Determine the current code page status of your monitor and keyboard.
5. Load the special keyboard translation for France. Now press each letter, number, and symbol key on your keyboard to see which keys are interpreted differently. Try the shifted versions of all keys to obtain additional special characters.
6. If you now have two separate keyboard tables in memory, try switching back and forth between them. Test the results by pressing some of the keys you learned from the preceding exercise.
7. If you used the MODE command to prepare your system for multiple code pages, switch to the multilingual code page now.
8. If you have a CGA (Color Graphics Adapter) on your system, you should make a habit of entering this command:

   ```
   GRAFTABL
   ```

Do this now to ensure that your extended ASCII symbol set will be more readable. Test this out by holding down the Alt key and then pressing any of the three-digit numbers (on your right side keypad) seen in Figure 11.10.

9. Use the SELECT command to prepare a bootable DOS system disk for international use. Prepare a system disk for use in the Netherlands, assuming that you have a French keyboard.

10. Try booting your computer from the newly prepared system disk. Place it in your A drive now and restart your system. Use TYPE to view the contents of the AUTOEXEC.BAT and CONFIG.SYS files, verifying that they were automatically generated during the SELECT command.

CHAPTER 12 EXERCISES

1. Practice using redirection to send DOS command output to the printer instead of the screen. Redirect the DIR and CHKDSK commands.
2. Send the output of the DIR command to a file called RESULTS. Use the TYPE command to view the contents of the RESULTS file.
3. Repeat Exercise 2 using the CHKDSK command. Use the TYPE command again to view the contents of RESULTS. (Notice that the old contents were completely obliterated by the new, redirected CHKDSK output.)
4. Now add a DIR output to the CHKDSK information currently residing in RESULTS. Once again, use the TYPE command to verify that the DIR command's output has been added to the RESULTS file.
5. Use the SORT filter command to arrange a series of names alphabetically. Type SORT at the DOS prompt and press Return. Type the following names, each on their own line. End the list by pressing Ctrl-Z and then the Return key:

   ```
   Robbins
   Carlton
   Busby
   Samuelson
   Kincaid
   ^Z
   ```

6. Rerun Exercise 5. This time, however, use redirection to send the alphabetized results to a new file called ARRANGED.DTA
7. The BUSINESS.TXT and PERSONAL.TXT files appear in Figures 12.1 and 12.2. If you have access to the instructor's diskette that accompanies this Academic Edition, you can copy these two files to your system. Otherwise, you can create the files using EDLIN (or your own word processor).

   Use redirection to take BUSINESS.TXT as input, sort the input text with SORT, and then use redirection again to send the sorted results to CLIENTS.TXT. Use the TYPE command now to view the sorted results of the CLIENTS.TXT file.
8. Use the FIND filter to extract the entries in BUSINESS.TXT that contain a phone number beginning with the 415 area code.

9. Combine DOS commands with DOS filters by using pipes. Produce a sorted directory listing on your screen.
10. Print a sorted listing of any diskette.
11. Sort any subject directory by the file size column. Print the results for later consideration by adding the redirection operator.
12. Combine various filters with redirection to obtain sophisticated results. Arrange the entries in the BUSINESS.TXT file by phone number for all contacts in the 415 calling area, by typing

```
SORT /+43 < BUSINESS.TXT | FIND "415/"
```

13. Take a directory of a disk that contains a lot of files, making sure that the listing is displayed one screen at a time.

CHAPER 13 EXERCISES

1. Write a short batch file called SIMPLE.BAT that will change the default directory to \DOS, clear the screen, take a DIR listing of all .COM files and then all .EXE files:

   ```
   CD \DOS
   CLS
   DIR/W *.COM
   DIR/W *.EXE
   ```

   After creating this batch file, run it by typing

   ```
   SIMPLE
   ```

   The results will appear on your screen in rapid succession, as if you individually typed in these four commands.

2. Insert a new line

   ```
   @ECHO OFF
   ```

   at the beginning of SIMPLE.BAT. Rerun the program and note the difference (the same results, but this time the batch commands themselves will not appear).

3. Create or obtain the DEMO.BAT file, which consists of the two lines:

   ```
   CLS
   DIR *.%1
   ```

   Assuming that you are currently in your \DOS directory, run the batch file to see how it works. First, run DEMO with an argument of EXE:

   ```
   DEMO EXE
   ```

   This lists all file names with an .EXE extension. Rerun the command with an argument of COM:

   ```
   DEMO COM
   ```

4. Write the following batch file and name it PARA.BAT:

```
MD %1
CD %1
COPY %2 %1
DIR/W %1
CHKDSK %3
```

   Analyze what this batch file does. Then run it to verify your analysis.

5. Write your own batch file to create a new directory called \EXECS in \DOS, copy all executable files from \DOS to \EXECS, and verify the copy with a DIR command. Write this batch file two ways. First, write it so you can run it by typing

```
CONSOLID
```

   Second, rewrite it so you use input arguments for the new directory name and the file name extensions to consolidate in the new subdirectory.

CHAPTER 14 EXERCISES

1. If you have access to the instructor's diskette, copy all the batch files onto your own disk. You can then run these programs without having to write them, and can ignore any directions to create the files from scratch. Write your own first user help file in the fashion suggested in Figure 14.1. After creating this file, test it by typing

   ```
   HELP1
   ```

2. Use the COPY command to create HELP2.BAT from HELP1.BAT:

   ```
   COPY HELP1.BAT HELP2.BAT
   ```

   Now edit the HELP2.BAT file by adding in additional ECHO statements, as demonstrated in Figure 14.3. Separate the first group of statements from this new group by the following:

   ```
   ECHO ***********************************************
   ECHO Press Ctrl-Break key to terminate these messages, or
   PAUSE
   CLS
   ```

   Write your own ECHO messages in the second half of this program. Then, test it by typing

   ```
   HELP2
   ```

   at the DOS prompt.

3. Rerun HELP2. This time, press the Ctrl-Break key combination at the PAUSE. This produces a controlled termination of your batch file.

4. Rerun HELP2 a third time. This time, press Ctrl-Break while the first screenful is being displayed. Answer N when asked whether to "Terminate batch job (Y/N)." Note that although the batch file continues at this point, one entire ECHO line is missed. Unfortunately, when you interrupt a batch file during execution, you lose one statement if you choose to continue running the batch program after the break.

5. Create the LOCATE.BAT file seen in Figure 14.7. This batch file tells you whether a specified file name is found on a diskette or in a particular directory. It uses a variable parameter (%1) to enable you to enter the target file name when you run the LOCATE program.

   After creating the batch file, select some file name that you know exists in the directory, or on the disk, containing the LOCATE.BAT file. Then type

   LOCATE *filename.ext*

   Substitute a known file name for *filename.ext*. Note how %1 is replaced in the resulting ECHO message with the actual *filename.ext* that you typed as an argument to the batch program. Note also how the IF statement, with the GOTO command, controls the decision making in this batch file.

6. Create the HUNT.BAT file seen in Figure 14.11. Run the program, specifying as arguments up to four file names that may or may not exist on your system.

7. Develop a modification of HUNT.BAT called HUNTHELP.BAT. Besides simply determining the existence of specified files, this batch file should display a Help screen about the named topic. If no help file exists, the batch file should say that no Help text is available for the topic.

   First, create two text files called TOPIC1.HLP and TOPIC2.HLP. Use ECHO commands to display your help text for either topic. If a user types

   HUNTHELP TOPIC1

   your batch file should clear the screen and display the help text file contents from TOPIC1.HLP. Do the same for TOPIC2. If the user specifies an argument for any other topic for which no help file exists, you should display an appropriate message.

8. Create the three batch files seen in Figures 14.14, 14.15, and 14.16. These demonstrate how to control the flow of execution from one batch file to another. Run the entire sequence of batch files. The final instruction in the SECOND.BAT file does not execute because DOS's chaining technique passes control irrevocably to the THIRD.BAT file. Control never returns to SECOND.BAT and the last instruction never has a chance to execute.

9. Write the FOURTH.BAT file seen in Figure 14.18. Run it by typing

```
FOURTH
```

at the DOS prompt. Notice how the CALL instruction effectively transfers control to THIRD, yet also returns control back to FOURTH. In this way, all remaining instructions in the calling program (FOURTH) will execute after the called program (THIRD) completes its execution. This CALL instruction becomes the correct way to implement true subroutine invocation in the DOS batch language.

CHAPTER 15 EXERCISES

1. Make a copy of your AUTOEXEC.BAT file:

   ```
   COPY C:\AUTOEXEC.BAT C:\AUTOEXEC.HLD
   ```

   When you're done with the exercises in this chapter, you can restore your original AUTOEXEC.BAT simply by typing

   ```
   COPY C:\AUTOEXEC.BAK C:\AUTOEXEC.BAT
   ```

2. Use your editor to adjust your AUTOEXEC.BAT file so that your most commonly needed program is automatically initiated when you turn on your computer. (Do this by adding to your AUTOEXEC.BAT a line that changes directory to the one containing your desired program, and a line that names and thereby initiates the program itself.) Save AUTOEXEC-.BAT and reboot your system to see the effect. Since AUTOEXEC.BAT is only a batch file that is automatically executed by DOS when you boot your computer, you could just type

   ```
   AUTOEXEC
   ```

   to rerun this batch file after you make your changes, without having to reboot. However, first read the rest of the instructions in AUTOEXEC-.BAT to check that the batch file can rerun now that your system is up and running.

3. If there is no PATH command in your AUTOEXEC.BAT, include one so that DOS can find the EDITOR.EXE file without a Change Directory command (CD \WP) line at the end of the AUTOEXEC.BAT.

4. You learned about the PROMPT command in Chapter 10. Add two PROMPT commands to your AUTOEXEC.BAT file. The first should set the DOS prompt to the current directory and date; the second should initialize function key F10 to CHKDSK. Reboot or rerun AUTOEXEC.BAT to test your new prompt and your new F10 definition.

5. Remove the added lines in your AUTOEXEC.BAT from Exercise 2. You will now restructure your startup to provide a simple menu system. Make

the last two lines in your AUTOEXEC.BAT the following:

```
CLS
TYPE MENU.SCR
```

Then create the MENU.SCR file, which should consist of a series of ECHO lines that display the possible user program choices. Refer to Figure 15.1 for an example of the sort of information you can include in your ECHO statements. Replace the choices 1, 2, 3, and 4 with your own application program names on your system.

6. A user who is presented with the echoed display developed in the preceding exercise can type 1 and press Return to initiate the first application program. To make this work, your first application program needs to be initiated in another batch file called 1.BAT. Create 1.BAT, 2.BAT, 3.BAT, and 4.BAT (if your MENU.SCR file shows four choices), using the models seen in Figure 15.2. Notice in each model batch file that after the application program itself runs, the MENU.SCR file is once again displayed on the screen. This reminds the user what main menu choices are available for continued processing.

7. Create abbreviation batch files for the two most common DOS commands: DIR and CHKDSK. Remember that each command can accept one argument, so you'll have to incorporate variable parameters into your batch file. For example, the D.BAT file might consist of the single line:

   ```
   DIR %1
   ```

   Create this batch file, and a similar one called C.BAT (for CHKDSK). Then, test them by running these two commands:

   ```
   D C:\DOS\*.EXE
   C A:
   ```

   Make sure that you have a diskette in drive A when you run the test.

8. Create an R.BAT file that uses two variable parameters (%1 and %2) to rename any one file (%1) to a new name (%2).

9. Create two batch files named COMPRESS.BAT and NORMAL.BAT. Each should use the MODE command to switch your Epson or IBM compatible printer, respectively, to 132 columns per inch (CPI) of printed output (COMPRESS.BAT) and back to 80 CPI (NORMAL.BAT).

10. Create and run the CONTENTS.BAT file seen in Figure 15.4. Use a series of floppy diskettes in your A drive to test the program. Press Ctrl-Break when you're ready to stop this batch file's programmed repetitions.
11. If your system includes a RAM disk, create a RAMINIT.BAT file to copy all desired programs from your hard disk onto the RAM disk.
12. Create the RGB.BAT file seen in Figure 15.9. Then test it by choosing a color combination pleasing to your eye. I find blue letters on a white background easy to read when working for hours at a time:

```
RGB BLUE WHITE
```

13. Create your own appointment reminder system, based on the techniques seen in the TODAY.BAT file of Figure 15.16. As a sample file, create a text file whose name is 12-12-90 (or any other date-like name you wish). Place some messages into it, and run the TODAY batch file:

```
TODAY 12-12-90
```

Try running TODAY for a different date to be sure that you've successfully handled the case of a date that has no appointments.

14. Incorporate the password protection demonstrated in Figure 15.24 into some or all of the application program batch files (1.BAT, 2.BAT, 3.BAT, 4.BAT) created in Exercise 6. When you're done adjusting the batch files, each application program that you want to be password protected should require a user to successfully enter that password. Test your complete main menu system.

If everything works correctly, your AUTOEXEC.BAT file should display MENU.SCR, and you should be able to access each of your system's application programs by simply typing 1, 2, and so on at the DOS prompt. Some or all of your programs should only be allowed to execute if the user correctly types a password of your choosing. Remember that this password must be stored in the DOS environment before running the application program batch file (1.BAT, and so on). In other words, if EELS is the password, you must type

```
SET PASSWORD = EELS
```

before running the batch file that checks for the password.

CHAPTER 16 EXERCISES

1. Use the ATTRIB command to protect any important file you like from accidental erasure by making it read-only. Verify that this file is now a read-only file. (First back it up, in case your ATTRIB command submission was wrong in some way.)

   ```
   COPY SAMPLE.TXT SAMPLE.BAK
   ```

   You can always recover your file by renaming the .BAK version. To verify whether the ATTRIB command worked, try erasing the file:

   ```
   ERASE SAMPLE.TXT
   ```

   You should get the error message "Access Denied." You must use the -R switch on the ATTRIB command to delete this file in the future.

2. Use the MD command to create a new directory called \DRIVE-A in the root of your C drive. Now join your A drive to the hard disk directory structure. Verify that all references to the \DRIVE-A directory on drive C are really translated automatically to references to drive A. (This request is satisfied by reading the directory table on your physical A drive. Watch the red light on your A drive when you make this request.)

   Try copying files to and from this \DRIVE-A directory. DOS will make the automatic translation to operations occurring to and from the diskette in drive A.

3. Disengage the JOIN set up in Exercise 3.

4. Some directory hierarchies become quite complex. If there are many levels in your disk tree, it can be time consuming to type complete and complex path names repeatedly. Use the SUBST command to reduce a complex path to a simple drive identifier letter. Verify that the substitution has been successful.

   At this point, you can refer to any of the picture files in this system with such references as E:FILE1.PIC or E:FILE2.WPG. When you're done, disengage the substitution.

5. You can also use the FASTOPEN command when your system contains many levels in the tree. This is a simple addition to your CONFIG.SYS file. Although it does take some space, it is generally worth including.

6. To discover what environmental variables are currently in use, type

   ```
   SET
   ```

   at the DOS prompt. Identify which ones you set during earlier exercises (such as the PASSWORD). The remaining variables are defaulted by DOS for such things as the disk location of the command processor (COMSPEC). You may discover that some variables are not defaulted but are rather set by application programs. For example, a context switching program called Software Carousel sets the PROMPT to indicate how much memory has been allocated to each individual program's executing context.

INDEX

% (percent sign)
as DOS environment string indicator, 409
as variable indicator, 320–321
$ (dollar sign)
in file extensions, 149
in prompt display arguments, 114
* (asterisk), as wild-card character, 41
+ (plus sign), as concatenation indicator, 65
: (colon)
in file and drive names, 54, 64, 112
in reserved device names, 181
in time formats, 248
; (semicolon), in path listings, 101, 103
< (less-than symbol or left angle bracket), as output destination
indicator, 284
> (greater-than symbol or right angle bracket)
in DOS prompt, 20, 113
as output destination indicator, 278, 280
? (question mark), as wild-card character, 58–59
\ (backslash)
as hierarchical directory structure indicator, 85, 112
to cause commands to be ignored, 24
{} (brackets), as optional switch/parameter indicator, 415
, (comma), in currency formats, 248
. (period), in currency formats, 248
" (quotation marks), as string delimiters, 287
¦ (vertical bar)
as either/or choice indicator, 415
as pipe symbol, 291
special characters
in foreign countries' date/time/currency conventions, 248
not allowed in file names, 52
abbreviations of commands, executing with batch files, 356–359
"Abort, Retry, Fail (or Ignore)" message, 51
Above Board expanded memory, 229
"Access denied" message, 389
active partition, 463, 493
adapters (graphics), 154
"All files canceled by operator" message, 168
angle bracket (>)
in DOS prompt, 20, 113
as output destination indicator, 278, 280, 284
ANSI driver, 463
ANSI.SYS, 227, 233
API (Application Programming Interface), 463
APPEND command, 102–103, 123, 126, 415, 419
Application Programming Interface (API), 463
application programs, 463. *See also under names of programs*
appointment reminder system
through batch files, 370–373
archive bit, 209, 463
argument, 21
ASCII
defined, 246–247, 463, 479–480
displaying on screen, 267–268, 438
mapping of, 480, 482–484
ASCII files, displaying, 74, 459
assembly language, 427, 463
ASSIGN command, 404, 416, 419
asterisk (*), as wild-card character, 41
asynchronous communications, 179
ATTRIB command, 388–390, 417
attributes
changing, 388–390, 417
described, 387

AUTOEXEC.BAT file
  for DOS, 224, 271-272, 350-353, 463
  AUX standard device name, 181

background tasks, 162, 463
backslash (\)
  as hierarchical directory structure indicator, 85, 112
  to cause commands to be ignored, 24
Backspace key, 22-23
BACKUP command, 196-213, 388-389, 418-419
backups. *See also* BACKUP command
  adding files to, 202-207
  importance of, 12, 62, 195, 232
.BAK file extension, 55
base name, 464
.BAS file extension, 54-55
BASIC computer language, 464
batch files. *See also* commands
  for appointment reminder system, 370-373
  and AUTOEXEC.BAT file, 224, 271-272, 350-353, 463
  for broadcasting messages to system users, 374-375
  chaining of, 342-345
  for controlling user access, 380-382
  creating, 314-318
  for customized help screens, 368-370
  for customized menus, 353-356
  decision-making (branching) in, 333-337
  described, 313, 349, 464
  ECHO command for, 318-319, 328-329, 430
  editing, 318-319
  improving performance with, 356-367
  limitations of, 316-317
  looping and repetition in, 337-342
  messages in, 328-329
  pausing execution of, 329-333, 446
  providing variables to, 455-456
  running, 317
  for status tracking, 375-378
  for using RAM disks effectively, 378-380
  using variables in, 320-325
.BAT file extension, 55, 316, 415
baud rate, 186, 464
binary numbering system, 174-176, 464, 482-483
.BIN file extension, 55, 432
bit, 464
bit mapping, 464
blinking, 237
booting. *See also* bootstrapping
  described, 8, 18, 351
  warm and cold, 465, 477
boot record, 11, 464
bootstrapping, 18, 224, 464
brackets ({}), as optional switch/parameter indicator, 415
branching, 327, 333-337, 464
BREAK command, 419
break key, 330-333, 464
broadcasting messages to system users through batch files, 374-375
buffers. *See also* memory
  described, 66, 226-227, 419-420, 464
  external, 469
BUFFERS command, 226-227, 419-420
bytes, 3, 40, 464

cache, 464
CAD (computer-aided design) programs, 465
CADVANCE, memory requirements of, 228
CALL command, 420
case sensitivity
  of character searches, 299
  described, 464
  in EDLIN program, 145

in file names, 52
of passwords, 381–382
CD command, 112–113
Central Point Software, 33
central system unit, 4
CGA (Color Graphics Adapter), 154, 189, 267
chaining
in batch files, 342–345
described, 464
for diskette-switching, 363–364
characters. *See also Special Characters Index*
as bytes, 3
deleting, 22–23, 26
inserting, 26
not allowed in file names, 52
retyping in commands, 26
character sets, 465, 479–484
CH (CHDIR) command, 87–88, 421
CHCP command, 272, 421
CHDIR (CD) command, 87–88, 421
CHKDSK command, 38–42, 90–91, 126–127, 422
clearing the screen, 25–26, 422
clock
internal, 18, 458–459
CLS command, 25–26, 422
clusters, 38–39, 465
COBOL language, 465
code pages, 249–268, 272, 421, 443–444, 465
cold booting, 351, 465
colon (:)
in file and drive names, 54, 64, 112
in reserved device names, 181
in time formats, 248
Color Graphics Adapter (CGA), 154, 189
.COM file extension, 54–55, 415, 432
comma (,), in currency formats, 248
COMMAND.COM, 30, 231, 405–406, 409–412, 465
COMMAND command, 409–412, 423
command line, 465
command processor, 405, 409–412, 423, 455, 465
commands. *See also* batch files; *individual commands*
abbreviating through batch files, 356–359
canceling, 24, 26
editing, 25
entering, 20–21
jumping/skipping, 336, 437–438
listed for reference, 415–462
renaming, 406–409
repeating with batch files, 359–360
repeating with function key, 24–25
resident vs. transient, 8–9, 406, 475, 477
switches for, 21, 476
used in EDLIN program, 133
COM*n* ports, 159
COMP command, 423–424
compressed print, 183, 465
computer-aided design (CAD) program, 465
COMSPEC, 364–365, 374, 407–408
concatenation, 65, 465
conditional statements, 333, 465
IF, 334–336, 439–440, 471
CONFIG.SYS, 223–225, 465
configuring
described, 4, 119, 223, 465
DOS partitions, 486–498
connector ports, 5
console, 466
constants, 334
contiguity, 41–42, 466
control characters, 3
control codes, 176, 466
COPY command, 60–67, 88, 91–92, 96–97, 111–112, 159, 424–425
COPY CON command, 315–316
COPY II PC program, 33, 196

copying
  with COPY command, 60-67, 88, 91-92, 96-97, 111-112, 159, 424-425
  diskettes, 32-38, 429-430
  with EDLIN program, 143-144
  files, 67-73, 461-462
copy protection, 32-33, 466
country codes, 249
COUNTRY command, 248, 425
COUNTRY.SYS file, 260, 421
CPU (central processing unit), 4, 466
Ctrl-Alt-Del reboot method, 351
Ctrl-Break key, 419
Ctrl-Z end-of-file marker, 26, 466
CTTY command, 426
currency formats, 245, 248
cursor, 466
cutting and pasting, 466
cylinders, 466, 488

daisy-wheel printers, 466
data area, 466
database management systems
  described, 466
  running in DOS, 122-123
databases, 466
data bits, 175, 186, 466
data disks, 466
data files, 3
data stream, 466
date-stamping of programs, 27
date
  formats of, 248, 425
  making backups by, 211
  of program version, 27
  system, 18, 26-27, 268-270, 426, 453
DATE command, 426
.DAT file extension, 54-55
dBASE III PLUS, 228
.DBF file extension, 55
dead key, 266, 467
DEBUG command, 427
debugging
  with DEBUG command, 427
  described, 467
  through batch file subroutines, 375-378
decimal numbering system
  converting from binary, 482
  converting from hexadecimal, 483-484
  described, 467, 483
decision making, 467
default, 467
deferred execution, 321, 467
DEL command, 427
deleting
  characters, 22-23, 26
  directories, 452
  files, 427
  lines in EDLIN program, 147
delimiter, 85, 467
Del key, 26
destination, 214, 467
destination diskette, 33
DEVICE command, 228-230, 233, 270-271, 428
device drivers, 179-191, 227-233, 250, 255-259, 467. *See also* MODE command
device name, 467
devices
  changing, 426
  described, 6-7, 179-182, 467
  drivers for, 179-191, 227-233, 250, 255-259, 467
  initializing, 182-183, 185-187
digital, 467
digitizer, 467
DIR command, 50-60, 77, 86, 112, 428-429
directories
  backing up, 200-201
  changing, 87-88, 421
  creating, 85, 442
  current, 237

default, 87–88
deleting, 452
described, 81, 467
as drives, 397, 457
listing, 98–99, 126–127, 459
listing contents of, 50–60, 77, 86, 112, 428
multilevel, 197
removing files from, 427
restoring, 216–217
sample structures of, 68, 208
searching for programs, 100–102, 123–126, 445–446
searching through, 102–103, 123, 126, 415, 419
sorting for display, 282–285, 290–295, 298, 303–304, 456
speeding access to, 404–405, 432–433
"Directory not empty" message, 396
directory table, 11
directory tree, 467
DISKCOMP command, 429
DISKCOPY command, 32–38, 429–430
disk drives
assigning, 404, 416, 419
described, 2, 57, 467
identifier for, 468
as subdirectories with JOIN command, 394–397, 404, 419, 440
substitutes of, 397–404, 419, 457
for systems with more than five, 230, 442
diskettes. *See also* backups; floppy diskette systems; FORMAT command; hard disk systems
care of, 11–12
comparing, 439
copying, 32–38, 429–430
described, 3, 7–11, 467
labeling, 83, 404, 441
recovering, 393–394, 448–449
disk operating system. *See* DOS (Disk Operating System); OS/2 operating system
disk optimizers, 468
disks. *See* diskettes; floppy diskette systems; hard disk systems
.$$$ file extension, 149
$g argument, for display of angle bracket at prompt, 114
$p argument, for display of directory at prompt, 114
DOS (Disk Operating System). *See also* commands; files; floppy diskette systems; hard disk systems; OS/2 operating system; utilities; Windows
customizing through CONFIG.SYS file, 223–242
described, xxiii, 2–4, 468
displaying current version of, 460
environment, 374, 406–408, 453–454, 468
prompt, 19–20, 30, 468
startup, 18–20
versions of, xxiii
DOS prompt, 19–20, 30, 468
dot-matrix printers, 184, 468
double-density diskette, 10–11, 468
drive identifier, 468
driver files, 102
drivers. *See* device drivers
DRIVER.SYS, 468
drives. *See* disk drives
.DRV file extension, 55
.DTA file extension, 55
dual tasking, 468

ECHO command, 318–319, 328–329, 430
echoing, 468
editing
batch files, 318–319
commands, 25
files with EDLIN, 137–143

with word processors, 478
EDLIN program
copying lines in, 143–144
deleting lines in, 147
described, 131–132, 431, 468
displaying files in, 136–137
editing files in, 137–143
exiting, 147–150
reading files into, 132–136
searching with, 144–147
starting, 132–136
EGA (Enhanced Graphics Adapter), 154, 189
end-of-file marker (Ctrl-Z), 26, 64, 468
Enhanced Graphics Adapter (EGA), 154, 189
ENTER (return) key, 21
environment (DOS), 374, 406–408, 453–454, 468
ERASE command, 77–78, 103, 105, 323, 431
error level, 468
Escape (Esc) key, 24, 26
EXE2BIN command, 432
.EXE file extension, 55, 415
expanded memory, 229
expansion cards, 468
expansion slots, 469
extended ASCII codes, 176, 246–247, 267–268, 438, 469
extended DOS partition, 469, 485
extended memory, 229, 469
extensions (of file names)
described, 52, 469
.$$$, 149
.BAK, 55
.BAS, 54
.BAT, 55, 316, 415
.BIN, 55, 432
.COM, 54–55, 415, 432
.DAT, 54–55
.DBF, 55
.DRV, 55
.DTA, 55
.EXE, 55, 415
.HLP, 54–55
.LOG, 211
.NDX, 55
.OVL, 54–55
.PRG, 55
.SYS, 55
.TXT, 54–55
.WK1, 55
.WKS, 55
external buffers, 469

FAPI (Family Application Programming Interface), 469
FASTOPEN command, 404–405, 432–433
FAT (file allocation table)
described, 11, 41, 393, 469
resolving errors in, 38, 41, 422
FCBS command, 433
FDISK command, 434, 486–498
file allocation table. *See* FAT (file allocation table)
file control blocks (FCBs), 225, 433, 435
file names, 52–54, 469
files. *See also* backups; EDLIN program; extensions (of file names)
attributes of, 388–390, 417
comparing, 423–424, 429
converting executable for command, 432
copying, 60–67, 88, 91–92, 96–98, 111–112, 424, 461–462
deleting, 427
described, 3, 469
erasing, 77–78, 103, 105, 323, 431
hidden, 7, 30, 40, 470
listing, 50–60, 86, 112, 428
printing, 159–168, 404, 446–447
program vs data, 3, 49

recovering, 393–394, 448–449
renaming, 74–77, 450
replacing selectively, 390–393, 450–451
restoring, 213–218, 404, 451–452
searching for strings/text in, 285–289, 298–304, 435
sharing/locking, 454
specifying number openable, 225, 435
speeding access to, 404–405, 432–433
as stored during backups, 197–199
verifying transfer of, 65–67, 199, 460, 474
FILES command, 225, 435
file version, 198, 469
filters
described, 282, 469
and pipes, 290
searching for data with, 285–289
sorting data with, 282–285
FIND command, 285–289, 298–304, 435
fixed disks, 2, 469
floppy diskette systems. *See also* diskettes; hard disk systems
backups for, 32–38
checking for available space on, 38–42
commands for diskette/directory handling in, 82–107
comparing diskettes on, 429
copying diskettes on, 32–38, 429–430
described, 2–3, 467
disk drive nomenclature on, 4
DOS prompt in, 19–20
formatting diskettes on, 27–32, 83, 281–282, 436–437
storage capabilities of, 81–82
flow of control, 327, 469
FOR command, 337–340, 436
foreground tasks, 162, 469
foreign language
format conventions, 248–249, 425
keyboards, 250–252, 256–259, 263–266, 471
FORMAT command, 28–32, 83, 110, 281–282, 436–437
formatting
described, 469
diskettes, 27–32, 83, 281–282, 436–437
hard disks, 27–32, 83, 110, 281–282, 436–437
fragmentation, 470
function keys
described, 24–26, 470
redefinition codes for, 241
F1, 25
F2, 26
F3, 24–25
F4, 26
F5, 26
F6, 26

gigabyte (Gb), 470
global characters, 470
GOTO command, 336, 437–438
GRAFTABL command, 267–268, 438
graphics, printing, 154–158, 438–439
graphics adapters, 154
GRAPHICS command, 154–158, 438–439
graphics mode, 470
greater-than symbol (>)
in DOS prompt, 20, 113
as output destination indicator, 278, 280

hard disk systems
backups for, 32–38, 196–213, 388–389, 404, 418–419
checking for available space on, 38–42
commands for directory handling in, 109–129
described, 2–3, 7–11, 470
DOS prompt in, 19–20
formatting of, 27–32, 83, 110, 281–282, 438
mapping, 126–128

partitioning, 434, 485–498
recovering disks on, 393–394, 448–449
resolving errors in, 38–42, 90–91, 126–127, 422, 477
restoring files on, 213–218, 404, 451–452
storage capabilities of, 81–82
hardware, xxiii, 4–12, 470
hardware interrupts, 470
head, 470
head crash, 470
help file, 470
help screens, customized through batch files, 368–370
hexadecimal numbering system, 470, 483–484
hidden files, 7, 30, 40, 470
high-capacity diskette, 470
high-resolution mode, 470
.HLP file extension, 54–55
horizontal landscape, 158, 470
hot key, 471
housekeeping, described, 471
hub, 471
hub hole, 10

IBMBIO.COM, 30
IBMDOS.COM, 30
icons, xxvii
IF command, 334–336, 439–440, 471
"Incorrect number of parameters" message, 397
initialization. *See* startup
ink-jet printers, 471
Ins key, 26
installing DOS, 18
interface, 471
interrupts
hardware and software, 250, 470, 476
processing with stack frames, 456
providing for, 419
"Invalid drive specification" message, 50–51, 397
"Invalid parameter" message, 397
IO.SYS, 30

JOIN command, 394–397, 404, 417, 440

KEYB command, 263–266, 271–272, 441
keyboards. *See also* function keys
altering with KEYB command, 263–266, 271–272, 441
described, 4–5, 21–25, 251–252
redefining, 240–242, 471
KEYBOARD.SYS, 257
keyboard translation table, 250–252, 256–259, 263–266, 471. *See also* KEYB command
key combination, 471
key redefinition, 240–242, 471
kilobyte (K), 3, 471

LABEL command, 404, 441
labeling, diskettes, 83, 404, 441, 461
languages
computer,
assembly, 427, 463
BASIC, 464
COBOL, 465
machine, 427, 472
Pascal, 473
foreign,
format conventions of, 248–249, 425
national language-support operations, 473
and NLSFUNC command, 260, 272, 445
simulating keyboards of, 250–252, 256–259, 263–266, 471
laser printers, 471
LASTDRIVE command, 230, 442
LCD (Liquid Crystal Display), 471
less-than symbol (<), as output destination indicator, 284
letter-quality printers, 184, 471
line editor, 471

line feed, 471
Liquid Crystal Display (LCD), 471
literals, 334, 471
lockup, 471
log file, 472
.LOG file extension, 211
logging on, 472
logical drives, 472, 491
logical expressions, 333
logical testing, 472
loops, establishing in batch files, 337–342, 436
Lotus 1-2-3, 117–119, 399
LPTn ports, 159, 181

machine language, 427, 472
macros, 472
mapping
  of ASCII codes to characters, 480, 482–484
Mb (megabytes), 3, 472
MD command, 111
medium-resolution mode, 472
megabytes (Mb), 3, 472
memory-resident programs, 472
memory. *See also* buffers; diskettes; partitions
  calculating available, 228
  described, 472
  extended, 229, 469
  "map" of, 20
  random access (RAM), 2, 474
  read-only (ROM), 475
menus
  circumventing, 224
  customizing, 353–356
  described, 472
messages, sending to system users through batch files, 374–375
meta symbols, 235–237, 472
microfloppy diskettes, 3, 472
Microsoft Corporation, 1
Microsoft Windows. *See* Windows
MKDIR (MD) command, 85, 442
MODE command, 173–174, 182–191, 260–263, 443–444
modems, described, 472
monitors
  color, 233–235, 238
  controlling mode of video display on, 188–191
  described, 5, 472
  initializing through batch files, 365–367
monochrome, 472
MORE command, 305, 444–445
mouse, 472
MS-DOS, 1
MSDOS.SYS, 30
multiprocessing. *See* multitasking
multitasking
  described, 473
  spooling as, 160
multithreading, 473

national language-support operations, 473
national language-support scheme (NLS), 259
.NDX file extension, 55
networks, 394, 473
nibble, 473
NLSFUNC command, 260, 272, 445
NLS (national language-support scheme), 259
"No files were found to restore" message, 214
nonexecutable instructions, 337
nonremovable disks, 2

octal numbering system, 473, 483
operating system. *See* DOS (Disk Operating System); OS/2 operating system
OS/2 operating system, 473
output. *See also* diskettes; printing

directing with MODE command, 173–174, 182–191, 260–263, 443–444
redirecting, 99, 277–282, 290, 296–298, 475
overlay files, 102, 473
overwriting, 62, 217–218, 473
.OVL file extension, 54–55

parallel communications, 176–179, 473
parallel ports, 5–6
parameters, 21, 473
parity, 186, 473
parity bits, 176
partitions
active, 463, 493
creating, 434, 486–498
deleting, 495–498
described, 473, 485
displaying information about, 493–494
Pascal language, 473
password protection, 380–382, 473
path, 92–94, 99–102, 473
PATH command, 100–102, 123–126, 445–446
path name, 90
PAUSE command, 330, 446
pausing
execution of batch files, 329–333, 446
screen displays, 55–56, 305, 444–445
PC-DOS, 1
percent sign (%)
as DOS environment string indicator, 409
as variable indicator, 320–321
period (.), in currency formats, 248
peripherals, 1, 4, 174, 474
PGA (Professional Graphics Adapter), 154
piping, 289–293, 296–297, 474
pixels, 154, 474
platters, 474, 488–489
plotters, 168, 474
plus sign (+), as concatenation indicator, 65
ports
described, 474
initializing, 182–183, 185–187
power failures, 232
Precursor utility, 233
Presentation Manager, 474
.PRG file extension, 55
primary DOS partition, 474, 485
PRINT command, 160–168, 404, 446–447
printers
daisy-wheel, 466
described, 474
dot-matrix, 184, 468
ink-jet, 471
laser, 471
letter-quality, 184, 471
Proprinter, 256, 259, 263, 271
Quietwriter III, 256, 271
rerouting output to, 188
printing
canceling, 168
in compressed mode, 183, 465
contents of screen, 154
from queues, 160–168, 404, 446–447
graphics, 154–158, 438–439
multiple files at once, 424–425
print modes, 183–185, 443–444
PRN standard device name, 181
processes. *See* tasks
Professional Graphics Adapter (PGA), 154
program files, 3
programs
accessing in other directories/drives, 100–102, 123–126, 445–446
application, 463
calling subroutines in, 420
date-stamping of, 27
debugging, 375–378, 427, 467

file version of, 198, 469
remarks in, 328–329, 356, 449, 475
running from hard disk systems, 123–126
setup through batch files, 360–363
specifying user command processor for, 455
PROMPT command, 113–114, 233–242, 447–448
prompts
changing, 113–114, 233–242, 352, 447–448
DOS, 19–20, 30, 468
Proprinter, 256, 259, 263, 271
protected mode (OS/2), 474
public domain, 474

Quadboard, 230
question mark (?), as wild-card character, 58–59
queues, 160–168, 404, 446–447, 474
Quietwriter III, 256, 271
quotation marks (''), as string delimiters, 287

RAM disks, 228–232, 365–365, 378–380, 474
RAMDRIVE.SYS, 228–229
RAM (Random Access Memory), 2, 422, 474
range, 474
RD command, 104–105
read-after-write verification, 67, 474
read-only memory (ROM), 475
read-only status, 388, 475
read/write bit, 475
real mode (OS/2), 475
RECOVER command, 393–394, 448–449
recovering, files and disks, 393–394, 448–449
redirection, 99, 277–282, 290, 296–298, 475
remarks, in programs, 328–329, 356, 449
REM command, 328–329, 356, 449
reminder system
through batch files, 370–373
removable cartridges, 2
REM statement, 475
RENAME command, 74–77, 450
REPLACE command, 390–393, 450–451
reserved device names, 159
reserved names, 475
resident commands, 8–9, 406, 475
resource allocation, 380, 475
RESTORE command, 213–218, 404, 451–452
return key, 21
reverse video, 156, 235, 237, 475
RMDIR (RD) command, 452–453
ROM (Read-Only Memory), 475
root directory, 81, 88–89, 94, 113, 475

saving
and exiting from EDLIN program, 149
through backups, 12, 62, 195, 232
scan code, 250, 475
scratch diskettes, 28
screen. *See also* Windows
attribute codes for, 234
changing color of, 233–235
clearing, 25–26, 422
outputting to disk file, 278–279
printing contents of, 154, 278
printing one at a time, 305, 444–445
in reverse video, 156, 235, 237, 475
scrolling and stopping scrolling of, 50, 475
scrolling, 475
searching
with EDLIN program, 144–147
with filters, 285–289
for strings/text, 285–289, 298–304, 435

through paths, 99–102
secondary command processor, 475
sectors, 9, 40, 475
SELECT command, 268–270, 453
semicolon (;), in path listings, 101, 103
serial communications, 176–179, 475
serial ports, 5–6, 185–188
Session Manager (of OS/2), 476–477
SET command, 406–408, 453–454
SHARE command, 454
shareware, 476
SHELL command, 455
Shift-PrtSc key, 154, 278
SHIFT command, 455–456
Six-Pak Plus, 230
SMARTPATH program, 125
snapshot program, 375–377, 476
software, 476
software interrupt, 476
SORT command, 282–285, 290–295, 298, 303–304, 456
source, 476
source diskette, 33
special characters. *See also Special Characters Index*
in foreign countries' date/time/currency conventions, 248
not allowed in file names, 52
spooling, 160, 476
spreadsheet programs, 117–119, 476
STACKS command, 456
start bits, 476
startup
automating for DOS through AUTOEXEC.BAT, 350–356
status tracking, through batch files, 375–378
stop bits, 176, 186, 476
strings
defined, 476
searching for with EDLIN program, 144–147
searching for, 285–289, 298–304, 435
subcommands, 327, 476
subdirectories
backing up, 207–208
creating, 85, 442
creating multiple, 119–120
described, 81, 476
disk drives as (with JOIN command), 394–397, 404, 419, 440–441
listing, 98–99, 126–127, 459
restoring, 216–217
running programs from, 121–122
subroutines, 420–421
SUBST command, 397–404, 419, 457
SuperKey, 233
switches, 21, 476
synchronization (of communications), 175, 185–186, 476
SYS command, 458
.SYS file extension, 55
system date and time, 18, 26–27, 426
system disks, 28–32, 458, 497

target diskette, 33
tasks. *See also* multitasking
defined, 477
text
editing with EDLIN program, 137–143
searching with filters, 285–289
sorting with filters, 282–285
text mode, 477
thread, 477
time
formats of, 248, 425
making backups by, 211
system, 19, 26–27, 268–270, 453
TIME command, 458–459
time slice, 477
toggles, 50, 477
tracks, 9, 477
transient commands, 8–9, 406, 477

translation tables (keyboard), 250–252, 256–259, 263–266, 471
TREE command, 98–99, 126–127, 459
.TXT file extension, 54–55
TYPE command, 74, 459

unconditional transfer of control, 336
utilities, 110–111, 415, 477

values (of parameters), 21
variable parameters, 320–325, 327, 477
VDISK.SYS, 228–229
verbose listing, 90–91, 477
VER command, 460
VERIFY command, 199, 460, 474
version, of DOS, 460
vertical bar (¦)
  as either/or choice indicator, 415
  as pipe symbol, 291
vertical portrait, 158, 477
VGA (Video Graphics Array), 154
video, reverse, 156, 235, 237, 475
Video Graphics Array (VGA), 154
virtual disk, 228. *See also* RAM disk
VOL command, 461
volume labels, 82–84, 477

warm booting, 351, 477
wide directory listing, 54–55, 478
wild-card characters
  in copying multiple files, 159
  described, 478
  in directory display requests, 58
  testing effects of using, 62
.WK1 file extension, 55
.WKS file extension, 55
word processors, 114–117, 478
write-protection, 478

XCOPY command, 67–73, 461–462
XTREE program, 395

UNDERSTANDING DOS 3.3 The Companion Diskette ($19.95)

If you have found *Understanding DOS 3.3* to be useful, you will be glad to learn that every one of the batch files in this book is contained in a companion diskette. Save time, energy, and money—and avoid the drudgery of typing these excellent programs—by ordering the *Understanding DOS 3.3* Companion diskette now.

An excellent introductory training guide to DOS is also available in audio cassette form. Two cassettes and an accompanying Professional Learning Manual can be your personal aid to quick and easy understanding of DOS.

Use the order form below to order any of the fine products produced by Judd Robbins. Mail today, with complete payment, to Computer Options, P.O. Box 9656, Berkeley, CA 94709-9656.

_____ copies of *Understanding DOS 3.3* Companion Diskette,
at $19.95 each _____

_____ copies of *ReComm*, the DOS Command Reissuing Utility,
at $19.95 each _____

_____ copies of *Introduction to DOS* Audio Cassette Training,
at $19.95 each _____

_____ Shipping and handling (add $2.50 per item)

_____ California sales tax (please add appropriate amount
for your city/county) _____

TOTAL ORDER: _____

Name ________________________________

Address ________________________________

City ____________ State ____________ Zip ____________

Phone ________________________________

SYBEX Computer Books are different.

Here is why . . .

At SYBEX, each book is designed with you in mind. Every manuscript is carefully selected and supervised by our editors, who are themselves computer experts. We publish the best authors, whose technical expertise is matched by an ability to write clearly and to communicate effectively. Programs are thoroughly tested for accuracy by our technical staff. Our computerized production department goes to great lengths to make sure that each book is well-designed.

In the pursuit of timeliness, SYBEX has achieved many publishing firsts. SYBEX was among the first to integrate personal computers used by authors and staff into the publishing process. SYBEX was the first to publish books on the CP/M operating system, microprocessor interfacing techniques, word processing, and many more topics.

Expertise in computers and dedication to the highest quality product have made SYBEX a world leader in computer book publishing. Translated into fourteen languages, SYBEX books have helped millions of people around the world to get the most from their computers. We hope we have helped you, too.

For a complete catalog of our publications:

SUMMARY OF DOS COMMANDS*			
COMMAND	**DESCRIPTION**	**FORMAT**	**PAGE**
KEYB	Loads in new keyboard translation table and code page	[*D*:*Path*]KEYB [*xx*[,[*yyy*],[*FileSpec*]]]	592
LABEL	Defines or changes existing volume label	[*D*:*Path*]LABEL [*D1*:][*String*]	593
MKDIR (MD)	Creates a new subdirectory	MD [*D*:]*Path*	595
MODE	Defines attributes for all ports and code pages	[*D*:*Path*]MODE LPT*x*: [*CPL*][,[*LPI*][,P]] [*D*:*Path*]MODE LPT*x*: =COM*y* [*D*:*Path*]MODE COM*y*[:]*Baud*[,[*Parity*] [,[*Bits*][,P] [*D*:*Path*]MODE *Type* [*D*:*Path*]MODE [*Type*], *Shift* [,T] [*D*:*Path*]MODE *Device* CODEPAGE PREPARE = ((*CP*) *FileSpec*) [*D*:*Path*]MODE *Device* CODEPAGE PREPARE = ((*CPList*) *FileSpec*) [*D*:*Path*]MODE *Device* CODEPAGE SELECT = *CP* [*D*:*Path*]MODE *Device* CODEPAGE[/STATUS] [*D*:*Path*]MODE *Device* CODEPAGE REFRESH	596
MORE	Pauses the display of long files	[*D*:*Path*]MORE	598
NLSFUNC	Loads in routines for code pages and the CHCP command	[*D*:*Path*]NLSFUNC [*FileSpec*]	599
PATH	Defines search list for .EXE, .COM, and .BAT files	PATH [*D1*:*Path1*][;*D2*:*Path2*...]	600
PRINT	Queues files for printing	[*D*:*Path*]PRINT [/D:*Device*][/B:*BuffSize*][/U:*BusyTicks*] [/M:*MaxTicks*][/S:*TimeSlice*][/Q:*QueueSize*][/C][/T] [/P][*FileSpec*,...]	602
PROMPT	Changes the system prompt	PROMPT [*String*]	603
RECOVER	Rescues damaged files	[*D*:*Path*]RECOVER[*D1*][*FileSpec*]	604
RENAME (REN)	Changes the name of a file	REN *OldFile NewFile*	606

*See Part 6, "DOS Command Reference," for a complete description of subcommands and their parameters.

SUMMARY OF DOS COMMANDS*

COMMAND	DESCRIPTION	FORMAT	PAGE
REPLACE	Copies, adds, and updates programs	[*D*:*Path*]REPLACE *SourceFile* [*Dest*][/A][/P][/R][/S][/W]	607
RESTORE	Reads backup file back onto disk	[*D*:*Path*]RESTORE *SourceD FileSpec* [/S][/P][/B:*mm-dd-yy*] [/A:*mm-dd-yy*][/M][/N][/L:*hh-mm-ss*][/E:*hh-mm-ss*]	608
RMDIR (RD)	Deletes empty directories	RD [*D*:*Path*]	610
SELECT	Creates a system disk with country information	[*D*:*Path*]SELECT [[A:¦B:][*DestD*:[*DestPath*]] *xxx yy*	611
SET	Changes defaults and definitions in DOS environment	SET [*Name* = [*Param*]]	612
SHARE	Loads network lock-out routines	[*D*:*Path*]SHARE [/F:*FileMem*][/L:*Locks*]	613
SORT	Sorts data by column	[*D*:*Path*]SORT [/R][/ + *Col*]	616
SUBST	Makes DOS think a directory is a disk drive	[*D*:*Path*]SUBST [*D*:*Path*]SUBST *NewD*[*Path2* [*D*:*Path*]SUBST *NewD* /D	618
SYS	Transfers hidden system files to another disk	[*D*:*Path*]SYS *DestD*:	619
TIME	Sets the system time	TIME [*hh*:*mm*[:*ss*[.*xx*]]]	620
TREE	Lists all directories, subdirectories, and files on a disk	[*D*:*Path*]TREE [*D2*:][/F]	621
TYPE	Displays the contents of an ASCII file	TYPE *FileSpec*	622
VER	Displays the current version of DOS	VER	623
VERIFY	Causes DOS to verify everything that is written to disk	VERIFY [ON¦OFF]	624

*See Part 6, "DOS Command Reference," for a complete description of subcommands and their parameters.

SUMMARY OF DOS COMMANDS*

COMMAND	DESCRIPTION	FORMAT	PAGE
VOL	Displays volume label of drive	VOL [*D*:]	625
XCOPY	Copies complete directories, subdirectories, and files	[*D*:*Path*]XCOPY[*FileSpec1*][*FileSpec2*][/A][/D:*mm-dd-yy*] [/E][/M][/P][/S][/V][/W]	626

*See Part 6, "DOS Command Reference," for a complete description of subcommands and their parameters.

CONFIGURATION FILE COMMANDS*

COMMAND	DESCRIPTION	FORMAT	PAGE
BREAK	Determines when DOS checks for a Ctrl-Break	BREAK = [ON¦OFF]	557
BUFFERS	Sets number of buffers	BUFFERS = *x*	558
COUNTRY	Specifies date and time formats	COUNTRY = *xxx*,[*yyy*] [,*FileSpec*]	568
DEVICE	Loads device drivers into memory	DEVICE = *FileSpec*[*Switches*]	573
FCBS	Defines how many file control blocks can be used at once	FCBS = *MaxNum*,*PermNum*	582
FILES	Specifies how many files can be accessed at once	FILES = *x*	584
LASTDRIVE	Specifies the highest drive letter	LASTDRIVE = *D*	594
SHELL	Specifies location of a different command processor	SHELL = *ComFileSpec* [/E:*xxxxx*][/P]	614
STACKS	Specifies new stack resources	STACKS = *n*,*s*	617

*See Part 6, "DOS Command Reference," for a complete description of commands and their parameters.